JOHN P.

0-07-037040-0	J. Kneiling	*Un*
0-07-022453-6	A. Friend	*CO* *M*
0-07-006583-7	H. Bookman	*COBOL/370: For VS COBOL and COBOL II Programmers*
0-07-008606-6	L. Brumbaugh	*VSAM: Architecture, Theory, and Applications*
0-07-041793-9	B. Merrow	*VSE/ESA: Performance Management and Fine Tuning*
0-07-054977-X	J. Savit	*VM/CMS: Concepts and Facilities*
0-07-018994-3	T. Eddolls	*ASO: Automated Systems Operations for MVS*
0-07-033783-7	T. Keller	*CICS: Capacity Planning and Performance Management*
0-07-035869-9	J. Lebert	*CICS Essentials for Application Developers and Programmers*
0-07-050623-X	J. Porter	*AS/400 Information Engineering*
0-07-024128-7	H. F. Graubart-Cervone	*VSE/ESA JCL: Utilities, POWER, and VSAM*

To order or to receive additional information on these or any other McGraw-Hill titles, please call 1-800-822-8158 in the United States. In other countries, please contact your local McGraw-Hill office.

MH93

IBM Mainframe
Programmer's
Desk Reference

IBM Mainframe Programmer's Desk Reference

V. Mitra Gopaul

McGraw-Hill, Inc.

New York   San Francisco   Washington, D.C.   Auckland   Bogotá
Caracas   Lisbon   London   Madrid   Mexico City   Milan
Montreal   New Delhi   San Juan   Singapore
Sydney   Tokyo   Toronto

Library of Congress Cataloging-in-Publication Data

Gopaul, V. Mitra.
    IBM mainframe programmer's desk reference / V. Mitra Gopaul.
      p.   cm.
    Includes index.
    ISBN 0-07-096425-4
    1. IBM computers—Programming. I. Title.
    QA76.8.I1015G65 1993
    005.2'25—dc20   93-27840
                                          CIP

1 2 3 4 5 6 7 8 9 0 DOC/DOC 9 9 8 7 6 5 4 3

ISBN 0-07-096425-4

The sponsoring editor for this book was Jerry Papke, the editing supervisor was Kimberly A. Goff, and the production supervisor was Pamela A. Pelton.

Printed and bound by R. R. Donnelley & Sons Company.

I dedicate this work to my dad, Goorooparsad Gopaul, for his unconditional love, inspiring courage, and elevating contentment; these are a few of his contributions that made this world a better place for the human family, before passing to the next.

Contents

Preface

As an IBM mainframe programmer, on any given project, I have worked with a variety of software and languages. If you are in this situation, you will probably have difficulty remembering all the syntax, commands, and keywords of products such as JCL, CICS, DB2, IMS, SQL, VSAM, and so on. It is impossible. So your desk is occupied by dozens of reference manuals and books on these subjects. Often, when you desperately need to know the correct way of coding a statement or command, you reach for the manual, but it's not available. Someone has borrowed it.

For many years I yearned for *one* book, right on my desk, like a dictionary, that would contain all the information commonly used by programmers. I know many of my colleagues have the same desire; therefore, I wrote *IBM Mainframe Programmer's Desk Reference*.

About This Book

This book is an attempt to provide IBM mainframe programmers with everything they could possibly want to know. The topics covered here are so varied that they will definitely be useful in most, if not all of your development and maintenance work. The subjects are CICS, CLIST, CMS, COBOL II, DB2, IMS, MVS utilities, JCL, REXX, SQL, VSAM, IDCAMS, and CMS XEDIT.

As you know, computers must be given precise information: a missing comma in a JCL produces errors, and variables with incorrect data can make utility programs unpredictable. When writing this book, I focused on giving the reader the kind of information that is essential in making work more productive. This book is a repository of the syntax, commands, and keywords of most of the tools that are widely used by programmers in the IBM mainframe environment. The illustrations and examples, included wherever possible, will make your coding task a little bit easier.

I assumed that the reader has a basic knowledge of the subjects covered here. Although it is useful for learning programming concepts and practices, the material is presented in such a way as to benefit both experienced and novice programmers. It will refresh your memory if you have forgotten something. The easy-to-understand descriptions and examples will enrich your understanding of languages, utilities, and databases.

How This Book Is Organized

The subject matter is organized to be both practical and useful. Since this book is primarily a desk reference, you will retrieve data randomly. There are twelve chapters, each dealing with a subject such as a database, a language, or a software product. Within each chapter, whenever sensible, the content is ordered alphabetically. However, in some cases, the order is different from the normal hierarchical order of the subject. I think the need to access information randomly lends itself to this arrangement. Furthermore, the way all the chapters are developed is consistent, with a convention used throughout the book.

Chapter 1 is a summary of all the CICS commands. Also, it contains useful data layout information for COBOL programmers. Chapter 2 gives you the syntax and description of all the CLIST statements and built-in functions. Chapter 3 is a reference for all the CMS commands. Chapter 4 presents information for COBOL II, including all the divisions, sections, paragraphs, statements, and clauses. In addition, this chapter also contains sections on often forgotten but necessary compiler directives and options.

Chapter 5 first gives you reference material on DB2 commands and utilities, then gives a few useful JCL samples for executing commands and utilities. Chapter 6 is a good source for information on different programming aspects of IMS databases, including DL/I DB and DC. Chapter 7 discusses some of the most used MVS utilities, such as the compiler, line editor, sort, IEBGENER, and so on. Chapter 8 deals with all the JCL and JES2 statements.

Chapter 9 is a reference for REXX programmers. There are ample examples to enhance readers' understanding. In Chapter 11, the Access Method Services are discussed. This chapter explains IDCAMS commands, giving many samples of JCL for you to clone. Also, there is a section on how to estimate storage for VSAM files.

Finally, Chapter 12 is a reference for CMS/XEDIT users, with sections on subcommands and macros.

Conclusion

IBM Mainframe Programmers' Desk Reference is unique. There are numerous books and manuals on each of the subjects discussed here or on combinations of subjects. This is the first time that all these diverse and sought-after subjects can be found in one place.

This book is written with the needs of the programmer in mind. I am certain that it will replace many of the books and manuals on your desk. It will serve you for a long time in your demanding task of software development and maintenance.

Acknowledgments

First, I must thank Jay Ranade for his technical guidance for this book. I am very grateful to Gerald Papke, senior editor, for supplying me with the research materials promptly and all his encouragements over many months of writing this book. Many thanks to the editing staff of McGraw-Hill for their meticulous work to ensure that the information given here is accurate, clear, and useful.

Thanks to many of my friends and colleagues for their encouragements, positive thoughts, and great interest in the progress of this work.

Finally, my special gratitude to my wife, Gaye, my daughter, Laila, and my son, Sanjiv, for their unfailing support and encouragement throughout this project; also for their understanding when I took time away from them.

V. Mitra Gopaul

CICS

This chapter is a reference for programmers using CICS and COBOL. It provides the syntax of all the CICS commands, as well as explanations of options and condition codes.

General Format: The general format for COBOL starts with EXEC CICS (EXECUTE CICS), followed by function, options, and END-EXEC in the form

EXEC CICS *function* [*option*[*(argument)*]]...
END-EXEC

The function denotes a CICS operation requested by your program. The option is a facility supplied by CICS for a particular function; a function may no options or many options. An option may have an argument, enclosed by parentheses. An argument may be one of the following:

- Data value
- Data area
- Pointer value
- Pointer reference
- Name
- Label
- Time in format hhmmss

1

Notational Convention: In the general format of the CICS commands used in this chapter, there are a few symbols that are not part of the syntax; therefore they must not be included when you code your program. These symbols and their meanings are:

Symbol	Meaning
[]	The option enclosed by the brackets ([]) is not required but can be included.
<>	Only one of the alternatives enclosed by the angle brackets (<>) must be chosen.
or	The alternatives enclosed by the angle brackets (<>) are separated by "or."
____	The underlined word is the default value.
...	The horizontal or vertical ellipsis means that the preceding can be coded more than once.
Uppercase characters	All keywords of the command are written in uppercase characters; they must be coded as shown.
Lowercase characters	All strings in lowercase characters and italic are variables that can be changed to any other strings to suit your programming style. In your code they represent values that you supply to commands.
Comment	In some instances, there is a remark to the right of a command parameter, specifying how it is used. For example,

```
[KEYLENGTH(data-value) [GENERIC]] VSAM only
```

means the KEYLENGTH and GENERIC parameters apply to VSAM file only.

In this chapter the CICS commands are grouped into the following categories:

Exception conditions
File control commands
DL/I services
Basic Mapping Support (BMS)
Batch data exchange
Interval control
Task control

Program control
Storage control
Transient data control
Temporary storage control
Abnormal termination and recovery
Trace control
Dump control
Journal control
Sync point control

Also, there are record definitions for the following:

Key assignments
EXEC interface block
BMS standard attribute

1.1   EXCEPTION CONDITIONS

An error can occur during the execution of a CICS program; this is called an exception condition. There are 70 such conditions. CICS provides commands to handle these conditions. If one of these conditions occurs and your program does not take appropriate action, then the system default action is taken, which is to end the task abnormally.

The CICS commands to handle exception conditions are HANDLE CONDITION, IGNORE CONDITION, PUSH HANDLE, and POP HANDLE.

There is an alternative to using HANDLE command for handling exception errors. You can specify an option with each CICS command; these options are NOHANDLE, RESP, RESP2, and RESP(xxx), where xxx is a user-defined fullword binary data area.

◻ **General formats**

● **HANDLE   CONDITION   command—Process   exception conditions**

```
EXEC CICS HANDLE CONDITION
  condition[(label)]
  .
```

```
        .
        .
END-EXEC
```

● **HANDLE AID command—Associate key with a process**

```
EXEC CICS HANDLE
   key (label)
     .
     .
     .
END-EXEC
```

● **IGNORE CONDITION command—Ignore exception conditions**

```
EXEC CICS IGNORE CONDITION
   condition
     .
     .
     .
END-EXEC
```

● **PUSH HANDLE command—Suspend all exception processing**

```
EXEC CICS PUSH HANDLE

END-EXEC
```

● **POP HANDLE command—Restore all exception processing**

```
EXEC CICS POP HANDLE

END-EXEC
```

◼ Description of options

condition
This specifies any CICS exception code (e.g., NOTOPEN, LENGERR, DUPREC, etc.). Later in this chapter, after the general format of each command, there is a list of possible condition codes that may occur as a result of the processing of a command.

key
This specifies any of the following keys:

   ● Clear or ENTER key

- Program function key (1 through 24)
- Program attention key (PA1, PA2, and PA3)
- Light pen
- Operid (for the operator)
- Anykey (any PA or PF key or the Clear key, but not the ENTER key)

label

This specifies a label of the application program to which control is tranferred when a condition code associated with it occurs.

1.2 FILE CONTROL

The file control commands perform various file operations on VSAM and sequential files. This section first lists the general format of each file control command. In addition, all the options and condition codes associated with these commands are explained. The file control commands are READ, WRITE, REWRITE, DELETE, UNLOCK, STARTBR, READNEXT, READPREV, RESETBR and ENDBR.

■ **General formats**

● **READ command—Read a record**

```
EXEC CICS READ
   <FILE(name) or DATASET(name)>
   [INTO(data-area) or SET(ptr-ref)]
   [LENGTH(data-area)]
   RIDFLD(data-area)
   [KEYLENGTH(data-value) [GENERIC]] VSAM only
   [SYSID(name)]
   [RBA or RRN or DEBKEY or DEBREC]
   [GTEQ  or EQUAL]                    VSAM only
   [UPDATE]
END-EXEC
```

Condition codes: DISABLED,   DSIDERR,   DUPKEY,
                  FILENOTFOUND,   ILLOGIC,   INVREQ,
                  IOERR, ISCINVREQ, LENGERR, NOTAUTH,
                  NOTFND, NOTOPEN, SEGIDERR, SYSIDERR

Notes: RBA and RRN are used for VSAM only.

DEBKEY and DEBREC are used with blocked BDAM only. LENGTH is mandatory with SYSID and with INTO and variable-length records.

● WRITE command—Write a record

```
EXEC CICS WRITE
   <FILE(name) or DATASET(name)>
   FROM(data-area)
   [LENGTH(data-value)]
   RIDFLD(data-area)
   [KEYLENGTH(data-value)]
   [SYSID(name)]
   [RBA or RRN]          VSAM only
   [MASSINSERT]          VSAM only
END-EXEC
```

Condition codes: DSIDERR,   DUPKEY,   DUPREC, FILENOTFOUND,   ILLOGIC,   INVREQ, IOERR, ISCINVREQ, LENGERR, NOSPACE, NOTAUTH, NOTOPEN, SYSIDERR

Notes: LENGTH and KEYLENGTH are mandatory with SYSID. LENGTH is also mandatory with SYSID and with FROM when writing variable-length records.

● REWRITE command—Update a record

```
EXEC CICS REWRITE
   <FILE(name) or DATASET(name)>
   FROM(data-area)
   [LENGTH(data-value)]
   [SYSID(name)]
END-EXEC
```

Condition codes: DISABLED,   DSIDERR,   DUPREC, FILENOTFOUND,   ILLOGIC,   INVREQ, IOERR, ISCINVREQ, LENGERR, NOSPACE, NOTOPEN, SYSIDERR

Notes: LENGTH is mandatory with SYSID and with FROM when updating variable-length records.

● DELETE command—Delete a record

```
EXEC CICS DELETE
   <FILE(name) or DATASET(name)>   VSAM only
   [RIDFLD(data-area)
     [KEYLENGTH(data-value)
     [GENERIC [NUMREC(data-area)]]]]
   [SYSID(name)]
```

```
      [RBA or RRN]
    END-EXEC
```

Condition codes: DISABLED,   DSIDERR,   DUPKEY,
                      FILENOTFOUND,   ILLOGIC,   INVREQ,
                      IOERR, ISCINVREQ, NOTAUTH, NOTFND,
                      NOTOPEN, SYSIDERR

Notes: RIDFLD is mandatory with GENERIC.
          KEYLENGTH is mandatory with SYSID.

• UNLOCK command—Release exclusive control

```
EXEC CICS UNLOCK
  <FILE(name) or DATASET(name)>          VSAM only
  [SYSID(name)]
END-EXEC
```

Condition codes: DISABLED, FILENOTFOUND, ILLOGIC,
                      IOERR, ISCINVREQ, NOTAUTH, NOTOPEN,
                      SYSIDERR

• STARTBR command—Start browse

```
EXEC CICS STARTBR
  <FILE(name) or DATASET(name)>
  RIDFLD(data-area)
  [KEYLENGTH(data-value) [GENERIC]]
  [REQID(data-value)]
  [SYSID(name)]
  [RBA or RRN or DEBKEY or DEBREC]
  [GTEQ or EQUAL]
END-EXEC
```

Condition codes: DISABLED, FILENOTFOUND, ILLOGIC,
                      INVREQ, IOERR, ISCINVREQ, NOTAUTH,
                      NOTFND, NOTOPEN, SYSIDERR

Notes: GENERIC, RBA and RRN are used for VSAM only.
          DEBKEY and DEBREC are used with blocked BDAM only.
          KEYLENGTH is mandatory with SYSID or GENERIC.

• READNEXT command—Retrieve record sequentially during a browse

```
EXEC CICS READNEXT
  <FILE(name) or DATASET(name)>
  <INTO(data-area) or SET(ptr-ref)>
  [LENGTH(data-area)]
  RIDFLD(data-area)
  [KEYLENGTH(data-value)]
  [REQID(data-value)]
```

```
    [SYSID(name)]
    [RBA or RRN]
END-EXEC
```

```
Condition codes:    DISABLED,     DUPKEY,     ENDFILE,
                    FILENOTFOUND,    ILLOGIC,    INVREQ,
                    IOERR, ISCINVREQ, LENGERR, NOTAUTH,
                    NOTFND, NOTOPEN, SYSIDERR
```

Notes: RBA and RRN are used for VSAM only.
LENGTH is mandatory with SYSID and with INTO and variable-length records.
KEYLENGTH is mandatory with SYSID.

• READPREV command—Retrieve previous record during a browse

```
EXEC CICS READPREV
    <FILE(name) or DATASET(name)>
    <INTO(data-area) or SET(prt-ref)>
    [LENGTH(data-area)]
    RIDFLD(data-area)
    [KEYLENGTH(data-value)]
    [REQID(data-value)]
    [SYSID(name)]
    [RBA or RRN]
```

```
Condition codes:    DISABLED,     DUPKEY,     ENDFILE,
                    FILENOTFOUND,    ILLOGIC,    INVREQ,
                    IOERR, ISCINVREQ, LENGERR, NOTAUTH,
                    NOTFND, NOTOPEN, SYSIDERR
```

Notes: RBA and RRN are used for VSAM only.
LENGTH is mandatory with SYSID and with INTO and variable-length records.
KEYLENGTH is mandatory with SYSID.

• RESETBR command—Reset start of browse operation

```
EXEC CICS RESETBR
    <FILE(name) or DATASET(name)>
    RIDFLD(data-area)
    [KEYLENGTH(data-value) [GENERIC]]
    [REQID(data-value)]
    [SYSID(name)]
    [GTEQ or EQUAL]
    [RBA or RRN]
END-EXEC
```

```
Condition codes:    DISABLED,  FILENOTFOUND,   ILLOGIC,
                    INVREQ, IOERR, ISCINVREQ, NOTAUTH,
                    NOTFND, NOTOPEN, SYSIDERR
```

Notes: LENGTH is mandatory with SYSID.
KEYLENGTH is mandatory with SYSID.

● **ENDBR command—End browse operation**

```
EXEC CICS ENDBR
  <FILE(name) or DATASET(name)>
  [REQID(data-value)]
  [SYSID(name)]
END-EXEC
```

```
Condition codes:   DISABLED,  FILENOTFOUND,  ILLOGIC,
                   INVREQ,     ISCINVREQ,    NOTAUTH,
                   NOTOPEN, SYSIDERR
```

▣ Description of options

FILE(*name*) or DATASET(*name*)
This mandatory option specifies a symbolic name that refers to a dataset name. This name must be defined in the file control table (FCT) before data access is possible. The association between the FCT name and the dataset name is done in the following ways:

● A JCL DD statement is used, where the FCT name is the DD name defining the dataset.
● A dataset name, up to 44 characters in length, is entered in the FCT with the DSNAME option.
● The name is set dynamically with the EXEC CICS SET command or the CEMT command.

The keywords FILE and DATASET are used interchangeably. Both have the same effect.

If SYSID option is used, CICS assumes that the dataset to which name is pointing is in a remote system. If a name is not found in the FCT, CICS generates an exception condition to be logged under DSIDERR. The name must be alphanumeric and 8 characters in length.

DEBKEY
This option is only used with BDAM, and it specifies that the deblocking is to be done by key.

If KEYLENGTH is used as an option, its value must be the sum of the lengths of all three subfields of the key.

DEBREC

This option is used only with BDAM, and it specifies that the deblocking is to be done by relative record. If KEYLENGTH is used as an option, its value must be the sum of the lengths of all three subfields of the key.

EQUAL

This option is used only with VSAM. It specifies that to satisfy a search of the record, the key must be the same as the key value specified in the RIDFLD option.

FROM(*data-area*)

This specifies the data area that contains a record to be written to a dataset. This option is used with the WRITE and REWRITE commands. If you are writing variable-length records, the LENGTH option must be used. *data-area* is the main storage area which is part of an application program.

GENERIC

This option is used only with VSAM. It specifies a partial key, whose length is determined by KEYLENGTH. During a search, a match occurs when the starting characters of the record are the same as the characters of the specified key.

GTEQ

This option is used only with VSAM. It means that the browsing operation will start at the first record having a key equal to the specified key or, if this fails, at the first record having a greater key.

INTO(*data-area*)

This specifies the data area where a record is placed after it is read from a file. It is used with the READ, READNEXT, and READPREV commands. For variable-length records, the LENGTH option must be used; it specifies the maximum record length that the program will accept. However, for fixed-length records, there is no need to use the LENGTH option. *data-area* is the main storage area which is part of an application program.

KEYLENGTH(*data-value*)
This specifies the length (halfword binary) of the key and it is used in the RIDFLD option. LENGTHKEY is mandatory if the GENERIC option is used.

LENGTH(*data-value or data-area*)
This specifies the length of the record that is read from or written to the dataset. The LENGTH option is mandatory with SYSID and with the INTO and FROM options if variable-length records are processed. This parameter is the maximum length of the record expected by the application program.

MASSINSER—VSAM only
This specifies that the WRITE command is part of a mass insertion operation.

NUMREC(*data-area*)
This specifies a data area (halfword binary) that contains the number of records that have been deleted.

RBA—VSAM only
This specifies that the value of the RIDFLD option represents a relative byte address.

REQID(*data-value*)
This option is used when two or more than one browsing operations are performed concurrently against a dataset. It specifies a unique number to identify each browse operation. The default is zero, in which case only one browse can be performed against a dataset.

RIDFLD(*data-area*)
This option, called the Record Identification Field, specifies the structural makeup of the key. *data-area* contains any one of the following:

● Relative byte address (RBA) for VSAM
● Relative record number (RRN) for VSAM
● Physical key for BDAM

RRN—VSAM only

This specifies that the data area of the RIDFLD option contains a relative record number (RRN).

SET(*ptr-ref*)

This specifies a pointer reference to a buffer to which data are written during a read operation. It should be acquired by CICS and be large enough to hold the record. With SET, the option LENGTH is not required. The reference is an address in main storage.

SYSID(*name*)

This specifies the name of a remote system. The name may be up to 4 characters in length.

UPDATE—VSM only

This specifies that the record is for updating or deletion. Without it, the default is read only.

▣ File control exception condition codes

DISABLED	File is disabled.
DSIDERR	A filename (dataset ID) is not found in the file control table (FCT). It is equivalent to FILENOTFOUND.
DUPREC	Two records with the same key exist in the dataset (VSAM only) when an alternative index that allows for duplicates is used to retrieve data.
DUPREC	A record already exists with the same key as a record that is being added to a file.
ENDFILE	The end-of-file condition is reached while executing a browse or READPREV command.
FILENOTFOUND	A filename is not found in the FCT.
ILLOGIC	The error does not fall into any other response category (VSAM only).

INVREQ   The request is invalid due to:
                 ·   Its not being compatible with FCT information
                 ·   Options having been incorrectly coded

IOERR   An input-output error occurred that is not covered
                 by the CICS exception condition.

ISCINVREQ   The remote system failed.

LENGERR   The specified length for a fixed-length record is
                 incorrect, or the length of the input record is less
                 than the record size in the FCT.

NOSPACE   There is no space in the dataset to write or
                 rewrite a record.

NOTAUTH   There is insufficient authorization to perform a
                 CICS command.

NOTFND   The record specified with the key in the RIDFLD
                 option is not found in the file. With a retrieve
                 command, the record is not found in the
                 temporary storage.

NOTOPEN   The file is closed when it is accessed.

SEGIDERR   The name specified in the SEGSET option is not
                 found in the FCT.

SYSIDERR   The name specified in the SYSID option is not
                 found in the INTESYSTEMS table or the link to
                 the system is closed.

1.3   DL/I SERVICES

The DL/I command provides various database services between
CICS and an IMS database. Only the format of the each service is
given. In Chapter 6 we discuss IMS database and DL/I calls in
detail, refer to this chapter for more explanations. The format of
services given in this section are:

Schedule the PSB
Get one or more segments
Insert one or more segments
Load a segment (batch only)
Replace one or more segments
Delete a segment
Return pool statistics
Terminate access to the PSB
Request a basic checkpoint
Back out updates and abend
Back out updates and return
Write record to system log
Request a symbolic log
Invoke extended restart

The following is the general format of each DL/I service.

◘ General formats

● Schedule the PSB

```
EXEC DLI SCHD
   <PSB(name) or PSB(data-area)>
END-EXEC
```

● Get one or more segments

```
EXEC DLI <GU or GN or GNP>
   [USING PCB(integer-expr)]
   [KEYFEEDBACK(data-area)
     [FEEDBACKLEN(integer-expr)]]

Parent segment:
   [VARIABLE]
   [FIRST or LAST or CURRENT]
   [SEGMENT(name) or SEGMENT(data-area)]
   [SEGLENGTH(integer-expr)]
   [OFFSET(integer-expr)]
   [LOCKED]
   [SETPARENT]
   [INTO(data-area)]
   [WHERE(where-clause)
     [FIELDLENGTH(integer-expr)]]
   [KEYS(data-area)
     KEYLENGTH(integer-expr)]

Object segment:
   [VARIABLE]
```

```
    [FIRST or LAST]
    [SEGMENT(name) or SEGMENT(data-area)]
    [SEGLENGTH(integer-expr)]
    [OFFSET(integer-expr)]
    [LOCKED]
    [INTO(data-area)]
    [WHERE(where-clause)
      [FIELDLENGTH(integer-expr)]]
    [KEYS(data-area)
      KEYLENGTH(integer-expr)]
END-EXEC
```

• Insert one or more segments

```
EXEC DLI IRST
    [USING PCB(integer-expr)]

Parent segment:
    [VARIABLE]
    [FIRST or LAST or CURRENT]
    [SEGMENT(name) or SEGMENT(data-area)]
    [SEGLENGTH(integer-expr)]
    [FROM(data-area)]
    [WHERE(where-clause)
      [FIELDLENGTH(integer-expr)]]
    [KEYS(data-area)
      KEYLENGTH(integer-expr)]

Object segment:
    [VARIABLE]
    [FIRST or LAST]
    [SEGMENT(name) or SEGMENT(data-area)]
    [SEGLENGTH(integer-expr)]
    [OFFSET(integer-expr)]
    [FROM(data-area)]
END-EXEC
```

• Load a segment (batch only)

```
EXEC DLI LOAD
    [USING PCB(integer-expr)]
    [VARIABLE]
    [SEGMENT(name) or SEGMENT(data-area)]
    [FROM(data-area)]
    [SEGLENGTH(integer-expr)]
END-EXEC
```

• Replace one or more segments

```
EXEC DLI REPL
    [USING PCB(integer-expr)]
    [VARIABLE]
    [SEGMENT(name) or SEGMENT(data-area)]
    [SEGLENGTH(integer-expr)]
    [OFFSET(integer-expr)]
```

```
   [FROM(data-area)]
END-EXEC
```

• Delete a segment

```
EXEC DLI DLET
   [USING PCB(integer-expr)]
   [VARIABLE]
   [SEGMENT(name) or SEGMENT(data-area)]
   [FROM(data-area)]
   [SEGLENGTH(integer-expr)]
END-EXEC
```

• Return pool statistics

```
EXEC DLI STAT
   [USING PCB(integer-expr)]
   [INTO(data-area)]
   [LENGTH(integer-expr)]
   [VSAM or NONVSAM]
   [FORMATTED or UNFORMATTED or SUMMARY]
END-EXEC
```

• Terminate access to the PSB

```
EXEC DLI TERM
END-EXEC
```

• Request a basic checkpoint

```
EXEC DLI CHKP
   ID(data-area) or ('char-expr')
END-EXEC
```

• Back out updates and abend

```
EXEC DLI ROLL
END-EXEC
```

• Back out updates and return

```
EXEC DLI ROLB
END-EXEC
```

• Write record to system log

```
EXEC DLI LOG
   FROM(data-area)
   [LENGTH(integer-expr)]
END-EXEC
```

- **Request a symbolic log**

```
EXEC DLI SYNCHKP
   ID(data-area)
   [AREA1(data-area)
    [LENGTH1(integer-expr)]]
     .
     .
     .
   [AREA7(data-area)
    [LENGTH7(integer-expr)]]
END-EXEC
```

- **Invoke extended restart**

```
EXEC DLI XRST
   [ID(data-area)]
   [MAXLENGTH(integer-expr)]
   [AREA1(data-area)
    [LENGTH1(integer-expr)]]
     .
     .
     .
   [AREA7(data-area)
    [LENGTH7(integer-expr)]]
   RETRIEVE
   USING PCB(integer-value)
   KEYFEEDBACK(data-area)
   [FEEDBACKLEN(integer-expr)]
END-EXEC
```

1.4 BASIC MAPPING SUPPORT (BMS)

This section first lists the syntax of the Basic Mapping Support (BMS) commands. In addition, all the options and condition codes associated with these commands are explained. The BMS commands are RECEIVE MAP, RECEIVE PARTN, SEND PARTNSET, SEND MAP, SEND TEXT, SEND TEXT MAPPED, SEND TEXT NOEDIT, SEND CONTROL, SEND PAGE, PURGE MESSAGE, and ROUTE.

◻ **General formats**

- **RECEIVE MAP command—Input data from terminal**

```
EXEC CICS RECEIVE MAP(name)
   [MAPSET(name)]
   [INTO(data-area) or SET(ptr-ref)]
```

```
   [FROM(data-area) LENGTH(data-value) or
     TERMINAL[ASIS]]
END-EXEC
```

Condition codes: EOC, EODS, INVMPSZ, INVPARTN,
                    INVREQ, MAPFAIL, PARTNFAIL, RDATT,
                    UNEXPIN

• RECEIVE PARTN command—Read data from a partition

```
EXEC CICS RECEIVE PARTN(data-area)
   <INTO(data-area) or SET(ptr-ref)>
   LENGTH(data-area)
   [ASIS]
END-EXEC
```

Condition codes: EOC, EODS, INVPARTN, INVREQ, LENGERR

• SEND PARTNSET command—Load a partition set

```
EXEC CICS SEND PARTNSET [(name)]
END-EXEC
```

Condition codes: INVPARTNSET, INVREQ

• SEND MAP command—Send mapped data to terminal

```
EXEC CICS SEND MAP(name)
   [MAPSET(name)]
   [FROM(data-area) LENGTH(data-value) or
     DATAONLY or MAPONLY]
   [CURSOR[(data-value)]]
   [FORMFEED]
   [ERASE or ERASEAUP]
   [PRINT]
   [FREEKB]
   [ALARM]
   [FRSET]
   [NLEOM]
   [MSR(data-value)]
   [OUTPARTN(name)]
   [ACTPARTN(name)]
   [FMHPARM(name)]
   [LDC(name)]
   [ACCUM]
   [SET(ptr-ref) or PAGING or
             TERMINAL[WAIT][LAST]]
   [REQID(name)]
   [L40 or L64 or L80 or HONEOM]
END-EXEC
```

Condition codes: IGREQCD, IGREQID, INVLDC, INVMPSZ,
                   INVPARTN,   INVREQ,   OVERFLOW,
                   RETPAGE, TSIOERR, WRBRK

● **SEND TEXT command—Send text without mapping**

```
EXEC CICS SEND TEXT FROM(data-area)
   LENGTH(data-value)
   [CURSOR(data-value)]
   [FORMFEED]
   [ERASE]
   [PRINT]
   [FREEKB]
   [ALARM]
   [NLEOM]
   [LDC(name)]
   [OUTPARTN(name)]
   [ACTPARTN(name)]
   [MSR(data-value)]
   [SET(ptr-ref) or PAGING or
            TERMINAL[WAIT][LAST]]
   [REQID(name)]
   [HEADER(data-area)]
   [TRAILER(data-area)]
   [JUSTIFY(data-value) or JUSFIRST or
    JUSTLAST]
   [ACCUM]
   [L40 or L64 or L80 or HONEOM]
END-EXEC
```

Condition codes: IGREQCD, IGREQID, INVLDC, INVPARTN,
                    INVREQ, RETPAGE, TSIOERR, WRBRK

● **SEND TEXT MAPPED command—Send text with mapping**

```
EXEC CICS SEND TEXT MAPPED FROM (data-area)
   LENGTH(data-value)
   [PAGING or TERMINAL[WAIT][LAST]]
   [REQID(name)]
END-EXEC
```

Condition codes: IGREQID, RETPAGE, TSIOERR, WRBRK

● **SEND TEXT NOEDIT command—Send user data stream**

```
EXEC CICS SEND TEXT NOEDIT FROM(data-area)
   LENGTH(data-value)
   [ERASE]
   [PRINT]
   [FREEKB]
   [ALARM]
   [OUTPARTN(name)]
   [PAGING or TERMINAL[WAIT][LAST]]
   [REQID(name)]
   [L40 or L64 or L80 or HONEOM]
END-EXEC
```

Condition codes: IGREQCD, IGREQID,   INVPARTN,
                    TSIOERR, WRBRK

- **SEND CONTROL command—Send device control to terminal**

```
EXEC CICS SEND CONTROL
    [CURSOR[(data-value)]]
    [FORMFEED]
    [ERASE or ERASEAUP]
    [PRINT]
    [FREEKB]
    [ALARM]
    [FRSET]
    [MSR(data-value)]
    [OUTPARTN(name)]
    [ACTPARTN(name)]
    [LDC(name)]
    [ACCUM]
    [SET(ptr-ref) or PAGING or
        TERMINAL[WAIT][LAST]]
    [REQID(name)]
    [L40 or L64 or L80 or HONEOM]
END-EXEC

Condition codes:   IGREQCD, IGREQID, INVLDC, INVPARTN,
                   INVREQ, RETPAGE, TSIOERR, WRBRK
```

- **SEND PAGE command—Complete a BMS logical message**

```
EXEC CICS SEND PAGE
    [RELEASE[TRANSID(name)] or RETAIN]
    [TRAILER(data-area)]
    [SET(ptr-ref)]
    [AUTOPAGE[CURRENT or ALL] or NOAUTOPAGE]
    [OPERPURGE]
    [FMHPARM]
    [LAST]
END-EXEC

Condition codes:   IGREQCD,  INVREQ, RETPAGE, TSIOERR,
                   WRBRK
```

- **PURGE MESSAGE command—Delete the current logical message**

```
EXEC CICS PURGE MESSAGE
END-EXEC

Condition codes:   TSIOERR
```

- **ROUTE command—Route BMS logical message**

```
EXEC CICS ROUTE
    [INTERVAL(hhmmss) or TIME(hhmmss)]
    [ERRTERM[(name)]]
    [TITLE(data-area)]
```

```
     [LIST(data-area)]
     [OPCLASS(data-area)]
     [REQID(name)]
     [LDC(name)]
     [NLEOM]
END-EXEC
```

Condition codes: INVERRTERM,   INVLDC,   INVREQ,
                    RTEFAIL, RTESOME

Notes: LDC is used with logical units only.

◘ Description of options

ACCUM

This specifies building a logical message such that this command
is one of a number of commands. This logical message is either
completed by the SEND PAGE command or removed by the
PURGE MESSAGE command.

ACTPARTN(*name*)

This option activates a partition. It also specifies a partition name
to which the cursor is to be moved. The partition name is up to 2
characters in length.

ALARM

This option activates the alarm feature of the IBM 3270 device.

ALL

This specifies that the transmission of the current page of the BMS
logical message is to be stopped when the ATTN key of an IBM
2741 device is pressed and WRBRK is not active. No additional
pages will be transmitted.

ASIS

This overrides FEATURE=UCTRAN in the TCT for the terminal.

AUTOPAGE

This specifies that each page of the BMS logical message is to be
sent as soon as it is available. This option applies only to 3270
printers, not to terminals.

CURRENT

This specifies that the transmission of the current page of the BMS logical message is to be stopped when the ATTN key of an IBM 2741 device is pressed and WRBRK is not active. The next page, if any, will be transmitted.

CURSOR[(*data-value*)]

This specifies the cursor position on the screen after completion of a SEND MAP, SEND TEXT, or SEND CONTROL command. The cursor position is a halfword binary value relative to zero.

DATAONLY

This specifies that the data of the application program, not the whole map, are to be sent.

ERASE

This first clears the screen, then moves the cursor to the upper left-hand corner of the screen, and finally displays the current page of output.

ERASEAUP

This erases all unprotected fields before displaying subsequent pages of output.

ERRTERM(*name*)

This specifies the destination which is notified in case an undeliverable message is deleted. The destination is the name of a terminal. The default is the original terminal.

FMHPARM(*name*)

This specifies an outboard map name up to 8 characters long.

FORMFEED

This specifies skipping to a new page.

FREEKB

This unlocks the 3270 keyboard after data are written to the terminal.

FROM(*data-area*)

This specifies the data area from which data are sent by a SEND MAP or SEND TEXT command, or mapped by a RECEIVE MAP command. The storage area belongs to the application program.

FRSET
This specifies that MDTs (modified data tags) of all fields in the 3270 buffer are to be reset before any map data are written to the buffer.

HEADER(*data-value*)
This specifies the header value to be placed at the top of each page.

HONEOM
This specifies use of the default length for the printer line.
INPARTN(*name*)
This specifies the name of the terminal partition where data are to be entered. The name is 1 or 2 characters long.

INTERVAL(*hhmmss*)
This specifies the time interval for transmitting data to the terminals in a ROUTE command. The time consists of hours, minutes, and seconds.

INTO(*data-area*)
This specifies the data area where a record is placed during a RECEIVE MAP command. The data area belongs to the application program.

JUSFIRST
This places the text data at the top of the page.

JUSTLAST
This places the text data at the bottom of the page.

JUSTIFY(*data-value*)
This specifies the line where the text data are to be positioned. The line is a value (halfword binary) in the range 1 to 240.

LAST
This specifies the last output of a transaction.

LDC(*name*)
This specifies the logical device code (LDC) to be transmitted in

the FMH to the logical unit. The LDC name is a 2-character mnemonic which is translated into a logical device code.

LENGTH(*data-value*)

This specifies the actual length of data to be sent or received. The length is a halfword value.

LIST(*data-area*)

This specifies a list of terminals and/or operators to which data are to be sent. The data area contains a list of terminals and/or operators.

L40

This specifies the line length for the 3270 printer. After 40 characters are printed on a line, a carriage return and line feed are sent to the printer.

L64

This specifies the line length for the 3270 printer. After 64 characters are printed on a line, a carriage return and line feed are sent to the printer.

L80

This specifies the line length for the 3270 printer. After 80 characters have been printed on a line, a carriage return and line feed are sent to the printer.

MAP(*name*)

This specifies the name of the map to be displayed.
The name must be from 1 to 7 characters long.

MAPONLY

This specifies that only the default portion of the map is to sent.

MAPSET(*name*)

This specifies the name of the mapset belonging to a set of maps. The name must be an unsuffixed name and no more than 7 characters long.

NOAUTOPAGE

This specifies that pages of a BMS logical message are to be sent one page at a time.

OPCLASS(*data-area*)

This specifies a list of operator classes to which data are sent. The data area contains a list of operators.

OPERPURGE

This instructs CICS to delete the BMS logical message only if the operator submits a deletion request.

OUTPARTN(*name*)

This specifies a partition name to which data are sent.
The partition name is 1 or 2 characters long.

PAGING

This specifies that the data are to be placed in temporary storage rather than being sent immediately to the terminal. The data are displayed upon the request of the operator.

PARTNSET[(*name*)

This specifies a partition set name that belongs to an application program. The name is up to 6 characters long.

PARTN(*data-area*)

This specifies an input partition name, which is 1 or 2 characters long.

PRINT

This specifies that data sent to the printer buffer are to be printed.

RELEASE

This returns control to a higher logical level program or to CICS after a SEND PAGE command is completed.

REQID(*name*)

This specifies a prefix to be used in association with temporary storage. The name is 2 characters long and becomes the prefix of the temporary storage name. The default is **.

RETAIN

This returns control to the application program after a SEND PAGE command is completed.

SET(*ptr-ref*)
This specifies a pointer reference to a buffer that data are written to, or read from, during transfer operations. The reference is an address in main storage.

TERMINAL
This specifies that input data are to be read from the terminal that originated the transaction or that data will be sent to the terminal.

TIME(*hhmmss*)
This specifies the time when data are transferred to terminals in a ROUTE command. The time consists of hours, minutes and seconds.

TITLE(*data-area*)
This specifies a data area that contains the title to be used for routing logical messages.

TRAILER(*data-area*)
This specifies the data area that contains the information to be placed at the bottom of each output page.

TRANSID(*name*)
This specifies the transaction identification (ID). The transaction ID can be up to 4 characters long and must be defined in the program control table (PCT).

WAIT
This instructs CICS not to return control to the application program until the WRITE operation is completed. The default is to return control to the application program when output operation starts.

◼ BMS Exception condition codes

EOC   End-of-chain has been reached.

EODS   No data are received.

IGREQCD   An RCD (request change direction) code (with SIGNAL data flow control command) has been received from an LUTYPE4 logical unit.

IGREQID   The prefix specified with the REQID option is different from the one established by the previous REQID option.

INVERRTERM The terminal identification is invalid.

INVLDC   The LDC mnemonic cannot be found in the LDC list for the logical unit.

INVMPSZ   The map size is too wide.

INVPARTN   The partition is not defined.

INVPARTNSET The partition set name is not valid.

INVREQ   The request is invalid.

LENGERR   The specified length of the storage area to hold input data is incorrect.

MAPFAIL   The data to be mapped have a length of zero or do not contain a set-buffer-address (SBA).

OVERFLOW   The mapped data are larger than the current page.

PARTNFAIL   The partition specified by the terminal operator is not the same as the one specified by the INPARTN option of the RECEIVE MAP command.

RDATT   The operator terminated the RECEIVE MAP command with the ATTN key.

RETPAGE   The SET option specified when one or more pages are ready to be returned to the application program.

RTEFAIL   The message is being sent to a terminal that initiated the transaction when executing a ROUTE command.

RTESOME   The terminals will not receive a message as specified in a ROUTE command.

TSIORR   There is a temporary storage I/O error.

UNEXPIN   Unexpected or unrecognized data are received.

WRBRK   The terminal operator interrupts a SEND command with the ATTN key.

1.5   BATCH DATA EXCHANGE

This section lists the commands used to exchange data between application program and a destination; both must be part of a batch data interchange logical unit. First, there is a list of the general formats of the commands. In addition, all the options and condition codes associated with these commands are explained. The batch data exchange commands are ISSUE ABORT, ISSUE END, ISSUE REPLACE, ISSUE RECEIVE, ISSUE WAIT, ISSUE NOTE, ISSUE SEND, ISSUE ADD, and ISSUE QUERY.

◘ General formats

● ISSUE ABORT command—End communication with dataset abnormally

```
EXEC CICS ISSUE ABORT
   <[DESTID(data-value) [DESTIDLENG(data-value)]]   or
   [[SUBADDR(data-value)] [CONSOLE or PRINT or CARD or
       WPMEDIA1 or WPMEDIA2 or WPMEDIA3 or WPMEDIA4]]>
   [VOLUME(data-value) [VOLUMELENG(data-value)]]
END-EXEC

Condition codes:   FUNCERR, SELNERR, UNEXPIN
```

● ISSUE END command—End communication with dataset

```
EXEC CICS ISSUE END
   <[DESTID(data-value) [DESTIDLENG(data-value)] or
   [[SUBADDR(data-value)] [CONSOLE or PRINT or CARD or
       WPMEDIA1 or WPMEDIA2 or WPMEDIA3 or WPMEDIA4]]>
   [VOLUME(data-value)
       [VOLUMELENG(data-value)]]
END-EXEC

Condition codes:   FUNCERR, SELNERR, UNEXPIN
```

● ISSUE REPLACE command—Replace (update) a record in a
dataset

```
EXEC CICS ISSUE REPLACE
   DESTID(data-value)
   [DESTIDLENG(data-value)]
   [VOLUME(data-value) [VOLUMELENG(data-value)]]
   FROM(data-area)
   [LENGTH(data-value)]
   [NUMREC(data-value)]
   RIDFLD(data-area)
   [[KEYLENGTH(data-value)][KEYNUMBER(data-value)]
                     or RRN]
   [DEFRESP]
   [NOWAIT]
END-EXEC
```

Condition codes: FUNCERR, SELNERR, UNEXPIN

● ISSUE RECEIVE command—Read a record from a dataset

```
EXEC CICS ISSUE RECEIVE
   <INTO(data-area) or SET(ptr-ref)>
   [LENGTH(data-value)]
END-EXEC
```

Condition codes: DSSTAT, EODS, LENGERR, UNEXPIN

● ISSUE WAIT command—Suspend task activity

```
EXEC CICS ISSUE WAIT
   <[DESTID(data-value) [DESTIDLENG(data-value)]] or
    [[SUBADDR(data-value)] [CONSOLE or PRINT or CARD or
       WPMEDIA1 or WPMEDIA2 or WPMEDIA3 or WPMEDIA4]]>
   [VOLUME(data-value)
    [VOLUMELENG(data-value)]]
END-EXEC
```

Condition codes: FUNCERR, SELNERR, UNEXPIN

● ISSUE NOTE command—Get the next record number

```
EXEC CICS ISSUE NOTE
   DESTID(data-value)
   [DESTIDLENG(data-value)]
   [VOLUME(data-value)
    [VOLUMELENG(data-value)]]
   RRN
   RIDFLD(data-area)
END-EXEC
```

Condition codes: FUNCERR, SELNERR, UNEXPIN

● **ISSUE SEND command—Send data to a device**

```
EXEC CICS ISSUE SEND
   <[DESTID(data-value) [DESTIDLENG(data-value)]      or
    [SUBADDR(data-value)] [CONSOLE or PRINT or CARD or
        WPMEDIA1 or WPMEDIA2 or WPMEDIA3 or WPMEDIA4]]>
   [VOLUME(data-value)
    [VOLUMELENG(data-value)]]
   [LENGTH(data-value)]
   FROM(data-area)
   [NOWAIT]
   [DEFRESP]
END-EXEC

Condition codes:   FUNCERR, IGREQCD, SELNERR, UNEXPIN
```

● **ISSUE ADD command—Add a record to a dataset**

```
EXEC CICS ISSUE ADD
   DESTID(data-value)
   [DESTIDLENG(data-value)]
   [VOLUME(data-value)
    [VOLUMELENG(data-value)]]
   FROM(data-area)
   [LENGTH(data-value)]
   [NUMREC(data-value)]
   [DEFRESP]
   [NOWAIT]
   [RIDFLD(data-area) RRN]
END-EXEC

Condition codes:   FUNCERR, SELNERR, UNEXPIN
```

● **ISSUE QUERY command—Request to transmit dataset to host**

```
EXEC CICS ISSUE QUERY
   DESTID(data-value)
   [DESTIDLENG(data-value)]
   [VOLUME(data-value)
    [VOLUMELENG(data-value)]]
END-EXEC

Condition codes:   FUNCERR, SELNERR, UNEXPIN
```

● **Description of options**

CARD

This specifies that the output medium is a card reader/punch machine.

CONSOLE
This specifies that the output medium is an operator terminal.

DEFRESP
This specifies that all terminal control commands request a definite response from the outboard batch program.

DESTID(*data-value*)
This specifies the dataset name in the outboard destination.

DESTIDLENG(*data-value*)
This specifies the name length (halfword binary value) with the DESTID option.

FROM(*data-area*)
This specifies the area from which data are to be written to a dataset.

INTO(*data-area*)
This specifies the data area that is to receive the data read from a dataset.

KEYLENGTH(*data-value*)
This specifies the key length (halfword binary value) with the RIDFLD option.

KEYNUMBER(*data-value*)
This specifies a number (halfword binary value) of the index to find a record. The number is 1 through 8, and the default value is 1.

LENGTH(*data-value or data-area*)
This specifies the length of the data to be passed or received. For write operations, the length is a halfword binary value. For read operations, a data area contains the length.

NOWAIT
This specifies not waiting for a batch data interchange command to complete. The processing of the tasks continues.

NUMREC(*data-value*)
This specifies the number of logical records (halfword binary

value) to be added to, replaced in, or deleted from a relative dataset.

PRINT
This specifies that the output medium is a printer.

RIDFLD(*data-area*)
This specifies a data area that contains the record identification field.

RRN
This specifies that the number associated with the RIDFLD option is a relative record number (RRN).

SET(*ptr-ref*)
This specifies the pointer reference to be set to the address of the data retrieved from the dataset.

SUBADDR(*data-value*)
This specifies a value in the range 1 through 15 representing a medium subaddress.

VOLUME(*data-value*)
This specifies a diskette name in an outboard destination. The name is a character string up to 6 characters in length.

VOLUMELENG(*data-value*)
This specifies the length of diskette name in the VOLUME option.

WPMEDIA1 to WPMEDIA4
These options are the definition of input-output devices for wordprocessing mediums.

◼ Batch data interchange condition codes

DSSTAT   The destination status changed because the data stream was aborted or suspended.

EODS   End of dataset.

FUNCERR   An error has occurred during the execution of a command.

IGREQCD   The ISSUE SEND command is being executed after a SIGNAL RCD data-flow control is received from an LUTYPE4 logical unit.

LENGERR   The length of received data is greater than the length specified with the LENGTH option.

SELNERR   A destination selection error has occurred.

UNEXPIN   Unexpected data are received from the outboard controller.

1.6   INTERVAL CONTROL

The interval control commands provide time-controlled functions. This section first lists the general format of each command. In addition, all the options and condition codes associated with these commands are explained. The interval control commands are ASKTIME, FORMATTIME, DELAY, POST, WAIT, START, RETRIEVE, and CANCEL.

◻ **General Formats**

● **ASKTIME command—Get current date and time**

```
EXEC CICS ASKTIME
   [ABSTIME(data-area)]
END-EXEC
```

● **FORMATTIME command—Format date and time**

```
EXEC CICS FORMATTIME
   ABSTIME(data-value)
   [YYDDD(data-area)]
   [YYMMDD(data-area)]
   [YYDDMM(data-area)]
   [DDMMYY(data-area)]
   [MMDDYY(data-area)]
   [DATE(data-area)]
   [DATEFORM(data-area)]
   [DATESEP(data-value)]
   [DAYCOUNT(data-area)]
```

```
    [DAYOFWEEK(data-area)]
    [DAYOFMONTH(data-area)]
    [MONTHOFYEAR(data-area)]
    [YEAR(data-area)]
    [TIME(data-area)
      [TIMESEP[(data-value)]]]
END-EXEC
```

● **DELAY command—Suspend processing**

```
EXEC CICS DELAY
    [INTERVAL(hhmmss) or TIME(hhmmss)]
    [REQID(name)]
END-EXEC
```

Condition codes: EXPIRED, INVREQ

● **POST command—Notify expiry of specified time**

```
EXEC CICS POST
    [INTERVAL(hhmmss) or TIME(hhmmss)]
    SET(ptr-ref)
    [REQID(name)]
END-EXEC
```

Condition codes: EXPIRED, INVREQ

● **WAIT command—Wait for an event to complete**

```
EXEC CICS WAIT EVENT
    ECADDR(ptr-value)
END-EXEC
```

Condition codes: INVREQ

● **START command—Start a transaction through another transaction**

```
EXEC CICS START
    [INTERVAL(hhmmss) or TIME(hhmmss)]
    TRANSID(name)
    [REQID(name)]
    [FROM(data-area) LENGTH(data-value)[FMH]]
    [TERMID(name)]
    [SYSID(name)]
    [RTRANSID(name)]
    [RTERMID(name)]
    [QUEUE(name)]
    [NOCHECK]
    [PROTECT]
END-EXEC
```

Condition codes: INVREQ,   ISCINVREQ,   NOTAUTH,
                    SYSIDERR, TERMIDERR, TRANSIDERR

● **RETRIEVE command—Access data**

```
EXEC CICS RETRIEVE
   [INTO(data-area) or SET(ptr-ref)]
   [LENGTH(data-area)]
   [RTRANSID(data-area)]
   [RTERMID(data-area)]
   [QUEUE(data-area)]
   [WAIT]
END-EXEC
```

Condition codes: ENDDATA, ENVDEFERR, INVREQ, IOERR,
                    ISCINVREQ, LENGERR, NOAUTH, NOTFND

● **CANCEL command—Cancel previously issued command**

```
EXEC CICS CANCEL
   [REQID(name)
    [TRANSID(name)][SYSID(name)]]
```

Condition codes: INVREQ, ISCINVREQ, NOAUTH, NOTFND,
                    SYSIDERR

◖ Description of options

ABSTIME(*data-area*)
This specifies the data area that is to receive the absolute time of
day (in milliseconds since Jan. 1, 1900) during the execution of
the ASKTIME command.

DATE(*data-area*)
This specifies the data area that is to receive the date during the
execution of the FORMATTIME command. The length of the
value is 8 characters (including separators), and the format is
determined by the SIT DATFORM operand of the DFHSIT system
macro.

DATEFORM(*data-area*)
This specifies the data area that is to receive the date during the
execution of the FORMATTIME command. The format is
determined by the SIT DATFORM operand of the DFHSIT system
macro. CICS returns YYMMDD, DDMMYY, or MMDDYY.

DATESEP(*data-value*)
This specifies a character that is used to separate year, month, and
day in the output of the FORMATTIME command.

DAYCOUNT(*data-area*)
This specifies the data area that is to receive the number of days since Jan. 1, 1900. The number is 31-bit binary.

DAYOFWEEK(*data-area*)
This specifies the data area that is to receive the day of the week as a 31-bit binary number. Sunday is 0 and Saturday is 6.

DAYOFMONTH(*data-area*)
This specifies the data area that is to receive the day of the month as a 31-bit binary number.

DDMMYY(*data-area*)
This specifies the data area that is to receive the date. CICS returns an 8-character value with day, month, and year separated by the character specified in the DATESEP option.

ECADDR(*ptr-value*)
This specifies the address of the timer event area that must be posted before the activity of a task can continue.

FMH
This specifies that the data contains function management headers (FMH).

FROM(*data-area*)
This specifies the area from which data are to be passed to the transaction that will start in the future.

INTERVAL(*hhmmss*)
This specifies the hours, minutes, and seconds from the current time before a transaction.

INTO(*data-area*)
This specifies the data area that is to receive the retrieved data.

LENGTH(*data-value*)
This specifies the length of the data to be passed or received.

MMDDYY(*data-area*)
This specifies the data area to receive the month, day, and year. The length of the received data is 8 characters including the

separators specified in the DATESEP option.

MONTHOFYEAR(*data-area*)

This specifies the data area to receive the month of the year as a 31-bit binary number. January is 1; December is 12.

NOCHECK

This reduces error checks when executing a START command in a remote system.

PROTECT

This specifies that a new task will not start until the starting task has taken a sync point. This option is used to reduce the risk of duplicating or losing data.

QUEUE<(*name*) or (*data-area*)>

This specifies the name of a queue or a data area containing a queue that may be accessed by the transaction that is issuing the RETRIEVE command. The length of the queue name must be 8 characters.

REQID(*name*)

This specifies a unique Request Identification. The ID is used by CICS to name temporary storage.

RTERMID<(*name*) or (*data-area*)>

This specifies the name of a terminal or a data area that contains the name of the terminal.

RTRANSID<(*name*) or (*data-area*)>

This specifies the name of a transaction or a data area that contains the name of the transaction.

SET(*ptr-ref*)

This specifies the pointer reference to be set to the address of the retrived data.

SYSID(*name*)

This specifies the name of the remote system whose resources are to be used for intercommunication facilities.

TERMID(*name*)
This specifies the name of a terminal that is made available to a task being started.

TIME(*data-area*)
This specifies the expiration time, in format *hhmmss*, for an interval control function.

TIMESEP(*data-value*)
This specifies a character that is used to separate hours and minutes in the output of the FORMATTIME command.

TRANSID(*name*)
This specifies the name of a transaction to be executed or cancelled. The name should be up to 4 characters in length and must be defined in the program control table (PCT).

WAIT
This specifies that if all expired data have been retrieved, the task is to be put into a wait state until further expired data records become available.

YEAR(*data-area*)
This specifies the data area that is to receive the full number of years. The number is 31-bit binary.

YYDDD(*data-area*)
This specifies the data area that is to receive the year and number of days. CICS returns 6 characters with separator between year and days (e.g., 92/123).

YYDDMM(*data-area*)
This specifies the data area that is to receive year, days and months. CICS returns 8 characters with separators between year, days, and months (e.g., 92/17/03).

YYMMDD(*data-area*)
This specifies the data area that is to receive year, months, and days. CICS returns 8 characters with separators, between year, months, and days (e.g., 92/12/23).

◘ Interval control exception condition codes

ENDDATA   This error occurs when a RETRIEVE command is issued and one of the following situations exists:

- There are no more data or the end of file is reached.
- A FROM option is missing in a START command.
- A task which is not started with a START command issues a RETRIEVE command.

ENVDEFERR   The options in the RETRIEVE and START commands are not compatible.

EXPIRED   Time has expired in a POST or DELAY command.

INVREQ   There is an invalid interval control command or the ECB is above the 16-Mbyte line.

INVTSREQ   There is no support for temporary storage during execution of a RETRIEVE command.

IOERR   An I/O error occurred during execution of a RETRIEVE or START for the following reasons:

- Temporary storage is full.
- REQID(*name*) already exists.

ISCINVREQ   The remote system indicates a failure.

LENGERR   During a RETRIEVE operation, the record length is longer than the specified maximum in the LENGTH option.

NOTAUTH   There is not sufficient authority to use a resource.

NOTFND   A request identifier is not found.

SYSIDERR   The name specified in the SYSID option is not defined in the intersystem table, or the link to the remote system is closed.

TERMIDERR   The terminal ID is not found in the terminal control table or a duplicate terminal ID is specified in the START command.

TRANSIDERR   The transaction ID is not found in the program control table (PCT).

1.7 TASK CONTROL

The task control commands provide functions to control resources and synchronize task activity. This section first lists the general format of each command. In addition, all the options and condition codes associated with these commands are explained. The task control commands are SUSPEND, ENQ, and DEQ.

◻ General formats

● SUSPEND command—Suspend a task

```
EXEC CICS SUSPEND
END-EXEC
```

● ENQ command—Enqueue use of a resource

```
EXEC CICS ENQ
   RESOURCE(data-area)
   [LENGTH(data-value)]
   [NOSUSPEND]
END-EXEC
```

```
Condition codes:   ENQBUSY, LENGERR
```

● DEQ command—Dequeue use of a resource

```
EXEC CICS DEQ
   RESOURCE(data-area)
   [LENGTH(data-value)]
END-EXEC
```

```
Condition codes:   LENGERR
```

◻ **Description of options**

LENGTH(*data-value*)
This specifies the length of the data to be enqueued or dequeued.

NOSUSPEND
This specifies inhibition of the application program suspension for the ENQBUSY condition.

RESOURCE(*data-area*)
This specifies the data area that contains the resource.

◻ **Task control exception condition codes**

ENQBUSY   The resource specified by the ENQ command is not available.

LENGERR   The length specified in the ENQ or DEQ command is outside the range 1 through 255.

1.8   Program Control

The program control commands provide functions to govern the flow of application programs. This section first lists the general format of each command. In addition, all the options and condition codes associated with these commands are explained. The program control commands are LINK, XCTL, RETURN, LOAD, and RELEASE.

◻ **General formats**

● **LINK command—Link to a program and return**

```
EXEC CICS LINK
   PROGRAM(name)
   [COMMAREA(data-area)
     [LENGTH(data-value)]]
END-EXEC

Condition codes:   NOTAUTH, PGMIDERR
```

- **XCTL command—Pass control to a program**

```
EXEC CICS XCTL
    PROGRAM(name)
    [COMMAREA(data-area)
     [LENGTH(data-value)]]
END-EXEC
```

Condition codes: LENGERR, NOTAUTH, PGMIDERR

- **RETURN command—Return program control**

```
EXEC CICS RETURN
    [TRANSID(name)
     [COMMAREA(data-area)
        [LENGTH(data-value)]]]
END-EXEC
```

Condition codes: INVREQ, LENGERR

LOAD command—Load program into main storage

```
EXEC CICS LOAD
    PROGRAM(name)
    [SET(ptr-ref)
    [LENGTH(data-value) or FLENGTH(data-area)]
    [ENTRY(ptr-ref)]
    [HOLD]
END-EXEC
```

Condition codes: NOTAUTH, PGMIDERR

RELEASE command—Remove program from main storage

```
EXEC CICS RELEASE
    PROGRAM(name)
END-EXEC
```

Condition codes: NOTAUTH, PGMIDERR

◻ Description of options

COMMAREA(*data-area*)
This specifies a storage area that can be used to communicate data between programs.

ENTRY(*ptr-ref*)
This specifies a pointer reference. This pointer is used as a starting address of a program, table, or map that is to be loaded into main storage.

FLENGTH(*data-area*)

This specifies a data area (fullword binary) with the LOAD command. CICS writes the length of the program, table, or map that is successfully loaded. With the FLENGTH option, you cannot use the LENGTH option.

HOLD

This specifies not deleting a program, table, or map already loaded in storage when the task that issued the LOAD command terminates. The deletion is to happen when a RELEASE command is issued.

LENGTH(*data-value*)

This specifies a value that is the length of the communication area of a program. This option is used in the XCTL, RETURN and LINK commands. It is a halfword value not greater than 32,763 bytes. With the LENGTH option, you cannot use the FLENGTH option.

PROGRAM(*name*)

This specifies (1) a program name in the LINK, XCTL or RETURN command, and (2) a program, table, or map in the LOAD or RELEASE command.

SET(*ptr-ref*)

This specifies the pointer reference, an address where a program, table, or map is loaded.

TRANSID(*name*)

This specifies the transaction ID used in a RETURN command. The name must be defined in a CICS table and associated with a terminal.

◻ Program control exception condition codes

INVREQ   An invalid request is made in a RETURN command. The reason for this exception code is one of the following:

● The COMMAREA option is issued in a program that is not at the highest logical level.

- The address supplied with the COMMAREA option is zero.
- The transaction ID specified in the TRANSID option is not associated with a terminal.

LENGERR   The length specified in the LENGTH option is greater than the data length specified in the COMMAREA option.

NOTAUTH   There is no authorization to use resources.

PGMIDERR   The specified program, table, or map is not found in the PPT, or library, or is disabled.

1.9   STORAGE CONTROL

The storage control commands request main storage for working areas. This section lists the general format of each command. In addition, all the options and condition codes associated with these commands are explained. The storage control commands are GETMAIN and FREEMAIN.

■ **General formats**

- **GETMAIN command—Request and initialize main storage**

```
EXEC CICS GETMAIN
   SET(ptr-ref)
   <LENGTH(data-value) or FLENGTH(data-value)>
   [INITIMG(data-area)]
   [NOSUSPEND]
END-EXEC

Condition codes:    LENGERR, NOSTG
```

- **FREEMAIN command—Release main storage**

```
EXEC CICS FREEMAIN
   DATA(data-area)
END-EXEC
```

■ Description of options

DATA(*data-area*)

This specifies the data area to be freed in a FREEMAIN command. This area must have been obtained previously by the GETMAIN command.

FLENGTH(*data-value*)

This specifies the length of the data area to be obtained. The fullword binary value can be up to 65,504 bytes if the application is operating below the 16-Mbyte line. If the program is being executed above the 16-Mbyte line, then the maximum length is 1 gigabyte (1,073,741,824 bytes).

INITIMG(*data-area*)

This specifies the data area that contains a hexadecimal value used to initialize acquired storage in the GETMAIN command.

LENGTH(*data-value*)

This specifies the length of the data area to be obtained. The halfword binary value can be a maximum length of 32,767 bytes. With the LENGTH option, you cannot use the FLENGTH option.

NOSUSPEND

This specifies that the application program is not to be suspended when a NOSTG condition occurs.

SET(*ptr-ref*)

This specifies a pointer reference that is set by CICS when main storage is successfully obtained. It is the address of the storage area.

SHARED

This specifies that the obtained main area is to be shared by many tasks, and therefore should not be released when the task that requested the storage terminates. Such storage is terminated with a FREEMAIN command.

■ Storage control exception condition codes

LENGERR   The length specified with the FLENGTH option

exceeds the maximum value allowed.

NOSTG   The requested main storage is not available.

1.10 TRANSIENT DATA CONTROL

The transient data control commands provides a queuing facility used by application programs. This section lists the general format of each command. In addition, all the options and condition codes associated with these commands are explained. The transient data control commands are WRITE TD, READ TD, and DELETEQ TD.

■ **General formats**

● **WRITE TD command—Write data to transient queue**

```
EXEC CICS WRITE TD
   QUEUE(name)
   FROM(data-area)
   [LENGTH(data-value)]
   [SYSID(name)]
END-EXEC
```

```
Condition codes:    DISABLED,    IOERR,    ISCINVREQ,
                    LENGERR, NOSPACE, NOTAUTH, NOTOPEN,
                    QIDERR, SYSIDERR
```

● **READ TD command—Read data from transient queue**

```
EXEC CICS READ TD
   QUEUE(name)
   <INTO(data-area) or SET(ptr-ref)>
   [LENGTH(data-area)]
   [SYSID(name)]
   [NOSUSPEND]
END-EXEC
```

```
Condition codes:    DISABLED,    IOERR,    ISCINVREQ,
                    LENGERR, NOTAUTH, NOTOPEN, QBUSY,
                    QIDERR, QZERO, SYSIDERR.
```

• DELETEQ TD command—Delete a transient data queue

```
EXEC CICS DELETE TD
   QUEUE(name)
   [SYSID(name)]
END-EXEC
```

Condition codes: DISABLED,   ISCINVREQ,   NOTAUTH,
                    QIDERR, SYSIDERR

◘ Description of options

FROM(*data-area*)

This specifies the area from which data are written to the transient data queue.

INTO(*data-area*)

This specifies the data area of the application program into which data are to be copied from the transient data queue.

LENGTH(*data-area* or *data-value*)

This species the length of the data to be copied from or written to a transient data queue. In the WRITEQ TD command, the parameter must be a data value. For a READQ TD, the parameter must be a data area containing the maximum length of the data a program can accept.

NOSUSPEND

This specifies that the application program is not to be suspended when a QBUSY condition occurs.

QUEUE(*name*)

This specifies the name of the transient data queue.

SET(*ptr-ref*)

This specifies a pointer reference that is set by CICS when data are read from a queue. It is the address of data in a queue.

SYSID(*name*)

This specifies the name of a remote system whose resources are to be used for intercommunication. The length of the name can be up to 4 characters.

◼ Transient data control exception condition codes

DISABLED	The queue is disabled on this system.
IOERR	An I/O error occurred because an an incorrect data length was specified for an extrapartition or intrapartition destination.
ISCINVREQ	A remote system has failed and the condition is unknown.
LENGERR	The length specified with a READQ TD or WRITEQ TD command is incorrect.
NOSPACE	The intrapartition queue is full.
NOTAUTH	There is not authorization to use a resource.
NOTOPEN	A destination is closed.
QBUSY	The record being accessed by READQ TD is being either written to or deleted by another task.
QIDERR	The queue name cannot be found.
QZERO	The queue is empty or end of data has been reached.
SYSIDERR	The name specified in the SYSID option is either not defined or not available.

1.11 TEMPORARY STORAGE CONTROL

The temporary storage control commands provide facilities to application programs to store data in temporary queues. The queues are defined in main storage or in DASD. This section lists the general format of each command. In addition, all the options and condition codes associated with these commands are explained. The temporary storage control commands are WRITE TS, READ TS, and DELETEQ TS.

▣ **General formats**

● **WRITE TS command—Write data to temporary storage queue**

```
EXEC CICS WRITE TS
   QUEUE(name)
   FROM(data-area)
   [LENGTH(data-value)]
   [ITEM(data-area) [REWRITE]]
   [SYSID(name)]
   [MAIN or AUXILIARY]
   [NOSUSPEND]
END-EXEC
```

Condition codes: INVREQ, IOERR, ISCINVREQ, ITEMERR,
                    NOSPACE, NOTAUTH, QIDERR, SYSIDERR

● **READ TS command—Read data from temporary storage queue**

```
EXEC CICS READ TS
   QUEUE(name)
   <INTO(data-area) or SET(ptr-ref)>
   [LENGTH(data-area)
   [NUMITEMS(data-area)]
   [ITEM(data-value) or NEXT]
   [SYSID(name)]
END-EXEC
```

Condition codes: INVREQ, IOERR, ISCINVREQ, ITEMERR,
                    LENGERR, NOTAUTH, QIDERR, SYSIDERR

● **DELETEQ TS command—Delete a temporary storage queue**

```
EXEC CICS DELETE TS
   QUEUE(name)
   [SYSID(name)]
END-EXEC
```

Condition codes: ISCINVREQ,   NOTAUTH,   QIDERR,
                    SYSIDERR

▣ **Description of options**

AUXILIARY
This specifies that the temporary data queue is on a direct-access storage device.

FROM(*data-area*)
This specifies the area from which data are written to the temporary data queue.

INTO(*data-area*)
This specifies the data area of the application program into which data are to be copied from the temporary data queue.

ITEM(*data-area* or *data-value*)
This specifies the relative item that is being read or written. In the WRITEQ TS command, the parameter is a data area to which the item is written by CICS. In a READQ TS command, the parameter is a value specified by the application program.

LENGTH(*data-area* or *data-value*)
This specifies the length of the data to be copied from or written to a temporary data queue. In the WRITEQ TS command, the parameter must be a halfword binary value. For a READQ TS command, the parameter must be a data area containing the maximum length of the data a program can accept.

MAIN
This specifies that the temporary data queue is to reside in main storage.

NEXT
This specifies that the next logical record is to be read from the queue. The NEXT option is used instead of the ITEM option.

NOSUSPEND
This specifies that the application program is not to suspended when a NOSPACE condition occurs.

NUMITEMS(*data-area*)
This specifies a data area where CICS stores the number of items in the queue.

QUEUE(*name*)
This specifies the name of the temporary data queue.

REWRITE
This specifies writing the given data over an existing record. It is used with the ITEM option.

SET(*ptr-ref*)
This specifies a pointer reference that is set by CICS when data are read from a queue. It is the address of data in a queue.

SYSID(*name*)
This specifies the name of a remote system whose resources are to be used for intercommunication. The length of the name can be up to 4 characters.

■ **Temporary data control exception condition codes**

INVREQ	The queue name is not valid or the queue is locked.
IOERR	An I/O error occurred.
ISCINVREQ	A remote system has failed and the condition is unknown.
ITEMERR	There is an invalid item number.
LENGERR	The length specified with the READQ TS or WRITEQ TS command is incorrect.
NOSPACE	The data set containing the queue is full.
NOTAUTH	There is not authorization to use a resource.
QIDERR	The queue name cannot be found.
SYSIDERR	The name specified in the SYSID option is either not defined or not available.

1.12 ABNORMAL TERMINATION AND RECOVERY

The abnormal terminaton and recovery commands provide the facility to execute an exit routine when a task abends. This section lists the general format of each command. In addition, all the options and condition codes associated with these commands are explained. The abnormal termination and recovery commands are HANDLE ABEND and ABEND.

◼ **General formats**

● **HANDLE ABEND command—Handle abnormal program termination**

```
EXEC CICS HANDLE ABEND
   [PROGRAM(name)        or
     LABEL(name)         or
     CANCEL              or
     RESET]
END-EXEC
```

```
Condition codes:    PGMIDERR
```

● **ABEND command—Abnormal task termination**

```
EXEC CICS ABEND
   [ABCODE(name)]
   [CANCEL]
END-EXEC
```

◼ **Description of options**

ABCODE(*name*)

This specifies a name that can be used to identify a dump of main storage. The name may be up to 4 characters in length.

CANCEL

This specifies that exits established by HANDLE ABEND and ABEND commands are to be ignored.

LABEL(*name*)

This specifies a program label to which control will go if an abnormal termination occurs.

PROGRAM(*name*)

This specifies a program name which is executed if an abnormal termination occurs. The name must be defined in the program control table (PCT) and must not be longer than 8 alphanumeric characters.

RESET

This specifies that an exit previously cancelled by a HANDLE ABEND CANCEL command or CICS is to be activated.

◼ **Abnormal termination and recovery exception condition code**

PGMIDERR   A specified program name cannot be found in a program control table (PCT).

1.13 TRACE CONTROL

The trace control commands provide facilities to debug and monitor application programs. This section lists the general format of each command. In addition, all the options and condition codes associated with these commands are explained. The trace control commands are ENTER and TRACE.

◼ **General formats**

● **ENTER command—Enter user trace entry point and event monitoring point**

```
EXEC CICS ENTER
   TRACEID(data-value)
   [FROM(data-area)]
   [RESOURCE(name)]
   [ENTRYNAME(name)]
   [ACCOUNT]
   [MONITOR]
   [PERFORM]
END-EXEC

Condition code: INVREQ
```

TRACE command—Turn trace off or on

```
EXEC CICS TRACE
   <ON or OFF>
   [SYSTEM]
   [EI]
   [USER]
   [SINGLE]
END-EXEC
```

◻ Description of options

ACCOUNT

This specifies that user information (event monitoring point) is to be written to the accounting class monitoring data records.

EI

This specifies that tracing of CICS commands through the EXEC interface program is changed by the TRACE ON or TRACE OFF command.

ENTRYNAME(*name*)

This specifies a name for a user event monitoring point. The maximum length of the name is 8 characters.

FROM(*data-area*)

This specifies an area containing 8 bytes of data which appears in bytes 8 to 15 of the trace table entry.

MONITOR

This specifies a user event monitoring point.

PERFORM

This specifies the collection of user information (event monitoring point) in the performance class monitoring data records.

RESOURCE(*name*)

This specifies an area containing 8 bytes of data which appears in bytes 16 to 23 of the trace table entry as the resource field.

SINGLE

This specifies that tracing applies to user entries of a single task.

SYSTEM
This specifies production of system trace table entries.

TRACEID(*data-value*)
This specifies a value that is used for a user trace table entry. The value must be halfword binary in the range 0 through 199.

USER
This specifies that user entries are affected by the TRACE ON or TRACE OFF command.

◻ **Trace control exception condition code**

INVREQ Trace ID is greater than 199.

1.14 DUMP CONTROL

The dump control command writes specific areas of main storage to a sequential dataset. This section gives the general format of the command. In addition, all the options associated with this command are explained. The dump control command is DUMP.

◻ **General format**

● **DUMP command—Dump main storage**

```
EXEC CICS DUMP
   DUMPCODE(name)
   [FROM(data-area)
     LENGTH(data-value) or FLENGTH(data-value)]
   [COMPLETE]
   [TASK]
   [STORAGE]
   [PROGRAM]
   [TERMINAL]
   [TABLES]
   [DCT]
   [FCT]
   [PCT]
   [PPT]
   [SIT]
   [TCT]
END-EXEC
```

◘ Description of options

COMPLETE
This specifies dumping *all* main storage of a task.

DCT
This specifies the destination control table.

FCT
This specifies the file control table.

FLENGTH(*data-value*)
This specifies the length of the data area to be dumped. The fullword binary value can be up to 16,777,215 bytes.

FROM(*data-area*)
This specifies a valid data area to be dumped.

LENGTH(*data-value*)
This specifies the halfword binary value of the length of data in the FROM option. With LENGTH, you cannot use the FLENGTH option.

PCT
This specifies the program control table.

PPT
This specifies the processing program table.

PROGRAM
This specifies dumping the program storage areas of a task.

SIT
This specifies the system initialization table.

STORAGE
This specifies dumping the storage areas of a task.

TABLES
This specifies dumping all tables: DCT, FCT, PCT, PPT, SIT, and TCT.

TASK

This specifies dumping the storage areas of this task.

TCT

This specifies the terminal control table.

TERMINAL

This specifies dumping the storage areas of the terminal.

1.15 JOURNAL CONTROL

The journal control commands provide the facility to create and manage journals. This section lists the general format of each command. In addition, all the options and condition codes associated with these commands are explained. The journal control commands are JOURNAL and WAIT JOURNAL.

◻ **General formats**

● **JOURNAL command—Make a journal record**

```
EXEC CICS JOURNAL
   JFILEID(data-value)
   JTYPEID(data-value)
   FROM(data-area)
   [LENGTH(data-value)]
   [REQID(data-area)]
   [PREFIX(data-area)
     PFXLENGTH(data-value)]
   [STARTIO]
   [WAIT]
   [NOSUSPEND]
END-EXEC
```

```
Condition codes:   INVREQ,  IOERR,  JIDERR,  LENGERR,
                   NOJBUFSP, NOTAUTH, NOTOPEN
```

● **WAIT JOURNAL command—Synchronize task with journal output**

```
EXEC CICS WAIT JOURNAL
   JFILEID(data-value)
   [REQID(data-value)]
   [STARTIO]
END-EXEC
```

```
Condition codes:    INVREQ,   IOERR,   JIDERR,   NOTAUTH,
                    NOTOPEN
```

◼ Description of options

FROM(*data-area*)
This specifies the data area that is used as input to a journal record.

JFILEID(*data-value*)
This specifies a value (halfword numeric) in the range 1 through 99 to be used as the journal name.

JTYPEID(*data-value*)
This specifies a 2-character name placed in the journal record to identify its origin.

LENGTH(*data-value*)
This specifies the number of bytes (halfword binary value) of data to build into a journal record.

NOSUSPEND
This specifies that the application program is not to be suspended when the NOJBUFSP condition occurs.

PFXLENGTH(*data-value*)
This specifies the number of bytes (halfword binary value) of prefix data of the journal record.

PREFIX(*data-area*)
This specifies the area that contains the prefix data of the journal record.

REQID(*parameter*)
This specifies a data area in which the identifier of a journal record for asynchronous output is to be stored.

STARTIO
This specifies initializing the output of the journal record immediately.

WAIT

This specifies waiting for the synchronous journal output.

◻ Journal control exception condition codes

INVREQ	A WAIT JOURNAL command was issued before a JOURNAL command.
IOERR	Output of the journal record was not successful.
JIDERR	The journal name is not defined in the journal control table (JCT).
LENGERR	The length of the journal record is longer than the record size of the output dataset.
NOJBUFSP	The journal buffer space is not sufficient.
NOTAUTH	There is not authorization to use a resource.
NOTOPEN	The journal is not opened or available.

1.16 SYNC POINT CONTROL

The sync point control command provides a facility to restore certain resources, such as datasets, if an abnormal termination of a program happens. This section lists the general format of the command. In addition, it explains the option and condition code associated with this command. The sync point control command is SYNCPOINT.

◻ General format

● SYNCPOINT command—Sync point

```
EXEC CICS SYNCPOINT
   [ROLLBACK]
END-EXEC
```

Condition code: ROLLEDBACK

◘ Description of option

ROLLBACK
This specifies backing out all changes to resources made by a task since the last SYNCPOINT command was executed.

◘ Sync point control exception condition code

ROLLEDBACK   A rollback occurred during a SYNCPOINT command at a remote system.

1.17 LAYOUT OF DFHAID BLOCK—KEY ASSIGNMENTS

The DFHAID is a record definition used in a COBOL program for key assignments.

```
01  DFHAID.
    02   DFHNULL      PIC X VALUE ' '.
    02   DFHENTER     PIC X VALUE QUOTE.      ENTER KEY
    02   DFHCLEAR     PIC X VALUE ' '.        CLEAR KEY
    02   DFHPEN       PIC X VALUE '='.        LIGHT PEN
    02   DFHOPID      PIC X VALUE 'W'.        OPERATOR ID
    02   DFHMSRE      PIC X VALUE 'X'.        MAG. STRIP
    02   DFHSTRE      PIC X VALUE ' '.        NON-MAG. STRIP
    02   DFHTRIG      PIC X VALUE '"'.        TRIGGER FLD
    02   DFHPA1       PIC X VALUE '%'.        ATT KEY 1
    02   DFHPA2       PIC X VALUE ' '.        ATT KEY 2
    02   DFHPA3       PIC X VALUE ' '.        ATT KEY 3
    02   DFHPF1       PIC X VALUE '1'.        PF KEY 1
    02   DFHPF2       PIC X VALUE '2'.        PF KEY 2
    02   DFHPF3       PIC X VALUE '3'.        PF KEY 3
    02   DFHPF4       PIC X VALUE '4'.        PF KEY 4
    02   DFHPF5       PIC X VALUE '5'.        PF KEY 5
    02   DFHPF6       PIC X VALUE '6'.        PF KEY 6
    02   DFHPF7       PIC X VALUE '7'.        PF KEY 7
    02   DFHPF8       PIC X VALUE '8'.        PF KEY 8
    02   DFHPF9       PIC X VALUE '9'.        PF KEY 9
    02   DFHPF10      PIC X VALUE ':'.        PF KEY 10
    02   DFHPF11      PIC X VALUE '#'.        PF KEY 11
    02   DFHPF12      PIC X VALUE '@'.        PF KEY 12
    02   DFHPF13      PIC X VALUE 'A'.        PF KEY 13
    02   DFHPF14      PIC X VALUE 'B'.        PF KEY 14
    02   DFHPF15      PIC X VALUE 'C'.        PF KEY 15
    02   DFHPF16      PIC X VALUE 'D'.        PF KEY 16
    02   DFHPF17      PIC X VALUE 'E'.        PF KEY 17
    02   DFHPF18      PIC X VALUE 'F'.        PF KEY 18
    02   DFHPF19      PIC X VALUE 'G'.        PF KEY 19
    02   DFHPF20      PIC X VALUE 'H'.        PF KEY 20
    02   DFHPF21      PIC X VALUE 'I'.        PF KEY 21
    02   DFHPF22      PIC X VALUE ' '.        PF KEY 22
```

```
02   DFHPF23    PIC X VALUE '.'.    PF KEY 23
02   DFHPF24    PIC X VALUE ' '.    PF KEY 24
```

1.18 LAYOUT OF DFHEIBLK BLOCK—INTERFACE

The DFHEIBLK is a record definition for the EXEC interface block (IEF), which can be accessed, but not changed, by an application program.

```
01   DFHEIBLK.
   02   EIBTIME   PIC S9(7) COMP-3.  TIME IN 0HHMMSS FORMAT
   02   EIBDATE   PIC S9(7) COMP-3.  DATE IN 00YYDDD FORMAT
   02   EIBTRNID  PIC X(4).          TRANSACTION IDENTIFIER
   02   EIBTASKN  PIC X(4).          TASK NUMBER
   02   EIBTRMID  PIC X(4).          TERMINAL IDENTIFIER
   02   DFHEIGDI  PIC S9(7) COMP.    RESERVED BY THE SYSTEM
   02   EIBCPOSN  PIC S9(4) COMP.    CURSOR POSITION
   02   EIBCALEN  PIC S9(4) COMP.    LENGTH OF COMMAREA
   02   EIBAID    PIC X.             ATTENTION IDENTIFIER
   02   EIBFN     PIC X(2).          FUNCTION CODE
   02   EIBRCODE  PIC X(6).          RESPONSE CODE
   02   EIBDS     PIC X(6).          DATASET NAME
   02   EIBREOID  PIC X(8).          REQUEST IDENTIFIER
   02   EIBRSRCE  PIC X(8).          RESOURCE NAME
   02   EIBSYNC   PIC X.             SYNCPOINT REQUIRED
   02   EIBFREE   PIC X.             FREE TERMINAL REQ.
   02   EIBRECV   PIC X.             DATA REC. REQ.
   02   EIBSEND   PIC X.             RESERVED BY SYSTEM
   02   EIBATT    PIC X.             ATTACHED DATA EXIST
   02   EIBEOC    PIC X.             REC. DATA COMPLETE
   02   EIBFMH    PIC X.             REC. DATA HAVE FMH
```

1.19 LAYOUT OF DFHBMSCA—BMS STANDARD ATTRIBUTE

```
01   DFHBMSCA.
   02   DFHBMPEM PIC X VALUE ' '. PRINTER END OF MESSSAGE
   02   DFHBMPNL PIC X VALUE ' '. PRINTER NEW LINE CHAR
   02   DFHBMASK PIC X VALUE '0'. AUTOSKIP
   02   DFHBMUNP PIC X VALUE ' '. UNPROTECTED
   02   DFHBMUNN PIC X VALUE '&'. UNPROTECTED NUMERIC
   02   DFHBMPRO PIC X VALUE '-'. PROTECTED
   02   DFHBMBRY PIC X VALUE 'H'. BRIGHT INTENSITY
   02   DFHBMDAR PIC X VALUE '<'. NONDISPLAY
   02   DFHBMFSE PIC X VALUE 'A'. MODIFIED DATA TAG MDT ON
   02   DFHBMPRF PIC X VALUE '/'. PROTECTED AND MDT ON
   02   DFHBMASF PIC X VALUE '1'. AUTOSKIP AND MDT ON
   02   DFHBMASB PIC X VALUE '8'. AUTOSKIP BRIGHT INTENSITY
   02   DFHSA    PIC X VALUE ' '. SET ATTRIBUTE ORDER
   02   DFHCOLOR PIC X VALUE ' '. COLOR
   02   DFHPS    PIC X VALUE ' '. PROGRAMMED SYMBOLS
   02   DFHHLT   PIC X VALUE ' '. HIGHLIGHT
```

```
02   DFH3270  PIC X VALUE ' '. BASE 3270 FIELD ATTRIBUTE
02   DFHVAL   PIC X VALUE 'A'. VALIDATION
02   DFHALL   PIC X VALUE ' '. RESET ALL TO DEFAULTS
02   DFHERROR PIC X VALUE ' '. ERROR CODE
02   DFHDFT   PIC X VALUE ' '. DEFAULT
02   DFHDFCOL PIC X VALUE ' '. DEFAULT COLOR
02   DFHBLUE  PIC X VALUE '1'. BLUE
02   DFHRED   PIC X VALUE '2'. RED
02   DFHPINK  PIC X VALUE '3'. PINK
02   DFHGREEN PIC X VALUE '4'. GREEN
02   DFHTURQ  PIC X VALUE '5'. TURQUOISE
02   DFHYELLO PIC X VALUE '6'. YELLOW
02   DFHNEUTR PIC X VALUE '7'. NEUTRAL
02   DFHBASE  PIC X VALUE ' '. BASED PGM SYMBOL SET
02   DFHFHI   PIC X VALUE ' '. NO HIGHLIGHT—DEFAULT
02   DFHBLINK PIC X VALUE '1'. BLINKING
02   DFHREVRS PIC X VALUE '2'. REVERSE VIDEO
02   DFHUNDLN PIC X VALUE '4'. UNDERLINING
02   DFHMFIL  PIC X VALUE ' '. MANDATORY FILL
02   DFHMENT  PIC X VALUE ' '. MANDATORY ENTER
02   DFHMFE   PIC X VALUE ' '. MANDATORY FILL AND ENTER
```

1.20 LIST OF CICS TERMINALS

LUTYPE4 logical unit
LUTYPE6.1 logical unit
LUTYPE6.2 logical unit (VTAM only)
Standard CICS terminal support
System/3
2260 and 2265 display station
2741 communication terminal
2980 general banking terminal system
3270 information display system
3270 logical unit
3270 CSC printer logical unit
3270-display logical unit (LUTYPE2)
3270-printer logical unit
3600 and 4700 finance communication system
3600 logical unit
3630 plant communication system
3650 host command processor logical unit
3650 host conversational logical unit
3650 interpreter logical unit
3735 programmable buffered terminal
3740 data entry system
3767 interactive logical unit
3770 interactive logical unit

3770 interactive logical unit
3770 full-function logical unit
3790 inquiry logical unit
3790 SCS printer logical unit
3790 logical unit
7770 audio response unit

1.21 CICS-SUPPLIED TRANSACTIONS

The following is a list of transactions supplied by CICS.

CBRC—Database recovery control
CEBR—Temporary storage browse
CEBT—Master terminal backup
CECI—Command-level interpreter
CECS—Command-level syntax checker
CEDA—Resource definition online (RDO)
CEDB—Resource definition online
CEDC—Resource definition online
CEDF—Execution diagnostic facility
CEHS—Remote server
CEMT—Master terminal transaction
CEOT—Terminal status
CESN—Sign on
CEST—Supervisory terminal services
CMSG—Message switching
CRTE—Routing
CSFE—Terminal, test, trace, storage
CSMT—Master terminal
CSOT—Terminal status
CSPG—Terminal paging
CSSF—Sign off
CSSN—Sign on
CSST—Supervisory terminal
CSTT—System statistics and monitoring
CWTO—Write to console operator

CLIST

This chapter is a reference for programmers using CLIST. The first two section are

CLIST statements
CLIST built-in functions

In both cases the syntax and explanation of keywords are given. The third section lists all the control variables used by CLIST which you can access.

Notational Conventions: In the general format of the CLIST statements or built-in functions used in this chapter, there are a few symbols that are not part of the syntax; therefore they must not be included when coding your program. These symbols and their meanings are:

Symbol	Meaning
[]	The option enclosed by the brackets ([]) is not required but can be included.
<>	Only one of the alternatives enclosed by the angle brackets (<>) must be chosen.
or	The alternatives enclosed by the angle brackets (<>) are separated by "or."
_____	The underlined word is the default value.
...	The vertical or horizontal ellipsis means that the preceding can be coded more than once.

64

Uppercase characters	All keywords of the command are written in uppercase characters; they must be coded as shown.
Lowercase characters	All strings in lowercase characters and italic are variables that can be changed to any other strings to suit your programming style. In your code they represent values that you supply to commands.

2.1   CLIST Statements

This section contains all the statements of the CLIST language. For each statement, it gives the general format for usage, followed by explanation of the statement, keywords, and variables. In addition, wherever applicable, examples of how to use the statement are provided to enhance your understanding.

◼ ATTN—Associate routine with attention key

- **General format**
  ```
  [label:]   ATTN <OFF or action>
  ```

- **Description**
  The ATTN statement associates a routine with the attention key. When the ATTN or PA1 key is pressed while a CLIST is being executed, control is passed to this routine. It can be programmed to terminate or change the processing path.

  label is an optional statement label to branch to the ATTN statement with a GOTO statement. It's length varies from one to 31 characters.

  OFF is used to nullify any previously defined ATTN routine. ATTN OFF is the default. This parameter must not be used within an ATTN routine.

  action consists of one the following:

  - Single TSO command
  - A null statement
  - Any number of statements enclosed by a DO-END statement

- **Example**

In the following example, first a label ATTAKEY is associated with the ATTN. Next, the routine to write a message to the user, enclosed with a DO-END statement, is defined to be executed when the ATTN or PA1 key is pressed.

```
ATTAKEY: ATTN
DO
   WRITE ATTENTION KEY WAS PRESSED; PROGRAM TERMINATED
END
```

◻ CLOSFILE—Close file

- **General format**

```
label:    CLOSFILE <filename or &symbolic-variable>
```

- **Description**

The CLOSFILE statement closes a sequential file that was previously opened by an OPENFILE statement. One CLOSFILE statement closes only one file.

label is an optional statement label to branch to the CLOSFILE statement with a GOTO statement. Its length varies from 1 to 31 characters.

filename is a DDNAME which has been allocated to a dataset name and is being closed.

&symbolic-variable is a symbolic variable name which contains the DDNAME being closed.

- **Example**

In the following example, a DDNAME SYSUT1 is first allocated to dataset 'TEMP.SAA.REPORT'; it is then opened with an OPENFILE statement and finally closed with a CLOSEFILE statement.

```
ALLOC F(SYSUT1) DA('TEMP.SAA.REPORT') SHR REUSE
OPENFILE SYSUT1 INPUT
   .
   .
   .
CLFILE:   CLOSEFILE SYSUT1
```

◘ CONTROL—Define processing options

● **General format**
```
[label:]    CONTROL
            [PROMPT or NOPROMT] [SYMLIST or NOSYMLIST]
            [LIST or NOLIST] [CONLIST or NOCONLIST]
            [CAPS or NOCAPS or ASIS] [MSG or NOMSG]
            [FLUSH or NOFLUSH] [MAIN] [END(string)]
```

● **Description**
The CONTROL statement defines the processing options for CLIST. Each option used when a CONTROL statement is executed, is in effect until the CLIST ends or another CONTROL statement with the same option is issued.

label is an optional statement label to branch to the CONTROL statement with a GOTO statement. Its length varies from 1 to 31 characters.

PROMPT or NOPROMT allows or prohibits prompting for input values by TSO commands in CLIST.

SYMLIST or NOSYMLIST displays or prevents the display of commands, subcommands, or CLIST statements at the terminal *before* symbolic variable substitution is done.

LIST specifies the display of commands or subcommands at the terminal *after* symbolic variable substitution is done, but before execution.

NOLIST specifies that commands or subcommands are not to be displayed at the terminal.

CONLIST or NOCONLIST displays or prevents the display of CLIST statements at the terminal *after* symbolic variable substitution is done, but before execution.

CAPS converts characters to uppercase before execution.

NOCAPS or ASIS prevents any conversion of characters to uppercase.

MSG or NOMSG allows or prohibits display of information

messages at the terminal.

FLUSH or NOFLUSH allows or prohibits TSO's purging the queue of nested CLISTs.

MAIN specifies a main CLIST in the TSO environment; it cannot be deleted from the system.

END specifies *string* as a replacement for END in a DO or SELECT statement. *string* contains 1 to 4 characters and must start with an alphabetical character.

● **Example**

The following CONTROL statement sets the option to display executable statements, prompt for input values, and prevent the purge of input stack.

```
CONTROL CONLIST PROMPT NOFLUSH
```

◻ DATA-ENDDATA—Instream data for TSO

● **General format**

```
label:    DATA
   .
   .
   statements for TSO
   .
   .
   .
   ENDDATA
```

● **Description**

The DATA-ENDDATA statement marks statements that are not to be processed by CLIST, but rather passed to TSO for execution.

label is an optional statement label to branch to the DATA-ENDDATA statement with a GOTO statement. Its length varies from 1 to 31 characters.

● Example

In the following example, the instream data after DATA and before ENDDATA in a CLIST, is passed to TSO.

```
DATA
   EDIT 'ZOOGOP.SAMPLE.CLIST' OLD NONUM
   C * 999 '$' ' ' ALL
   END SAVE
ENDDATA
```

◻ DO—DO loop

• General format

Format 1
```
[label:]  DO variable = from-expression +
      TO to-expression      +
      [BY by-expression]

      statements
   END
```

Format 2
```
[label:]  DO WHILE condition
      statements
   END
```

Format 3
```
[label:]  DO UNTIL condition
      statements
   END
```

• Description
The DO statement is used to execute a sequence of statements in three ways: once, repeatedly, or conditionally. As shown above, the first format is for a one-time or repeated iteration of the DO loop. The next two formats are for conditional execution of statements, specified with the keywords WHILE or UNTIL and a *condition*. A DO loop starts with the keyword DO and ends with the keyword END; in between are one or more statements to be executed.

label is an optional statement label to branch to the DO-END statement with a GOTO statement. Its length varies from 1 to 31 characters.

variable is the name of a variable whose content changes depending on the *by-expression*. The value of *variable* starts from *from-expression* and reaches *to-expression*. With each change, the statements in the loop are executed.

statements consists of TSO commands, TSO subcommands, and CLIST statements.

condition is tested before the DO loop is executed. If the result is true, the loop is executed; otherwise the DO-END sequence stops.

• **Example**
The following example lists numbers from 1 to 5 and multiplies each number by 10.

```
DO &I = 1 to 5
SET &SUM = 10*I
WRITE TEN TIME &I = &SUM
END
```

In the next DO-WHILE loop, keys are read from the terminal. The loop continues to read the keys until "QUIT" is typed.

```
DO WHILE (&KEY |= QUIT)
READ &KEY
WRITE &KEY
END
```

◘ ERROR—Define error routine

• **General format**
```
[label:]   ERROR <OFF or routine>
```

• **Description**
The ERROR statement defines a routine to which control is passed when an error occurs while a CLIST statement, TSO command, or TSO subcommand is being executed. The ERROR routine is executed when the environment returns a nonzero value.

label is an optional statement label to branch to the ERROR statement with a GOTO statement. Its length varies from 1 to 31 characters.

OFF nullifies a previously defined ERROR routine.

routine consists of a single CLIST statement, TSO command, or DO-END statement.

● **Example**
In the following example, the ERROR routine prints the return code and a message that the CLIST is terminating.

```
ERROR DO
    WRITE RETURN CODE IS &LASTCC; CLIST TERMINATED.
    EXIT(4)
    END
```

◘ EXIT—Return from CLIST

● **General format**
[*label*:] EXIT [CODE(*expression*)] [QUIT]

● **Description**
The EXIT statement returns from a currently running CLIST, with control passed to the program that called the CLIST. Optionally, a return code can be passed on to the calling program.

label is an optional statement label to branch to the EXIT statement with a GOTO statement. Its length varies from 1 to 31 characters.

CODE specifies the return code to be be passed on to the calling program. If CODE is not listed, then the content of LASTCC is returned.

expression is either an integer or an expression evaluated to an integer.

QUIT passes control to CLIST with MAIN or NOFLUSH option.

● **Example**
In the following example, the ERROR routine prints the content of LASTCC and returns 4 to the calling program.

```
ERROR DO
    WRITE RETURN CODE IS &LASTCC
    EXIT(4)
    END
```

◻ GETFILE—Read a record

● General format
```
[label:]  GETFILE filename
```

● Description
The GETFILE reads a record from a dataset or a member of a partitioned dataset (PDS).

label is an optional statement label to branch to the GETFILE statement with a GOTO statement. Its length varies from 1 to 31 characters.

filename is a DDNAME allocated to a dataset name from which a record is read.

● Example
In the following example, a DDNAME FINPUT is allocated to a dataset TEMP.SAA.REPORT, then the file is opened as input. Next, using a DO-END statement, five records are read from the file using a GETFILE statement and displayed at the terminal. Finally, the file is closed.

```
ALLOC F(FINPUT) DA('TEMP.SAA.REPORT') SHR REUSE
OPENFILE FINPUT INPUT
DO &I = 1 to 5
   GETFILE FINPUT
   WRITE &FINPUT
END
CLOSEFILE FINPUT
```

◻ GLOBAL—Define global variables

● General format
```
[label:]     GLOBAL variable...
```

● Description
The GLOBAL statement defines one or more variables shared globally among nested CLISTs. The highest-level CLIST defines the variables, but all nested CLISTs where global variables are referenced must include a GLOBAL statement with matching variable names. All GLOBAL statements must appear before the global variables are used.

label is an optional statement label to branch to the GLOBAL statement with a GOTO statement. Its length varies from 1 to 31 characters.

variable is the name of a variable that is being created or used.

◘ GOTO—Branch to a label

- **General format**
  [*label*:] GOTO <*label-name* or *variable*>

- **Description**
  The GOTO statement passes control to a valid label, and execution continues.

  label is an optional statement label to branch to the GOTO statement with a GOTO statement. Its length varies from 1 to 31 characters.

  label-name is the name of the label to which branching occurs. It must be in the same CLIST as the GOTO statement; in other words, it cannot be in another CLIST.

  variable contains a label name.

- **Example**
  In the following example, the GOTO statement is used to branch back to a label LOOP.

```
LOOP:  GETFILE FINPUT
       WRITE &FINPUT
       GOTO LOOP
```

◘ IF-THEN-ELSE—Conditional processing

- **General format**
  [*label*:] IF *expression*
       THEN *action*
       [ELSE *action*]

• Description

The IF-THEN-ELSE statement executes one or many statements based on the result of an evaluation. An expression with the IF-THEN-ELSE statement is evaluated; if the result is TRUE, the statements associated with the THEN clause are executed; if the result is FALSE and if the optional ELSE clause is coded, the statements defined by this clause are executed. If the ELSE clause is not coded and the result is FALSE, then the next statement after the IF-THEN statement is executed.

label is an optional statement label to branch to the GOTO statement with a GOTO statement. Its length varies from 1 to 31 characters.

expression is a comparative expression or a series of comparative expressions separated by logical operators.

action consists of a single CLIST statement, TSO command, or DO-END statement.

• Example

In the following example, the IF-THEN-ELSE statement consists of the expression &X < 3; and after it is evaluated, either the WRITE statement associated with the THEN clause or that associated with the ELSE clause is executed.

```
IF &X < 3 THEN DO
    WRITE X IS LESS THAN 3
    END
    ELSE WRITE X IS GREATER THAN OR EQUAL TO 3
```

The next example is similar to the previous one except that the expression consists of two expressions &X < &Y and &Z = 5, and they are separated by a logical operator AND.

```
IF &X < &Y AND &Z = 5 THEN +
    EXIT CODE(0)
    ELSE WRITE &RECORD
```

◻ LISTDSI— Get dataset information

• General format

```
[label:]  LISTDSI dataset-name or filename [FILE]
          [VOLUME(vol-ser) or PREALLOC]
```

```
      [DIRECTORY or NODIRECTORY]
    [RECALL or NORECALL]
```

● **Description**
The LISTDSI statement retrieves characteristic information from an existing dataset file and stores it in special CLIST variables. For VSAM files, LISTDSI returns only *vol-ser*, unit type, and DSORG.

label is an optional statement label to branch to the LISTDSI statement with a GOTO statement. Its length varies from 1 to 31 characters.

dataset-name is the name of the dataset for which information is requested.

filename is the DD name of an allocated dataset name.

FILE is a keyword which is assocated with *filename*.

VOLUME(*vol-ser*) is the volume specification if the dataset is not catalogued.

PREALLOC specifies that allocation is required to extract the dataset information.

DIRECTORY specifies that the directory of a PDS is to be read in order to get the information.

NODIRECTORY means that no directory information is to be read.

RECALL specifies the recall of a dataset migrated by HSM.

NORECALL specifies that no recall of the dataset is required.

The following is a list of special CLIST variables:

Variable Name	Description
&SYSDSNAME	Dataset name
&SYSVOLUME	Volume serial number

&SYSUNIT	Device type for volume
&SYSDSORG	Dataset organization
&SYSRECFM	Record format
&SYSLRECL	Logical record length
&SYSBLKSIZE	Block size
&SYSKEYLEN	Key length
&SYSALLOC	Space allocation quantity
&SYSUSED	Space used quantity
&SYSPRIMARY	Primary allocation quantity
&SYSSECONDS	Secondary allocation quantity
&SYSUNITS	Space units (CYLINDER, TRACK, or BLOCK)
&SYSEXTENTS	Number of DASD extents already used
&SYSCREATE	Creation date (yyyy/ddd) of dataset
&SYSREFDATE	Last reference date (yyyy/ddd) of dataset
&SYSEXDATE	Expiration date (yyyy/ddd) of dataset
&SYSPASSWORD	Password status: NONE, READ, or WRITE
&SYSRACFA	RACF indication: NONE, GENERIC, or DISCRETE
&SYSUPDATED	Change indicator (YES or NO)
&SYSTRKSCYL	Number of tracks per cylinder
&SYSBLKSTRK	Number of directory blocks per track
&SYSADIRBLK	Directory blocks allocated (for PDS only)
&SYSUDIRBLK	Directory blocks used (for PDS only)
&SYSMEMBERS	Number of PDS members
&SYSMSGLVL1	First-level message
&SYSMSGLVL2	Second-level message
&SYSREASON	Reason code upon error

The statement returns one of the following codes:

0   Normal completion of function.
4   Some directory information for dataset was not obtained.
16   Severe error and no variables were properly set.

• Example

In the following example, the LISTDSI statement retrieves information from partitioned dataset TEST.COB.PGMSRC and displays the number of members in the PDS.

```
LISTDSI('TEST.COB.PGMSRC' 'DIRECTORY')
WRITE NUMBER OF MEMBERS IN PDS: &SYSMEMBERS
```

◘ NGLOBAL—Define named global variables

● **General format**
```
[label:]   NGLOBAL variable...
```

● **Description**
The NGLOBAL statement first defines one or many variables by name, then allows these variables to be shared by subprocedures. Subprocedures with the same CLIST can use or change the values of these variables by referring to them. However, subprocedures of other CLISTs cannot share or reference these NGLOBAL variables.

label is an optional statement label to branch to the NGLOBAL statement with a GOTO statement. Its length varies from 1 to 31 characters.

variable is a symbolic variable name that is being defined as a global variable. There is no limit to the number of names listed in the NGLOBAL statement.

◘ OPENFILE—Open a file

● **General format**
```
[label:]   OPENFILE <filename or &symbolic-variable>
    [INPUT or OUTPUT or UPDATE]
```

● **Description**
The OPENFILE statement opens a sequential file or PDS member previously allocated to a DDNAME. After the file is successfully opened, records can be read from it, written to it or updated. After I/O processing is done, the file must be closed.

label is an optional statement label to branch to the OPENFILE statement with a GOTO statement. Its length varies from 1 to 31 characters.

filename is a DDNAME allocated to a dataset name which is being opened.

&*symbolic-variable* is a symbolic variable name which contains the DDNAME being opened.

INPUT specifies the *filename* to be opened for input.

OUTPUT specifies the *filename* to be opened for output.

UPDATE specifies the *filename* to be opened for update.

• Example
In the following example, a DDNAME SYSUT1 is first allocated to dataset 'TEMP.SAA.REPORT', it is then opened with an OPENFILE statement and finally closed with a CLOSEFILE statement.

```
ALLOC F(SYSUT1) DA('TEMP.SAA.REPORT') SHR REUSE
OFILE:  OPENFILE SYSUT1 INPUT
    .
    .
    .
CLOSEFILE SYSUT1
```

◘ PROC— Define a procedure

• General format
```
[label:] PROC positional-number
    [positional-parameter...]
        [keyword-parameter][(default-value)]

    statements
    [END]
```

• Description
The PROC statement defines a procedure (or routine) in a CLIST. It is executed when called with the SYSCALL statement. Optionally, you can pass one or many parameters to the defined procedure. Each procedure is terminated with an END statement.

label is an optional statement label to branch to the PROC statement. Its length varies from 1 to 31 characters. This label is used with a SYSCALL statement to invoke the procedure.

positional-number specifies the number of parameters to pass to the subprocedure. This number is a 1- to 5-digit decimal number.

positional-parameter specifies the name of the positional parameter. The parameter is an alphanumeric symbol from 1 to 252 characters long, beginning with an alphabetical character.

default-value is specified for the *keyword-parameter*.

statements consists of TSO commands, TSO subcommands, and CLIST statements.

- **Example**
The following example illustrates how to define and execute a CLIST procedure. First, let's look at the definition. The name of the procedure is PRINTDSN. It copies a dataset to the printer using the IEBGENER program. The positional number is 1, indicating that there is only one positional parameter, which is DSN. In addition, there are three keyword parameters—each with a default value. These parameters are CLASS, COPIES and DEST. The body of the procedure consists of four ALLOC statements to assign DDNAMEs to input and output files. Then, there is a CALL statement to execute IEBGENER. Next, the DDNAMEs are deallocated with the FREE statement. Finally, the procedure is terminated with an END statement.

The execution of PRINTDSN is accomplished by the SYSCALL statement; in this case, it prints dataset MGOPAUL.TEST.COBOL(MYPROG).

```
     .
     .
     .
SYSCALL PRINTDSN 'MGOPAUL.TEST.COBOL(MYPROG)'
     .
     .
     .
PRINTDSN: PROC 1 DSN CLASS(A) COPIES(1) DEST(RMT0)
   ALLOC FILE(SYSUT1) DATASET(&DSN) SHR REUSE
   ALLOC FILE(SYSUT2) DATASET(&DSN) +
       SYSOUT(&CLASS) +
       COPIES(&COPIES) DESC(&DEST) REUSE
   ALLOC FILE(SYSPRINT) SYSOUT($CLASS) REUSE
   ALLOC FILE(SYSIN) DUMMY REUSE
   CALL 'SYS1.LINKLIB(IEBGENER)'
   FREE FILE(SYSUT1 SYSUT2 SYSPRINT SYSIN)
END
```

◘ **PUTFILE—Write a record**

- **General format**
  ```
  [label:]   PUTFILE filename
  ```

- **Description**
  The PUTFILE writes a record from a dataset or a member of a partitioned dataset (PDS).

  label is an optional statement label to branch to the PUTFILE statement with a GOTO statement. Its length varies from 1 to 31 characters.

  filename is a DDNAME allocated to a dataset name to which a record is written.

- **Example**
  In the following example, a DDNAME FOUTPUT is allocated to a dataset TEMP.SAA.REPORT, then the file is opened as output. Next, using a DO-END statement, five records are written to the file using a PUTFILE statement. Finally, the file is closed.

  ```
  ALLOC F(FOUTPUT) DA('TEMP.SAA.REPORT') SHR REUSE
  OPENFILE FOUTPUT OUTPUT
  DO &I = 1 to 5
     PUTFILE FOUTPUT   (QW)
  END
  CLOSEFILE FOUTPUT
  ```

◘ **READ—Read from terminal**

- **General format**
  ```
  [label:]   READ [variable...]
  ```

- **Description**
  The READ statement reads one or more strings of characters from the TSO terminal and places them into one or more specified symbolic variables. If no variable is listed in the READ statement, the input string is stored in a special variable &SYSDVAL.

  label is an optional statement label to branch to the READ statement with a GOTO statement. Its length varies from 1 to 31 characters.

variable is the name of a variable into which data are placed after they are read from the terminal. One or more variable names can be specified.

- **Example**

In the following example, the user is prompted to enter a filename and number of records at the TSO terminal.

```
READFL:  WRITE ENTER FILENAME AND NUMBER OF RECORDS
         READ &FNAME, &NREC
         IF &FNAME = " " THEN DO
               WRITE INVALID FILE NAME, TRY AGAIN
               GOTO READFL
               END
```

▣ READDVAL—Copy from &SYSDVAL

- **General format**

```
[label:]  READDVAL    variable...
```

- **Description**

The READDVAL statement copies the content of the special variable &SYSDVAL into one or more specified variables; this content is assigned from &SYSDVAL to variables from left to right. If not enough variables are entered, then unassigned values in &SYSDVAL are ignored.

label is an optional statement label to branch to the READDVAL statement with a GOTO statement. Its length varies from 1 to 31 characters.

variable is a symbolic variable to which the content of &SYSDVAL is assigned.

▣ RETURN—Return control

- **General format**

```
[label:]  RETURN [CODE(expression)]
```

- **Description**

The RETURN statement is primarily used to pass control from a subprocedure to the statement after a SYSCALL statement which is called the subprocedure. Optionally, the RETURN statement passes a value to the calling procedure. The return code is stored in a special variable &LASTCC.

label is an optional statement label to branch to the RETURN statement with a GOTO statement. Its length varies from 1 to 31 characters.

CODE specifies the return of a value.

expression can be a character string, a decimal integer, or any valid CLIST expression evaluated to a decimal integer; any of these is stored in &LASTCC before passing control to the calling procedure.

● **Example**

In the following example, the ERROR routine prints the error code and a message that the CLIST is terminating.

```
ERROR: DO
    IF &ERRCODE = NO THEN RETURN
    WRITE ERROR CODE IS &ERRCODE; CLIST TERMINATED.
    END
```

◘ **SELECT—Conditional execution of statement**

● **General format**

Simple SELECT statement

```
[label:] SELECT
    WHEN [logical-expression] [action]
    [WHEN [logical-expression] [action]
    [WHEN [logical-expression] [action]
       .
       .
       .
    [OTHERWISE [action]]
[label:]   END
```

Compound SELECT statement

```
[label:] SELECT test-expression
    WHEN [expression] [action]
    [WHEN [expression] [action]
    [WHEN [expression] [action]
```

```
    .
    .
    .
    [OTHERWISE [action]]
[label:]    END
```

● **Description**

The SELECT statement executes only one statement from a group of statements. The selection depends on the result of evaluating an expression. There are two formats for the SELECT statement: simple and compound.

In the simple SELECT statement, a logical expression is first evaluated; if the result is TRUE (1), then the corresponding action is executed. After the action is executed, control is passed to the END statement. If none of the evaluated expressions is TRUE, then the action associated with the OTHERWISE clause, if any, is executed.

In the compound SELECT statement, a test expression is first evaluated. The result is compared with the expression associated with the WHEN clause. If the test expression is equal to the expression or is in the range of the expression, then the action associated with the expression is executed. After the action is executed, control is passed to the END statement with a GOTO statement. If no match is found, then the action associated with the OTHERWISE clause, if any, is executed.

label is an optional statement label to branch to the SELECT or END statement with a GOTO statement. Its length varies from 1 to 31 characters.

logical-expression is a comparison expression, using logical operators (=, NE, <, >=).

test-expression is a character string or a logical expression.

expression is a character string, a single logical expression, or a range.

action consists of a single CLIST statement, a TSO command, or a DO-END statement.

● **Example**

The following example illustrates a simple SELECT statement.

```
SELECT
   WHEN &DEBUG = 0 CONTROL SYMLIST CONLIST
   WHEN &DEBUG = 1 CONTROL NOSYMLIST NOCONLIST
   OTHERWISE WRITE DEBUG CODE INVALID
END
```

The next example illustrates a compound SELECT statement. There is an expression (&VAL) associated with the SELECT keyword. This expression is first evaluated, then the result is compared to value (0, 1, and 2) next to the WHEN clause. If there is a match, the statement (WRITE VAL...) associated with the WHEN clause is executed.

```
SELECT &VAL
   WHEN 0 WRITE VAL IS 0

   WHEN 1 WRITE VAL IS 1

   WHEN 2 WRITE VAL IS 2

   OTHERWISE WRITE VAL IS < 0 or > 2
END
```

◼ **SET—Assign values**

● **General format**
```
[label:] SET &variable  =   value
      or
[label:] SET &variable  EQ value
```

● **Description**

The SET statement assigns a value to a specified symbolic variable. The values special CLIST variables that are not read-only can be changed using the SET statement.

label is an optional statement label to branch to the SET statement with a GOTO statement. Its length varies from 1 to 31 characters.

&variable is the name of the variable whose value is set.

value is stored in *&variable*.

- **Example**

The following are a few examples of the SET statement.

```
VALUES:    SET &HEXTAB = 0123456789ABCDEF
      SET B = 5
      SET &SWITCH EQ DOORS ARE CLOSED
```

◘ SYSCALL—Call a subprocedure

- **General format**

```
[label:] SYSCALL subproc-name [parameter...]
```

- **Description**

The SYSCALL statement passes control to a subprocedure, defined using a PROC statement, in the CLIST. Optionally, it also allows one or many parameters to be passed to the subprocedure. Parameters are separated with commas, blanks, or tabs.

label is an optional statement label to branch to the SYSCALL statement with a GOTO statement. Its length varies from 1 to 31 characters.

subproc-name is the name of a CLIST subprocedure, defined using the PROC statement.

parameter is an expression which may be a contant, a symbolic variable, a built-in function or an arithmetic expression.

- **Example**

In the following example, the subprocedure SQR is called by the SYSCALL statement.

```
SET &A = 20
SYSCALL SQR A
WRITE RESULT IS &A
   .
   .
   .
SQR:   PROC 1 B
   SYSREF   &B
   SET &B = &B * &B
   END
```

◘ SYSREF—Modify variable in subprocedure

• General format
```
[label:] SYSREF [variable...]
```

• Description
The SYSREF statement is used to allow a subprocedure to reference and change one or more variables passed to it. When the SYSREF variables are assigned new values in the subprocedure, the new values are passed back to the CLIST after the procedure was called by a SYSCALL statement.

label is an optional statement label to branch to the SYSREF statement with a GOTO statement. Its length varies from 1 to 31 characters.

variable is the name of the parameter list in the PROC statement that defines a subprocedure.

• Example
In the following example, after the PROC statement defining the subprocedure SQR, there is a SYSREF statement to allow this subprocedure to change the value of variable B. The new value of B is passed back to CLIST after the SYSCALL SQR A statement.

```
    SET &A = 20
    SYSCALL SQR A
    WRITE RESULT IS &A
    .
    .
    .
SQR:    PROC 1 B
    SYSREF  &B
    SET &B = &B * &B
    END
```

◘ TERMIN—Pass control to terminal

• General format
```
[label:] TERMIN [string...]
```

• Description
The TERMIN statement passes control to the TSO terminal of the user who invoked the CLIST. It is also used to specify one or

more character strings, when one is entered, that would return control to the statement after the TERMIN statement. The input data typed by the user is stored in the special variable &SYSDVAL and can be read with the READDVAL statement. The variable &SYSDLM contains a number indicating which input *string* terminates the TERMIN statement.

label is an optional statement label to branch to the TERMIN statement with a GOTO statement. Its length varies from 1 to 31 characters.

string terminates the TERMIN statement. If it is omitted, a null line would return control to the CLIST.

- **Example**
In the following example, the TERMIN statement is used to receive input from the user. This statement specifies two options: FIND and QUIT. The user types FIND followed by a dataset name to be located. If the user types QUIT, the CLIST terminates.

```
TERMIN  FIND, QUIT    /* PASS CONTROL TO TERMINAL */
READDVAL DSN          /* GET INPUT STRING */
IF &SYSDLM = 2 THEN DO
            WRITE CLIST ENDED
            EXIT      /* TERMINATE CLIST */
            END
ELSE DO
   LISTDI &DSN              /* FIND DSN */
   END
```

◘ WRITE—Write text to terminal

- **General format**
[*label*:] WRITE *text*

- **Description**
The WRITE statement sends a specified text to the TSO terminal of the user who invoked the CLIST. After the text is written, the cursor moves to the first column of the next row.

label is an optional statement label to branch to the WRITE statement with a GOTO statement. Its length varies from 1 to 31 characters.

text may consist of one or any combination of the following: character string, constants, symbolic variable, and arithmetic expression. Any expression must be evaluated using an &EVAL() function.

● **Example**
The following examples show a few ways to use the WRITE statement.

```
SET  &Y = THE WORLD IS BUT ONE COUNTRY AND +
                ALL MEN ARE ITS CITIZEN
WRITE &Y

WRITE NEW WORLD ORDER!!!

WRITE &STR(3 + 4) = &EVAL(3+4)
```

◘ **WRITENR—Write text to terminal**

● **General format**
[*label*:] WRITENR *text*

● **Description**
The WRITENR statement sends a specified text to the TSO terminal of the user who invoked the CLIST. Unlike with the WRITE statement, after the text is written, the cursor stays at the end of the text just written.

label is an optional statement label to branch to the WRITENR statement with a GOTO statement. Its length varies from 1 to 31 characters.

text may consist of one or any combination of the following: character string, constants, symbolic variable, and arithmetic expression. Any expression must evaluated using an &EVAL() function.

● **Example**
The following is an example of using the WRITENR statement.

```
WRITENR ENTER THE CUSTOMER NAME:
```

2.2 BUILT-IN FUNCTIONS

This section contains all the built-in functions supplied by the CLIST language. These functions perform various operations on variables, expressions, and character strings. For each function, the section provides a general format for usage, followed by a description of the function and its variables, expressions, parameters, and keywords. In addition, examples of how these functions are used are given to further clarify their purpose.

&DATATYPE—Determine data type

- **General format**

  &DATATYPE(*expression*)

- **Description**

  The &DATATYPE function determines the data type of a specified expression. It returns one of the following strings: CHAR, NUM, DBCS, or MIXED.

  CHAR means that at least one of the characters of the expression is nonnumeric.

  NUM means that the expression contains only numeric characters.

  DBCS means that the expression contains only DBCS characters.

  MIXED means that the expression contains both EBCDIC and DBCS characters.

- **Example**

  The following lists the return values from some uses of the &DATATYPE function.

```
SET &X = &DATATYPE(123E)  /* Assigns CHAR to X */

SET &Y = 4162504803
SET &PHONE = &DATATYPE(&Y)  /* Assigns NUM to PHONE */

SET &Y = 416-250-4803
SET &PHONE = &DATATYPE(&Y)  /* Assigns CHAR to PHONE */
```

◘ &EVAL—Evaluate an expression

- **General format**

  ```
  &EVAL(expression)
  ```

- **Description**

  The &EVAL function evaluates an arithmetic *expression*. It is mainly used in a WRITE or WRITENR statement to force evaluation of an expression; otherwise the expression is treated as characters.

- **Example**

  In the following example, the &EVAL function is part of a WRITE statement. It evaluates the sum of two numbers before displaying it on the terminal.

  ```
  SET X = 30
  SET Y = 40
  WRITE &X * &Y = &EVAL(&X * &Y)
  ```

◘ &LENGTH—Determine number of bytes

- **General format**

  ```
  &LENGTH(expression or string)
  ```

- **Description**

  The &LENGTH function determines the length in number of bytes of a specified *expression* or character *string*. If the evaluation of an expression results in a null string, &LENGTH returns 0. The &LENGTH function ignores any leading zeros or blanks.

- **Example**

  The following statements list the return values for the usage of &LENGTH.

  ```
  SET A = &LENGTH(2+7+2)        /* Assigns 2 to A */
  SET A = &LENGTH(&STR(1 2 3 )) /* Assigns 3 to A */
  ```

◘ &NRSTR—Define nonrescannable string

- **General format**

  ```
  &NRSTR(string)
  ```

- **Description**
  The &NRSTR function prevents CLIST from removing an ampersand (&) when a string is prefixed with two ampersands. It also prevents more than one level of symbolic variable substitution from being performed on a variable or expression.

- **Example**
  The following statement assigns &&FILE to &A.

```
SET A = &NRSTR(&&FILE)
```

&STR—Character string

- **General format**
  &STR(*string*)

- **Description**
  The &STR function is used to pass a string as it is, without performing any evaluation on it. The string may consists of an expression, a statement and a TSO command. And, the &STR function can be part of a CLIST statement.

- **Example**
  In the following statement, the variable OUTSTRING will have the string "4*5" and not 20, the product of 4 and 5. Note that &STR() is part of the SET statement.

```
SET OUTSTRING = &STR(4*5)
```

&SUBSTR—Return sub-string

- **General format**
  &SUBSTR(*start*[:*end*],*string*)

- **Description**
  The &SUBSTR function returns part of a specified *string*.

- **Example**
  The following shows a few examples of using &SUBSTR.

```
SET &Y=&SUBSTR(3:5,ABCDEFGH) /* Assigns CDE to Y */
SET &Y=&SUBSTR(5,ABCDEFGH)   /* Assigns E to Y */
```

◻ &SYSCAPS—Convert to uppercase characters

- **General format**
  &SYSCAPS(*string*)

- **Description**
  The &SYSCAPS function converts all characters of a specified string to uppercase characters.

- **Example**
  The following statement returns "ABCDEFGH."

```
&SYSCAPS(abcdefgh)
```

◻ &SYSDSN—Verify dataset

- **General format**
  &SYSDSN(*dsname*[(*member*)])

- **Description**

  The &SYSDSN function checks whether a dataset or a member of a partitioned dataset exists. It returns one of the following strings:

```
OK
MEMBER SPECIFIED, BUT DATASET IS NOT PARTITIONED
MEMBER NOT FOUND
DATASET NOT FOUND
ERROR PROCESSING REQUESTED DATASET
PROTECTED DATASET
VOLUME NOT ON SYSTEM
UNAVAILABLE DATASET
INVALID DATASET NAME, dsn
MISSING DATASET NAME
```

- **Example**
  In the following example, the dataset CANT.SAA.REPORT is checked to see whether it exists.

```
IF &SYSDSN('CANT.SAA.REPORT')=OK THEN +
   DO
      ALLOC F(REPORT) DA('CANT.SAA.REPORT')
```

```
      CALL (SAARPT)
   END
ELSE
   WRITE DATASET 'CANT.SAA.REPORT' DOES NOT EXIST
   WRITE CLIST TERMINATED
   EXIT
```

◘ &SYSINDEX—Find position of a character string

• **General format**
```
&SYSINDEX(string1, string2[,start])
```

• **Description**
The &SYSINDEX function finds the position of a string in another string. This function returns a number; if the string is not found, the result is zero.

string1 is the string that is searched for.

string2 is the string that is searched in.

start is the position in *string2* from which the search starts.

• **Example**
In the second SET statement, variable LOC is assigned 5 because the string DOG starts at position 5 of variable Y. However, in the third SET statement, LOC is assigned 0 because CAT is not found in variable Y.

```
SET &Y = ALL DOGS GO TO HEAVEN
SET &LOC = &SYSINDEX(DOGS,&Y,2) /* Assigns 5 to LOC */
SET &LOC = &SYSINDEX(CATS,&Y)   /* Assigns 0 to LOC */
```

◘ &SYSLC—Convert to lowercase characters

• **General format**
```
&SYSLC(string)
```

• **Description**
The &SYSLC function converts all characters in a specified string to lowercase characters.

• **Example**
The following statement converts all characters to lowercase and

returns "abcdefgh."

```
&SYSLC(ABCDEFGH)
```

◘ &SYSNSUB—Limit level of symbolic substitution

- **General format**
  ```
  &SYSNSUB(level,expression)
  ```

- **Description**

  The &SYSNSUB function places a limit on the number of times symbolic substitution is performed in a statement.

  level is a positive number or a symbolic variable containing a number in the range 0 to 99.

  expression is a CLIST expression whose symbolic substitution is controlled.

◘ &SYSONEBYTE—Convert DBCS to EBCDIC

- **General format**
  ```
  &SYSONEBYTE(string)
  ```

- **Description**

  The &SYSONEBYTE function converts a character string from the DBCS format to the EBCDIC format.

- **Example**

  In the following example, string "A<x1x2x3>B" is converted to "A123B."

  ```
  &SYSONEBYTE(A<x1x2x3>B)
  ```

◘ &SYSTWOBYTE—Convert EBCDIC to DBCS

- **General format**
  ```
  &SYSTWOBYTE(string)
  ```

● **Description**

The &SYSTWOBYTE function converts a character string from EBCDIC format to DBCS format.

● **Example**

In the following example, string "ABCD" is converted to "dAdBdCdD."

```
&SYSTWOBYTE(ABCD)
```

2.3 CONTROL VARIABLES

This section lists all the control variables used by CLIST. These variables are grouped into two categories: modifiable variables and nonmodifiable variables. The modifiable variables can be changed by the user—for example using the SET or CONTROL statement. However, the content of a nonmodifiable variable cannot be changed by the user. It is updated only by the system and can be accessed by the user.

◻ **Modifiable variables**

Variable	Content
&LASTCC	Contains the return code from the last execution of the following: TSO command, TSO subcommand, CLIST statement, or nested CLIST. &LASTCC can be set to any value.
&MAXCC	Contains the highest return code from execution of the following: TSO command, TSO subcommand, CLIST statement, or nested CLIST. &MAXCC can be set to any value.
&SYSDVAL	Contains the value after executing one of the following: TERMIN statement, READ statement without operands, or SET SYSDVAL=.

&SYSOUTLINE   Contains the number of lines produced by a TSO command.

&SYSOUTTRAP   Contains the maximum number of lines from a TSO command to be saved.

&SYSSCAN   Contains the maximum number of times a CLIST can rescan a line to evaluate variables. The range is 0 to +2,147,483,647. The default value is 16 times.

&SYSPROMPT   Contains ON or OFF when CONTROL PROMPT or CONTROL NOPROMPT, respectively, is specified.

&SYSSYMLIST   Contains ON or OFF when CONTROL SYMLIST or CONTROL NOSYMLIST respectively, is specified.

&SYSCONLIST   Contains ON or OFF when CONTROL CONLIST or CONTROL NOCONLIST, respectively, is specified.

&SYSLIST   Contains ON or OFF when CONTROL LIST or CONTROL NOLIST, respectively, is specified.

&SYSASIS   Contains ON or OFF when CONTROL NOCAPS/ASIS or CONTROL CAPS, respectively, is specified.

&SYSMSG   Contains ON or OFF when CONTROL MSG or CONTROL NOMSG, respectively, is specified.

&SYSFLUSH   Contains ON or OFF when CONTROL FLUSH or CONTROL NOFLUSH, respectively, is specified.

☐ Nonmodifiable variables

Variable	Content
&SYSCPU	Contains the number of seconds of CPU time used during the current session. The format is sss.hhh, where sss is seconds and hhh is hundredths of seconds.
&SYSDATE	Contains the current date in the form mm/dd/yy, where mm is the month, dd is the day, and yy is the year.
&SYSDLM	Contains the character string which when entered by the user returns control from the terminal to the CLIST after executing the TERMIN statement.
&SYSENV	Contains FORE or BACK to indicate whether a CLIST is executing in the foreground or the background, respectively.
&SYSHSM	Contains the status of the Hierarchical Storage Manager (HSM). If it contains a null string, this means HSM is not installed. Otherwise it contains the status in the form VRRM, where V is the version number, RR is the release number, and M is the modification number.
&SYSICMD	Contains the name of the CLIST currently being executed and invoked "implicitly"; otherwise it contains a null string.
&SYSISPF	Contains an indicator as to whether or not the CLIST is being executed under ISPF.
&SYSJDATE	Contains the Julian date in the form YY.DDD, where YY is the year and DDD is the number of days in the year.
&SYSLTERM	Contains the number of rows available on the TSO terminal screen.

&SYSLRACF   Contains the level of RACF (Resource Access Control Facility) installed. The information is in the form VRRM, where V is the version number, RR is the release number, and M is the modification number.

&SYSNEST   Contains a value indicating whether or not the currently running CLIST was called by another CLIST. A NO value means that the CLIST is the highest level invoked by the user. A YES value means that the current CLIST is nested.

&SYSPCMD   Contains the name of the most recent TSO command that was executed by the CLIST.

&SYSPREF   Contains the most current prefix for a dataset name used by TSO. However, if PROFILE NOPREFIX is in effect, &SYSPREF contains a null string.

&SYSPROC   Contains the name of the logon procedure used in the current TSO session.

&SYSRACF   Contains the status of RACF (Resource Access Control Facility). The possible strings are AVAILABLE, NOT AVAILABLE, and NOT INSTALLED.

&SYSSCMD   Contains the name of the TSO subcommand that was executed most recently.

&SYSSDATE   Contains the current date in the form YY/MM/DD, where YY is the year, MM is the month, and DD is the day.

&SYSSRV   Contains the number of service units used.

&SYSSTIME   Contains the current time in the form HH:MM, where HH is hours and MM is minutes.

&SYSTIME

Contains the current time in the form HH:MM:SS, where HH is hours, MM is minutes, and SS is seconds.

&SYSTSOE

Contains the release level of TSO/E. The information is in the form VRRM, where V is the version number, RR is the release number, and M is the modification number.

&SYSUID

Contains the TSO user ID for the current session.

&SYSWTERM

Contains the number of columns available on the screen of the TSO terminal.

The CMS (Conversational Monitor System) is an operating system that runs under the Control Program (CP) of a Virtual Machine (VM). This chapter is a reference guide for CMS commands. The commands are numerous and varied in their functions. The following list gives an idea of some of the types of functions available though CMS:

- Management of CMS, OS/VS, and VSE (DOS) files.
- Execution of language processors belonging to OS/VS and VSE (DOS) enviroments.
- Invoking the assembler and compilers such as COBOL, PL/I, and FORTRAN.
- Defining and manipulating windows.
- Reading data from a virtual card reader.
- Punching data to a virtual punch.
- Sending data to a virtual printer.
- Communicating with other CMS users in a local or remote system.

In 370 mode, VSE (DOS) is simulated in your CMS virtual machine. In this mode, all CMS/DOS commands are available to you.

General Format: For each command, this chapter provides a general form for usage and a brief description of the command. The general form starts with a command name, followed by one or more operands and options.

The format is

```
command-name [operand...] [(options...[)]]
```

The *command-name* is a symbolic name that represents a function that you want CMS to perform. The *operand* can be a keyword and/or positional operand.

Notational Convention: In the general format of the CMS commands, used in this chapter, there are few symbols that are not part of the syntax, therefore they must not be included when coding your program. These symbols and their meanings are:

Symbol	Meaning
[]	The option enclosed by the brackets ([]) is not required but can be included.
<>	Only one of the alternative enclosed by the angle brackets (<>) must be chosen.
or	The alternatives enclosed by the angle brackets (<>) are separated by "or."
____	The underline word is the default value.
...	The horizontal or vertical ellipsis means that the preceding can be coded more than once.
Uppercase characters	All keywords of the command are written in uppercase characters; they must be coded as shown.
Lowercase characters	All strings in lowercase characters and italic are variables that can be changed to any other strings to suit your programming style. In your code they represent values that you supply to commands.
fn	Filename.
ft	Filetype.
fm	Filemode.
Abbreviation	In many cases an abbreviated form of the command, operand, or option is permitted. The acceptable part is in uppercase characters. For example, the command named MAClib has a short form MAC; however, MACL, MACLI, and MACLIB are also valid specifications.

◘ ACCESS—Identify a disk to CMS

● **General format**
```
ACcess [vdev or 191] mode or A [/ext]
    [fn or *] [ft or *] [fm or *] [(options...[)]]

where options are [NOPROF] [NODISK]
                   [ERASE or SAVEONLY or NOSAVE]
```

● **Description**
The ACCESS command identifies a disk storage space to CMS.
It also creates a file directory and associates all files of this disk
space with a filemode letter for access.

◘ ALARM—Ring the terminal alarm

● **General format**
```
ALARM VSCreen vname
```

● **Description**
The ALARM command rings the terminal alarm when a virtual
screen is refreshed on the terminal.

◘ AMSERV—Access Method Services

● **General format**
```
AMserv fn1 [fn2 or fn1] [(options...[)]]

where options are [PRINT] [TAPIN <18n or TAPn>]
                  [TAPOUT [TAPOUT<18n or TAPn>]
```

● **Description**
The AMSERV command invokes the following utilities:

● Define catalogs, data storage spaces, or clusters for VSAM
  datasets.
● Alter, list, copy, export, or import VSAM datasets.

This command is available only in a System/370 virtual machine.

◘ ASSEMBLE—Assemble an assembly language program

● **General format**
```
Assemble fn [(options...[)]]

where options for listing control are
    [ALOGIC or NOALOGIC]
    [ESD or NOESD] [FLAG (nnn) or FLAG(0)]
    [LINECOUN (nn) or LINECOUN (55)]
    [LIST or NOLIST] [MCALL or NOCALL]
    [MLOGIC or NOMLOGIC]
    [RLD or NORLD] [LIBMAC or NOLIBMAC]
    [XREF (FULL) or XREF (SHORT) or NOXREF]
    [PRINT or NOPRINT or DISK]

options for output control are
    [DECK or NODECK]
    [OBJECT or NOOBJECT]
    [TEST or NOTEST]

options for SYSTERM are
    [NUMBER or NONUM]
    [STMT or NOSTMT]
    [TERMINAL or NOTERM]

other options are
    [ALIGN or NOALIGN]
    [BUFSIZE (MIN) or BUFFSIZE (STD) or
    BUFSIZE (MAX)] [RENT  or NORENT]
    [YFLAG or NOYFLAG]
    [SYSPARM (string) or SYSPARM () or SYSPARM (?)]
    [WORKSIZE (2048K) or WORKSIZE (nnnnnK)]
```

● **Description**
The ASSEMBLE command assembles an assembly language program contained in a specified file. The output and processing are done according to options entered as parameters of this command.

◘ ASSGN—Assign a system or programmer logical unit to a physical device

● **General format**
```
ASSGN SYSxxx < Reader or PUnch or
               PRinter or Terminal or
               TAP[n or 1] or mode or IGN or UA >
                   [(options...[)]]

where options are [UPCASE or LOWCASE]
                  [7TRACK or 9TRACK]
                  [TRTCH a] [DEN den]
```

- **Description**
The ASSGN command assigns or deassigns a specified system or programmer logical unit to a physical device. The valid programmer logical units are SYS000 through SYS241. The following is a list of system logical units: SYSRDR, SYSIPT, SYSIN, SYSPCH, SYSLST, SYSLOG, SYSOUT, SYSSLB, SYSRLB, SYSCLB, and SYSCAT.

This command is available only in a System/370 virtual machine.

CATCHECK—Check a VSE/VSAM catalog

- **General format**
```
CATCHECK  [catname or catname/password]
```

- **Description**
The CATCHECK command checks a catalog by invoking the VSE/VSAM Catalog Check Service Aid. The output of the analysis is sent to a print file. If *catname* is omitted, then the default catalog, specified in the DLBL command, is used.

CCDUMP—Dump communication controller file

- **General format**
```
CCDUMP fn [ft][fm] [(options[)]]
```
```
where options are [Erase] [LC nn] [OPT (string)]
                  [Printer or Disk]
```

- **Description**
The CCDUMP command formats a communication controller dump file produced by the CCLOAD command and then sends it to either a printer or a disk file. If it is a file, then its name is "input-filename LISTING A."

CCLOAD—Load a communication controller

- **General format**
```
CCLOAD vdev lmod [(options...[)]]
```
```
where options are LIBe loadlib
```

```
CMD(command)
RELoad<No or Yes or Prompt>
NOMONitor
DUMP<Yes or No or Prompt>
```

- **Description**

  The CCLOAD command is used to load an EP control program into a communication controller. This loading can be done in two ways: manually or using a service virtual machine. In case of failure, the CTLR is automatically dumped.

◘ CLEAR VSCREEN—Clear a virtual screen

- **General format**

  CLEAR VSCreen vname

- **Description**

  The CLEAR VSCREEN command clears a virtual screen by writing nulls to the data buffer. It also purges the data in the queue and reconnects all windows from the top. However, the cursor position is not changed.

◘ CLEAR WINDOW—Clear a window connected to a virtual screen

- **General format**

  CLEAR WINdow [wname or =]

- **Description**

  The CLEAR WINDOW command clears a window connected to a virtual screen. It does not erase data; rather, it scrolls past all data on the screen.

◘ CMDCALL—Convert PLIST function calls into CMS command calls.

- **General format**

  CMDCALL [cmd] [operand1][operand2...operandn]

- **Description**

  The CMDCALL command converts an EXEC 2 extended PLIST

function call into a CMS extended PLIST command call.

◘ CMSBATCH—Batch processing

- **General format**
  CMSBATCH [*sysname*]

- **Description**
  The CMSBATCH command submits a job to be processed in batch mode rather than interactively. This job is transferred to the virtual card reader of an active CMS batch machine. If *sysname* is not entered, then the job goes to the system where the job is submitted. The CMSBATCH command is invoked immediately after CMS is IPLed.

◘ CMSGEND—Generate a CMS module or LOADLIB

- **General format**
  CMSGEND   *fn* [CTLCMS or CTLALL or
                  NOCLEAR or MAP or NOINV] [*fm* or **A**]

- **Description**
  The CMSGEND command generates a CMS module or LOADLIB from a text file using the CMSGEND EXEC. The new module is sent to a specified disk or to the default disk A.

◘ CMSSERV—Establish communication between the VM host system and a personal computer

- **General format**
  CMSSERV

- **Description**
  The CMSSERV command establishes a communication between the VM host system and a personal computer using the Enhanced Connectivity Facilities.

◘ **COMPARE—Compare files**

• **General format**
```
COMpare field1 field2 [(option...[)]]
```
   where *option* is COL   [*mmmm* or 1] - [*nnn* or *lrecl*]

• **Description**
The COMPARE command compares two CMS files. The comparison is done on a record-for-record basis, and dissimilar records are displayed.

◘ **CONVERT—Convert DLCS statements into internal form**

• **General format**
```
CONVert COMmands fn [ft or DLCS]
            [fm or *] [(options...[)]]
```
   where *options* are [SYStem or USER or ALL]
              [CHeck or OUTmode [*fm* or *]]
              [STACK [FIFO or LIFO]] or FIFO or LIFO]

• **Description**
The CONVERT command is used to convert DLCS (definition language for command syntax) statements into internal form. The converted statements are then used for parsing purposes.

◘ **CONWAIT—Wait for console**

• **General format**
```
CONWAIT
```

• **Description**
The CONWAIT command is used to synchronize a program and a terminal. When this command is issued, it causes a program to wait until all output and input processing to the console is completed.

◘ **COPYFILE—Copy or modify CMS files.**

• **General format**
```
COPYFILE fileidil [fileidi2...]
```

```
                    [fileido] [(options...[)]]

where options are [Type or NOType] [NEWDate or OLDDate]
                  [NEWFile or REPlace]
                  [PRompt or NOPRompt]
                  [FRom recno or PRLabel xxxxxxxx]
                  [FOR numrec or TOLabel xxxxxxxx]
                  [SPecs or NOSPecs]
                  [OVLy or APpend]
                  [RECfm <F or V>] [Lrecl nnnn]
                  [TRUnc or NOTRunc]
                  [PAck or UNPack]
                  [FILL <c or hh or 40>]
                  [EBcdic] [UPcase or LOwcase]
                  [TRAns] [SIngle]
```

- **Description**

The COPYFILE command can be used in the following ways:

- To copy a single CMS file from one disk to another
- To duplicate a CMS file on the same disk
- To combine two or more files into one file
- To Modify the format of a file

◘ **CP—Issue CP commands**

- **General format**

CP [commandline]

- **Description**

The CP command issues commands to the VM control program from the CMS environement. It can also be used from CMS EXEC, EXEC 2 EXEC, or REXX programs.

◘ **CPEREPXA—Access the EREP program**

- **General format**

CPEREPXA [fn ft [fm or *]]

- **Description**

The CPEREPXA command accesses the EREP (Environment Record Editing and Printing) program. It is valid in System/370 mode only.

▢ CURSOR VSCREEN—Position the cursor on a virtual screen

• **General format**

    CURsor VSCreen vname line col [(options[)]]

    where the options are [Reserved or Data]

• **Description**

The CURSOR VSCREEN command positions the cursor on a virtual screen. The cursor position is specified by a line number and a column position on the line.

▢ DDR —DASD Dump Restore

• **General format**

    DDR [fn ft] [fm or *]

• **Description**

The DDR (DASD Dump Restore) program is used to print, restore, copy, or dump a user minidisk. It is valid in System/370 mode only.

▢ DEBUG—Display status after an ABEND.

• **General format**

    DEBUG

• **Description**

The DEBUG command displays information after a program ABENDs during execution.

▢ DEFAULTS— Set default options for commands

• **General format**

    DEFAULTS [Set command-options or List [command]]

• **Description**

The DEFAULTS command sets and lists options for a command. Below is a list of commands and valid options that can be specified as defaults. The underscored options are system defaults.

Command	Options
Filelist	Profile PROFFLST, Profile *fn*, Filelist, and Nofilelist
Help	Brief, All, DETail, DEScript, Format, Parms, Options, NOTes, Errors, Screen, and NOScreen
Maclist or Mlist	Profile PROFMLST, Profile *fn*, Compact, and Nocompact
Note	Profile PROFNOTE, Profile *fn*, Short, LONg, LOG, NOLog, NOAck, Ack, NOTebook *fn*, NOTebook ALL, NOTebook *, NONotebook
Peek	Profile PROFNOTE, Profile *fn*, FRom *recno*, FRom 1, FOr *numrec*, FOr *, and FOr 200
RDrlist or RList	Profile PROFRLST and Profile *fn*
Receive	Log, NOLog, Olddate, NEwdate, NOTebook *fn*, NOTebook ALL, NOTebook *, Fullprompt, Minprompt, and NOPrompt
Sendfile or Sfile	New, Old, NOType, Type, NOFilelist, Filelist, Log, NOLog, NOAck, and Ack
Tell	[Msgcmd MSG or Msgcmd Message] Msgcmd MSGNOH, Msgcmd SMSG, and [Msgcmd WNG or Msgcmd Warning]

◘ DEFINE VSCREEN—Define a virtual screen.

● **General format**

```
DEFine VSCreen vname lines cols rtop rbot
              [(options[)]]
```

```
where options are [TYPe or NOType]
                  [PRotect or NOProtect]
                  [High or NOHigh] [color] [exthi] [psset]
                  [USer or SYstem]
```

- **Description**

The DEFINE VSCREEN command creates a presentation space to simulate the functions of a physical display screen. Data to be displayed are written to this virtual screen.

◘ **DEFINE WINDOW—Define a window.**

- **General format**

```
DEFine WINdow wname lines psline pscol [(options[)]]

where options are [VARiable or FIXed] [BORder or
               NOBorder] [POP or NOPon]
               [TOP or NOTop] [USer or SYstem]
```

- **Description**

The DEFINE WINDOW command creates a window on a physical screen. This window is defined by giving a name, size, and position.

◘ **DELETE VSCREEN—Delete a virtual screen**

- **General format**

```
DELete VSCreen vname
```

- **Description**

The DELETE VSCREEN command deletes a virtual screen that has already been defined.

◘ **DELETE WINDOW—Delete a window**

- **General format**

```
DELete WINdow vname
```

- **Description**

The DELETE WINDOW command deletes a window that has already been defined.

◙ DESBUF—Clear the console and stack buffers

● General format
```
DESBUF
```

● Description
The DESBUF command clears buffers associated with the console and program stack.

◙ DISK—Send or load CMS files

● General format
```
DISK <DUMP or LOAD> fn ft [fm] [(options...[)]]

where   options are [Fullprompt or Minprompt or
                     NOPrompt]
                    [Replace or NOReplace] [OLDDate]
```

● Description
The DISK command either sends CMS files to the spooled card punch or loads CMS files, previously punched, from the spooled card reader.

◙ DLBL—Define or identify files

● General format
```
DLBL ddname <mode or DUMMY> [[CMS fn ft] or
            [CMS FILE ddname]]
                       [(option-1 option-2 [)]]

        or

DLBL ddname <mode or DUMMY>
   [[DSN qual1 [.qual2...qualn]] or
   [DSN qual1 [.qual2...qualn]] or
   [DSN ?]]   [(option-1 option-2 option-3 [)]]

        or

DLBL <ddname or *> CLEAR

where option-1 is [SYSxxx]
      option-2 is [PERM] [CHANGE or NOCHANGE]
      option-3 is [VSAM] [EXTENT or MULT] [CAT catdd]
            [BUFSP nnnnn]
```

- **Description**

The DLBL command either identifies or defines CMS, VSE, or VSAM files. It can be used for the following purposes:

- To define VSE and CMS sequential files for input/output operations
- To identify VSE libraries
- To define and identify VSAM datasets, clusters, and catalogs

It is valid in System/370 mode only.

DISLIB—Maintain phases in a CMS/DOS library

- **General format**

```
DOSLIB <DEL libname phasename1 [...phasenamen]> or
      <COMP libname>                            or
      <MAP libname> [(options[)]]
```

```
where the options are TERM, DISK, or PRINT
```

- **Description**

The DOSLIB command deletes, compacts, or lists information about phases of a CMS/DOS phase library. It is valid in System/370 mode only.

DOSLKED—DOS link-edit a source file or module

- **General format**

```
DOSLked fn [libname or fn] [(options[)]]
```

```
where the options are TERM or DISK or PRINT
```

- **Description**

The DOSLKED command link-edits the following:

- CMS file with TEXT filetype
- VSE private library
- VSE system library

The output is written to a CMS phase library in executable form. This command is valid in System/370 mode only.

◘ DROPBUF—Delete program stack buffer

• **General format**

```
DROPBUF [n]
```

• **Description**

The DROPBUF command deletes program stack buffer in the following ways:

• If a number is specified, then the specified program stack buffer and all buffers created after it are eliminated.
• If a number is not specified, then the most recent program stack buffer is dropped.

◘ DROP WINDOW—Move a window down

• **General format**

```
DROP WINdow <wname or = or WM> <n or *>
```

• **Description**

The DROP WINDOW command moves windows down in the order they are displayed. It can move a specified window, the topmost window, or WM window.

◘ DSERV—Get information about VSE libraries

• **General format**

```
DSERV   <<CD [PHASE <name [nn or 12]> or
            RD or SD or PD or TD or ALL>
            [d2...dn] [(options[)]]
```

where the *options* are [DISK or TERM or PRINT] [SORT]

• **Description**

The DSERV command, issued in CMS/DOS, gets information about VSE libraries. It is valid in System/370 mode only.

◻ DUMPLOAD—Load or print dumps

● General format

```
DUMPLOAD [SPOOL or TAPE or PRBxxxxx] [PRINT or NOPRINT]
         [CP or ALL]
```

● Description

The DUMPLOAD command performs the following functions:

- Loading a system abend or virtual machine dump from a reader spool file into a CMS file
- Loading a dump from a tape into a CMS file
- Printing a CMS dump file

◻ EDIT— Invoke the CMS editor

● General format

```
EDit fn ft [fm or *] [(options[)]]
```

where the *options* are [LRECL *nn*] [NODISP]

● Description

The EDIT command invokes the CMS editor. It is used to create and change CMS files.

◻ ERASE—Delete a CMS file

● General format

```
ERASE <fn or *> <ft or *> [fm or *] [(options[)]]
```

where the *options* are [Type or Notype]

● Description

The ERASE command removes one or more CMS files from a disk.

◻ ESERV—Copy VSE macros

● General format

```
ESERV fn
```

- **Description**

The ESERV command copies edited VSE macros to CMS disk files or lists deedited macros. The edited macros are from private or system source sublibraries.

◯ EXEC—Execute CMS commands or EXEC statements

- **General format**

```
EXec fn [args...]
```

- **Description**

The EXEC command executes CMS commands from a CMS EXEC file and EXEC control statements from an EXEC 2 file.

◯ EXECDROP—Remove EXECs in storage

- **General format**

```
EXECDrop [execname or *] [exectype or *] [(options[)]]
```

where the *options* are [User or SYstem or SHare]

- **Description**

The EXECDROP command removes one or more EXECs or System Product Editor macros from storage. Also, it can be used to discontinue EXECs or macros.

◯ EXECIO—Input and Ouput Operation

- **General format**

```
EXECIO <lines or *>
    <<DISKR fn ft [fm] [linenum]
    [([FINIs] [optiona] [optionb] [)]]>      or
    <DISKW fn ft fm [linenum] [recfm] [lrecl]
    [([FINIs] [optionb] [optionc] [optiond] [)]]> or
    <CARD    [([optiona] [optionb] [)]]>     or
    <CP      [([optiona] [optionb]
             [optiond] [optione] [)]]>        or
    <PUNCH   [([optionb] [optionc] [optiond] [)]]>  or
    <EMSG    [([optionb] [optionc] [optiond] [)]]>  or
    <PRINT   [([CC <code or DATA>]
    [optionb] [optionc] [optiond] [)]]>
    >
```

where *optiona* is [FInd/*chars*/ or LOcate/*chars*/
                    or Avoid/*chars*]

```
                [Zone <n1 or 1> or <n2 or *>]
                [LIFO or FIFO] [SKip]

    optionb is [Margins <n1 or 1> or <n2 or *>]
               [SRTRIP] [NOTYPE] [STEm xxxxn or VAR xxxx]

    optionc is [CAse <U or M>]

    optiond is [STring xxx...]

    optione is [BUFfer length]
```

● **Description**

The EXECIO command performs input and output operations between an external device and a program. This command can be used to read records from a disk file or virtual reader and to write to a stack or variable of a program. Also, it reads lines from the program stack and variable and writes them to CMS files, punch, or printer.

◘ **EXECLOAD—Load EXEC into storage**

● **General format**

```
<EXECLoad or EXLoad> fn ft [fm] [execname] [exectype]
                    [User or SYstem] [Push]
```

● **Description**

The EXECLOAD command loads an EXEC into storage and assigns it the name. This storage-resident EXEC is ready for execution. An EXEC can be removed from storage with the EXECDROP command, and the status of an EXEC can be determined by using the EXECSTAT command.

◘ **EXECMAP—List EXECs loaded into storage**

● **General format**

```
<EXECMap or EXMap> [execname or *]
                  [exectype or *] [(options... [)]]

where the options are [User] [SYstem] [SHared]
                      [STACK <FIFO or LIFO>]
                      [FIFO] [LIFO]
```

● **Description**

The EXECMAP command lists all the EXECs already loaded into

storage as well as in DCSS (Installation Discontiguous Shared Segment).

◼ EXECOS—Reset the OS and VSAM environment

- **General format**
  ```
  EXECOS [cmd] [operand1] [operand2...operandn]
  ```

- **Description**
  The EXECOS command is used to clear the following VSAM and OS items:

  - STAE exits
  - STIMER exits
  - SPIE exits
  - STAX exits
  - TXTLIB exits
  - MACLIB pointers
  - SSTAT extensions
  - LINKLIST
  - OSSFLAGS
  - VSAM environment

◼ EXECSTAT—Check a storage-resident EXEC

- **General format**
  ```
  <EXECStat or EXStat> [execname or *] [exectype or *]
  ```

- **Description**
  The EXECSTAT command checks whether an EXEC is loaded into storage. It also be used to list all storage-resident EXECs.

◼ EXECUPDT—Update a source program and create an executable file

- **General format**
  ```
  EXECUPDT fn [ft or EXEC] [fm or *] [(options...[)]]
  ```

  where options are [CTL fn1] [HISTory or NOHISTory]
  [COMPress or NOCOMPress]
  [COMMents or NOCOMMents]

              [ETMODE] [SID or NOSID] [NOUPdate]

- **Description**
  The EXECUPDT command is used to update an interpretive
  source program and create an executable file of the program. The
  input must be an 80-byte fixed-format record file, and the output
  is a variable-format file. The filetype must start with the character
  $.

◻ FETCH—Load an executable phase

- **General format**
  FETch *phasename* [(*options*...[)]]

  where *options* are [START] [COMP] [ORIGIN *hexdoc*]

- **Description**
  The FETCH command loads a CMS/DOS or VSE executable
  phase into storage. If the START option is used, then execution
  starts immediately; otherwise execution can be initiated with the
  START command. This command is valid in System/370 mode
  only.

◻ FILEDEF—File definition

- **General format**
```
FILedef <ddname or nn or *>
   <Terminal [(optiona optiond[)]]                  or
   PRinter   [(optiona OPTCD J[)]]                  or
   PUnch     [(optiona [)]]                         or
   Reader    [(optiona [)]]                         or
   DISK      [[<fn ft> or <FILE ddname>] [fm or A1]]
             [(optiona optionb [)]]                 or
   DISK      [ [<fn ft> or <FILE ddname>] [fm or A1]]
             [<DSN ?> or <DSN qual1 qual2...> or
                   <DSN qual1.qual2...>]            or
   DISK vaddr                                       or
   DUMMY     [(optiona[)]]                          or
   TAP n     [LABOFF or BLP[n] or NL[n]
                 <SL [n] [VOLID volid] [DISP MOD]> or
                 <SUL [n] [VOLID volid]> or
                     NSL filename]
         [(optiona optionc optione optionf [)]]         or
   GRAF vdev [([PERM] [CHANGE or NOCHANGE] [)]]        or
   CLEAR
   >
```

```
     where optiona is [PERM] [CHANGE or NOCHANGE]
                       [RECFM a] [LRECL nnnnn]
                       [BLOCK nnnnn or BLKSIZE nnnnn]

          optionb is [KELEN nnn] [XTENT nnnnn or 50]
                     [LIMCT nnn] [OPTCD a] [DISP MOD]
                     [MEMBER membername] [CONTACT]
                     [DSORG [PS or PO or DA]]

          optionc is [7TRACK or 9TRACK or 18TRACK]
                     [TRTCH a] [DEN den]

          optiond is [UPCASE or LOWCASE]

          optione is [LEAVE] [NOEOV]

          optionf is [ALT <TAP n or cuu>]
```

- **Description**
  The FILEDEF command is used to

  - Define datasets for OS ddnames
  - Define files that can be copied using the MOVEFILE command

◻ FILELIST—Display CMS file information

- **General format**
  ```
  FILELIST [fn] [ft] [fm] [(options[)]]

  where the options are [([APPEND]
                         [Filelist or Nofilelist]
                         [PROFile fn] [)]]
  ```

- **Description**
  The FILELIST command displays file information for a disk. Pattern matching of filename and filetype can be accomplished using the special characters * (asterisk) and % (percent).

◻ FINIS—Close a CMS file

- **General format**
  ```
  FINIS  <fn or *> <ft or *> [fm or *]
  ```

- **Description**
  The FINIS command closes one or more CMS files. All CMS

commands close files automatically; the FINIS command can be used when a program does not close a file.

◘ FORMAT—Format a minidisk

● **General format**
```
FORMAT vdev mode [nocyl or noblk]
    [([Blksize [n]] [Noerase] [Label] [Recomp] [)]]
```

where n is 512, 800, 1024, 2048, 4096, 1K, 2K or 4K.

● **Description**
The FORMAT command does the following:

● Initializes a minidisk to store CMS files
● Resets number of cylinders
● Inserts a label into the minidisk

◘ GENDIRT—Fill in an auxiliary directory

● **General format**
```
GENDIRT directoryname [targetmode] [sourcemode]
```

● **Description**
The GENDIRT command makes entries to an auxiliary file directory. It contains the name and location of modules.

◘ GENMOD—Create a MODULE file

● **General format**
```
GENMODE [fn] [MODULE [fm or A1]] [(options...[)]]
```

where options are [FROM entry1] [TO entry2]
            [MAP or NOMAP] [STR or NOSTR]
            [OS or DOS or ALL] [SYSTEM]
            [CLEAN or NOCLEAN]
            [AMODE <24 or 31 or ANY>]
            [RMODE <24 or ANY>] [370] [XA]

● **Description**
The GENMOD command creates a MODULE file which can be either relocatable or nonrelocatable. This command is used as the

final step when link-editing a program. The MODULE file is loaded using the LOADMOD or NUCXLOAD command, and it is executed with the START command.

◘ GENMSG—Convert a message file

• General format
```
GENMSG fn ft fm applid [langid] [(options...[)]]

where options are [CP] [Dbcs or NODbcs]
                  [List or NOList]
                  [Xref or NOXref]
                  [Object or NOObject]
                  [Margin nn or Margin 72]
```

• Description
The GENMSG command converts a message file into a form that the message processor can accept.

◘ GET VSCREEN—Update a virtual screen

• General format
```
GET VSCreen   vname fn ft [fm or *]
    [fromrec or 1] [numrec or *]
```

• Description
The GET VSCREEN command gets lines from a CMS file and updates a specified virtual screen.

◘ GLOBAL—Specify global libraries

• General format
```
GLobal <MACLIB or TXTLIB or DOSLIB or LOADLIB>
    [libname1...libname63]
```

• Description
The GLOBAL command specifies CMS, CMS/DOS, or OS libraries to be searched for macros, copybooks, VSE executable phases, or OS load modules when executing subsequent CMS commands.

◘ GLOBALV—Build global variables

• General format

```
GLOBALV INIT                                or
    SELECT [group or UNNAMED]               or
    SELECT [group or UNNAMED] option1 or
    SELECT [group or UNNAMED] option2 or
    SELECT [group or UNNAMED] PURGE         or
    GRPLIST                                 or
    GRPSTACK                                or
    PURGE

where option1 is

    <SET or SETS or SETP> [value1] [name2 value2] ...
    <SET or SETLS SETSL or SETLP or SETPL> name [value]
    LIST [name1] [name2]...
    <STACK or STACKR> name1 [name2] ...

    option2 is

    <PUT or PUTS or PUTP> name1 [name2] ...
    GET [name1] [name2]...
```

• Description

The GLOBALV command builds global variables in storage that can be used by EXECs. The EXECs access the values of the variables by common names. The GLOBALV command maintains the variables on a temporary or permanent basis.

◘ HELP—Help facility

• General format

```
Help [TASKs or Help] or [taskname TASKs] or
        [menuname MENU] or
            [component-name cmd-name]
    [([option1] [option2] [option3] [)]]
            [MESSAGE or MSG] message-id

where option1 is [BRIef or DETail or RELated]

    option2 is [ALL] [DESCript] [FORMat] [PARMs]
            [OPTions] [NOTEs] [ERRors]

    option3 is [SCReen or NOScreen] [TYPe or NOType]
            [EXTend]
```

• Description

The HELP command simulates the CMS HELP facility. It shows three levels of information: BRIEF, DETAIL, and RELATED.

◘ HELPCONV—Convert to HELP format

- **General format**
  ```
  HELPCONV fn ft [fm or *]
  ```

- **Description**
  The HELPCONV command converts the contents of a CMS file into a format compatible with the HELP command. The filetype of the output file is $HLPxxxx.

◘ HIDE WINDOW—Do not display a window

- **General format**
  ```
  HIDE WINdow [wname or = [ON vname [line col]]]
  ```

- **Description**
  The HIDE WINDOW command prevents a specified window from being displayed. It also connects the window to a virtual screen.

◘ IDENTIFY—Put information on a stack

- **General format**
  ```
  IDentify [([STACK [FIFO or LIFO]] or
          FIFO or LIFO or TYPE [)]]
  ```

- **Description**
  The IDENTIFY command either shows or displays the following information:

  - Userid and node of the person logged on
  - Userid of the RSCS virtual machine
  - Date and time

◘ IMMCMD—Clear or establish a command

- **General format**
  ```
  IMMCMD <SET or CLEAR or QUERY or STATUS> name
  ```

● **Description**
The IMMCMD command acts upon immediate commands. It is issued only from an EXEC file (CMS EXEC or EXEC 2). It does the following: establishes, clears, queries, or indicates an immediate command.

◻ **INCLUDE—Load a TEXT file into storage**

● **General format**
```
INclude   fn... [(options...[)]]

where options are
   [CLEAR or NOCLEAR]
   [RESET <entry or *>]
   [ORIGIN <hexloc or TRANS>] [MAP or NOMAP]
   [TYPE or NOTYPE] [INV or NOINV] [REP or NOREP]
   [AUTO or NOAUTO] [LIBE or NOLIBE] [START]
   [SAME] [DUP or NODUP] [RLDsave] [HIST or NOHIST]
```

● **Description**
The INCLUDE command loads into virtual storage one or more TEXT files from disk. Proper linkages are resolved between files. The INCLUDE must always follow a LOAD command to achieve desirable results.

◻ **LABELDEF—Label definition of tape**

● **General format**
```
LAbeldef <* or fn>
   CLEAR
   [FID <? or fid >] [VOLID<volid or ? or SCRATCH>]
        [VOLSEQ volseq]
   [FSEQ fseq] [GENN genn] [GENV genv]
   [CRDTE yyddd] [EXDTE yyddd] [SEC <0 or 1 or 3>]
        [(options...[)]]

   where options are [PERM] [CHANGE or NOCHANGE]
```

● **Description**
The LABELDEF command is used to describe label information about tape to CMS. The specification can be for standard HDR1 and EOF1 tape labels. This command is valid in System/370 mode only.

◘ LISTDS—Display OS and DOS file information

• General format
```
LISTDS  [? or dsname] <fm or *> [(options...[)]]

where options are [EXTENT or FREE] [FORMAT] [PDS]
```

• Description
The LISTDS command lists information about OS datasets and DOS files. The information is displayed on the terminal. This command is valid in System/370 mode only.

◘ LISTFILE—Get information about CMS files

• General format
```
Listfile [fn or *] [ft or *] [fm or *] [(options...[)]]

where options are
    [Header or NOHeader]
    [Exec [TRACE] [ARGS] or Trace [ARGS] or
      APpend [ARGS] or STACK [FIFO or LIFO] or
      FIFO  or LIFO  or XEDIT ]
    [FName or FType or FMode or FOrmat or ALloc or
        Date  or Label] [Blocks] [% x]
```

• Description
The LISTFILE command gets information about CMS files. The kind of information can be specified by the command options.

◘ LISTIO—List assignment of I/O devices

• General format
```
LISTIO [SYS or PROG or SYSxxx or A or UA or ALL]
            [(options...[)]]

    where options are [EXEC or APPEND] [STAT]
```

• Description
The LISTIO command issued in CMS/DOS displays the physical devices that have been assigned to logical units. The logical units can be for system or programmer, or for both. This command is valid in System/370 mode only.

◘ LKED—Link edit object file

• General format
```
LKED fname  [(options...[)]]

where options are
              [NCALL] [LET] [ALIGN2] [NE] [OL] [RENT]
              [REUS] [REFR] [OVLY] [XCAL]
              [NAME membername] [LIBE libraryname]
              [XREF or MAP or LIST] [TERM or NOTERM]
              [PRINT or DISK or NOPRINT]
              [SIZE <value1 value2>]
              [AMODE <24 or 31 or ANY>]
              [RMODE <24 or ANY>]
```

• Description
The LKED command takes an object file with filetype of TEXT
and converts it into a load module. The output is a CMS
LOADLIB or LOADLIB member.

◘ LOAD—Load an object file into storage

• General format
```
LOAD fn ... [(options...[)]]

where options are
    [CLEAR or NOCLEAR] [RESET <entry or *>]
    [MAP or NOMAP] [TYPE or NOTYPE] [INV or NOINV]
    [REP or NOREP] [AUTO or NOAUTO] [LIBE or NOLIBE]
    [START] [DUP or NODUP] [NORLDsav or RLDsave]
    [NOPRES or PRES] [RMODE <24 or ANY>]
    [ORIGIN <hexloc or TRANS>] [AMODE <24 or 31 or ANY>]
```

• Description
The LOAD command takes one or more relocatable object files
and loads them into virtual storage. The input file must have a
filetype of TEXT. The command resolves the linkages between the
input files. To execute the program after loading it, you use the
START command.

◘ LOADLIB—Manage LOADLIBs

• General format
```
LOADLIB [LIST or COMPRESS or COPY] <fileid1>
    [fileid2] [fileid3] [(options...[)]]

where options are [TERM or PRINT or DISK]
```

```
                    [REPLACE or MODIFY]
```

● **Description**
The LOADLIB command is used to manage CMS LOADLIBs. Its
functions are to list specified member names, compress a member,
and copy one member to another.

◻ **LOADMOD—Load a module into storage**

● **General format**
```
LOADMod fn [MODULE [fm]] [(options[)]]

where the options  are [NOPRES or PRES]
```

● **Description**
The LOADMOD command loads a module from a CMS disk into
storage. The filetype must be MODULE. After the module is
loaded, it can be executed by issuing a subsequent START
command.

◻ **MACLIB—Maintain macro libraries**

● **General format**
```
MAClib <GEN or ADD or REP> libname fn1 [fn2...]
    DEL libname  membername1 [membername2...]
    COMP libname
    MAP libname [membername1...] [membername2...]
        [(options[)]]

where options are [DISK or PRINT or TERM or
                  [STACK [FIFO or LIFO]] or
                  FIFO or LIFO or XEDIT]
```

● **Description**
The MACLIB command maintains CMS macro libraries. It
performs the following functions

● Generates or compresses a library
● Adds, replaces, or deletes a member of a library
● Lists the members of a library

◼ MACLIST—List members of a macro library

● **General format**

```
<MACLIST or MList> libname [(options[)]]

where options are [Append] [Compact or NOCompact]
                  [PROFile fn]
```

● **Description**

The MACLIST command lists information about members of a CMS macro library.

◼ MAKEBUF—Make a new program stack buffer

● **General format**

```
MAKEBUF
```

● **Description**

The MAKEBUF command allocates a new buffer within the stack of a program.

◼ MAXIMIZE WINDOW—Expand a window

● **General format**

```
MAXimize WINdow [wname or =]
```

● **Description**

The MAXIMIZE WINDOW command increases the size of a window to cover the full physical size of the screen.

◼ MINIMIZE WINDOW—Reduce the size of a window

● **General format**

```
MINimize WINdow [wname or =]
```

● **Description**

The MINIMIZE WINDOW command reduces the size of a window to one line.

◼ MODMAP—Module map

● **General format**

```
MODmap fn
```

- **Description**

  The MODMAP command lists the map of a module. The filetype of the file must be MODULE.

◘ MONWRITE—Save monitor records

- **General format**

```
MONWRITE [dscc or MONDCSS]
        [iucv appl or *MONITOR]
        [[TAPE [vdev or 181]] or
        [DISK [fn or Ddate]
        [ft or Ttime] [fm or A1]]]
```

- **Description**

  The MONWRITE command writes the monitor records produced by VM to a specified destination. The destination can be one of the following:

- MONITOR DSCC
- IUCV server or application program
- Tape
- Disk

◘ MOREHELP—Get "help" information

- **General format**

```
MOREhelp [([option1] [option2] [)]]
```

```
where option1 is [DETail or BRIef or RELated]
      option2 is [ALL] [DESCRipt] [FORMat] [PARMs]
              [OPTions] [NOTEs] [ERRors]
```

- **Description**

  The MOREHELP command gets information about the last HELP command issued. This command is used when a PF key is not available. There are three types of information: detail, brief, and related.

◘ MOVEFILE—Copy data

- **General format**

```
MOVEfile [inddname or INMOVE]
```

```
[outddname or OUTMOVE] [(PDS[)]]
```

- **Description**

The MOVEFILE command moves data to and from devices supported by VM.

◘ NAMEFIND—Display or place information from a names file

- **General format**

```
NAMEFind :tag value... [(options...[)]]
```

```
where options are [[STACK [n or * or 1]
                        [FIFO or LIFO]]       or
                        [FIDO [n or * or 1]] or
                        [LIFO [n or * or 1]] or
                        [TYPE [n or * or 1]]]
       [FILe fn] [LINenum] [STARt recnum]
       [SIze [n or * or 8]] [XEDIT]
```

- **Description**

The NAMEFIND command displays information from a specified names file or writes the information to the program stack. The filetype of the input file must be NAMES. If a file is omitted, the default is *userid*.NAMES.

◘ NAMES—Maintain a names file

- **General format**

```
NAMES [nickname]
```

- **Description**

The NAMES command shows a menu from which you can choose to create, change, and delete entries in a names file belonging to the user.

◘ NOTE—Send notes to computer users

- **General format**

```
NOTE   [name...] [CC: name...] [(options...[)]]
```

```
where options are [ACk or NOAck] [ADd] [Cancel]
                   [NOTebook <fn or *> or NONotebook]
                   [LOG or NOLog] [LONg or Short]
                   [Replace] [PROFile fn]
```

• **Description**
The NOTE command allows a user to compose a note or short communication and send it to one or more computer users. The users can be on the local or a remote system. For a remote user, the computers must be connected via RSCS (Remote Spooling Communications Subsystem). The note is prepared using XEDIT, and it references the *userid*.NAMES file for nicknames. A note can be sent to one user or all users on a list. The heading and recipients are automatically inserted on each note.

◻ **NUCXDROP—Remove a nucleus extension**

• **General format**
```
NUCXDROP - name1 or * [name2...]
```

• **Description**
The NUCXDROP command removes one or more nucleus extensions. It also releases the storage allocated for the program.

◻ **NUCXLOAD—Install a nucleus extension**

• **General format**
```
NUCXLOAD <name [fn]> <name member ddname>
    [([SYstem] [ENdcmd] [SErvice] [IMmcmd] [Push] [)]]
```

• **Description**
The NUCXLOAD command installs one or more load modules as nucleus extensions. The types of modules are ADCON-free module, relocatable module of OS or CMS library, and CMS module file.

◻ **NUCXMAP—List information about existing nucleus extensions**

• **General format**
```
NUCXMAP [* or name or ALL]
        [([ALL] [STACK] [LIFO or FIFO] [)]]
```

• **Description**
The NUCXMAP command lists information for all existing

nucleus extensions. As specified, the information is either displayed on the terminal or placed in the program stack.

◻ OPTION—Set options for DOS/VS COBOL compiler

● **General format**
```
OPTION [(options...[)]]
```

where *options* are [DUMP or NODUMP]
                     [DECK or NODECK]
                     [LIST or NOLIST]
                     [LISTX or NOLISTX]
                     [SYM or NOSYM]
                     [XREF or NOXREF]
                     [ERRS or NOERRS]
                     [48C or 60C]
                     [TERM or NOTERM]

● **Description**
The OPTION command sets one or many options for the DOS/VS COBOL compiler.

◻ OSRUN—Execute a load module

● **General format**
```
OSRUN member [PARM=parameters]
```

● **Description**
The OSRUN command executes a load module from a CMS LOADLIB or OS library. Only the member of the load module is specified with this command; the library where the member resides must have been identified by a previous GLOBAL or FILEDEF command.

◻ PARSECMD—Parse command arguments

● **General format**
```
PARSECMD uniqueid [(options...[)]]
```

where *options* are [TYPE or NOTYPE]
                    [STRING cmdstring]
                    [APPLID [applid or DMS]]

- **Description**

  The PARSECMD command provides the parsing and translation facility for command arguments.

◼ PEEK—List files of virtual reader

- **General format**

  ```
  PEEK [spoolid] [(options...[)]]

  where options are [FRom recno] [FOr numrec]
                    [PROFile fn]
  ```

- **Description**

  The PEEK command lists all the file in your reader. Once the files are displayed, the XEDIT subcommand can be used to browse through them.

◼ POP WINDOW—Move a window up

- **General format**

  ```
  POP WINdow <wname or WM> [n or *]
  ```

- **Description**

  The POP WINDOW command moves the window up by the number of positions specified. If the number of positions is omitted, then the window is moved to the top. The POP WINDOW command is effective only if the window is not hidden.

◼ POSITION WINDOW—Move the position of a window

- **General format**

  ```
  POSition WINdow <wname or => psline pscol
  ```

- **Description**

  The POSITION WINDOW command changes the position of a window on the physical screen by assigning a new line and column.

◘ PRINT—Print a CMS file

• General format
```
PRint fn ft [fm or *] [(options...[)]]

where options are [CC [HEADer] or NOCC]
                  [UPcase] [TRC or NOTRC]
                  [LINECOUN<nnn or 55>]
                  [MEMber <* or membername>]
                  [HEX]
```

• Description
The PRINT command prints a CMS file on the spooled printer.

◘ PROGMAP—Get information on the programs currently loaded

• General format
```
PROGMAP [progname or *] [(options...[)]]

where options are [PROGNAME or NUCX or ALL]
                  [STACK] [FIFO or LIFO]
```

• Description
The PROGMAP command get the information about all the programs loaded in the storage area. The information is either displayed or placed in the program stack, depending on the option entered in the command.

◘ PSERV—Maintain the VSE procedure library

• General format
```
PSERV procedure [ft or PROC] [(options...[)]]

where options are [DISK] [PRINT] [PUNCH] [TERM]
```

• Description
The PSERV command is used in CMS/DOS to maintain the VSE procedure library. The functions provided by this command are copy, display, print, and punch procedure.

◘ **PUNCH—Send a CMS file to a virtual punch**

● **General format**
```
PUnch fn ft [fm or *] [([Header or NOHeader]
                  [MEMber<* or membername>] [)]]
```

● **Description**
The PUNCH command sends a CMS file to the punch of your virtual machine.

◘ **PUT SCREEN—Copy a screen to a file**

● **General format**
```
PUT SCREEN fn ft [fm or * or A1]
```

● **Description**
The PUT SCREEN command copies the contents of an entire screen to a specified file.

◘ **PUT VSCREEN—Copy a virtual screen to a file**

● **General format**
```
PUT VSCreen vname fn ft [fm or * or A1]
    [fromlin or 1] [numlin or *]
```

● **Description**
The PUT SCREEN command copies the content of a data area of a virtual screen to a specified file.

◘ **QUERY—Get information about a CMS virtual machine**

● **General format**
```
Query <ABBREV or
    APL or
    AUTODUMP or
    AUTOREAD or
    BLIP <BORDER wname [OPTIONS]> or
    CHARMODE or
    CMSLEVEL or
    CMSPF [nn or *] or
    CMSTYPE or
    CURSOR [vname] or
    [DISK [mode or * or R/W or MAX]] or
    DISPLAY or
```

```
       DLBL or
       DOSLIB or
       DOSLNCNT or
       DOSPART or
       EXECTRAC or
       FILEDEF or
       FULLREAD or
       FULLSCREEN or
       HIDE [wname or *] or
       IMESCAPE or
       IMPCP or
       IMPEX or
       INPUT or
       INSTSEG or
       KEY or
       KEYPROTECT or
       LABELDEF or
       LANGLIST or
       LANGUAGE [ALL] or
       LDRTBLS or
       LIBRARY or
       LINEND or
       LOADAREA or
       LOADLIB or
       LOCATION wname or
       LOGFILE vname or
       MACLIB or
       NONDISP or
       OPTION or
       OUTPUT or
       PROTECT or
       RDYMSG or
       RELPAGE or
       REMOTE or
       RESERVED wname or
       ROUTE [segname or *] or
       SEARCH or
       SEGMENT [segment or *] or
       SHOW [wname or *] or
       STORECLR or
       SYNONYM [SYSTEM or USER or ALL] or
       SYSNAMES or
       TEXT or
       TRANslate [SYStem or USER or ALL] [TRANslate or
          SYNonym or BOTH] [APPLID applid or *] or
       TXTLIB or
       UPSI or
       VSCREEN [vname or * [ALL]] or
       WINDOW [wname or = or * [ALL]] or
       WMPF [nn or *]
    > [(options...[)]]

    where options are [STACK [FIFO or LIFO] or
                          FIFO or LIFO]
```

● **Description**

The QUERY command gets information on various aspects of the user virtual machine.

◼ RDR—Get information about files in the reader

● General format
RDR [*spool-class* or =] [(*options*[)]]

where *options* are [NOTYPE or [STACK [FIFO or LIFO]] or
FIFO or LIFO]

● Description
The RDR command gets information about files in the user reader.
The information is either displayed on the screen or written to the
program stack.

◼ RDRLIST—Maintain reader files

● General format
<RDRList or RList> [([PROFile *fn*] [Append][)]]

● Description
The RDRLIST command maintains reader files. This command
first lists information about the files. Subsequently, you can
discard files, copy them to a CMS disk, or send them to a local or
remote user.

◼ READCARD—Read data from the card reader

● General format
READcard *fn ft* [*fm* or A] [(*options*...[)]]

where *options* are [Fullprompt or Minprompt or NOPrompt]
[Replace or NOReplace]

● Description
The READCARD command reads spooled data from the card
reader and writes them to a specified CMS file. The data in the
reader must be fixed-length records with sizes ranging from 80 to
204 characters.

◘ RECEIVE—Read files or notes from reader

● **General format**
```
RECEIVE [spoolid] [fn] [ft] [fm] [(options...[)]]

where options are [NOTebook <fn or *>]
                  [Log or NOLog] [Purge]
                  [Fullprompt or Minprompt or NOPrompt]
                  [Replace or NOReplace]
                  [Olddate or NEwdate] [STack]
```

● **Description**
The RECEIVE command reads one or more files or notes from the reader of a user and writes then onto disk. These files or notes can be from local or remote users of the computer network (RSCS).

◘ REFRESH—Redraw the virtual screen

● **General format**
```
REFresh
```

● **Description**
The REFRESH command redraws a virtual screen by updating any changes to the windows associated with it.

◘ RELEASE—Free a disk

● **General format**
```
RELease <vdev or mode> [(DET[)]]
```

● **Description**
The RELEASE command releases a disk from being accessed from a CMS virtual machine.

◘ RENAME—Change the name of a CMS file

● **General format**
```
Rename file-old file-new
       [([Type or NOType] [UPdirt or NOUPdirt] [)]]
```

● **Description**
The RENAME command changes the filename and filetype of one

or more CMS files.

◻ RESERVE—Allocate available disk space

● **General format**
RESERVE fn ft fm

● **Description**
The RESERVE command allocates available blocks of space to a specified CMS file. The space is part of a formatted minidisk and in blocks of 512 bytes, 1 k byte, 2 k bytes, or 4 k bytes.

◻ RESTORE WINDOW—Restore window size

● **General format**
REStore WINdow [wname or =]

● **Description**
The RESTORE WINDOW command restores a window to its original size.

◻ RETRIEVE—Get accounting information

● **General format**
RETRIEVE [ACCOUNT or EREP or ALL]

● **Description**
The RETRIEVE command gathers error and accounting information and places it in a CMS file. The information is used for analysis.

◻ ROUTE—Reroute message data

● **General format**
ROUTE msglass TO vname [(options...[)]]

where options are [ALArm or NOALarm]
                   [NOTify or NONotify]

- **Description**
  The ROUTE command re-routes message data to a virtual screen.

◘ RSERV—Maintain VSE relocatable module

- **General format**
  ```
  RSERV modname [ft or TEXT] [(options...[)]]

  where options are [DISK] [PRINT] [PUNCH] [TERM]
  ```

- **Description**
  The RSERV command maintains VSE relocatable modules. It copies, displays, prints, or punches load modules from a private or system library. This command is valid in System/370 mode only.

◘ RUN—Perform a function

- **General format**
  ```
  RUN fn [ft] [fm] [(args...[)]]
  ```

- **Description**
  The RUN command performs a series of functions on a source, MODULE, TEXT, or EXEC file.

◘ SCROLL—Change a window location

- **General format**
  ```
  SCROLL BAckward [wname or = [n or * or 1]] or
         Bottom   [wname or = ] or
         Down     [wname or = [n or * or 1]] or
         Forward  [wname or = [n or * or 1]] or
         Left     [wname or = [n or 1]] or
         Next     [wname or = [n or * or 1]] or
         Right    [wname or = [n or 1]] or
         Top      [wname or = ] or
         Up       [wname or = [n or * or 1]]
  ```

- **Description**
  The SCROLL command changes the location of a window. The window must be connected to a virtual screen.

◘ SEGMENT—Manage saved segments

● **General format**
```
SEGMENT LOAD segname [(options...[)]]

where options are [SYSTEM or USER]
                  [SHare or NOShare]

SEGMENT PURGE segname

SEGMENT RELEASE segname

SEGMENT RESERVE segname [(options...[)]]

where options are [SYSTEM or USER]
                  [SHare or NOShare]
```

● **Description**

The SEGMENT command manages the saved segments (DCSSs).
It performs the following functions:

- Loading a saved segment
- Purging a saved segment
- Releasing a saved segment
- Reserving a CMS storage for a saed segment

◘ SENDFILE—Send a note or file

● **General format**
```
<SENDFile or SFile> [[fn ft [fm] [TO] name...]
                    [(options...[)]]]

where options are [Ack or NOAck] [NOTE]
                  [Filelist or NOFilelist]
                  [Log or NOLog] [NEw or Old]
                  [Type or NOType]
```

● **Description**

The SENDFILE command is used to send a CMS file or a note.
The recipients are local users or other users connected through
RSCS network.

◘ SENTRIES—Get the number of lines in a program stack

● **General format**
```
SENTRIES
```

- **Description**

The SENTRIES command gets the number of lines in a program stack. The number is returned via CMS as a return code.

◻ SET—Set characteristics of a CMS virtual machine

- **General format**
```
SET ABBREV <ON or OFF>
SET APL <ON or OFF>
SET AUTODUMP [CMS or ALL or OFF]
SET AUTOREAD <ON or OFF>
SET BLIP
SET BORDER wname <ON or OFF> [([optiona] [optionb][)]]
```

where *optiona* is [TOP *char*] [BOTTOM *char*] [LEFT *char*]
             [RIGHT *char*] [ALL *char*]
where *optionb* is [High or NOHigh] [*color*] [*exthi*]
             [*psset*]

```
SET CHARMODE <ON or OFF>
SET CMSPF nn [<pseudonym or NOWRITE>
             [keyword or DELAYED] string]
SET CMSTYPE <HT or RT>
SET DOS <ON [mode [(VSAM[)]]]> or OFF
SET DOSLNCNT nn
SET DOSPART <nnnnnK or OFF>
SET EXECTRAC <ON or OFF>
SET FULLREAD <ON or OFF>
SET FULLSCREEN <ON or OFF or SUSPEND or RESUME>
SET IMESCAPE <ON or OFF or char>
SET IMPCP <ON or OFF>
SET IMPEX <ON or OFF>
SET INPUT [a xx or xx yy]
SET INSTSEG <ON [mode or LAST] or OFF>
SET KEYPROTect [ON or OFF]
SET LANGUAGE [langid] [(options...[)]]
```

where *options* are [ADD *applid* or DELETE *applid*]
    [USER or SYSTEM or ALL] [TYPE or NOTYPE]

```
SET LDRTBLS [nn]
SET LINEND <ON or OFF> [char]
SET LOADAREA <20000 or RESPECT>
SET LOCATION wname <ON or OFF>
SET LOGFILE vname <ON or OFF> [fn] [LOGFILE or
    [fm or * or A1]]
SET NONDISP [char]
SET NONSHARE <CMSDOS or CMSVSAM or CMSAMS or CMSBAM>
SET OUTPUT [xx a]
SET PROTECT <ON or OFF>
SET RDYMSG <LMSG or SMSG>
SET REPLACE <ON or OFF>
SET REMOTE <ON or OFF>
SET RESERVED wname <rtop or *> <rbot or *>
SET STORECLR <ENDCMD or ENDSVC>
```

```
SET SYSNAME <CMSDOS or CMSVSAM or CMSAMS or CMSBAM>
          entryname
SET TEXT <ON or OFF>
SET TRANslate <ON or OFF> [SYStem or USER or ALL]
      [TRANslate or SYNonym or BOTH] [APPLID applid or *]
SET UPSI <nnnnnnnn or OFF>
SET VSCREEN vname [TYPe or NOType]
         [PRotect or NOPRotect]
         [High or NOHigh] [color] [exthi] [psset]
SET WINDOW wname [VARiable or FIXed] [POP or NOPop]
         [TOP or NOTop]
SET WMPF nn [<pseudonym or NOWRITE>
         [keyword or DELAYED] string]
```

- **Description**

The SET command turns functions of a CMS virtual machine on
or off where applicable. Otherwise it sets or resets function
characteristics.

◘ **SETKEY—Change CMS storage keys**

- **General format**
```
SETKEY key sysname [startadr]
```

- **Description**
The SETKEY command changes the storage protection key.

◘ **SETPRT—Set printer parameters**

- **General format**
```
SETPRT Chars [(]ccc...[)]
      COpies [(]nnn[)]
      COPYnr [(]nnn[)]
      Fcb [(]ffff[)]
      FLash [(]id nnn[)]
      Init
      Modify [(]mmmm[n][)]
```

- **Description**
The SETPRT command loads a 3800 printer. It also sets printing
parameters such as the name of character arrangement tables, the
number of copies per page, FCB, and so on.

◘ SHOW WINDOW—Place a window at the top

● **General format**
```
SHOW WINdow wname [ON vname [line col]]
```

● **Description**
The SHOW WINDOW command moves a window to the top of the virtual screen.

◘ SIZE WINDOW—Change the size of a window

● **General format**
```
SIZE WINdow < wname or = > lines [cols]
```

● **Description**
The SIZE WINDOW command changes the size of a window by altering the line and column.

◘ SORT—Sort a CMS file

● **General format**
```
SORT field1 field2
```

● **Description**
The SORT command sorts a specified input file.   The input records must be of fixed length. The result is placed in a specified output file with sorted records in ascending order. The sort fields are interactively entered.

◘ SSERV—Maintain the VSE statement library

● **General format**
```
SSERV sublib bookname [ft or COPY] [(options...[)]]
```
```
where options are [DISK] [PRINT] [PUNCH] [TERM]
```

● **Description**
The SSERV command maintains the VSE source statement library. This command is issued in CMS/DOS. It copies, displays, prints or punches a book from a source statement library. This command is valid in System/370 mode only.

◘ START—Start execution of a program

- **General format**
```
START [entry [args...] [((OPTIONB[)]]]
    [ * [((optionb[)]]]
    [ (optiona[)]]]
    [ (optionb[)]]]]

    where optiona is [NO]
          optionb is [AMODE <24 or 31 or ANY>]
```

- **Description**
The START command starts the execution of a CMS, OS, or VSE program. The program must be already loaded or fetched.

◘ STATE/STATEW (ESTATE/ESTATEW)—Check a CMS, OS, or CMS file

- **General format**
```
<STATE or STATEW or ESTATE or ESTATEW>
   <fn or *> <ft or *> [fm or *]
```

- **Description**
The STATE, STATEW, ESTATE, or ESTATEW command checks a CMS, OS, or CMS file on an accessed disk.

◘ SVCTRACE—Set supervisor call trace

- **General format**
```
SVCTrace <ON or OFF>
```

- **Description**
The SVCTRACE command starts or stops tracing of SVC instructions.

◘ SYNONYM—Invoke a synonym

- **General format**
```
SYNonym [fn] [SYNONYM] [fm or A1 or *] [(options...[)]]

where options are [STD or NOSTD] [CLEAR]
```

- **Description**
The SYNONYM command invokes a table containing synonyms
created by the user. The synonyms are used with or instead of
CMS or user-defined command names.

◻ **TAPE—Manage a tape file**

- **General format**
```
TAPE  DUMP <fn or *> <ft or *> [fm or *]
    [(optiona optionb optiond optionf[)]]        or
    LOAD <fn or *> <ft or *> [fm or *]
    [(optionb optionc optiond [)]]      or
    SCAN <fn or *> <ft or *>
    [(optionb optionc optiond [)]]      or
    SKIP <fn or *> <ft or *>
    [(optionb optionc optiond [)]]        or
    DVOL1 [(optiond optione [)]]        or
    WVOL1 volid owner [(optiond optione [)]]       or
    MODESET [(optiond [)]]        or
    tapcmd [n or 1] [(optiond [)]]

    where optiona is [WTM or NOWTM]
                [BLKSIZE 4096 or BLKSIZE 800]
        optionb is [NOPRint or PRint or Term or DISK]
        optionc is [EOT or EOF n or EOF 1]
        optiond is [TAPn or TAP1]
                [7TRACK or 9TRACK or 18TRACK]
                [DEN den] [TRTCH a] [vdev 181]
        optione is [REWIND or LEAVE]
        optionf is [TRANsfer <BUFFered or IMMEDiate>]
```

- **Description**
The TAPE command is mainly used to manage tape files. The file
can have fixed- or variable-length records. The TAPE command
cannot handle files that reside in multiple volumes. It performs the
following functions:

- Dumping files in CMS format from disk to tape
- Copying previously dumped files from tape to disk
- Doing control operations on a tape drive

◻ **TAPEMAC—Create a MACLIB library**

- **General format**
```
TAPEMAC fn [SL labeldefid or NSL filename
    [ID =identifier]] [(options...[)]]
```

where *options* are [TAP*n* or TAP1]
             [ITEMCT *yyyy* or ITEMCT 5000]

• **Description**

The TAPEMAC command creates a CMS MACLIB. The input is a PDS (partitioned data set) unloaded from a tape. The PDS must be created by the IEHMOVE utility program of OS.

◻ **TAPPDS—Create CMS disk files from tape**

• **General format**

TAPPDS [*fn* or *] [*ft* or *] [*fm* or A1 or *]
    [SL *labeldefid* or NSL *filename* [ID =*identifier*]
         [(*options*...[)]]]

    where *options* are [PDS or NOPDS or UPDATE]
                  [COL1 or NOCOL1] [TAP*n* or TAP1]
                  [END or NOEND] [MAXTEN or NOMAXTEN]

• **Description**

The TAPPDS command creates a CMS disk file from tape. The tape is either an input or an output from the OS utility programs IEBUPDTE or IEBTTPCH, respectively.

◻ **TELL—Send a message to a user**

• **General format**

TELL *name message*

• **Description**

The TELL command sends a message to one or more users. If the user is on a remote system, that system must be connected via a RSCS network. To receive the message, the user must be logged on.

◻ **TXTLIB—Manage text libraries**

• **General format**

TXTlib GEN *libname fn1* [*fn2*...] [(*optiona* [)]]   or
       ADD *libname fn1* [*fn2*...] [(*optiona* [)]]   or
       DEL *libname membername1*...   or
       MAP *libname* [(*optionb* [)]]

```
where optiona is [FILename]
      optionb is [TERM or DISK or PRINT]
```

- **Description**

  The TXTLIB command manages CMS text libraries. This command performs the following functions:

  - Creating a TXTLIB on the A disk
  - Adding a member to an existing TXTLIB
  - Deleting a member from an existing TXTLIB
  - Listing all the members of a TXTLIB

◻ **TYPE—Display the content of a CMS file**

- **General format**

```
Type fn ft [fm or *] [rec1 or * or 1]
     [recn or *] [(options...[)]]
```

```
where options are [HEX]
                  [COL <xxxxx or 1><yyyyy or lrecl>]
                  [MEMber <* or name>]
```

- **Description**

  The TYPE command displays the content of a CMS file on the terminal. By specifying the first and last numbers, it is possible to display all or part of the file. Also, the display can be in either EBCDIC or hexadecimal mode.

◻ **UPDATE—Change a program source file**

- **General format**

```
Update fn1 [ft1 or ASSEMBLE] [fm1 or A1]
       [fn2] [ft2] [fm2] [(options... [)]]
```

```
where options are [REP or NOREP] [SEQ8 or NOSEQ8]
                  [INC or NOINC] [CTL or NOCTL]
                  [OUTMODE fm] [STK or NOSTK]
                  [TERM or NOTERM] [DISK or PRINT]
                  [STOR or NOSTOR]
```

- **Description**

  The UPDATE command changes a file containing a source program. The input to this command is one program file and one or more files with control statements. The output is the updated source file and a log file indicating the kinds of changes that took place.

◘ VALIDATE—Verify syntax of a filename

- **General format**
  ```
  VALIDATE <fn or *> <ft or *> <fm or *>
  ```

- **Description**
  The VALIDATE command checks the syntax of a filename. If the filemode is specified, then the command validates whether or not the disk is accessed.

◘ WAITREAD VSCREEN—Refresh the virtual screen and wait

- **General format**
  ```
  WAITREAD VSCreen vname
  ```

- **Description**
  The WAITREAD VSCreen command can be issued only from an EXEC. It is used to refresh the virtual screen with data and wait for the next attention interrupt.

◘ WAITT VSCREEN—Refresh the virtual screen

- **General format**
  ```
  WAITT VSCreen [vname or *]
  ```

- **Description**
  The WAITT VSCREEN command refreshes the virtual screen with data.

◘ WRITE VSCREEN—Enter data in a virtual screen

- **General format**
  ```
  WRITE VSCreen - vname line col length
       [([REServed] [optiona] [optionb]
                    [optionc] [optiond] [)]]

  where optiona is [BLANKs or NULls]
  ```

```
optionb is [PROtect or NOPROtect]
         [High or NOHigh or Invisible]
optionc is [color] [exthi] [psset]
optiond is [FIELD or DATA or COLOR or
         EXTHI or PSS] text
```

• **Description**

The WRITE VSCREEN command enters data in a virtual screen. The data are placed in the queue and displayed the next time the screen is refreshed.

◻ **XEDIT—Invoke the editor**

• **General format**
```
Xedit [fn] [ft] [fm] [(options...[)]]
```

```
where options are [WINdow wname] [Width nn] [NOSCreen]
            [PROFile macroname] [NOPROFil] [NOCLear]
            [NOMsg] [MEMber membername]
```

• **Description**

The XEDIT command invokes the editor. This editor can be used to create or change a CMS file. The editor also has many subcommands that can be issued to manipulate a file. All the XEDIT commands are described in Chapter 12.

◻ **XMITMSG—Retrieve a message**

• **General format**
```
XMITMSG msgnumber [sublist] [(options...[)]]
```

```
where options are [FORmat nn] [LINE nn] [LETter a]
            [APPLID applid] [CALLER name] [VAR]
            [COMPress or NOCOMPress]
            [HEADer or NOHEADer]
            [DISPLay or NODISPlay or ERRMSG]
            [SYSLANG]
```

• **Description**

The XMITMSG command retrieves a message from a repository file.

COBOL II

This chapter is a reference guide for programmers using the COBOL II language. It provides the syntax and descriptions of the divisions, sections, paragraphs, clauses, and statements of the language. In addition, it explains how operands are coded with clauses and operands.

General Format: The general format of a COBOL source program is:

```
<IDENTIFICATION DIVISION. or ID DIVISION.>
PROGRAM-ID. program-name.
   [identification-division-content]
[ENVIRONMENT DIVISION.]
   [environment-division-content]
[DATA DIVISION.]
   [data-division-content]
[PROCEDURE DIVISION.]
   [procedure-division-content]
[END PROGRAM program-name.]
```

All these DIVISIONs and their content are discussed in detail later in this chapter.

Notational Convention: In the general format of the COBOL statements and clauses used in this chapter, there are a few symbols that are not part of the syntax; therefore they must not be included when you code your program. These symbols and their meanings are:

Symbol	Meaning
[]	The option enclosed by the bracket ([]) is not required but can be included.
<>	Only one of the alternatives enclosed by the angle brackets (<>) must be chosen.
or	The alternatives enclosed by the angle brackets (<>) are separated by "or."
____	The underlined word is the default value.
...	The horizontal or vertical ellipsis means that the preceding can be coded more than once.
Uppercase characters	All keywords of the command are written in uppercase characters; they must be coded as shown.
Lowercase characters	All strings in lowercase characters and italic are variables that can be changed to any other strings to suit your programming style. In your code they represent values that you supply to commands.

4.1   IDENTIFICATION   DIVISION

In a COBOL source program, the IDENTIFICATION DIVISION must always be the first division. This division has several paragraphs, each specifying pieces of information to document a program. The general format of this division is

```
IDENTIFICATION DIVISION or ID DIVISION.
PROGRAM-ID. program-name [IS] INITIAL COMMON PROGRAM.
[AUTHOR. comment-entry]
[INSTALLATION. comment-entry]
[DATE-WRITTEN. comment-entry]
[DATE-COMPILED. comment-entry]
[SECURITY. comment-entry]
```

The PROGRAM-ID paragraph is for the program name and it is mandatory. The other paragraphs, AUTHOR, INSTALLATION, DATA-WRITTEN, DATE-COMPILED, and SECURITY, are optional, but when used they must appear in the order shown in the general format.

Note: The optional paragraphs will be deleted from future release of the ANSI standard, as they are obsolete elements of the IDENTIFICATION DIVISION.

All these elements of this division are discussed below.

PROGRAM-ID paragraph

- **General format**

```
PROGRAM-ID. program-name [IS] INITIAL COMMON PROGRAM.
```

- **Description**

The PROGRAM-ID paragraph specifies the name of the program; it must be the first paragraph in the IDENTIFICATION DIVISION.

program-name is a user-defined name of a program. The first 8 characters of the name must be unique within the system. The first character must be alphabetic; if it is not, a translation will take place. A hyphen in positions 2 through 8 of the name is converted to a zero.

IS is an optional keyword with no special meaning.

INITIAL specifies that every time a program is called, the program and any programs within it are placed in their initial state.

COMMON specifies that *program-name* is found within another program.

AUTHOR paragraph

- **General format**

```
AUTHOR. comment-entry
```

- **Description**

The AUTHOR paragraph specifies the name of the person who wrote the program.

INSTALLATION paragraph

- **General format**

```
INSTALLATION. comment-entry
```

- **Description**
  The INSTALLATION paragraph is used to enter the name of the location where the program is written.

◻ **DATE—WRITTEN paragraph**

- **General format**
  ```
  DATE-WRITTEN. comment-entry
  ```

- **Description**
  The DATE-WRITTEN paragraph is used to specify the date when the program was written.

◻ **DATE—COMPILED paragraph**

- **General format**
  ```
  DATE-COMPILED. comment-entry
  ```

- **Description**
  The DATE-COMPILED paragraph is used to specify the date when the program was compiled.

◻ **SECURITY paragraph**

- **General format**
  ```
  SECURITY. comment-entry
  ```

- **Description**
  The SECURITY paragraph is used to specify the level of security of a program.

4.2 ENVIRONMENT DIVISION

The ENVIRONMENT DIVISION of a program is optional and consists of two sections:

- CONFIGURATION SECTION
- INPUT-OUTPUT SECTION

The general format of this division is:

```
ENVIRONMENT DIVISION.
[CONFIGURATION SECTION.]
   [configuration-section-entry]
[INPUT-OUTPUT SECTION.]
   [input-output-section-entry]
```

In the rest of this section, we discuss in detail all the sections, paragraphs, and clauses, listed in alphbetical order, associated with the ENVIRONMENT DIVISION.

◘ ACCESS MODE clause

• General format
```
QSAM and VSAM Sequential File ENTRIES:

  ACCESS [MODE IS] SEQUENTIAL

VSAM Indexed File ENTRIES:

  ACCESS [MODE IS] <SEQUENTIAL or RANDOM or DYNAMIC>

VSAM Relative File ENTRIES:

  ACCESS [MODE IS] <SEQUENTIAL or RANDOM or DYNAMIC>
```

• Description
The ACCESS MODE clause specifies how a file is to be accessed. This clause is an optional entry in the FILE-CONTROL paragraph of the INPUT-OUTPUT SECTION. Files are accessed in three different modes: sequential, random, and dynamic. If this clause is omitted, the default is sequential mode.

SEQUENTIAL is used to process records sequentially for three types of files:

- Sequential files
- VSAM indexed files
- VSAM relative files

RANDOM is used to process records randomly for two types of files:

- VSAM indexed files

- VSAM relative files

DYNAMIC is used to process records sequentially and randomly for two types of files:

- VSAM indexed files
- VSAM relative files

◘ ALPHABET clause

- **General format**

```
ALPHABET alphabet-name [IS]
              < STANDARD-1 or
                STANDARD-2 or
                NATIVE     or
                EBCDIC     or
                <literal-1 <THROUGH or THRU>
                  literal-2 ALSO literal-3>
              >
```

- **Description**

The ALPHABET clause specifies a relation between an alphabet and a character code or collating sequence. This clause is an optional entry in the SPECIAL-NAMES paragraph of the CONFIGURATION SECTION.

alphabet-name is the name of the character. A collating sequence is specified when *alphabet-name* is used in either

- The PROGRAM COLLATING SEQUENCE clause of the OBJECT-COMPUTER paragraph
- The COLLATING SEQUENCE phrase of the SORT or MERGE statment

A character code set is specified when *alphabet-name* is specified in either

- The FD entry CODE-SET clause (discussed later in the DATA DIVISION section)
- The SYMBOLIC CHARACTERS clause

STANDARD-1 specifies the ASCII character set.

STANDARD-2 specifies the International Reference Version of the ISO 7-bit code.

NATIVE specifies the native character code set.

EBCDIC specifies the EBCDIC character set.

literal-1, *literal-2*, and *literal-3* specify that the collating sequence is to be determined by the program.

◘ ALTERNATE RECORD KEY clause

● General format
```
ALTERNATE [RECORD KEY IS] data-name [WITH] [DUPLICATES]
```

● Description
The ALTERNATE RECORD KEY clause, an optional entry in the FILE-CONTROL paragraph of the INPUT-OUTPUT SECTION, specifies an alternative path to the data of a VSAM file.

data-name contains the alternative key. Also, it must be an alphanumeric item within only one of the record description entries of a file.

DUPLICATES specifies that the alternative keys may not be unique.

◘ APPLY WRITE-ONLY clause

● General format
```
APPLY WRITE-ONLY [ON] filename
```

● Description
The APPLY WRITE-ONLY clause, an optional entry in the I-O-CONTROL paragraph of the INPUT-OUTPUT SECTION, optimizes buffer and device space allocation for sequential files with blocked variable-length records.

filename is the name of the file, entered in the FILE-CONTROL paragraph, to which the WRITE-ONLY applies.

◘ ASSIGN clause

• General format
```
ASSIGN [TO] assignment-name...
```

• Description
The ASSIGN clause, an entry in the FILE-CONTROL paragraph of the INPUT-OUTPUT SECTION, associates a file used in a program with the external name of a dataset or device. This clause is used along with the SELECT clause, which specifies the file.

assignment-name is either a user-defined word or a nonnumeric literal. It has the following three formats:

- QSAM file format:
  label S *name*

- VSAM sequential file format:
  label AS *name*

- VSAM indexed or retrieve file format:
  label *name*

AS specifies a VSAM file.

label is the device or device class to which a file is assigned.

name is the external name (i.e., the DDNAME in a JCL DD statement).

S specifies a QSAM file.

◘ CLASS clause

• General format
```
CLASS class-name [IS]   literal-1
    [<THROUGH or THRU> literal-2]
```

• Description
The CLASS clause, an entry in the SPECIAL-NAMES paragraph of the CONFIGURATION SECTION, associates a name with a set

of characters.

class-name may be a DBCS user-defined word.

literal-1 and   *literal-2* define a set of characters to be associated with *class-name.*

◘ CONFIGURATION SECTION

● **General format**
```
CONFIGURATION SECTION.
  [SOURCE-COMPUTER. source-computer-entry]
  [OBJECT-COMPUTER. object-computer-entry]
  [SPECIAL-NAMES. special-names-entry]
```

● **Description**
The CONFIGURATION SECTION, an optional entry within the ENVIRONMENT DIVISION, specifies:

● The computer where the program is compiled
● The computer where the program is run
● The configurations

The SOURCE-COMPUTER, OBJECT-COMPUTER and SPECIAL-NAMES paragraphs are discussed in more detail elsewhere in this chapter.

◘ CURRENCY SIGN clause

● **General format**
```
CURRENCY [SIGN][IS] literal DECIMAL-POINT [IS] COMMA.
```

● **Description**
The CURRENCY sign clause, an optional entry in the SPECIAL-NAMES paragraph of the CONFIGURATION SECTION, specifies a currency symbol.

literal is the current symbol used in the PICTURE clause (discussed later in the DATA DIVISION section). It must be a single character and nonnumeric. It cannot be any of the following characters:

Digits 0 to 9
Uppercase characters A B C D P R S V X Z
Lowercase characters a to z
Space character
Characters * + - / ' . ; ( ) = "
A figurative constant

The default is the dollar sign character ($).

◘ FILE STATUS clause

● General format
```
FILE STATUS [IS] data-name
```

● Description
The FILE STATUS clause, an optional entry in the FILE-
CONTROL paragraph of the INPUT-OUTPUT SECTION,
associates a file with a file status key.

data-name is an alphanumeric data area 2 bytes long.

◘ FILE-CONTROL paragraph

● General format
QSAM and VSAM sequential file entry

```
FILE-CONTROL. SELECT clause
        ASSIGN clause
        [RESERVE clause]
        [ORGANIZATION clause]
        [PADDING CHARACTER clause]
        [RECORD DELIMITER clause]
        [ACCESS MODE clause]
        [PASSWORD clause]
        [FILE STATUS clause]
```

VSAM indexed file entry

```
FILE-CONTROL. SELECT clause
        ASSIGN clause
        [RESERVE clause]
        [ORGANIZATION clause]
        INDEXED
        [ACCESS MODE clause]
        RECORD KEY clause
        [ALTERNATE RECORD KEY clause]
        [PASSWORD clause]
```

```
            [FILE STATUS clause]

VSAM relative file entry

    FILE-CONTROL. SELECT clause
            ASSIGN clause
            [RESERVE clause]
            [ORGANIZATION clause]
            RELATIVE
            [ACCESS MODE clause]
            [PASSWORD clause]
            [FILE STATUS clause]
```

● **Description**
The FILE-CONTROL paragraph, an entry in the INPUT-OUTPUT
SECTION of the ENVIRONMENT DIVISION, associates each
file that is being accessed in a program with its external dataset.
It also describes the file organization, access mode, and other
information useful in file processing.

Each file described in this paragraph must have an FD or SD entry
in the DATA DIVISION.

◼ **INPUT-OUTPUT SECTION**

● **General format**
```
INPUT-OUTPUT SECTION.
    FILE-CONTROL. file-control-entry...
    [I-O-CONTROL.] [input-output-entry]
```

● **Description**
The INPUT-OUTPUT SECTION, an optional entry in the
ENVIRONMENT DIVISION, describes the external files that a
program processes. It contains two paragraphs:

● FILE-CONTROL paragraph
● I-O-CONTROL paragraph

◼ **I-O-CONTROL paragraph**

● **General format**
```
QSAM Files

    I-O-CONTROL. [RERUN clause           or
                 SAME SORT AREA clause or
                 SAME RECORD AREA clause      or
```

```
                MULTIPLE FILE TAPE clause ]
            [APPLY WRITE-ONLY clause...]
```

VSAM Files

```
    I-O-CONTROL. <RERUN clause or SAME clause >
```

Sort/Merge Files

```
    I-O-CONTROL. [RERUN clause or] [SAME clause]
```

- **Description**
  The I-O-CONTROL paragraph, an optional entry in the INPUT-OUTPUT SECTION of the ENVIRONMENT DIVISION, specifies storage areas that are to be shared among different files. It also specifies when checkpoints are to take place. There are three formats for the I-O-CONTROL paragraph, those for QSAM files, VSAM files and Sort/Merge files.

◘ MULTIPLE FILE TAPE clause

- **General format**
  MULTIPLE FILE [TAPE CONTAINS] <*filename*
      [POSITION *integer*]>...

- **Description**
  The MULTIPLE FILE TAPE clause is an entry in the I-O-CONTROL paragraph of the INPUT-OUTPUT SECTION. It specifies that two or more files are found in the same reel of tape.

  filename is the name of the file.

  POSITION specifies an integer value at which the file starts.

◘ OBJECT-COMPUTER paragraph

- **General format**
  ```
  OBJECT-COMPUTER. computer-name
        MEMORY SIZE integer
            <WORDS or CHARACTERS or MODULES>
        PROGRAM COLLATING SEQUENCE [IS] alphabet-name
        SEGMENT-LIMIT IS priority-number
  ```

- **Description**

The OBJECT-COMPUTER paragraph, an optional entry in the CONFIGURATION SECTION of the ENVIRONMENT DIVISION, specifies the computer environment where the object program runs.

computer-name is the computer system name.

MEMORY SIZE is obsolete; its systax is checked, but it is otherwise ignored.

PROGRAMING COLLATING SEQUENCE IS specifies the collating sequence used for this program.

alphabet-name is the alphabet name which is used for the collating sequence.

SEGMENT-LIMIT IS is obsolete.

▣ ORGANIZATION clause

- **General format**

QSAM and VSAM Sequential File ENTRIES:

    ORGANIZATION [IS] SEQUENTIAL

VSAM Indexed File ENTRIES:

    ORGANIZATION [IS] INDEXED

VSAM Relative File ENTRIES:

    ORGANIZATION [IS] RELATIVE

- **Description**

The ORGANIZATION clause, an entry in the FILE-CONTROL paragraph of the INPUT-OUTPUT SECTION, specifies the logical structure of a file processed in a program. There are three types: sequential, indexed, and relative. The default is sequential.

SEQUENTIAL specifies that the records in a file are accessed in the same order in which they were written. A record is added at the end of the file.

INDEXED specifies that the position of each logical record is determined by an index.

RELATIVE specifies that the position of each logical record is determined by its relative record number.

◘ PADDING CHARACTER clause

- **General format**
  PADDᴵNG [CHARACTER IS] *data-name* or *literal*

- **Description**
  The PADDING CHARACTER clause, an optional entry in the FILE-CONTROL paragraph of the INPUT-OUTPUT SECTION, specifies the character to be used for block padding on sequential files.

  data-name is an alphanumeric data area defined in the DATA DIVISION as 1 byte long.

  literal is a 1 byte nonnumeric literal.

  Note: In COBOL II, this clause has no effect during runtime, however, its syntax is checked during compilation.

◘ PASSWORD clause

- **General format**
  PASSᴡORD [IS] *data-name*

- **Description**
  The PASSWORD clause, an entry in the FILE-CONTROL paragraph of the INPUT-OUTPUT SECTION, specifies a password for VSAM files.

  data-name is a data area, defined as an alphanumeric item in the WORKING-STORAGE SECTION of the DATA DIVISION, that contains a password associated with a file. The first 8 characters must contain the password. If the length of the password is less than 8 characters, then it is padded with blanks to the right.

◻ RECORD KEY clause

- **General format**
  RECORD [KEY IS] *data-name*

- **Description**
  The RECORD KEY clause, an entry in the FILE-CONTROL
  paragraph of the INPUT-OUTPUT SECTION, defines the data
  within a record as the prime key. This clause is mandatory for
  VSAM files.

  data-name is the prime key and must be an alphanumeric item
  within one of the record description entries associated with the
  file.

◻ RECORD DELIMITER clause

- **General format**
  RECORD DELIMITER [IS]
      <STANDARD-1 or *assignment-name*>

- **Description**
  The RECORD DELIMITER clause, an entry in the FILE-
  CONTROL paragraph of the INPUT-OUTPUT SECTION,
  specifies the method for determining the size of variable-length
  records.

  STANDARD-1 specifies that the external medium of the file is
  magnetic tape.

  assignment-name is any COBOL word.

  Note: In COBOL II, this clause has no effect during runtime,
  however, its syntax is checked during compilation.

◻ RELATIVE KEY clause

- **General format**
  RELATIVE [KEY IS] *data-name*

- **Description**

    The RELATIVE KEY clause, an entry in the FILE-CONTROL paragraph of the INPUT-OUTPUT SECTION, specifies the data area that contains the relative record number of the next record in a relative VSAM file.

    data-name is a data area that contains the relative record number used for each input and output operation. It is defined as an unsigned integer.

    This clause is required for random and dynamic access of VSAM files. For sequential files, it is required only if the file is referenced by a START statement.

■ RERUN clause

- **General format**

```
QSAM files

RERUN [ON assignment-name] [EVERY]
      < integer RECORDS or END [OF] <REEL or UNIT>>
      [OF] filename

VSAM files

RERUN ON assignment-name [EVERY] integer RECORDS
             [OF] filename
```

- **Description**

    The RERUN clause, an optional entry in the I-O-CONTROL paragraph of the INPUT-OUTPUT SECTION, specifies that checkpoints are to take place. This clause is obsolete and will be removed from future releases of the ANSI standard.

    assignment-name is the external dataset for the checkpoint file.

    integer is a number; for every occurrence of this number of records in *filename*, a checkpoint record is written.

    filename is a sequential file.

◘ RESERVE clause

● General format
```
RESERVE integer <AREA or AREAS>
```

● Description
The RESERVE clause, an entry in the FILE-CONTROL paragraph of the INPUT-OUTPUT SECTION, specifies the number of buffers to be allocated.

integer is the number of buffers; it must not exceed 255. The default is the number of buffers associated with the DD statement or the system.

◘ SAME SORT AREA clause

● General format
SAME <RECORD or SORT or SORT-MERGE> [AREA FOR]
    filename-1 filename-2

● Description
The SAME SORT AREA clause, an optional entry in the I-O-CONTROL paragraph of the INPUT-OUTPUT SECTION, optimizes storage area if the SORT statement is used.

filename-1 and *filename-2* are files that must be defined in the FILE-CONTROL paragraph of the same program in which the SAME SORT AREA clause is used.

◘ SAME RECORD AREA clause

● General format
```
SAME [RECORD] [AREA FOR] filename-1 filename-2
```

● Description

The SAME RECORD AREA clause, an optional entry in the I-O-CONTROL paragraph of the INPUT-OUTPUT SECTION, specifies that two or more VSAM files can use the storage area while processing the current logical record.

filename-1 and *filename-2* are the names of files that share the storage area. Both must be defined in the FILE-CONTROL paragraph of the same program in which the SAME RECORD AREA clause is used.

◻ SELECT clause

● General format
```
SELECT [OPTIONAL] filename
```

● Description
The SELECT clause, the first entry in the FILE-CONTROL paragraph of the INPUT-OUTPUT SECTION, specifies a filename in a COBOL program that is associated with an external dataset. The ASSIGN clause describes the external dataset; it must follow the SELECT clause.

filename is a user-defined name that is unique to a program. Also, there must be a corresponding FD or SD entry in the DATA DIVISION.

OPTIONAL specifies that the file(s) are not necessarily present each time the program is run.

◻ SOURCE-COMPUTER paragraph

● General format
```
SOURCE-COMPUTER. computer-name [WITH] DEBUGGING MODE.
```

● Description
The SOURCE-COMPUTER paragraph, an optional entry in the CONFIGURATION SECTION of the ENVIRONMENT DIVISION, specifies the computer environment in which the source program is to be compiled.

computer-name is the computer system name.

DEBUGGING MODE specifies that a switch is to be turned on during compilation to write debugging lines in the source program.

◻ SPECIAL-NAMES paragraph

● General format

```
SPECIAL-NAMES.  <environment-name-1 [IS]
                  mnemonic-name-1> or
           <environment-name-2 [IS] mnemonic-name-2
              ON  [STATUS IS] condition-1
              OFF [STATUS IS] condition-2>
    [ALPHABET. alphabet-entry]
    [SYMBOLIC. symbolic-entry]
    [CLASS. class-entry]
    [CURRENCY. currency-entry]
```

● Description

The SPECIAL-NAMES paragraph, an entry in the CONFIGURATION SECTION of the ENVIRONMENT DIVISION, specifies configuration options.

environment-name-1	Meaning	Statement
SYSIN	System logical	ACCEPT
SYSIPT	Input unit	
SYSOUT	System logical	DISPLAY
SYSLST	Ouput unit	
SYSPUNCH	System unit	DISPLAY
SYSPCH	Device	
CONSOLE	Console typewriter	ACCEPT or DISPLAY
C01 — C12	Skip to channel 1 — 12	WRITE ADVANCING
CSP	Suppress spacing	WRITE ADVANCING
S01 — S05	Pocket select 1 or 2 on punch devices	WRITE ADVANCING

environment-name2 is an UPSI switch of 1 byte long. It can be UPSI-0 through UPSI7.

mnemonic-name-1 is a user-defined name used in the ACCEPT, DISPLAY, and WRITE statements.

mnemonic-name-2 is an user-defined name used in the SET statement.

condition-1 and *condition-2* are conditions that follow the rules for user-defined names.

○ SYMBOLIC CHARACTERS clause

- **General format**
  ```
  SYMBOLIC [CHARACTERS] symbolic-character <ARE or IS>
                       integer IN alphabet-name
  ```

- **Description**
  The SYMBOLIC CHARACTERS clause, an optional entry in the SPECIAL-NAMES paragraph of the CONFIGURATION SECTION, specifies one or more symbolic characters.

  symbolic-character is a user-defined word (DBCS word) or a series of user-defined words.

  integer is a single number or a series of corresponding numbers.

4.3   DATA DIVISION

The DATA DIVISION is an optional entry which defines the data area to be used by a program during processing. It consists of three sections:

- FILE SECTION
- WORKING-STORAGE SECTION
- LINKAGE SECTION

The general format of the DATA DIVISION is:

```
DATA DIVISION.
[FILE SECTION.]
   [file-description-entryrecord-description-entry...]

[WORKING-STORAGE SECTION.]
   [record-description data-item-description]...

[LINKAGE SECTION.]
   [record-description data-item-description]...
```

All these sections of the division and related clauses are discussed, in alphabetical order, in detail below.

◘ BLANK WHEN ZERO clause

● General format
```
BLANK [WHEN] <ZERO or ZEROS or ZEROES>
```

● Description
The BLANK WHEN ZERO clause, an optional entry in the WORKING-STORAGE SECTION of the DATA DIVISION, specifies that whenever a zero value occurs in a data area it is to be replaced with spaces.

◘ BLOCK CONTAINS clause

● General format
```
BLOCK [CONTAINS] [integer1 TO] integer2
       <CHARACTERS or RECORDS>
```

● Description
The BLOCK CONTAINS clause, an optional entry in the FILE SECTION of the DATA DIVISION, specifies the number of physical records in a blocked sequential file. This clause is not necessary for VSAM files, as the blocking concept is not used in VSAM files.

integer1 is an unsigned nonzero number that specifies the minimum number of characters or logical records.

integer2 is an unsigned nonzero number that specifies the maximum number of characters or logical records.

CHARACTERS specifies the size of the record in characters.

RECORDS specifies the number of logical records in a physical record.

When BLOCK CONTAINS 0 is specified, the size of the block of the dataset is determined from the JCL DD statement during execution.

▢ CODE-SET clause

● General format
```
CODE-SET [IS] alphabet-name
```

● Description
The CODE-SET clause, an optional entry in the FILE SECTION of the DATA DIVISION, specifies the character set used to represent data in a magnetic tape file.

alphabet-name is a name defined in the SPECIAL-NAMES paragraph of the ENVIRONMENT DIVISION. It can be STANDARD-1, STANDARD-2, or EBCDIC. The default is EBCDIC.

▢ DATA RECORDS clause

● General format
```
DATA <RECORD IS or RECORDS ARE> data-name...
```

● Description
The DATA RECORDS clause, an optional entry in the FILE SECTION of the DATA DIVISION, specifies a name for the data records of a file.

data-name is a data area that contains the name of the data records associated with a file.

Note: The DATA RECORDS clause is obsolete and will be removed from future versions of the ANSI standard.

▢ EXTERNAL clause

● General format
```
FD filename [IS] EXTERNAL
level-number data-name EXTERNAL
```

● Description
The EXTERNAL clause, an optional entry in the FILE SECTION or the WORKING-STORAGE SECTION of the DATA DIVISION, allows the same file or data area to be shared by

several programs running concurrently.

filename is the name of the file to be shared.

data-name is the name of the data area to be shared. The data area must defined at *level-number* 01.

◘ FILE SECTION

• General format
```
FILE SECTION
file-description-entry record-description-entry
```

Format for sequential file:

```
FD filename
```

```
    EXTERNAL clause
    GLOBAL clause
    BLOCK CONTAIN clause
    RECORD clause
    LABEL RECORDS clause
    VALUE OF clause
    DATA RECORDS clause
    LINAGE clause
    RECORDING MODE clause
    CODE-SET clause
```

Format for relative/indexed file:

```
FD filename
```

```
    EXTERNAL clause
    GLOBAL clause
    BLOCK CONTAIN clause
    RECORD clause
    LABEL RECORDS clause
    VALUE OF clause
    DATA RECORDS clause
```

Format for sort/merge file:

```
SD filename
```

```
    RECORD clause
    DATA RECORDS clause
```

• Description
The FILE SECTION, the first, and optional, entry in the DATA DIVISION, defines the filenames to be used within a program and associates each of them with its attributes. In this section, there are

two types of entries: file description and record description. There must only be one file description entry for each file followed by one or many record descriptions entries.

You can specify three kinds of files: sequential files, indexed or relative files, and sort or merge files. The above formats for each type of file show all the different entries for record descriptions.

filename is the filename used in the program. It must also be specified in the SELECT clause of the IDENTIFICATION DIVISION. Following the filename, you can enter one or many record descriptions.

FD specifies a sequential, indexed, or relative file. Following this is a series of clauses describing the file.

SD specifies a sort or merge file. Following this is a series of clauses describing the file.

◘ GLOBAL clause

● General format
```
FD filename [IS] [GLOBAL]
level-number <data-name> [GLOBAL]
```

● Description
The GLOBAL clause, an optional entry in the FILE SECTION or the WORKING-STORAGE SECTION of the DATA DIVISION, allows the same file or data area to be shared by subprograms of a program.

filename is the name of the file to be shared.

data-name is the name of the data area to be shared. The data area must be defined at *level-number* 01.

◘ JUSTIFIED clause

● General format
```
<JUSTIFIED or JUST> [RIGHT]
```

- **Description**
  The JUSTIFIED clause, an optional entry in the WORKING-STORAGE SECTION of the DATA DIVISION, specifies that the data moved into a data area be right-justified, instead of following the default justification rules.

◼ LABEL RECORDS clause

- **General format**
  LABEL <RECORD IS or RECORDS ARE>
      < STANDARD or OMITTED or *data-name*>

- **Description**
  The LABEL RECORDS clause, an optional entry in the FILE SECTION of the DATA DIVISION, specifies whether a file has a label or not.

  STANDARD specifies that the label in the file conforms to system standard.

  OMITTED specifies that the file does not have a label.

  data-name specifies that user labels are present in addition to standard labels.

  Note: The LABEL RECORDS clause is obsolete and will be removed from future versions of the ANSI standard.

◼ LINAGE clause

- **General format**
```
LINAGE [IS] <data-name-1 or integer-1> [LINES]
      [WITH] FOOTING [AT] <data-name-2 or integer-2>
      [LINES AT] TOP <data-name-3 or integer-3>
      [LINES AT] BOTTOM <data-name-4 or integer-4>
```

- **Description**
  The LINAGE clause, an optional entry in the FILE SECTION of the DATA DIVISION, specifies the number of lines per page, top margin, bottom margin and footing for a report.

data-name-1 is the data area that contains the number of lines for each page.

integer-1 is the number of lines on each page.

data-name-2 is the data area that contains the last print line of each page.

integer-2 is the last print line of each page.

data-name-3 is the data area that contains the number of blank lines at the top of each page.

integer-3 is the number of blank lines at the top of each page.

data-name-4 is the data area that contains the number of lines at the bottom of each page.

integer-4 is the number of lines at the bottom of each page.

◻ LINKAGE SECTION

- **General format**
```
LINKAGE SECTION.
   record-description data-item-description
```

- **Description**
The LINKAGE section, the third, and optional entry in the DATA DIVISION, defines the data area that is made available to a calling program. The data are actually stored in the program storage area and passed to another program. There are two entries: record and data descriptions.

record-description defines a record, which is made up of a group of related data items. There must be one record entry for each record.

data-item-description defines each data area, which can be an independent item or one of the elements of a record.

◻ OCCURS clause

• General format
Fixed-length tables

```
OCCURS integer1 [TIMES]
<ASCENDING or DESCENDING> [KEY IS] data-name2...
INDEXED [BY] index-name1...
```

Variable-length tables

```
OCCURS integer1 TO integer2 [TIMES]
DEPENDING [ON] data-name1
<ASCENDING or DESCENDING> [KEY IS] data-name2...
INDEXED [BY] index-name1...
```

• Description
The OCCURS clause, an optional entry in the WORKING-STORAGE SECTION of the DATA DIVISION, specifies that the data area must be arranged as a table or array. Each element of the table is referenced with an index or subscript. There are two formats for the OCCURS clause: fixed-length table and variable-length table.

integer1 is the exact number of elements in a fixed-length table and the minimum number of elements in a variable-length table.

integer2 is the maximum number of elements in a variable-length table.

data-name1 is a data area that contains a value which is the current number of elements in a variable-length table.

data-name2 is a data area that contains a value by which the data is arranged in either an ascending or a descending order.

index-name1 is a data area which is used in a program to access a particular element of a table.

◻ PICTURE clause

• General format
```
<PICTURE or PIC> [IS] character-string
```

● **Description**

The PICTURE clause, an optional entry in the WORKING-STORAGE SECTION of the DATA DIVISION, defines the type and size of an elementary data area. Also, it specifies the editing requirements of the data.

character-string is a combination of symbols that defines the characteristics of the data. The following is a list of all the symbols and their descriptions.

SYMBOL	Description
A	Alphabetic character or space
B	Space
E	Exponential
G	Double-byte character
P	Decimal position
S	Operational sign
V	Decimal sign
X	Alphanumeric character
Z	Leading zeros replaced by spaces
9	Numeric character
/	Insert a slash
,	Insert a comma
.	Insert a period
+	Editing control character
-	Editing control character
CR	Editing control character
DB	Editing control character
*	Replace leading zeros with asterisk
$	Currency symbol

◻ **RECORD clause**

● **General format**

Fixed-length records

```
RECORD [CONTAINS] integer-1 [CHARACTERS]
```

Fixed- or variable-length records

```
RECORD [CONTAINS] integer-2 TO integer-3 [CHARACTERS]
```

Variable-length records

```
RECORD [IS] VARYING [IN SIZE]
    [FROM] integer-4 TO integer-5 [CHARACTERS]
    DEPENDING [ON] data-name
```

• Description

The RECORD clause, an optional entry in the FILE SECTION of the DATA DIVISION, specifies the number of characters in a logical record of a dataset. There are three different types of records: fixed length, fixed- or variable-length, and variable-length. The format for each type of record is different.

integer-1 through *integer-5* must be unsigned nonzero values.

integer-1 is the number of character positions in each record.

integer-2 is the minimum number of character positions in each record.

integer-3 is the maximum number of character positions in each record.

integer-4 is the minimum number of character positions in each record.

integer-5 is the maximum number of character positions in each record.

data-name is the number of table elements to be included in a record.

If the RECORD CONTAINS clause is omitted, then the compiler calculates the length of the record from the record descriptions.

If the RECORD CONTAINS 0 is specified for a QSAM file, then the length of the record is obtained from the JCL DD statement during the run time of the program.

◻ RECORDING MODE clause

• General format
```
RECORDING [MODE IS] mode
```

• Description
The RECORDING MODE clause, an optional entry in the FILE SECTION of the DATA DIVISION, specifies the format type of a sequential file.

mode is the format:

    F Fixed
    V Variable
    U Undefined (variable or fixed)
    S Spanned

◻ REDEFINES clause

• General format
```
level-number <data-name1 or FILLER>
     REDEFINES data-name2
```

• Description
The REDEFINES clause, an optional entry in the WORKING-STORAGE SECTION of the DATA DIVISION, changes the definition of an existing data area and gives it a different name. A redefinition may alter the length and data type of the subfields.

data-name1 is the data area that already exists.

data-name2 is the new name of the redefined data area *data-name1*.

FILLER specifies that the data area does not have a name.

◻ RENAMES clause

• General format
```
66 data-name1 RENAMES data-name2
   <THROUGH or THRU> data-name3
```

- **Description**
The RENAMES clause, an optional entry in the WORKING-STORAGE SECTION of the DATA DIVISION, changes the grouping of elementary data areas. It allows overlapping of data areas.

data-name1 is the name of the new grouping.

data-name2 is a defined data area to be regrouped. If *data-names* is specified, then *data-name2* is the starting data area to be renamed. It cannot be level 01, 77, 88, or another 66.

data-name3 is the last data area in a group of data areas.

◘ SIGN clause

- **General format**
```
SIGN [IS] <LEADING or TRAILING> SEPARATE [CHARACTER]
```

- **Description**
The SIGN clause, an optional entry in the WORKING-STORAGE SECTION of the DATA DIVISION, specifies the position and format of the sign for numeric data.

If SEPARATE CHARACTER is not specified, then the operational sign is associated with the first digit position if LEADING is specified and with the last digit position if TRAILING is specified.

If SEPARATE CHARACTER is specified, then the operational sign is placed in a separate TRAILING or LEADING byte position.

◘ SYNCHRONIZED clause

- **General format**
```
<SYNCHRONIZED or SYNC> [LEFT or RIGHT]
```

- **Description**
The SYNCHRONIZED clause, an optional entry in the WORKING-STORAGE SECTION of the DATA DIVISION,

aligns an elementary data item on either the halfword or fullword storage boundary. Proper alignment improves the performance of arithmetic computations.

LEFT specifies that the item begins at the left character position.

RIGHT specifies that the item begins at the right character position.

▢ USAGE clause

● General format

```
USAGE [IS] < DISPLAY                               or
             INDEX                                 or
             POINTER                               or
             BINARY                                or
             PACKED-DECIMAL                        or
             <COMPUTATIONAL or COMP                or
             <COMPUTATIONAL-1 or COMP-1>           or
             <COMPUTATIONAL-2 or COMP-2>           or
             <COMPUTATIONAL-3 or COMP-3>           or
             <COMPUTATIONAL-4 or COMP-4>
           >
```

● Description

The USAGE clause, an optional entry in the WORKING-STORAGE SECTION of the DATA DIVISION, specifies the format for internal storage of a group or elementary item of data. The USAGE clause can be used with all level numbers except 66 and 88.

DISPLAY specifies storing 1 character of data in 1 byte, corresponding to print format. This phrase can be used with the following types of data:

- Alphanumeric
- Alphabetic
- Alphanumeric-edited
- Numeric-edited
- External decimal (numeric)
- External floating-point

INDEX specifies that the data area is an index; therefore it is used to store index name values. An elementary data area is 4 bytes long.

POINTER specifies that the data area is a pointer; therefore it is used to store limited base addresses. An elementary data area is 4 bytes long.

BINARY specifies that the data area is for binary values and its size depends on the number of digits.

Digits	Size
1—4	2 bytes (halfword)
5—9	4 bytes (fullword)
10—18	8 bytes (doubleword)

PACKED-DECIMAL specifies internal decimal items. Each item contains up to 18 decimal digits stored, and two items are stored in 1 byte.

COMPUTATIONAL or COMP specifies a binary data item.

COMPUTATIONAL-1 or COMP-1 specifies single-precision internal floating-point.

COMPUTATIONAL-2 or COMP-2 specifies double-precision internal floating-point.

COMPUTATIONAL-3 or COMP-3 specifies a packed-decimal data item.

COMPUTATIONAL-4 or COMP-4 specifies a binary data item.

◘ VALUE clause

● General format
```
Format 1:
  VALUE [IS] literal

Format 2:
  88 condition-name <VALUE or VALUES> [IS or ARE]
        literal1 <THROUGH or THRU> literal2
```

- **Description**

  The VALUE clause, an optional entry in the WORKING-STORAGE SECTION of the DATA DIVISION, specifies the initial value of a data area or value(s) for a condition name.

  literal is a value assigned to a data area.

  condition-name is the name of the condition to which a single value, a set of values, a range of values, and/or combinations of sets and ranges of values are assigned.

  literal1 specifies a single value for a condition name.

  literal1 THRU *literal2* specifies a range of values for a condition name.

◘ VALUE OF clause

- **General format**
  ```
  VALUE OF system-name [IS] <data-name or literal>
  ```

- **Description**

  The VALUE OF clause, an optional entry in the FILE SECTION of the DATA DIVISION, specifies an item in the label record of a file.

  data-name is a data area containing the item and defined in the WORKING-STORAGE SECTION.

  literal is a numeric or nonnumeric value.

  Note: The VALUE OF clause is obsolete and will be removed from future versions of the ANSI standard.

◘ WORKING-STORAGE SECTION

- **General format**
  ```
  level-number <data-name or FILLER>

  [REDEFINES clause]
  ```

```
[BLANK WHEN ZERO clause]
[EXTERNAL clause]
[GLOBAL clause]
[JUSTIFIED clause]
[OCCURS clause]
[PICTURE clause]
[SIGN clause]
[SYNCHRONIZED clause]
[USAGE clause]
[VALUE clause]
[RENAMES clause]
```

● **Description**

The WORKING-STORAGE SECTION, an optional entry in the
DATA DIVISION, defines data structures that use a program.
These working data areas include counters, variables, flags, and
accumulators required to accomplish programming tasks. This
section consists of one to many data description entries. Each entry
is made up of a level number, a data name, and optional clauses.

level-number is a number that represents a hierarchy within a
group of related data. The level number is a value between 01 and
49, 66, 77, or 88.

01 to 49 may begin in area A or B and be followed by a period or
space.

66 and 88 may begin in area A or B followed by a space.

data-name is the name of the data area. In the program the data
item is referenced by this name. This name follows a level
number.

FILLER is a data area that does not have a specific name and is
not referenced in a program.

4.4   PROCEDURE DIVISION

The PROCEDURE DIVISION is the part of the source program that
contains the logic. It consists of declaratives, sentences, and
statements that are executed during the runtime of a program. The
sentences and statements are grouped into paragraphs and sections
of a COBOL program.

The general format of the PROCEDURE DIVISION is

```
PROCEDURE DIVISION
   USING data-name

DECLARATIVES. section-name SECTION priority-no.
   USE statement.
   paragraph-name. sentence...
END-DECLARATIVES.

section-name SECTION priority-no.
paragraph-name. sentence...
```

USING is an optional phrase as part of the PROCEDURE DIVISION header. It is used only if the program is called by another program and data are passed using *data-name*.

data-name is the name of a data area which is used to receive data from a calling program. It must be defined as level-number 01 or 77 in the LINKAGE SECTION of the called program.

section-name is the name of a section, it is followed by the keyword SECTION. A section consists of one or more paragraphs.

priority-no is an optional entry in a section header. It follows the keyword SECTION. It is a number in the range 0 to 99.

paragraph-name is the name of a paragraph; it is followed by a period and one or more sentences. In a program, there may be none to many paragraphs.

sentence is one or more COBOL sentences followed by a period.

In the rest of this section we describe all the statements, in alphabetical order, belonging to the PROCEDURE DIVISION.

◼ ACCEPT statement

● General format
Format 1:
```
ACCEPT identifier FROM mnemonic-name
```

Format 2:
```
ACCEPT identifier FROM <DATE or DAY or
                   DAY-OF-WEEK, TIME>
```

● **Description**
The ACCEPT statement transfers data from an input device or system information, such as date and time, into a defined data area. There are two formats for the ACCEPT statment. Format 1 transfers data from a device. In this case, if the FROM phrase is omitted, then a system input device is assumed. This format is used to receive data from the operator. Format 2 moves the date, day, day of the week, or time into an identifier.

identifier is a data area, which may be any group or elementary item. For format 1, the data type of the *identifier* can be alphabetic, alphanumeric, alphanumeric-edited, numeric-edited, or external decimal. For format 2, the data type of the *identifier* can be alphanumeric, alphanumeric-edited, numeric-edited, decimal, binary, or floating-point.

mnemonic-name is a name associated with an input-output device: system input device or console. The name must be defined in the SPECIAL-NAMES paragraph of the ENVIRONMENT DIVISION.

DATE specifies moving the current date to the identifier. The information is, from left to right, 2 digits for the year, 2 digits for the month, and 2 digits for the day.

DAY specifies moving the current Julian date to the identifier. The information is, from left to right, 2 digits for the year and 3 digits for the day.

DAY-OF-WEEK specifies moving the day of the week to the identifier. The following lists the resulting values and corresponding day of the week.

Value	Day of the week
1	Monday
2	Tuesday
3	Wednesday
4	Thursday
5	Friday
6	Saturday
7	Sunday

TIME specifies moving the current time of day to the identifier. The information, from left to right, is

2 digits for the hour
2 digits for the minute
2 digits for the second
2 digits for the hundredths of a second

▢ ADD statement

● General format

```
Format 1:
  ADD <identifier1 or literal> TO identifier2 ROUNDED
    [ON] [SIZE ERROR statement1]
    [NOT [ON] SIZE ERROR statement2]
  [END-ADD]

Format 2:
  ADD <identifier1 or literal> TO identifier3
    GIVING identifier4 ROUNDED
    [ON] [SIZE ERROR statement1]
    [NOT [ON] SIZE ERROR statement2]
  [END-ADD]

Format 3:
  ADD <CORRESPONDING or CORR> identifier5 TO identifier6
    ROUNDED
    [ON] [SIZE ERROR statement1]
    [NOT [ON] SIZE ERROR statement2]
  [END-ADD]
```

● Description

The ADD statement adds one or more numeric operands and stores the result.

identifier1 must be an elementary numeric data area.

identifier2 must be an elementary numeric data area. It receives the sum.

identifier3 must be an elementary numeric data area.

identifier4 must be either an elementary numeric data area or a numeric-edited data area. It receives the sum.

identifier5 and *identifier6* must be group data areas. The elementary elements of *identifier5* are added and stored in the elements of *identifer6*.

literal is a numeric literal.

ROUNDED specifies that any fractional result is to be rounded to the nearest decimal position.

statement1 is the statement to which control is transferred when ON SIZE ERROR condition occurs.

statement2 is the statement to which control is transferred when a NOT ON SIZE ERROR condition occurs.

CORRESPONDING specifies two group operands. The operation is to be performed on all corresponding elementary data items of both groups.

END-ADD is an optional phrase to terminate the ADD statement.

◻ ALTER statement

● General format
```
ALTER procedure-name1 TO [PROCEED TO] procedure-name2
```

● Description
The ALTER statement changes the name of the procedure to which control is transferred in a GO TO statement. The change occurs during execution.

procedure-name1 is the name of the old paragraph.

procedure-name2 is the name of the new paragraph.

Note: The ALTER statement is obsolete and will be removed from the next release of the ANSI standard.

◘ Arithmetic Operators

● Description
There are two kinds of arithmetic operators: binary and unary. The following is a list of the operators and their operations.

Binary Operator	Operation
+	Addition
-	Subtraction
*	Multiplication
/	Division
**	Exponential

Unary Operator	Operation
+	Multiplication by +1
-	Multiplication by -1

◘ CALL statement

● General format
```
Format 1:
  CALL <identifier1 or literal1>
  USING <identifier2                          or
        [BY] REFERENCE identifier2            or
        [BY] REFERENCE ADDRESS OF identifier2     or
        [BY] CONTENT <identifier2 or literal2 or LENGTH>
           OF identifier2
        >
  [ON] OVERFLOW statement1
  [END-CALL]

Format 2:
  CALL <identifier1 or literal1>
  USING <identifier2                          or
        [BY] REFERENCE identifier2            or
        [BY] REFERENCE ADDRESS OF identifier2     or
        [BY] CONTENT <identifier2 or literal2 or LENGTH>
           OF identifier2
        >
  [ON] EXCEPTION statement1
  NOT [ON] EXCEPTION statement2
  [END-CALL]
```

● **Description**

The CALL statement transfers control from one program to another during execution. When the execution of the called program is terminated, the control goes back to the calling program.

identifier1 is an alphanumeric data area which contains the name of a program.

literal1 is the literal name of a program.

USING is used to pass parameters to the called program.

BY REFERENCE applies to all parameters that follow it. It specifies that the data area in the called program occupies the same storage area as the calling program.

BY CONTENT applies to all parameters that follow it. It specifies that the value of each parameter is assigned to the corresponding parameter of the called program.

identifier2 is a data area.

literal2 may be a nonnumeric literal, a figurative constant, or a DBCS literal.

ON EXCEPTION specifies that if an exception condition occurs, program control must be transferred to *statement1*.

NOT ON EXCEPTION specifies that no exception condition occurs, program control must be transferred to *statement2*.

ON OVERFLOW specifies that if an exception condition occurs, program control must be transferred to *statement1*. The ON OVERFLOW phrase has the same effect as the ON EXCEPTION phrase.

END-CALL is an optional clause to terminate the CALL statement.

◘ CANCEL statement

● General format
```
CANCEL <identifier1 or literal1>
```

● Description
The CANCEL statement ensures that every time a program is called, a fresh copy, with all its initial values set, is loaded for execution.

identifier1 is a data area which contains the name of a program.

literal1 is the literal name of a program.

◘ CLOSE statement

● General format
```
Sequential file

CLOSE filename
    [ [WITH] LOCK            or
      [WITH] NO REWIND       or
      <UNIT or REEL> [WITH] NO REWIND or
      <UNIT or REEL> [FOR] REMOVAL
    ]

Indexed or relative file

    CLOSE filename [WITH] LOCK
```

● Description
The CLOSE statement closes a sequential or VSAM file for processing.

filename is the name of the file to be closed.

UNIT or REEL specifies a medium with a multivolume file.

WITH LOCK ensures that the file cannot be opened again while this program is executing.

WITH NO REWIND specifies that the current volume is to be left in its current position.

◻ COMPUTE statement

● **General format**
```
COMPUTE identifier1 ROUNDED
   < EQUAL OR = > arithmetic-expression
   [ON] SIZE ERROR statement1
   NOT [ON] SIZE ERROR statement2
[END-COMPUTE]
```

● **Description**

The COMPUTE statement evaluates an arithmetic expression and moves the result into one or more data areas.

identifier1 must be an elementary numeric item, an elementary numeric-edited item, or a floating point item. It can be one or more of these items.

arithmetic-expression is made up of one or more arithmetic binary operators and numeric items.

statement1 is the statement to which control is transferred when an ON SIZE ERROR condition occurs.

statement2 is the statement to which control is transferred when a NOT ON SIZE ERROR condition occurs.

ROUNDED specifies that any fractional result is to be rounded to the nearest decimal position.

END-COMPUTE is an optional clause to terminate the COMPUTE statement.

◻ CONTINUE statement

● **General format**
CONTINUE

● **Description**

The CONTINUE statement is a no operation statement. It has no effect during the execution of a program.

◘ Conditional Expressions

A conditional expression is evaluated, and its result is either true or false. Usually the result of a conditional expression is used to choose logical paths in a program. Condition expressions are specified in EVALUATE, IF, PERFORM, and SEARCH statements. There are two types of conditional expressions: simple conditions and complex conditions. There are five simple conditions:

- Class condition
- Condition-name condition
- Relation condition
- Sign condition
- Switch-status condition

There are two complex conditions:
    Negated simple condition
    Combined condition

◘ DELETE statement

● General format
```
DELETE filename RECORD
    INVALID [KEY] statement1
    NOT INVALID [KEY] statement2
END-DELETE
```

● Description
The DELETE statement deletes a record in an indexed or relative file. After the record has been removed, the space is available for a record addition or a new record in indexed and relative files, respectively.

filename is the name of an indexed or relative file, defined as an FD entry in the DATA DIVISION.

statement1 is the statement to which control is transferred when an INVALID KEY condition occurs.

statement2 is the statement to which control is transferred when a NOT INVALID KEY condition occurs.

END-DELETE is an optional phrase to terminate the DELETE statement.

◘ DISPLAY statement

• General format
```
DISPLAY <identifier or literal>
   UPON mnemonic-name
   [WITH] NO ADVANCING
```

• Description
The DISPLAY statement sends the content of one or more of its operands to an output device.

identifier is a data area which contains the data to be printed to an output device.

literal is a literal operand.

UPON is an optional clause that specifies that a device or *mnemonic-name* must be associated with an output device described in the SPECIAL-NAMES paragraph of the ENVIRONMENT DIVISION.

WITH NO ADVANCING specifies that the positioning of the output device is not to be reset.

◘ DIVIDE statement

• General format
```
Format 1:
   DIVIDE <identifier1  or   literal1>  INTO  identifier2
ROUNDED
    ON SIZE ERROR statement1
    NOT [ON] SIZE ERROR statement2
[END-DIVIDE]

Format 2:
   DIVIDE <identifier1 or literal1> <INTO or BY>
       <identifier2 or literal2>
     GIVING identifier3 ROUNDED
     ON SIZE ERROR statement1
     NOT [ON] SIZE ERROR statement2
[END-DIVIDE]

Format 3:
   DIVIDE <identifier1 or literal1> <INTO or BY>
```

```
    <identifier2 or literal2>
    GIVING identifier3 ROUNDED
    REMAINDER identifier4
    ON SIZE ERROR statement1
    NOT [ON] SIZE ERROR statement2
[END-DIVIDE]
```

- **Description**

The DIVIDE statement divides one numeric data item by or into another.

identifier1 and *identifier2* are elementary numeric data areas.

identifier3 and *identifier4* are elementary numeric or numeric-edited data areas.

literal1 and *literal2* are numeric literals.

statement1 is the statement to which control is transferred when an ON SIZE ERROR condition occurs.

statement2 is the statement to which control is transferred when a NOT ON SIZE ERROR condition occurs.

ROUNDED specifies that any fractional result is to be rounded to the nearest decimal position.

REMAINDER specifies that the remainder of the division is to be stored in *identifier4*.

END-DIVIDE is an optional phrase to terminate the DIVIDE statement.

☐ **ENTER statement**

- **General format**
```
ENTER language-name routine-name
```

- **Description**

The ENTER statement allows more than one language to be used in a source program.

language-name must be COBOL.

routine-name is a user-defined word that contains at least one alphanumeric character.

Note: The ENTER statement is obsolete and will be removed from the next release of the ANSI standard.

◘ ENTRY statement

- **General format**
```
ENTRY literal [USING] identifier
```

- **Description**
The ENTRY statement establishes an alternative entry point into a called COBOL program, other than at the start of the PROCEDURE DIVISION.

literal is nonnumeric and follows the rules for forming program names.

USING is used to pass parameters to the called program.

identifier is a data area.

◘ EVALUATE statement

- **General format**
```
EVALUATE < identifier1 or literal1 or
    expression1 or TRUE or FALSE
      >
    ALSO < identifier2 or literal2 or
    expression2 or TRUE or FALSE
      >
    WHEN phrase1 ALSO phrase2 statement1
    WHEN OTHER statement2
END-EVALUATE
```

where *phrase1* is

```
<ANY or condition1 or TRUE or FALSE or subphrase1>
```

where *subphrase1* is

```
<identifier3 or literal3      or
   arithmetic-expression1      or
 NOT identifier3 or NOT literal3  or
 NOT arithmetic-expression1
```

```
> <THROUGH or THRU>
   <identifier4 or literal4 or
    arithmetic-expression2>
```

• Description

The EVALUATE statement evaluates a series of conditions and takes actions depending on the results of the evaluation. It is like an expanded IF statement.

Operands before the WHEN phrase are individually called selection subjects and collectively a set of selection subjects. Operands after the WHEN phrase are individually called selection objects and collectively a set of selection objects.

ALSO separates selection subjects within a set of selection subjects and selection objects within a set of selection objects.

END-EVALUATE is an optional clause to terminate the EVALUATE statement.

◘ EXIT statement

• General format
```
paragraph-name. EXIT.
```

• Description

The EXIT statement provides a common exit point for a series of paragraphs. It is also used to document the end of a paragraph.

paragraph-name is the name of a COBOL paragraph.

◘ EXIT PROGRAM statement

• General format
```
EXIT PROGRAM
```

• Description

The EXIT PROGRAM statement terminates the execution of a program and passes control to the calling program.

◘ GOBACK statement

● General format
```
GOBACK
```

● Description
The GOBACK statement terminates the execution of a program and passes control to the calling program.

◘ GO TO statement

● General format
Unconditional:
```
GO [TO]  procedure-name1
```

Conditional:
```
GO [TO] procedure-name2 DEPENDING [ON] identifier1
```

● Description
The GO TO statement transfers control from one procedure of a program to another.

procedure-name1 is the name of a paragraph or section to which control is unconditionally transferred.

procedure-name2 is the name of a paragraph or section; optionally one or more names may be specified.

identifier1 is a value that corresponds to a procedure name. If it is 1, control goes to the first procedure; if it is 2, control goes to the second procedure; and so on.

◘ IF statement

● General format
```
IF condition [THEN]
   <statement1 or NEXT SENTENCE>...
ELSE
   <statement2 or NEXT SENTENCE>...
END-IF
```

• Description

The IF statement first evaluates a condition and then, depending on the result of the evaluation, executes alternative logical parts of a program. If the result of the condition is TRUE, then only *statement1* is executed. If the result is FALSE, then only *statement2* is executed. Only one or the other is executed, never both. Both *statement1* and *statement2* are optional, but at least one should be specified within the IF statement. Within the IF statement, many levels of IF statement nesting can be used.

condition may be a simple or a compound condition.

statement1 is one or more statements.

statement2 is one or more statements.

ELSE is the clause that divides the two alternative actions if both are specified.

NEXT SENTENCE means to go to the next statement.

END-IF terminates the IF statement.

■ INITIALIZE statement

• General format

```
INITIALIZE identifier1
   REPLACING <ALPHABETIC          or
             ALPHANUMERIC         or
             ALPHANUMERIC-EDITED  or
             NUMERIC-EDITED       or
             DBCS>
   [DATA] BY <identifier2 or literal1>
```

• Description

The INITIALIZE statement moves values to the specified data areas. It is equivalent to the MOVE statement.

identifier1 is the data area that receives the values.

identifier2 is the data area that contains the value to be moved to *identifier1*.

literal1 is the literal value to be moved to *identifier2*.

REPLACING specifies the data type of *identifier2* and *literal1*.
The data types are alphabetic, alphnumeric, alphanumeric-edited,
numeric-edited, and DBCS.

◻ INSPECT statement

● General format
```
Format 1:
  INSPECT identifier1
    TALLYING identifier2
    FOR <CHARACTERS phrase1 <ALL or LEADING>
        <identifier3 or literal1> phrase1
        >

Format 2:
  INSPECT identifier1
    REPLACING
    <CHARACTERS BY <identifier5 or literal3> phrase1> or
                < <ALL or LEADING or FIRST>
                  <identifier3 or literal1>
      BY <identifier5 or  literal3>
      phrase1
    >


Format 3:
  INSPECT identifier1
    TALLYING identifier2
    FOR <CHARACTERS phrase1
        <ALL or LEADING> <identifier3 or literal1>
        phrase1
        >
    REPLACING
    <CHARACTERS BY <identifier5 or literal3> phrase1> or
           < <ALL or LEADING or FIRST>
     <identifier3 or literal3>
     BY <identifier5 or  literal3>
     phrase1
    >

Format 4:
  INSPECT identifier1
  CONVERTING <identifier6 or literal4>
    TO <identifier7 or  literal5> phrase1

  where phrase1 is
    <BEFORE or AFTER> [INITIAL] <identifier4 or literal2>
```

• Description

The INSPECT statement counts or replaces characters in a data area.

identifier1 is the data area to be inspected; it must be an elementary data item or a group of data items with USAGE DISPLAY.

identifier2 is the data area that holds the count (or tally). It receives the number of matches when the TALLYING clause is specified. It must be an elementary data item.

identifier3 is a data area and the tallying operand. It must be an elementary data item with USAGE DISPLAY.

literal1 is a literal value and the tallying operand.

literal2 is a literal value that is not counted during the execution of the INSPECT statement.

identifier4 is a data item that holds characters that are not counted during the execution of the INPECT statement.

literal3 is a literal value and the replacing operand.

identifier5 is a data area and holds the replacing operand.

literal4 and *literal5* are strings of replacement values and both must have the same size.

identifier6 and *identifier7* are data areas, each containing a string of replacement values. Both must have the same size.

◘ MERGE statement

• General format
```
MERGE filename1
   [ON] <ASCENDING  or DESCENDING> [KEY] data-name1
   [COLLATING] SEQUENCE [IS] alphabet-name1
   USING filename2 filename3
   GIVING filename4
   OUTPUT PROCEDURE [IS] proc-name1
        <THROUGH or THRU> proc-name2
```

● **Description**

The MERGE statement takes two files, based on some common keys, and writes the output records to an output file or makes them available them available to an output procedure.

filename1 describes the records to be merged; it must be defined in the SD entry of the DATA DIVISION.

data-name1 is a data area which specifies the KEY and is associated with *filename1*.

alphabet-name1 is specified in the ALPHABET clause of the SPECIAL-NAMES paragraph of the ENVIRONEMNT DIVISION and is used in the collating sequence.

ASCENDING or DESCENDING specifies that the records are merged in ascending or descending order, based on the specified keys.

COLLATING SEQUENCE specifies the collating sequence to be used during the merge operation.

USING specifies the input files, namely *filename2* and *filename3*.

filename2 and *filename3* are the files to be merged. They should be defined as FD entries of the DATA DIVISION. They are operands of the USING phrase.

GIVING specifies the output file, namely *filename4*.

filename4 is the name of the output file. It must be defined as an FD entry of the DATA DIVISION. It is an operand of the GIVING phrase.

OUTPUT PROCEDURE specifies the procedure for selecting or modifying output records during the merge operation.

proc-name1 is the first section or paragraph in the OUTPUT PROCEDURE phrase.

proc-name2 is the last section or paragraph in the OUTPUT PROCEDURE phrase.

◻ MOVE statement

● General format
Format 1
```
MOVE <identifier1 or literal1> TO identifier2...
```

Format 2
```
MOVE <CORRESPONDING or CORR> identifier1 TO identifier2
```

● Description
The MOVE statement copies data from one data area to one or more data areas.

identifier1 is the data area that contains the data to be moved.

litereall is the literal value to be moved.

identifier2 is the data area which receives the data.

CORRESPONDING specifies two group operands. The operation is to be performed on all corresponding elementary data items of both groups. If specified, the elementary data items of *identifier1* are moved to *identifier2*.

◻ MULTIPLY statement

● General format
Format 1:

```
MULTIPLY <identifier1 or literal1>
   BY identifier2 ROUNDED
   [ON] SIZE ERROR statement1
   NOT [ON] SIZE ERROR statement2
[END-MULTIPLY]
```

Format 2:

```
MULTIPLY <identifier1 or literal1>
   BY <identifier2 or literal2>
     GIVING identifier3 ROUNDED
   [ON] SIZE ERROR statement1
   NOT [ON] SIZE ERROR statement2
[END-MULTIPLY]
```

● Description
The MULTIPLY statement multiplies two numeric data items and stores the result in a data area.

identifier1 is the name of a numeric data area which is multiplied by *identifier2*.

literal1 is the literal value that is multiplied by *literal2*.

identifier2 is the name of a numeric data area that receives the result in format 1.

identifier3 is the name of a numeric data area that receives the result of the multiplication in format 2.

statement1 is the statement to which control is transferred when an ON SIZE ERROR condition occurs.

statement2 is the statement to which control is transferred when a NOT ON SIZE ERROR condition occurs.

ROUNDED specifies that any fractional result is to be rounded to the nearest decimal position.

END-MULTIPLY is an optional clause to terminate the MULTIPLY clause.

▣ OPEN statement

● General format
```
QSAM file:
  OPEN INPUT filename1 <REVERSED or [WITH] NO REWIND>
     OUTPUT filename2... [WITH] NO REWIND
     I-O filename3...
     EXTEND filename4...

VSAM file:
  OPEN INPUT filename1...
     OUTPUT filename2...
     I-O filename3...
     EXTEND filename4...
```

● Description
The OPEN statement opens a sequential or VSAM file for processing. All the filenames must be defined in an FD entry in the DATA DIVISION.

INPUT opens *filename1* as an input file.

OUTPUT opens *filename2* as an output file.

I-O opens *filename3* as both an input and an output file.

EXTEND opens *filename4* as an output file. It must not be specified for a multiple-reel file.

REVERSED is valid for a sequential single reel file.

NO REWIND is valid for a sequential single file.

◻ PERFORM statement

● General format

```
Basic PERFORM format:

  PERFORM <procedure-name1 [<THROUGH or THRU>
                   procedure-name2]            or
          statement1 [END-PERFORM]
          >

PERFORM TIMES format:

  PERFORM <procedure-name1 [<THROUGH or THRU>
                   procedure-name2] <identifier1 or integer1>
             TIMES
                  or
          <identifier1 or integer1> TIMES statement1
             [END-PERFORM]
          >

PERFORM UNTIL format:

  PERFORM <procedure-name1 [<THROUGH or THRU>]
             procedure-name2 [WITH] TEST
             <BEFORE or AFTER> UNTIL condition1>
                    or
             [WITH] TEST <BEFORE or AFTER>
             UNTIL condition1
             statement1 [END-PERFORM]
          >

PERFORM VARYING format:

  PERFORM <procedure-name1 <THROUGH or THRU>
                   procedure-name2 phrase1
                    or
             phrase1 statement1 [END-PERFORM]
          >
  where phrase1 is
     [[WITH] TEST <BEFORE or AFTER>]
     VARYING <identifier1 or index-name1>
     FROM <identifier2 or index-name2 or literal1>
```

```
BY <identifier3 or literal2>
UNTIL condition1
```

● Description

The PERFORM statement transfers control to one or more procedures and controls the number of times they are executed. After the execution of the specified procedures, control goes to the next statement after the PERFORM statement. There are four types of PERFORM statements:

- Basic PERFORM
- TIMES phrase PERFORM
- UNTIL phrase PERFORM
- VARYING phrase PERFORM

The basic PERFORM executes a procedure only once; however, the other types specify conditions which determine the number of times a procedure is executed.

procedure-name1 and *procedure-name2* are names of sections or paragraphs in the PROCEDURE DIVISION.

condition1 is a conditional expression.

identifier1, *identifier2*, and *identifier3* are data areas that contain values to control the number of execution of procedures.

statement1 is the last statement in an in-line PERFORM statement.

The TIMES phrase specifies the number of times procedures are executed.

The UNTIL phrase specifies that execution of procedures continues until a specified condition is true.

The VARYING phrase specifies that the procedures are executed as certain identifiers, subscripts, or indexes are initialized and incremented, and until a certain condition is true.

END-PERFORM is an optional phrase to terminate the PERFORM statement.

◻ READ statement

● General format

```
Sequential access
  READ filename1 NEXT RECORD INTO identifier1
     [[AT] END statement1]
     [NOT [AT] END statement2]
  [END-READ]

Random access
  READ filename1 [RECORD] INTO [identifier1]
     [KEY [IS] data-name1]
     [INVALID [KEY] statement3]
     [NOT INVALID [KEY] statement4]
  [END-READ]
```

● Description

The READ statement reads a record from an external file and places the data in a specified data area. There are two types of files: sequential-access and random-access. For sequential-access files, the next logical record is read. For random-access files, a specific record with a key is read. Before a file is read, it must be opened with an INPUT or I-O phrase.

filename1 is the name of the file to be accessed. It must be defined in an FD entry in the DATA DIVISION.

identifier1 is the data area that receives the read record. It must be defined in the WORKING-STORAGE SECTION as a group or elementary data item. It must be long enough to hold all the data in the record.

statement1 is the statement to execute when an AT END condition occurs.

statement2 is the statement to execute when a NOT AT END condition occurs.

statement3 is the statement to execute when an INVALID KEY condition occurs.

statement4 is the statement to execute when a NOT INVALID KEY condition occurs.

KEY IS specifies the key to retrieve a record from a VSAM file.

data-name1 is the data area, defined in the WORKING-STORAGE SECTION, which holds the key to retrieve a record from a VSAM file.

END-READ is an optional phrase to terminate the READ statement.

◼ RELEASE statement

● **General format**

```
RELEASE record-name [FROM identifier]
```

● **Description**

The RELEASE statement makes a record available for sorting and is used within the INPUT PROCEDURE of an internal sort.

record-name is defined as an SD entry in the FILE SECTION of the DATA DIVISION. Its content is placed in the sort file each time the RELEASE statement is executed.

identifier is a data area defined in the WORKING-STORAGE SECTION. Its content is moved to *record-name*.

◼ RETURN statement

● **General format**

```
RETURN filename [RECORD]
    [INTO identifier]
    [AT] END statement1
    [NOT [AT] END statement2]
[END-RETURN]
```

● **Description**

The RETURN statement retrieves the next record during an internal sort (or merge) operation. It is used within the OUTPUT PROCEDURE of a MERGE or SORT statement.

filename is the name of a file described as an SD entry in the DATA DIVISION.

identifier is the name of a data area which receives the record being retrieved from *filename.*

statement1 is the statement to execute when an AT END condition occurs.

statement2 is the statement to execute when a NOT AT END condition occurs.

END-RETURN is an optional phrase to terminate the RETURN statement.

◘ REWRITE statement

● General format
```
REWRITE record-name [FROM identifier]
   [INVALID [KEY] statement1]
   [NOT INVALID [KEY] statement2]
[END-REWRITE]
```

● Description
The REWRITE statement updates a record in a VSAM file. The file must be open to execute the rewrite operation.

record-name is the name of a logical record described as an FD entry of the DATA DIVISION.

identifier is the name of the data area from which the data are written.

statement1 is the statement to execute when an INVALID KEY condition occurs.

statement2 is the statement to execute when a NOT INVALID KEY condition occurs.

END-REWRITE is an optional phrase to terminate the REWRITE statement.

◻ **SEARCH statement**

● **General format**
```
Serial search:
  SEARCH identifier1
    [VARYING <identifier2 or index-name>]
    [[AT] END statement1]
    [WHEN condition1 <statement2 or NEXT SENTENCE>]...
  [END-SEARCH]

Binary search:
  SEARCH ALL identifier1
    [AT] END statement1
    WHEN <condition1                    or
      <data-name1  [IS] EQUAL [TO]
            <identifier3 or literal1 or expression1>
      [AND <data-name2  [IS]  EQUAL [TO]
            <identifier4 or literal2 or expression2>]
      <statement2 [END-SEARCH] or NEXT SENTENCE>
```

● **Description**
The SEARCH statement searches a data area (table) until a certain condition is satisfied. There are two kinds of searches: serial and binary.

identifier1 is the name of a data area, defined as a table with an OCCURS clause.

VARYING is used for a serial search which increments *index-name* or *identifier2*, the subscript to the table *identifier1*. The search starts from the current settings of the index.

identifier2 is a data area which holds a subscript to the table *identifier1*.

index-name is an index to table *identifier1*.

WHEN specifies the conditions for the search.

condition1 and *condition2* are conditional expressions.

identifier3 and *identifier4* are names of data areas.

statement1 is the statement to execute when an AT END condition occurs.

statement2 is the statement to execute that is associated with the WHEN statement.

literal1 and *literal2* are literal values.

expression1 and *expression2* are arithmetic expressions.

data-name1 and *data-name2* are associated with the WHEN phrase. Both must specify a data item (ASCENDING/DESCENDING KEY) in the *identifier1* table element.

END-SEARCH is an optional phrase to terminate the SEARCH statement.

◘ SET statement

● General format
```
TO phrase:
  SET <index-name1 or identifier1> TO
      <index-name2 or identifier2  or integer1>

UP/DOWN phrase:
  SET index-name3... <UP or DOWN> BY
      <identifier3 or integer2>

ON/OFF phrase:
  SET mnemonic-name1... TO <ON or OFF>

TO TRUE phrase:
  SET condition-name1... TO TRUE

Pointer data item phrase:
  SET <identifier4 or ADDRESS OF identifier5>...
    TO <identifier6 or ADDRESS OF identifier7 or
              NULL or NULLS>
```

● Description
The SET statement does the following:

- Changes table indexes
- Sets status codes to external switches
- Sets values of conditional variables
- Sets values to pointer data areas

The TO phrase sets the value of *index-name2* or *identifier2* or *integer1* to the current value of *index-name1* or *identifier1*.

The UP/DOWN phrase increases or decreases the value of *index-name3* by *identifier3* or *integer2*.

The ON/OFF phrase sets *mnemonic-name1* to ON or OFF status.

The TO TRUE phrase sets *condition-name1* to its true value.

The ADDRESS OF phrase sets the value of *identifier6* or ADDRESS OF *identifier7* or NULL or NULLS to *identifier4* or ADDRESS OF *identifier5*.

◘ SORT statement

• General format

```
SORT filename1 [ON] <ASCENDING or DESCENDING>
   [KEY] data-name1...
   [[WITH] DUPLICATES IN ERROR]
   [[COLLATING] SEQUENCE [IS] alphabet-name1]
   < <USING filename2> or
            <INPUT PROCEDURE [IS] proc-name1
               <THRU or THROUGH> proc-name2
     >
   >
   < <GIVING filename3> or
            <OUTPUT PROCEDURE [IS] proc-name3
               <THRU or THROUGH> proc-name4
     >
   >

where filename1 is
   <ASCENDING or DESCENDING> KEY PHRASE
```

• Description

The SORT statement sorts input records in ascending or descending order specified by one or more keys. The input records can be made available to the SORT statement either from one or more input files or through a procedure specified in the INPUT PROCEDURE phrase. The sorted records can be either written to an external file or passed on for further processing to a procedure specified in the OUTPUT PROCEDURE phrase.

filename1 describes the records to be sorted; it must be defined in an SD entry in the DATA DIVISION.

data-name1 is a data area which specifies the KEY and is associated with *filename1*.

ASCENDING or DESCENDING specifies that the records are to be sorted in ascending or descending order, based on the specified keys.

COLLATING SEQUENCE specifies the collating sequence to be used during the merge operation.

alphabet-name1 is specified in the ALPHABET clause of the SPECIAL-NAMES paragraph of the ENVIRONMENT DIVISION and is used in the collating sequence.

USING specifies the input files, namely *filename2*.

filename2 contains the files to be merged. They should be defined as FD entries in the DATA DIVISION. They are operands of the USING phrase.

GIVING specifies the output file, namely *filename3*.

filename3 is the name of the output file. It must be defined as an FD entry in the DATA DIVISION. It is an operand of the GIVING phrase.

INPUT PROCEDURE specifies the procedures for selecting or modifying input records before the sort operation starts.

proc-name1 is the first section or paragraph in the INPUT PROCEDURE phrase.

proc-name2 is the last section or paragraph in the INPUT PROCEDURE phrase.

OUTPUT PROCEDURE specifies the procedure for selecting or modifying output records during the sort operation.

proc-name3 is the first section or paragraph in the OUTPUT PROCEDURE phrase.

proc-name4 is the last section or paragraph in the OUTPUT

PROCEDURE phrase.

◻ START statement

• General format

```
START filename1
    KEY [IS] < EQUAL [TO]                         or
             =                                    or
             GREATER [THAN]                       or
             >                                    or
             NOT LESS                             or
             NOT <                                or
             GREATER [THAN] OR EQUAL [TO] or
             >=
        > data-name1
  [INVALID [KEY] statement1]
  [NOT INVALID [KEY] statement2]
[END-START]
```

• Description

The START statement establishes the position for retrieving a record of an indexed or relative VSAM file. Before this statement is executed, the file must be opened in INPUT or I-O mode.

filename1 is the name of the file for which the position of a record is sought. It must be described as an FD entry in the DATA DIVISION.

KEY specifies that the file indicator is to be positioned at the first logical record whose key field satisfies a comparison with the value in *data-name1*. The default is to position the file indicator at the logical record whose key field is equal to the current value of the prime record key.

statement1 is the statement to execute when an INVALID KEY condition occurs.

statement2 is the statement to execute when a NOT INVALID KEY condition occurs.

END-START is an optional phrase that terminates the START statement.

◻ STOP statement

● General format
```
STOP <RUN or literal>
```

● Description
The STOP statement terminates the execution of a program. All files are closed, and control is transferred to the calling program.

Note: The STOP statement is obsolete and will be removed from the next release of the ANSI standard.

◻ STRING statement

● General format
```
STRING <identifier1 or literal1>...
    DELIMITED [BY] <identifier2 or literal2 or SIZE>
    INTO identifier3
    [WITH] [POINTER identifier4]
    [ON] [OVERFLOW statement1]
    [NOT [ON] OVERFLOW statement2]
[END-STRING]
```

● Description
The STRING statement is used to concatenate several fields of data into one form. All the data areas must be defined with the USAGE DISPLAY phrase. There may be one or more input fields.

identifier1 is a data area that holds the input field.

literal1 is a nonnumeric value that is the input field.

DELIMITED BY specifies the limit of each input field with a delimiter.

identifier2 is a data area that holds one or more characters as the delimiters.

literal2 is a nonnumeric value that is the delimiter.

identifier3 is a data area that receives the output string.

POINTER specifies that the output is a pointer field.

identifier4 is a data area defined as a pointer data type.

statement1 is the statement to execute when an ON OVERFLOW condition occurs.

statement2 is the statement to execute when a NOT ON OVERFLOW condition occurs.

END-STRING is an optional phrase that terminates the STRING statement.

◘ SUBTRACT statement

• General format
```
Format 1:

  SUBTRACT <identifier1 or literal1> FROM identifier2
[ROUNDED]
    [ON] [SIZE ERROR statement1]
    [NOT [ON] SIZE ERROR statement2]
  [END-SUBTRACT]

Format 2:

  SUBTRACT <identifier1 or literal1> FROM
          <identifier2 or literal2>
    GIVING identifier4 [ROUNDED]
    [ON] [SIZE ERROR statement1]
    [NOT [ON] SIZE ERROR statement2]
  [END-SUBTRACT]

Format 3:

  SUBTRACT <CORRESPONDING or CORR> identifier5
    FROM identifier6 [ROUNDED]
    [ON] [SIZE ERROR statement1]
    [NOT [ON] SIZE ERROR statement2]
  [END-SUBTRACT]
```

• Description
The SUBTRACT statement subtracts one or more numeric operands from one or more numeric operands and stores the result.

identifier1 must be an elementary numeric data area.

identifier2 must be an elementary numeric data area.

identifier3 must be an elementary numeric data area.

identifier4 must be either an elementary numeric data area or numeric-edited data area. It receives the sum.

CORRESPONDING specifies two group operands. The operation is to be performed on all corresponding elementary data items of both groups.

identifier5 and *identifier6* must group data areas. The elementary elements of *identifier5* are subtracted from, and stored in, elements of *identifier6*.

literal1 is a numeric literal.

statement1 is the statement to which control is transferred when an ON SIZE ERROR condition occurs.

statement2 is the statement to which control is transferred when a NOT ON SIZE ERROR condition occurs.

ROUNDED specifies that any fractional result is to be rounded to the nearest decimal position.

END-SUBTRACT is an optional phrase to terminate the SUBTRACT statement.

◘ UNSTRING statement

● **General format**
```
UNSTRING identifier1
   [DELIMITED [BY] [ALL] <identifier2 or literal1>
     OR ALL <identifier3 or literal2>]
   [INTO identifier4 DELIMITER [IN] identifier5
            COUNT [IN] identifier6]
   [WITH] [POINTER identifier7]
   [TALLYING [IN] identifier8]
   [ON] OVERFLOW statement1
   NOT [ON] OVERFLOW statement2
[END-UNSTRING]
```

● **Description**
The UNSTRING statement takes contiguous data fields, separates them, and stores them into several data fields. Depending on the

processing, it can replace several MOVE statements.

identifier1 is a data area that holds the input field.

DELIMITED BY specifies the limit of each input field with a delimiter.

identifier2 and *identifier3* are data areas that hold one or more characters as the delimiters.

literal1 and *literal2* are nonnumeric values that are the delimiters.

identifier4 is the data area that receives the output fields. It must be defined with the USAGE DISPLAY phrase.

DELIMITER IN specifies the delimiter for the output fields.

identifier5 is the data area that hold the output field delimiter.

COUNT IN specifies the data area of the count for the input fields.

identifier6 is the data area that holds the count of examined characters for the input fields.

POINTER specifies that the ouput is a pointer field.

identifier7 is a data area defined as a pointer data type.

TALLYING IN specifies the data area of the count for the output fields.

identifier8 is a data area that holds the number of output fields during the execution of the UNSTRING statement.

statement1 is the statement to execute when an ON OVERFLOW condition occurs.

statement2 is the statement to execute when a NOT ON OVERFLOW condition occurs.

END-UNSTRING is an optional phrase that terminates the UN-

STRING statement.

◻ WRITE statement

General format
```
Sequential file:

  WRITE record-name1
    [FROM identifier1]
    [<BEFORE or AFTER> ADVANCING
      <mnemonic-name1 or PAGE> or
                 [<identifier2 or literal>
                  <LINE or LINES>]]
    [<INVALID [KEY] statement1> or
     <[AT] END-OF-PAGE statement3>]
    [<NOT INVALID [KEY] statement2> or
            <NOT [AT] END-OF-PAGE statement4>]
  [END-WRITE]

VSAM sequential file:

  WRITE record-name1
    [FROM identifier1]
  [END-WRITE]

VSAM indexed and relative file
  WRITE record-name1
    [FROM identifier1]
    [INVALID [KEY] statement1]
    [NOT INVALID [KEY] statement2]
  [END-WRITE]
```

● Description
The WRITE statement causes a logical record to be written to a file. Before this operation, the file must be open in OUTPUT, I-O, or EXTEND mode. After the WRITE statement is executed, the FILE STATUS is updated. There are three types of files to which records are written:

- Sequential files
- VSAM sequential files
- VSAM indexed and relative files

record-name1 is defined as an FD entry in the DATA DIVISION; its current content is written to the file.

identifier1, if specified, is a data area from which the record is written to the file.

identifier2 is a data area and must contain an integer value.

ADVANCING controls the positioning of the current output record on the page of a sequential file.

statement1 is the statement to execute when an INVALID KEY condition occurs.

statement2 is the statement to execute when a NOT INVALID KEY condition occurs.

statement3 is the statement to execute when an END-OF-PAGE condition occurs.

statement4 is the statement to execute when a NOT END-OF-PAGE condition occurs.

END-WRITE is an optional phrase to terminate the WRITE statement.

4.5   COMPILER DIRECTIVE

This section describes the compiler directive statements which are used in a COBOL source program.

◘ BASIC statement

● General format
```
[sequence-number] BASIS basis-name
```

● Description
The BASIC statement provides a way to include a complete COBOL program during compilation.

sequence-number is a number in columns 1 through 6.

basis-name is a program name.

◘ CONTROL statement

- **General format**

Source code

```
<*CONTROL or *CBL> <SOURCE or NOSOURCE>
```

Object code

```
<*CONTROL or *CBL> <LIST or NOLIST>
```

Storage maps

```
<*CONTROL or *CBL> <MAP OR NOMAP>
```

- **Description**

The CONTROL statement displays or suppresses listing of source code, object code, or storage maps.

◘ COPY statement

- **General format**

```
COPY text-name <OF or IN> library-name SUPPRESS
    REPLACING operand1 BY operand2
```

- **Description**

The COPY statement is used to include the text of a COBOL program during compilation. The text is commonly known as the copy book.

text-name is the name of a member of a library.

library-name is the name of the library where *text-name* is found.

operand1 and *operand2* are either pseudo-text, identifiers, literals, or COBOL words.

◘ DELETE statement

- **General format**

```
[sequence-number] DELETE sequence-number-field
```

- **Description**

The DELETE statement removes COBOL statements from the BASIS source program.

sequence-number is a number in columns 1 through 6.

sequence-number-field is a number equal to a sequence number in the BASIS source program.

◘ EJECT statement

● General format
```
EJECT [.]
```

● Description
The EJECT statement specifies that the next line of the source program is to be printed at the top of the page.

◘ INSERT statement

● General format
```
[sequence-number] INSERT sequence-number-field
```

● Description
The INSERT statement adds COBOL statements from the BASIS source program.

sequence-number is a number in columns 1 through 6.

sequence-number-field is a number equal to a sequence number in the BASIS source program.

◘ REPLACE statement

● General format
```
Format 1:

  REPLACE text1 by text2

Format 2:

  REPLACE
```

● Description
The REPLACE statement replaces the source program.

text1 must contain one or more text words.

text2 may contain no word, or one or many words.

◘ SKIP1/2/3 statements

● General format
```
<SKIP1 or SKIP2 or SKIP3> [.]
```

● Description
The SKIP statements insert one, two, or three blank lines in the source listing.

SKIP1 inserts one blank line.

SKIP2 inserts two blank lines.

SKIP3 inserts three blank lines.

◘ TITLE statement

● General format
```
TITLE literal [.]
```

● Description
The TITLE statement specifies that a title is to be printed at top of each page of the source listing.

literal is the title.

4.6   COMPILER OPTIONS

In this section we list all the compiler options giving their general format and a brief description. They are used when you compile a COBOL source program. The underlined options are the default values.

◻ ADV

- **General format:**
  ```
  <ADV or NOADV>
  ```

- **Description**
  With ADV, the compiler adds 1 byte to the record length of files that contain printer control characters. It is effective with WRITE AFTER ADVANCING in the source program.

◻ APOST/QUOTE

- **General format**
  ```
  <APOST or Quote>
  ```

- **Description**
  This option specifies that the compiler is to accept literals enclosed with either apostrophes (') or quatation marks (").

◻ BUFSIZE

- **General format**
  ```
  <BUF(nnnnn or nnnK) or BUF(4096)>
  ```

- **Description**
  This option allocates buffer storage for compiler work data sets.

◻ COMPILE

- **General format**
  ```
  <Compile or NOCompile(W or E or S) or NOC(S)>
  ```

- **Description**
  This option forces compilation, even though severe compilation errors have occurred.

◻ DATA

- **General format**
  ```
  <DATA(24) or DATA(31)>
  ```

- **Description**
  This option allocates data areas in storage below or above the 16-Mbyte line. DATA(24) is below the line, and DATA(31) is above the line.

◘ DECK

- **General format**
  ```
  <Deck or NODeck>
  ```

- **Description**
  This option produces object code on SYSPUNCH.

◘ DUMP

- **General format**
  ```
  <DUmp or NODUmp>
  ```

- **Description**
  This option produces a system dump during compilation.

◘ DYNAM

- **General format**
  ```
  <DYNam or NODYnam>
  ```

- **Description**
  This option resolves CALL literal statements in the program dynamically.

◘ FASTSRT

- **General format**
  ```
  <FaStsRT or NOFaStsoRT>
  ```

- **Description**
  This option allows DFSORT instead of COBOL to perform input-output.

◘ FDUMP

- **General format**
  ```
  <FDUmp or NOFDUmp>
  ```

- **Description**
  This option generates a formatted dump if an ABEND occurs.

◘ FLAG

- **General format**
  ```
  < Flag(x, [y]) or NOFlag or Flag(I) >

      where x and y are I, W, E, S, or U.
  ```

- **Description**
  This option produces diagnostic messages for errors.

◘ LIB

- **General format**
  ```
  <LIB or NOLIB>
  ```

- **Description**
  This option specifies the library for a COPY or BASIS statement.

◘ LINECOUNT

- **General format**
  ```
  <LineCount or LC(60)>
  ```

- **Description**
  This option specifies the number of lines per page.

◘ LIST

- **General format**
  ```
  <LIST or NOLIST>
  ```

- **Description**

This option generates an assembler-language listing of the PROCEDURE DIVISION.

■ MAP

• **General format**
```
<MAP or NOMAP>
```

• **Description**
This option produces a listing and map of the DATA DIVISION.

■ NUMBER

• **General format**
```
<NUMber or NONUMBer>
```

• **Description**
This option uses numbers in columns 1 through 6 of the source program.

■ OBJECT

• **General format**
```
<OBJect or NOOBject>
```

• **Description**
This option produces object code on SYSLIN.

■ OFFSET

• **General format**
```
<OFFset or NOOFFset>
```

• **Description**
This option generates a condensed listing. It suppresses LIST.

◘ **OPTIMIZE**

● **General format**
```
<OPTimize or NOOPTimize>
```

● **Description**
This option reduces the run time of an object program.

◘ **OUTDD**

● **General format**
```
<OUTdd(ddname) or OUTDD(SYSOUT)>
```

● **Description**
This option redirects the display from SYSOUT.

◘ **PFDSGN**

● **General format**
```
<PFDsgn or NOPFDsgn>
```

● **Description**
This option assumes that all numeric fields have the correct signs, X"C" or X"D" or X"F".

◘ **RENT**

● **General format**
```
<RENT or NORENT>
```

● **Description**
This option generates reentrant code.

◘ **RESIDENT**

● **General format**
```
<RESIDENT or NORESIDENT>
```

- **Description**
This option requests the COBOL Library Management Feature.

◘ SEQUENCE

- **General format**
```
<SEQuence or NOSEQuence>
```

- **Description**
This option checks the sequence numbers in columns 1 through 6 of the source program.

◘ SIZE

- **General format**
```
<SiZe(nnnnn or nnnK or MAX) or Sz(MAX)>
```

- **Description**
This option uses a specified amount of memory.

◘ SOURCE

- **General format**
```
<NOSource or Source>
```

- **Description**
This option prints a source listing.

◘ SPACE

- **General format**
```
<SPACE(1 or 2 or 3) or SPACE(1)>
```

- **Description**
This option selects single, double, or triple spacing of the source code listing.

◻ SSRANGE

- **General format**
  ```
  <SSRange or NOSSRange>
  ```

- **Description**
  This option tests that all array references are within bounds.

◻ TERMINAL

- **General format**
  ```
  <TERMinal or NOTERMinal>
  ```

- **Description**
  This option sends messages to SYSTERM.

◻ TEST

- **General format**
  ```
  <TESt or NOTEst>
  ```

- **Description**
  This option generates a code that can be used with the COBTEST debugger.

◻ TRUNC

- **General format**
  ```
  <TRUnc or NOTRUnc>
  ```

- **Description**
  This option truncates binary (COMP) fields to conform to their PIC during arithmetic and MOVE statements.

◻ VBREF

- **General format**
  ```
  <VBREF or NOVBREF>
  ```

- **Description**
This option cross-references verb types and line numbers.

▢ WORD

- **General format**
`<WorD(xxx) or OWorD>`

- **Description**
This option uses a user-supplied reserved word table during compilation.

▢ XREF

- **General format**
`<Xref or NOXref>`

- **Description**
This option produces a sorted cross-reference listing.

▢ ZWB

- **General format**
`<NOZWB or ZWB>`

- **Description**
This optons ignores the sign when comparing PIC 9 and PIC x data items.

DB2 COMMANDS AND UTILITIES

This chapter is a reference guide for programmers using DB2. The subjects covered here can be grouped into these categories:

- DSN Commands
- DB2 Commands
- Attachment Facility Commands
- DB2 Utilities

For each command and utility, this chapter provides the syntax, a description of the function and its parameters, and required authorization. In some cases you will also find examples of how the functions use them. This chapter also gives sample JCLs for running a DB2 program and using utilities to perform database operations.

Notational Convention: In the general format of the commands for utilities used in this chapter, there are a few symbols that are not part of the syntax; therefore they must not be included when you code your program. These symbols and their meanings are:

Symbol	Meaning
[]	The option enclosed by the brackets ([]) is not required but can be included.
<>	Only one of the alternatives enclosed by the angle brackets (<>) must be chosen.
or	The alternatives enclosed by the angle brackets (<>) are separated by "or."

	The underlined word is the default value.
...	The horizontal or vertical ellipsis means that the preceding can be coded more than once.
Uppercase characters	All keywords of the command are written in uppercase characters; they must be coded as shown.
Lowercase characters	All strings in lowercase characters and italic are variables that can be changed to any other strings to suit your programming style. In your code they represent values that you supply to the commands.

5.1   DB2 COMMANDS

This section lists all the DB2 commands. For each command it provides the following:

- The syntax of the command
- An explanation of the command and its parameters
- The authorization or privileges needed to perform actions
- Indication of how the command can be issued, whether through batch or online
- Examples of how to use the command

◻ BIND—Create an application plan

- **General format**

```
BIND  PLAN(plan-name)
   MEMBER(dbrm-member,...)
   LIBRARY(dbrm-pds,...)
   [ACTION(REPLACE [RETAIN] or ADD)]
   [VALIDATE(RUN or BIND)]
   [ISOLATION(RR or CS)]
   [FLAG(I or W or E or C)]
   [ACQUIRE(USE or ALLOCATE)]
   [RELEASE(COMMIT or DEALLOCATE)]
   [EXPLAIN(NO or YES)]
```

- **Description**

  The BIND command creates an application plan which is used to access DB2 data during the execution of a program. During a bind processing, the following happens:

  - Validation of the rules, structure, and syntax of SQL statements

used in a program
- Verification of authority to access DB2 data
- Choice of an access path to data
- Creation of an application plan which is used to allocate resources during program execution

PLAN(*plan-name*)
This parameter allows you to specify a name for an application plan. An entry is made to the SYSIBM.SYSPLAN catalog table only if no error occurs during the bind processing.

plan-name may have up to 8 characters; the first character must be alphabetic. *plan-name* must not have any underscore (_) characters or begin with DSN.

MEMBER(*dbrm-member,...*)
This parameter allows you to enter the names of one or more database request modules (DBRMs). Each DBRM is a member of a partitioned dataset, generated during the DB2 precompilation of a program. The PDS either is specified with the parameter LIBRARY of the BIND command or is part of a JCL statement with ddname DBRMLIB.

LIBRARY(*dbrm-pds,...*)
This parameter allows you to enter the names of one or more partitioned datasets (libraries) that contain the members listed after the parameter MEMBER. Alternatively, a PDS can be part of a JCL statement with ddname DBRMLIB.

ACTION(REPLACE or ADD)
This parameter specifies whether an application plan is to be added to or replaced in a catalog table.

REPLACE means that the bind process replaces an old application plan with a new one, if no errors occur. The same name is kept in SYSIBM.SYSPLAN if it exists; otherwise a new plan is added. REPLACE is the default.

ADD means that the bind process adds a new entry to the SYSIBM.SYSPLAN catalog table, if no error occurs.

RETAIN
This parameter allows you to retain authorities after an application plan is replaced. It has no effect during an add operation.

VALIDATE(RUN or BIND)
This parameter specifies whether validation should occur during bind processing or when the program is run.

RUN means to validate during execution of the program. RUN is the default.

BIND means to validate during bind processing.

ISOLATION(RR or CS)
This parameter specifies the isolation level of this application plan from others.

RR is used for *repeated read.* It means that no other application can value, read, or be changed by this application until the application issues an SQL statement to commit or roll back. RR is the default.

CS is used for *cursor stability.* It means that when the cursor is positioned on a page, the page lock is held. The lock is released only if the cursor moves to a new page and a new lock is acquired.

FLAG(I or W or E or C)
This parameter specifies the types of messages with one of the following values:
I—All. I is the default.
W—Warning, error, and completion messages.
E—Error and completion messages.
C—Completion messages.

ACQUIRE(USE or ALLOCATE)
This parameter specifies when tablespace-level locks are acquired.

USE means that locks are acquired on the first use. USE is the default.

ALLOCATE means that locks are acquired when the plan is

allocated (when the program begins execution).

RELEASE(COMMIT or DEALLOCATE)
This parameter specifies when tablespace-level locks are released.

COMMIT means that locks are released at each synch point.
COMMIT is the default.

DEALLOCATE means that locks are released when the plan is
deallocated (when the program is terminated).

EXPLAIN(NO or YES)
This parameter specifies whether information regarding the access
strategy of SQL statements of a program will be added to the table
userid.PLAN-TABLE. This table must exist before EXPLAIN can
be used.

NO means to provide no information. NO is the default.

YES means to insert information in the table *userid*.PLAN-
TABLE.

Either of these two values can be overwritten with an SQL
EXPLAIN statement.

- **Authorization**

Action	Authority	Privilege
Add a plan	SYSADM	BINDADD
Replace a plan	SYSADM	BIND
Use VALIDATE(BIND)		To execute SQL statements during bind processing
Use VALIDATE(RUN)		To execute SQL statements during execution of the program
Create a plan		All (with GRANT option)

- **Usage**
The BIND command can be issued through DB2I or TSO (online
or batch).

● **Example**

In the following BIND command, the *plan-name* is LGL701 and *dbrm-member* is LGL701. All validation is to be done during bind processing, and all privileges are to be retained after the application plan is replaced. ISOLATION(CS) means that a page is locked while it is being used.

```
BIND PLAN(LGL701)
     MEMBER(LGL701)
     VALIDATE(BIND)
     ACTION(REPLACE)
     RETAIN
     ISOLATION(CS)
```

◻ **DCLGEN—Create language declarations**

● **General format**

```
DCLGEN TABLE(table-name or view-name)
  LIBRARY(<dataset-name or pds-name(member)>
               [/password])
  [ACTION(ADD or REPLACE)]
  [LANGUAGE(COBOL or PLI)]
  [NAMES(field-prefix)]
  STRUCTURE(structure-name)
  [APOST or QUOTE]
  [LABEL(NO or YES)]
```

● **Description**

DCLGEN is a commmand that allows you to create host language declarations of rows as defined in an actual table. Using the DB2 catalog, DCLGEN produces a complete SQL DECLARE statement for a view or table. The output can be used with COPY or INCLUDE statements of COBOL or PL/I programs, respectively. The SQL DECLARE statement and the data declaration can be coded manually, but the advantage of using DCLGEN is that it ensures that the data definitions of a program are compatible with the column definitions of DB2. The DCLGEN output must be in sync with any change in the actual table. Otherwise, the bind processing will fail.

TABLE(*table-name* or *view-name*)

This parameter specifies the table or view for which a language declaration is to be created.

table-name is the name of the DB2 table.

view-name is the name of the DB2 view.

If either name contains any special characters, other than underscores, it must be enclosed in apostrophes. If the declaration is for COBOL, any underscores (_) in the name will be changed to hyphens (-), and all lowercase characters will be translated to uppercase.

LIBRARY(<*dataset-name or pds-name(member)*>[*/password*])
This parameter specifies either a sequential or a partitioned dataset name where the output of DCLGEN should be written. The dataset must exist. If the name is not enclosed in apostrophes, a standard TSO prefix (userid) and language suffix (COBOL or PLI) will be added to it.

dataset-name is a sequential dataset name.

pds-name is a partitioned dataset name.

member is a member of the partitioned dataset.

password is optional.

ACTION(ADD or REPLACE)
This parameter specifies whether to add or replace a DCLGEN member.

ADD means to add a member to the dataset, if one does not exist. ADD is the default.

REPLACE means to replace an existing member. If the output is to a PDS member and it does not exist, then a new member is created.

LANGUAGE(COBOL or PLI)
This parameter specifies the language for which the declaration is to be generated. COBOL is the default.

NAMES(*field-prefix*)
This parameter allows you to give the fields in the generated data definition names other than the column names of the table or view. If it is blank, DCLGEN generates field names that are the same as

the columns of the table or view.

field-prefix is the prefix you supply. It can be 1 to 28 alphanumeric characters, with the first being alphabetic. For example, if *field-prefix* is XYZ, then the field names will be XYZ1, XYZ2, XYZ3, and so on.

STRUCTURE(*structure-name*)
This parameter specifies the name of a data definition created by DCLGEN. The default is the name of the table or view prefixed with DCL.

structure-name can be from 1 to 31 alphanumeric characters, with the first being alphabetic

APOST or QUOTE
These two parameters specify the delimiter used in the host language.

APOST means apostrophe ('). APOST is the default.

QUOTE means quotation mark (").

LABEL(NO or YES)
This parameter specifies whether comments are to be created in the output from column labels.

NO means not to create comments. NO is the default.

YES means to create comments from column labels.

- **Authorization**

Action	Privilege
Use DCLGEN	To use SELECT statements on a specified table or view.

- **Usage**
The DCLGEN command can be issued through DB2I or TSO (online or batch).

• **Examples**

In the following DCLGEN command, a language declaration is
created for table CLIENTS and placed in PDS
TEST.DB2.DCLGEN(DCL01) for COBOL. It replaces a previous
member generated by DCLGEN and uses the apostrophe as the
string delimiter.

```
DCLGEN TABLE(CLIENTS)
       LIBRARY(TEST.DB2.DCLGEN(DCL01))
       ACTION(REPLACE)
       APOST
```

The output from DCLGEN is as follows:

```
************************************************************
* DCLGEN TABLE(CLIENTS)
*        LIBRARY(TEST.DB2.DCLGEN(DCL01))
*        ACTION(REPLACE)
*        APOST
* ... IS THE DCLGEN COMMAND THAT MADE THE FOLLOWING
*     STATEMENTS
************************************************************
         EXEC SQL DECLARE CLIENTS TABLE
         ( CL_CL_NAME                CHAR(25) NOT NULL,
           CL_CITY                        CHAR(15),
           CL_LANG                        CHAR(1),
           CL_P_CDE                       CHAR(7),
           CL_PROV                        CHAR(15),
           CL_SITE                        CHAR(4),
           CL_COMPANY_NO                  CHAR(10),
           CL_SERV_NAME                   CHAR(25),
           CL_NODE_ID                     CHAR(8),
           CL_STUB_NO                     CHAR(4)
         ) END-EXEC.
************************************************************
* COBOL DECLARATION FOR TABLE CLIENTS
************************************************************
         01   DCLCLIENTS.
              10 CL-CL-NAME          PIC X(25).
              10 CL-CITY             PIC X(15).
              10 CL-LANG             PIC X(1).
              10 CL-P-CDE            PIC X(7).
              10 CL-PROV             PIC X(15).
              10 CL-SITE             PIC X(4).
              10 CL-COMPANY-NO       PIC X(10).
              10 CL-SERV-NAME        PIC X(25).
              10 CL-NODE-ID          PIC X(8).
              10 CL-STUB-NO          PIC X(4).
```

In the next example, the paramater NAMES specifies a *field-prefix*
as XYZ.

```
DCLGEN TABLE(CLIENTS)
     LIBRARY(TEST.DB2.DCLGEN(DCL02))
     NAMES(XYZ)
     ACTION(REPLACE)
     APOST
```

Note: The field names of the data definition have the prefix XYZ and sequence numbers from 1 to 10.

The output from DCLGEN is as follows:

```
************************************************************
* DCLGEN TABLE(CLIENTS)
*        LIBRARY(TEST.DB2.DCLGEN(DCL02))
*        NAMES(XYZ)
*        APOST
* ... IS THE DCLGEN COMMAND THAT MADE THE FOLLOWING
*     STATEMENTS
************************************************************
         EXEC SQL DECLARE RBA.CLIENTS TABLE
           ( CL_CL_NAME               CHAR(25) NOT NULL,
             CL_CITY                  CHAR(15),
             CL_LANG                  CHAR(1),
             CL_P_CDE                 CHAR(7),
             CL_PROV                  CHAR(15),
             CL_SITE                  CHAR(4),
             CL_COMPANY_NO            CHAR(10),
             CL_SERV_NAME             CHAR(25),
             CL_NODE_ID               CHAR(8),
             CL_STUB_NO               CHAR(4)
           ) END-EXEC.

************************************************************
* COBOL DECLARATION FOR TABLE RBA.CLIENTS
************************************************************
     01  DCLCLIENTS.
     *                           CL_CL_NAME
         10 XYZ1                     PIC X(25).
     *                           CL_CITY
         10 XYZ2                     PIC X(15).
     *                           CL_LANG
         10 XYZ3                     PIC X(1).
     *                           CL_P_CDE
         10 XYZ4                     PIC X(7).
     *                           CL_PROV
         10 XYZ5                     PIC X(15).
     *                           CL_SITE
         10 XYZ6                     PIC X(4).
     *                           CL_COMPANY_NO
         10 XYZ7                     PIC X(10).
     *                           CL_SERV_NAME
         10 XYZ8                     PIC X(25).
     *                           CL_NODE_ID
         10 XYZ9                     PIC X(8).
     *                           CL_STUB_NO
         10 XYZ10                    PIC X(4).
```

⬛ **-DISPLAY DATABASE OR -DIS DB—Display status information for DB2 databases.**

- **General format**

```
-DISPLAY DATABASE (* or database-name,...)
        [SPACENAME(* or space-name,...)]
        [USE or LOCKS]
        [AFTER]
        [LIMIT(* or number)]
        [ACTIVE]
        [RESTRICT]
```

- **Description**

This -DISPLAY command displays status information for one or more DB2 databases.

DATABASE(* or *database-name*,...)
This parameter allows you to specify the names of one or more DB2 databases for which status information is to be displayed.

* means to display status information for all DB2 databases for which you have authority.

database-name is the name of a database already defined in the DB2 subsystem for which status information is to be displayed.

SPACENAME(* or *space-name*,...)
This parameter specifies what kind of information is to be displayed. SPACENAME can be used only if no more than one database is specified.

* means to display status information for all indexes and table spaces for a specified database.

space-name is the name of a table space for which status information is to be displayed. More than one name may be entered.

USE
This parameter is used to display information about correlation ids and connection ids.

LOCKS
This parameter is used to display information about correlation ids and connection ids for all applications holding or awaiting locks.

AFTER
This parameter is used to display the status of all databases greater than *database-name*. It can be used for only one database name.

LIMIT(* or *number*)
This parameter specifies the number of messages to be displayed.

* means the limit is 12 kbytes, which is the size of the message buffer.

number is an interger value which is the maximum number of messages to be displayed. The default is 50.

ACTIVE
This parameter is used to display status information for table spaces or index spaces already allocated to applications.

RESTRICT
This parameter is used to display status information for databases, table spaces, or index spaces whose use is restricted.

- **Authorization**

Action	Authority	Privilege
Display status of all databases	SYSADM SYSOPR	DISPLAY
Display status of a selected list of databases	SYSOPR DBADM DBCTRL DBMAINT	DISPLAYDB

- **Usage**
The -DISPLAY DATABASE command can be issued from an MVS console, IMS/VS terminal or CICS/OS/VS terminal, or

through DSN command under TSO or DB2I.

- **Example**

  The following -DISPLAY DATABASE command displays status information for database CDBEXP. The parameter SPACENAM(*) is used to display information for all table spaces and index spaces for database CDBEXP. USE displays correlation id and connection id.

  ```
  -DISPLAY DB(CDBEXP)
     SPACENAM(*)
     USE
  ```

◘ -DISPLAY THREAD or -DIS THD—Display information for DB2 connections

- **General format**

  ```
  -DISPLAY THREAD [(* or connection-name,...)]
                  [TYPE (* or ACTIVE or INDOUBT)]
  ```

- **Description**

  The -DISPLAY THREAD command displays information about all DB active or in-doubt connections.

  THREAD(* or *connection-name,...*)
  This parameter specifies one or more connection names. Only threads from address spaces associated with the specified connection names are selected.

  * means to display all connections in all the address spaces already attached to the DB2 subsystem.

  connection-name is the name of a connection; it can be 1 to 8 characters in length.

  TYPE(* or ACTIVE or INDOUBT)
  This parameter is used to choose the type of thread to display.

  * mean to display both active and in-doubt threads.

  ACTIVE means to display only active threads.

INDOUBT means to display only in-doubt threads.

- **Authorization**

Action	Authority	Privilege
To display thread	SYSADM	DISPLAY
	SYSOPR	

- **Usage**

The -DISPLAY THREAD command can be issued through DB2I or TSO (online or batch), from MVS console, IMS/VS terminal, or CICS/OS/VS terminal.

- **Example**

The following -DISPLAY THREAD command displays all active and in-doubt threads with the connection name associated with your userid.

```
-DISPLAY THREAD
        TYPE(*)
```

◘ **-DISPLAY TRACE—Display active traces**

- **General format**

```
DISPLAY TRACE(* or GLOBAL or PERFM or ACCTG or STAT)
        DEST(*  or (GTF or RES or SMF or SRV))
        PLAN(* or plan-name,...)
        AUTHID(* or authorization-id,...)
        CLASS(* or class-number,...)
        RMID(* or rmid-number,...)
        TNO(* or tno-number,...)
        [COMMENT(string)]
```

- **Description**

The -DISPLAY TRACE command displays active traces depending on the following parameters.

TRACE(* or GLOBAL or PERFM or ACCTG or STAT)
This parameter specifies a limit on the display of traces. The following is a list of all the options.

Type	Description
*	All traces

GLOBAL	Service data
PERFM	Performance
ACCTG	Accounting
STAT	Statistic

The default is to list all traces

DEST(* or (GTF or RES or SMF or SRV))
This parameter specifies a limit on traces for destinations.

* means to list all traces. It is the default.

Limitations are imposed by four keywords. You can use more than one of them, but never the same one twice. The following is the list of the keywords and their descriptions.

Keyword	Description
GTF	Generalized trace facility
RES	Resident table in CSA storage
SMF	System management facility
SRV	Diagnostic routines

PLAN(* or *plan-name*,...)
This parameter specifies one or more application plans for which to list traces.

* means not to limit the list. This is the default.

AUTHID(* or *authorization-id*,...)
This parameter is used to specify authorization.

* means not to limit the list. This is the default.

authorization-id is an integer for the authorization identifier.

CLASS(* or *class-number*,...)
This parameter is used to specify one or more classes.

* means not to limit the list. This is the default.

class-number is an integer for a class.

RMID(* or *rmid-number,...*)
This parameter is used to specify one or more resource managers.

* means not to limit the list. This is the default.

rmid-number is an integer for a resource manager.

TNO(* or *tno-number,...*)
This parameter is used to specify one or more trace numbers.

* means not to limit the list. This is the default.

tno-number is an integer for a trace number.

COMMENT *(string)*
This parameter is used to specify a comment that is reproduced in
the output record.

string is a valid SQL string.

- **Authorization**

Action	Authority	Privilege
Display trace	SYSADM SYSOPR	DISPLAY

- **Usage**
The -DISPLAY TRACE command can be issued through DB2I or
TSO (online or batch), from an MVS console, IMS/VS terminal,
or CICS/OS/VS terminal.

- **Example**
The following -DISPLAY TRACE command lists all traces that
have as their destination the System Management Facility.

```
-DISPLAY TRACE(*)
        DEST(SMF)
```

■ **-DISPLAY UTILITY or -DIS UTIL—Display the status of a utility job**

● **General format**
```
-DISPLAY UTILITY (* or utilid or partial-utilid*))
```

● **Description**
The -DISPLAY UTILITY command displays the status of a job that is running, completed, or failed.

UTILITY(* or *utilid* or *partial-utilid*)
This parameter is used to specify the JOBID you wish to monitor.

* means all utility jobs currently known to DB2 that you are authorized to see.

utilid is the name of a specific utility job.

*partial-utilid** is only part of the utility job name. If *partial-utilid* is *aaa*, then the job name begins with *aaa* and ends with any other characters. This command will show every job that starts with *aaa*.

● **Authorization**
None required.

● **Usage**
The -DISPLAY UTILITY command can be issued through DB2I or TSO (online or batch), from an MVS console, IMS/VS terminal, or CICS/OS/VS terminal.

● **Example**
The following -DISPLAY UTILITY command shows the status of all utility jobs currently known to DB2.

```
-DISPLAY UTILITY (*)
```

■ **DSN (TSO)—Invoke the DSN command processor**

● **General format**
```
DSN [SYSTEM (db2-name)]
    [RETRY(retry-number)]
    [TEST(test-number)]
```

- **Description**

The DSN command processor executes DSN commands and passes commands to DB2. It processes the following subcommands.

Command	Description
ABEND	Diagnose problem with DSN or DB2
BIND	Create an application plan
DCLGEN	Create language declarations
END	End DSN command
FREE	Delete an application plan from DB2
REBIND	Rebind an existing application plan
RUN	Run an application program
SPUFI	Execute SQL statements from TSO
*	Comment subcommand
-	DB2 commands

SYSTEM (*db2-name*)
This parameter specifies which DB2 subsystem to connect to.

db2-name is the name of a DB2 subsystem.

RETRY(*retry-number*)
This parameter specifies the number of times connection to the DB2 subsystem should be attempted. The default is 0.

retry-number is a number of retries; it should be less than 120.

TEST
This parameter is used to start the trace facility.

test-number must be an integer.

- **Authority**

None required; but authorization is required to process subcommands.

- **Usage**

The DSN command processor can be invoked only from TSO. However, all the DSN commands, such as BIND, RUN, SPUFI, and so on, can be issued from DB2I, batch JCL, or CLIST programs.

- **Example**

The following DSN command is issued from ISPF option 6 or TSO READY.

```
DSN SYSTEM (PAJ0)
```

PAJ0 is the name of the DB2 subsystem. After this command is entered, DSN returns the prompt.

```
DSN
```

Then you may type any DSN command, such as RUN, -DISPLAY DATABASE, -DISPLAY THREAD, and so on. To terminate the DSN session, type END.

◻ DSNC—Issue DB2 commands from CICS/OS/VS

- **General format**

```
DSNC [dest] -db2-command
```

- **Description**

DSNC is a CICS transaction that controls the attachment facility between CICS and DB2. Before it is used to issue DB2 commands, the command

DSNC STRT x must be executed, where x is the suffix of the RCT that you want to use. The default for x is 0. Some installation is set up to execute this start-up process when the region comes up.

dest

This parameter is optional; it is the name of a destination to which the output is to be directed.

db2-command

This parameter is the DB2 command.

- **Authorization**

Action	Authority
To issue DSNC	To execute the CICS transaction DSNC
	To enter DB2 commands

- **Usage**

The DSNC command is issued from a CICS/OS/VS terminal.

- **Example**

The following command uses DSNC to issue a DB2 command. It displays the status of all DB2 databases for which you have authority.

```
DSNC -DISPLAY DATABASE(*)
```

▣ DSNC DISCONNECT or DSNC DISC—Disconnect threads from CICS/OS/VS

- **General format**
```
DSNC DISCONNECT plan-name
```

- **Description**

The DSNC DISCONNECT command is used to disconnect threads.

plan-name is the name of an application plan.

- **Authorization**

Action	Authority
Issue DSNC	To execute the CICS transaction DSNC

- **Usage**

The DSNC DISCONNECT command is issued from a CICS/OS/VS terminal.

- **Example**

The following DSNC DISCONNECT command disconnects active threads for the application plan MYPLAN.

DSNC DISCONNECT MYPLAN

◻ DSNC DISPLAY or DSNC DISP—Display information on CICS transactions for a DB2 subsystem.

- **General format**
```
DSNC DISPLAY <PLAN [plan-name]                     or
             TRANSACTION [transaction-id]          or
             STATISTICS>
            [destination-id]
```

- **Description**
The DSNC DISPLAY command is used to display information about CICS transactions that access DB2 data.

PLAN *plan-name destination-id*
This parameter is used to specify an application plan for which information about the transaction is displayed.

plan-name is the name of an application plan.

destination-id is the name of the output device to which the output is to be directed.

TRANSACTION *transaction-id*
This parameter is used to specify a CICS transaction.

transaction-id is the name of the CICS transaction.

STATISTICS
This parameter is used to display the statistical counters associated with each entry in the resource control table.

- **Authorization**

Action	Authority
Issue DSNC DISPLAY	To execute the CICS transaction DSNC.

- **Usage**
The DSNC DISPLAY command is issued from a CICS/OS/VS terminal.

● **Example**
The following DSNC DISPLAY command displays all application
plans listed in the resource control table.

```
DSNC DISPLAY PLAN *
```

◘ **DSNC MODIFY or DSNC MODI—Modify the error
destination entry in the resource control table (RCT)**

● **General format**
```
DSNC MODIFY
   DESTINATION  old-dest new-dest
   [TRANSACTION transaction-id number]
```

● **Description**
DSNC DISPLAY, a command of the CICS DSNC transaction,
modifies the error destination entry of the RCT. The entry is
ERRDEST of the resource control table.

DESTINATION *old-dest new-dest*
This parameter is used to specify the old destination ID that is to
be replaced with the new destination ID in the RCT.

old-dest is the name of the old destination ID.

new-dest is the name of the new destination ID.

TRANSACTION *transaction-id number*
This parameter is used to specify a CICS transaction ID and the
maximum number of threads.

transaction-id is the name of a CICS transaction ID.

number is the new maximum value.

● **Authorization**

Action	Authority
Issue DSNC MODIFY	To execute the CICS transaction DSNC.

● **Usage**
The DSNC MODIFY command is issued from a CICS/OS/VS

terminal.

● **Example**
The following DSNC MODIFY command changes the ERRDEST
parameter of the RCT from XX01 to XX02.

```
DSNC MODIFY DESTINATION XX01 XX02
```

◘ **DSNC STOP—Stop the attachment facility from CICS to DB2**

● **General format**
```
DSNC STOP QUIESCE
     [FORCE]
```

● **Description**
The DSNC STOP command is used to remove the attachment
facility that allows CICS programs to access DB2 data.

QUIESCE or Q
This parameter is used to stop the attachment facility after current
CICS transactions terminate.

FORCE
This parameter is used to stop the attachment facility immediately,
thus disconnecting DB2.

● **Authorization**

Action	Authority
Issue DSNC STOP	To execute the CICS transaction DSNC.

● **Usage**
The DSNC STOP command is issued from a CICS/OS/VS
terminal.

● **Example**
The following DSNC STOP command stops the attachment facility
between CICS and DB2 immediately.

```
DSNC STOP FORCE
```

◻ DSNC STRT—Start the attachment facility between CICS and DB2

- **General format**
  ```
  DSNC STRT x
  ```

- **Description**

  The DSNC STRT command must be issued to start the attachment facility between CICS and DB2. Subsequently any DB2 commands can issued. Some installations are set up to execute this start-up process when the region comes up.

  x is a suffix of the RCT that you want to use. The default is 0.

- **Authorization**

Action	Authority
Issue DSNC STRT	To execute the CICS transaction DSNC.

- **Usage**

  The DSNC STRT command is issued from a CICS/OS/VS terminal.

- **Example**

  The following DSNC STRT command will first append 1 to DSNCRCT; then the resource control table DSNCRCT1 will be loaded.

  ```
  DSNC STRT 1
  ```

◻ END—End a DSN session and return to TSO

- **General format**
  ```
  END
  ```

- **Description**

  END is a subcommand of DSN. It terminates a DSN session and returns control to TSO.

- **Authorization**

  None required.

- **Usage**
The END command is issued from a TSO terminal.

- **Example**
In the following example, the user types END during a DSN TSO session. This terminates the DSN session. Control is passed to TSO, which prompts READY.

```
END
READY
```

◻ FREE—Delete an application plan from DB2

- **General format**
```
FREE PLAN(* or plan-name,...)
      [FLAG(I or W or E or C)]
```

- **Description**
The FREE command removes application plans from DB2. It delete entries from the SYSIBM.SYSPLAN, SYSIBM.SYSDBRM, and SYSIBM.SYSSTMT tables. The dropped plans are available to be reused by the BIND command.

PLAN(* or *plan-name,...*)
This parameter specifies one or more application plans.

* means to delete all plans for which you have BIND authority.

plan-name is the name of an application plan.

FLAG(I or W or E or C)
This parameter specifies the types of messages with one of the following values:

I—All. I is the default.
W—Warning, error, and completion messages.
E—Error and completion messages.
C—Completion messages.

- **Authorization**

Action	Authority	Privilege
Issue FREE command	SYSADM	BIND

- **Usage**

The FREE command can be be issued from TSO, DB2I, or CLIST.

- **Example**

The following FREE command deletes plan LBA101.

```
FREE PLAN (LBA101)
```

■ **REBIND—Rebind an existing application plan**

- **General format**

```
REBIND PLAN(* or plan-name,...)
    [FLAG(I or W or E or C)]
    [VALIDATE(RUN or BIND)]
    [ISOLATION(RR or CS)]
    [ACQUIRE(USE or ALLOCATE)]
    [RELEASE(COMMIT or DEALLOCATE)]
    [EXPLAIN(NO or YES)]
```

- **Description**

The REBIND command is used for the following reasons:

- Authoriation to use database tables is altered
- A new index is added
- RUNSTATS has been used

If SQL statements have been changed, then the application plan must undergo the binding process using the BIND command with the REPLACE parameter.

In the following catalog tables, items are either updated or added:

```
SYSIBM.SYSPLAN
SYSIBM.SYSPLANAUTH
SYSIBM.SYSPLANDEP
```

PLAN(* or plan-name,...)

This parameter allows you to specify a name for one or more application plans to rebind.

* means all application plans for which you have authority.

plan-name is the name of an application plan to rebind.

FLAG(I or W or E or C)
This parameter specifies the types of messages with one of the following values:

I—All. I is the default.
W—Warning, error and, completion messages.
E—Error and completion messages.
C—Completion messages.

VALIDATE(RUN or BIND)
This parameter specifies whether validation should occur during rebind processing or when the program is run.

RUN means to validate during execution of the program. RUN is the default.

BIND means to validate during rebind processing.

ISOLATION(RR or CS)
This parameter specifies the isolation level of this application plan from others. If you omit this parameter, the value specified in a previous bind or rebind process is used.

RR is used for *repeated read.* It means that no other application can value, read, or be changed by this application until the application issues an SQL statement to commit or roll back.

CS is used for *cursor stability.* It means that when the cursor is positioned on a page, the page lock is held. The lock is released only if the cursor moves to a new page and a new lock is acquired.

ACQUIRE(USE or ALLOCATE)
This parameter specifies when tablespace-level locks are acquired. If you omit this parameter, the value specified in a previous bind

or rebind process is used.

USE means that locks are acquired on the first use.

ALLOCATE means that locks are acquired when the plan is allocated (when the program begins execution).

RELEASE(COMMIT or DEALLOCATE)
This parameter specifies when tablespace-level locks are released. If you omit this parameter, the value specified in a previous bind or rebind process is used.

COMMIT means that locks are released at each sync point.

DEALLOCATE means that locks are released when the plan is deallocated (when the program is terminated).

EXPLAIN(NO or YES)
This parameter specifies whether information regarding the access strategy of SQL statements of a program will be added to the table *userid*.PLAN-TABLE. This table must exist before EXPLAIN can be used. If you omit this parameter, the value specified in a previous bind or rebind process is used.

NO means to provide no information. NO is the default.

YES means insert information to the table *userid*.PLAN-TABLE.

Either of these two values can be overwritten with an SQL EXPLAIN statement.

- **Authorization**

Action	Authority	Privilege
Rebind a plan	SYSADM	BIND

- **Usage**
The REBIND command can be issued through DB2I or TSO (online or batch).

● **Example**

In the following REBIND command, the *plan-name* is LGL701. The command also specifies that all validation is to be done during rebind processing. ISOLATION(CS) means that a page is locked while it is being used.

```
REBIND PLAN(LGL701)
    VALIDATE(BIND)
    ISOLATION(CS)
```

◘ **RUN—Run an application program**

● **General format**
```
RUN <<CP PLAN(plan-name)> or
        <PROGRAM(program-name) [PLAN(plan-name)] >>
    [LIBRARY(library-name)]
    [PARMS('parms-list')]
```

● **Description**

The RUN command is used to execute a program that has been precompiled, compiled, and link-edited and has undergone the binding process.

CP

This parameter is used to enter a TSO command, especially when running debuggers. With CP an application plan must be specified using the PLAN parameter.

PROGRAM(*program-name*)

This parameter is used to run a specific program.

program-name is the name of a program that has already been precompiled, compiled, and link-edited.

PLAN(*plan-name*)

The PLAN parameter can be used with either the CP or the PROGRAM parameter. The application plan is required with the former and is optional with the latter.

LIBRARY(*library-name*)

This parameter is used to specify the dataset from which the program is to be executed.

library-name is the name of a fully or partially qualified name. If the name is partially qualified, it is suffixed with the *userid*. The default is *userid*.RUNLIB.LOAD.

PARMS('*parms-list*')
This parameter is used to specify one or more parameters to pass to a program.

parms-list is a list of parameters separated with commas, blanks, or both and enclosed in apostrophes.

- **Authorization**

Action	Authority	Privilege
Issue RUN command	SYSADM	EXECUTE

- **Usage**
The RUN command is issued from a DSN command processor or DB2I.

- **Example**
The following RUN command is issued from a DSN command processor. The program LGLP703 is executed from the library TEST.DB2.LOAD.

```
DSN
RUN PROGRAM(LGLP703)
     LIBRARY('TEST.DB2.LOAD')
```

◻ SPUFI—Execute SQL statements from TSO

- **General format**
SPUFI

- **Description**
SPUFI (SQL processor using file input) is a TSO facility to create a DB2 database and dynamically use SQL statements. SPUFI is useful in testing or debugging SQL statements before they are included in a program.

- **Authorization**
Access to DB2I.

- **Usage**
  SPUFI is used from DB2I or CLIST.

◘ -START DATABASE or -STA DB —Start a DB2 database

- **General format**
  ```
  -START DATABASE (* or database-name,...) or
                  <(database-name)
                  SPACENAME(* or space-name,...)>
          ACCESS (RW or RO or UT or FORCE)
  ```

- **Description**
  Normally, when DB2 comes up, all databases are started automatically. The only time -START DATABASE is used is if -STOP DATABASE has been issued previously. It starts the databases and associated table spaces.

  DATABASE (* or *database-name*,...)
  This parameter is used to specify one or more databases. This can be done in three ways: with an asterisk, with one or more database names, or with one database name with the SPACENAME parameter.

  * means to start all databases for which you are authorized.

  database-name is the name of a database you want to start.

  SPACENAME(* or *space-name*,...)

  This parameter specifies one or more table spaces or index spaces that you want to start within a database. SPACENAME must be used with only one database.

  * means to start all table spaces and index tables for a database.

  space-name is the name of a table space or index space to be started.

  ACCESS (RW or RO or UT or FORCE)
  This parameter specifies the types of access to databases with the following values:

RW—Read and write access by programs. RW is the default.

RO—Read only by programs.

UT—Access by DB2 utilities.

FORCE—Full access to database.

- **Authorization**

Action	Authority	Privilege
Issue -START DATABASE	SYSADM	STARTDB
	DBADM	
	DBCTRL	
	DBMAINT	

- **Usage**
The -START DATABASE command is issued from a DSN command processor or DB2I.

- **Example**
The following -START DATABASE command starts all the databases for which you are authorized.

```
-START DATABASE (*)
```

◘ **-START DB2 or -STA DB2—Initialize the DB2 subsystem**

- **General format**
```
-START DB2
  [PARM(DSNZPARM or module-name)]
  [ACCESS(* or MAINT)]
  [MSTR(jcl-sub)]
  [DBMI(jcl-sub)]
```

- **Description**
When the -START DB2 command is completed, the subsystem becomes active and is available to TSO, IMS, and application programs.

PARM (DSNZPARM or *module-name*)
This parameter is used to specify the load module where

initialization information is stored.

DSNZPARM is the default.

module-name is the name of a load module.

ACCESS(* or MAINT)
This parameter specifies the type of access.

* means general access.

MAINT means restricted access.

MSTR(*jcl-sub*)
This parameter is used to specify substitutions in the EXEC statement of the JCL used.

jcl-sub is the string of characters enclosed in apostrophes to be substituted.

DBMI (*jcl-sub*)
This parameter is used to specify substitutions in the EXEC statement of the JCL used.

jcl-sub is the string of characters enclosed in apostrophes to be substituted.

◘ -START TRACE or -STA TRACE—Start DB2 traces

- **General format**

```
-START   TRACE(GLOBAL or PERFM or ACCTG or STAT)
         [DEST * or (GTF or RES or SMF or SRV))]
         PLAN(* or plan-name,...)
         AUTHID(* or authorization-id,...)
         CLASS(* or class-number,...)
         RMID(* or rmid-number,...)
         [COMMENT(string)]
```

- **Description**

The -START TRACE command starts DB2 traces depending on the following parameters.

TRACE(* or GLOBAL or PERFM or ACCTG or STAT)

This parameter specifies the types of traces. The following is a list of all the options.

Type	Description
*	All traces
GLOBAL	Service data
PERFM	Performance
ACCTG	Accounting
STAT	Statistic

DEST(* or (GTF or RES or SMT or SRV))
This parameter specifies the destination of the output with four keywords. You can use more than one of them, but never the same one twice. The following is the list of the keywords and their descriptions.

Keyword	Description
*	List all traces
GTF	Generalized trace facility
RES	Resident table in CSA storage
SMF	System management facility
SRV	Diagnostic routines

PLAN(* or *plan-name*,...)
This parameter specifies one or more application plans for which to start traces.

* means not to limit the trace. This is the default.

AUTHID(* or *authorization-id*,...)
This parameter is used to specify authorization.

* means not to limit the trace. This is the default.

authorization-id is an integer for the authorization identifier.

CLASS(* or *class-number*,...)
This parameter is used to specify one or more classes.

* means not to limit the trace. This is the default.

class-number is an integer for a class.

RMID(* or *rmid-number*,...)
This parameter is used to specify one or more resource managers.

* means not to limit the trace. This is the default.

rmid-number is an integer for a resource manager.

COMMENT *(string)*
This parameter is used to specify a comment that is reproduced in
the output record.

string is a valid SQL string.

- **Authorization**

Action	Authority	Privilege
Start a trace	SYSADM SYSOPR	DISPLAY

- **Usage**
The -START TRACE command can be issued through DB2I or
TSO (online or batch) from an MVS console, IMS/VS terminal, or
CICS/OS/VS terminal.

- **Example**
The following -START TRACE command is used to start all
traces; the the destination of the output is the System Management
Facility.

```
-DISPLAY TRACE(*)
          DEST(SMF)
```

◼ **-STOP DATABASE or -STO DB—Close a DB2 database**

- **General format**
-STOP DATABASE (* or *database-name*,...) or

[SPACENAME(* or *space-name*,...)]

- **Description**
  The -STOP DATABASE command closes databases, making them unavailable for access.

  DATABASE (* or *database-name*,...)
  This parameter is used to specify one or more databases.

  * means to close all databases for which you are authorized.

  database-name is the name of a database you want to close.

  SPACENAME(* or *space-name*,...)
  This parameter specifies one or more table spaces or index spaces that you want to stop within a database.

  * means to stop all table spaces and index spaces for a database.

  space-name is the name of a table space or index space to stop.

- **Authorization**

Action	Authority	Privilege
Issue -STOP DATABASE	SYSADM DBADM DBCTRL DBMAINT	STARTDB

- **Usage**
  The -STOP DATABASE command is issued from a DSN command processor or DB2I.

- **Example**
  The following -STOP DATABASE command closes all the databases for which you are authorized.

```
-STOP DATABASE (*)
```

◘ -STOP DB2 or -STO DB2—Close the DB2 subsystem

- **General format**
```
-STOP DB2 [MODE(QUIESCE or FORCE)]
```

- **Description**
The -STOP DB2 command closes the DB2 subsystem and terminates all application programs and utilities that access DB2 databases.

MODE(QUIESCE or FORCE)
This parameter specifies how to terminate programs that access DB2 during a subsystem shutdowm.

QUIESCE means to allow all current programs to complete processing. QUIESCE is the default.

FORCE means to stop executing all programs, including utilities, that are accessing the DB2 subsystem immediately.

- **Authorization**

Action	Authority
Issue -STOP DB2	SYSADM or SYSOPR or STOPALL

- **Usage**
The -STOP DB2 command can be issued through DB2I or TSO (online or batch), from an MVS console, IMS/VS terminal, or CICS/OS/VS terminal.

- **Example**
The following -STOP DB2 command shuts down the DB2 subsystem and terminates all programs accessing the database immediately.

```
-STOP DB2 MODE(FORCE)
```

◘ -STOP TRACE—Stop active traces

● **General format**

```
-STOP    TRACE(* or GLOBAL or PERFM or ACCTG or STAT)
         DEST(*  or (GTF or RES or SMF or SRV))
         PLAN(* or plan-name,...)
         AUTHID(* or authorization-id,...)
         CLASS(* or class-number,...)
         RMID(* or rmid-number,...)
         TNO(* or tno-number,...)
         [COMMENT(string)]
```

● **Description**

The -STOP TRACE command stops the display of active traces
depending on the following parameters.

TRACE(* or GLOBAL or PERFM or ACCTG or STAT)
This parameter specifies which type of tracing to stop. The
following is a list of all the options.

Type	Description
*	All traces
GLOBAL	Service data
PERFM	Performance
ACCTG	Accounting
STAT	Statistic

The default is to stop all traces.

DEST(* or (GTF or RES or SMT or SRV))
This parameter specifies the destinations for which tracing is to
stop.

* means not to limit the STOP command. It is the default.

Limitations are imposed by four kewords. You can use more than
one of them, but never the same one twice. The following is the
list of the keywords and descriptions.

Keyword	Description
*	Do not limit the command
GTF	Generalized trace facility

RES	Resident table in CSA storage
SMF	System management facility
SRV	Diagnostic routines

PLAN(* or *plan-name,...*)
This parameter specifies one or more application plans for which
to stop traces.

* means to stop all the plans. This is the default.

AUTHID(* or *authorization-id,...*)
This parameter is used to specify authorization.

* means to stop all traces. This is the default.

authorization-id is an integer for the authorization identifier.

CLASS(* or *class-number,...*)
This parameter is used to specify one or more classes.

* means to stop all traces. This is the default.

class-number is an integer for a class.

RMID(* or *rmid-number,...*)
This parameter is used to specify one or more resource managers.

* means to limit all traces. This is the default.

rmid-number is an integer for a resource manager.

TNO(* or *tno-number,...*)
This parameter is used to specify one or more trace numbers.

* means to stop all traces. This is the default.

tno-number is an integer for a trace number.

COMMENT *(string)*
This parameter is used to specify a comment that is reproduced in
the output record.

string is a valid SQL string.

- **Authorization**

Action	Authority	Privilege
Stop trace	SYSADM	DISPLAY
	SYSOPR	

- **Usage**
  The -STOP TRACE command can be issued through DB2I or
  TSO (online or batch), from an MVS console, IMS/VS terminal,
  or CICS/OS/VS terminal.

- **Example**
  The following -STOP TRACE command stops all active traces.

  ```
  -STOP TRACE
  ```

■ **-TERM UTILITY or -TERM UTIL—Terminate a utility job**

- **General format**
  ```
  -TERM UTILITY (* or utilid or partial-utilid*)
  ```

- **Description**
  The -TERM UTILITY command terminates a job that is running
  and releases all resources assigned to it.

  UTILITY(* or *utilid* or *partial-utilid*)
  This parameter is used to specify the JOBID you wish to
  terminate.

  * means all utility jobs currently known to DB2 that you are
  authorized to terminate.

  utilid is the name of a specific utility job.

  *partial-utilid** is only part of the utility job name. If *partial-utilid*
  is *aaa*, then the job name begins with *aaa* and ends with any other
  characters. This command will terminate every job that starts with
  aaa.

- **Authorization**

  None required.

- **Usage**

  The -TERM UTILITY command can be issued through DB2I or TSO (online or batch), MVS console, IMS/VS terminal, or CICS/OS/VS terminal.

- **Example**

  The following -TERM UTILITY command terminates all utility jobs currently known to DB2.

  ```
  -TERM UTILITY (*)
  ```

5.2   DB2 UTILITES

This section lists all the DB2 utilities. For each utility, it provides the following:

- The syntax of the utility
- An explanation of the function and its parameters
- The authorization and privileges needed to perform actions
- Indication of how a utility can be issued, whether through batch or online

◘ CHECK—Check the index of a database

- **General format**

  ```
  CHECK INDEX <<NAME(index,..)
              [TABLESPACE[dbname].tsname] > or
                          TABLESPACE[dbname].tsname>
              [WORKDDN(SYSUT1 or ddname)]
              [SORTDEVT device-type]
              [SORTNUM number]
  ```

- **Description**

  CHECK INDEX is a utility to ensure that indexes are consistent with the data they are pointing to. This utility does not repair any damaged objects; rather, it reports any inconsistencies found.

NAME(*index,..*)
This parameter is used to specify one or more indexes belonging to tables in the same table space.

index is the name of the index.

TABLESPACE *dbname.tsname*
This parameter specifies the name of the table space for which indexes are checked.

dbname is the database name. The default is DSNDB04.

tsname is the name of the table space.

WORKDDN (SYSUT1 or *ddname*)
This parameter specifies the name for a DD statement for a temporary work file.

ddname is the DD name; the default is SYSUT1.

SORTDEVT *device-type*
This parameter specifies the device type for temporary datasets.

device-type is the name of the device type.

SORTNUM *number*
This parameter specifies the number of temporary datasets to be dynamically allocated.

number is the number of datasets.

- **Authorization**

Action	Authority
Use the CHECK utility	SYSADM
	STATS
	DBADM
	DBMAINT
	DBCTRL

- **Usage**
The CHECK utility can be used from DB2I, JCL batch, or CLIST.

◻ COPY—Check the index of a database

● General format
```
COPY <TABLESPACE [database].tablespace>
        <DEVT device-type>
    [DSNUM <ALL or number>]
      [COPYDDN <SYSCOPY or ddname>]
      [FULL <YES or  NO>]
      [SHRLEVEL<REFERENCE or CHANGE>]
```

● Description
The COPY utility creates an image copy of a table space or a dataset within a table space. The copy is done in two ways: full image or incremental image. A full-image copy is a page-for-page copy of a dataset; whereas an incremental image copy consists of pages changed since the COPY utility was last run. This process does not copy the indexes.

TABLESPACE *database.tablespace*
This parameter specifies the table space to be copied.

database is the name of the database. The default is DSNDB04.

tablespace is the name of the table space to be copied.

DEVT *device-type*
This parameter specifies the device type for the dataset.

device-type is the name of the device type.

DSNUM <ALL or *number*>
This parameter specifies the partition or dataset to be copied.

ALL means copy all the pages of the table space. ALL is the default.

number is the number of the partition or dataset to be copied.

COPYDDN <SYSCOPY or *ddname*>
This parameter specifies the name of the DD statement for the dataset where the output of the image copy should go.

ddname is the DD name.

SYSCOPY is the default output name.

FULL <<u>YES</u> or NO>
This parameter specifies full image or incremental image copy.

YES means full-image copy.

NO means incremental-image copy.

SHRLEVEL<<u>REFERENCE</u> or CHANGE>
This parameter controls whether or not other programs can access a table space while COPY utility is in progress.

REFERENCE means other programs can only read the table space; it is the default.

CHANGE allows other programs to read or write to the table space. This will happens only if LOCKRULE in the SYSIBM.SYSTABLESPACE catalog table is either ANY or PAGE.

- **Authorization**

Action	Authority	Privilege
Use COPY utility	SYSADM DBCTRL DBMAINT	IMAGCOPY

- **Usage**
The COPY utility can be used from DB2I, JCL batch, or CLIST.

○ **LOAD—Load data into DB2 tables**

- **General format**
```
LOAD [DATA]
    [INDDN <SYSREC or ddname>]
    [REPLACE]
    [RESUME <NO [REPLACE] or YES>]
    [WORKDDN <SYSUT1 or ddname>]
    [FORMAT <UNLOAD or SQL/DS>]
    [DISCARDDN <SYSDISC or ddname>]
    [DISCARDS disc-num]
    [SORTDEVT device-type]
    [SORTNUM number]
```

- **Description**

The LOAD utility adds data into one or more DB2 tables. It can also be used to replace data. Loading data with this utility is more efficient than inserting data with an application program.

DATA
This is an optional parameter for clarity only.

INDDN <SYSREC or *ddname*>
This parameter specifies the DD name which is used in the DD statement and points to an input dataset.

ddname is the name of the data definition used in the DD statement. The default is SYSREC.

RESUME
This parameter specifies whether the table is empty or has data.

NO means an empty table space.

YES means a used table space.

REPLACE
This parameter means to replace all table space and indexes.

WORKDDN <SYSUT1 or *ddname*>
This parameter specifies the DD name of the DD statement for a temporary work file.

ddname is the DD name; the default is SYSUT1.

FORMAT <UNLOAD or SQL/DS>
This parameter specifies the format of the input record.

UNLOAD means the input record format is compatible with the DB2 unload format.

SQL/DS means the input record format is compatible with the SQL/DS unload format.

DISCARDDN <SYSDISC or *ddname*>
This parameter specifies the DD name of the DD statement for the

discard dataset.

ddname is the DD name; the default is SYSDISC.

DISCARDS *disc-num*
This parameter specifies the maximum number of records to write
to the discard dataset.

disc-num must be in the range 0 to 2,147,483,647; the default
value is 0.

SORTDEVT *device-type*
This parameter specifies the device type for temporary datasets.

device-type is the name of the device type.

SORTNUM *number*
This parameter specifies the number of temporary datasets to be
dynamically allocated.

number is the number of datasets.

* **Authorization**

Action	Authority	Privilege
Use the LOAD utility	SYSADM	LOAD
	DBCTRL	
	DBMAINT	

* **Usage**
The LOAD utility can be used from DB2I, JCL batch, or CLIST.

■ **MERGECOPY—Merge incremental image copies**

* **General format**
```
MERGECOPY <TABLESPACE [database].tablespace>
        <DEVT device-type>
    [WORKDDN <SYSUT1 or ddname>]
    [DSNUM <ALL or number>]
    [NEWCOPY <NO or YES>]
    [COPYDDN <SYSCOPY or ddname>]
```

- **Description**
The MERGECOPY utility consolidates several incremental-image copies. It will either merge the incremental copies with the last full-image copy or create a new full-image copy.

TABLESPACE *database.tablespace*
This parameter specifies the table space to be copied.

database is the name of the database. The default is DSNDB04.

tablespace is the name of the table space to be copied.

DEVT *device-type*
This parameter specifies the device type for the dataset.

device-type is the name of the device type.

WORKDDN <SYSUT1 or *ddname*>
This parameter specifies the name of the DD statement for a temporary work file.

ddname is the DD name; the default is SYSUT1.

DSNUM <ALL or *number*>
This parameter specifies the partition or dataset to be merged.

ALL means merge all the pages of the table space. ALL is the default.

number is the number of the partition or dataset to be merged.

NEWCOPY <NO or YES>
This parameter specifies whether to consolidate with a full-image copy or not.

NO means to consolidate incremental-image copies into one incremental-image copy.

YES means to consolidate incremental-image copies into a full-image copy.

COPYDDN <SYSCOPY or *ddname*>
This parameter specifies the name of the DD statement for the dataset where the output of the image copy should go.

ddname is the DD name; the default is SYSCOPY.

- **Authorization**

Action	Authority	Privilege
Use the MERGECOPY utility	SYSADM	
	DBCTRL	IMAGCOPY
	DBMAINT	

- **Usage**
The MERGECOPY utility can be used from DB2I, JCL batch, or CLIST.

◼ **MODIFY—Delete information from the SYSIBM.SYSCOPY catalog table for unwanted data**

- **General format**
```
MODIFY < RECOVER  TABLESPACE [database].tablespace >
          [DSNUM <ALL or  number>]
          <DELETE AGE n-day or DATE date >
```

- **Description**
Information related to image copies is kept in SYSIBM.SYSCOPY by DB2 and used during recovery. The MODIFY utility removes any information related to image copies that are not needed.

TABLESPACE *database.tablespace*
This parameter specifies the table space to be modified.

database is the name of the database. The default is DSNDB04.

tablespace is the name of the table space to be modified.

DSNUM <ALL or *number*>
This parameter specifies the partition or dataset to be modified.

ALL means modify all the pages of the table space. ALL is the default.

number is the number of the partition or dataset to be modified.

DELETE AGE *n-day* or DATE *date*
This specifies deletion of records according to age or date.

AGE means to delete all records older than *n-day* days.

DATE means to delete all records before the date specified by *date*. The date format is *yymmdd*.

- **Authorization**

Action	Authority	Privilege
Use the MODIFY utility	SYSADM	
	DBCTRL	IMAGCOPY
	DBMAINT	

- **Usage**
The MODIFY utility can be used from DB2I, JCL batch, or CLIST.

◻ **RECOVER—Recover DB2 data**

- **General format**
Format 1:

```
RECOVER <TABLESPACE database.tablespace>
    [DSNUM <ALL or number>]
    [PAGE page-num [CONTINUE]]
    [ERROR RANGE]
      [TORBA X'hex-num']
    [TOCOPY dsname]
```

Format 2:

```
RECOVER  <INDEX index-name >
```

- **Description**
The RECOVER utility restores data from the image copies or DB2 log. The recovery is to one of the following: the current state, an image copy, or a specific log RBA.

TABLESPACE *database.tablespace*
This parameter specifies the table space to be recovered.

database is the name of the database. The default is DSNDB04.

tablespace is the name of the table space to be recovered.

DSNUM <<u>ALL</u> or *number*>
This parameter specifies the partition or dataset to be recovered.

ALL means recover all the pages of the table space. ALL is the default.

number is the number of the partition or dataset to be recovered.

PAGE *page-num* or CONTINUE
This parameter specifies a specific page to be recovered.

page-num is the hexadecimal or decimal number of the page.

CONTINUE means to continue the recovery process.

ERROR RANGE
This parameter specifies recovery of all pages that are within the range of reported errors.

TORBA X'*hex-num*'
This parameter specifies the relative byte address (RBA).

hex-num is the hexadecimal number of an RBA.

TOCOPY *dsname*
This parameter specifies at what dataset to stop recovery.

dsname is the name of a dataset.

INDEX *index-name*
This parameter is used to recover an index only.

index-name is the name of the index to recover.

- **Authorization**

Action	Authority	Privilege
Use the RECOVER utility	SYSADM	
	DBCTRL	RECOVERDB
	DBMAINT	

- **Usage**

    The RECOVER utility can be used from DB2I, JCL batch, or CLIST.

◘ **REORG—Reorganize table space and indexes**

- **General format**

```
REORG  <TABLESPACE[dbname].tsname or INDEX index-name>
    [PART part-num]
    [LOG <YES or NO]
    [UNLDDN <SYSREC or ddname>]
    [WORKDDN <SYSUT1 or ddname>]
    [SORTDEVT device-type]
    [SORTNUM number]
    [UNLOAD <CONTINUE or  PAUSE or ONLY>]
```

- **Description**

    The REORG utility loads and unloads to reorganize a tablespace and its indexes. It is used to improve performance and efficiency in clustering.

    TABLESPACE *dbname.tsname*
    This parameter specifies the name of the table space to be reorganized.

    dbname is the database name. It may not be DSNDB03, DSNDB06, or DSNNDB07. The default is DSNDB04.

    tsname is the name of the table space.

    INDEX *index-name*
    This parameter is used to specify an index to be reorganized.

    index-name is the name of the index.

    PART *part-num*

This parameter specifies the partition to be reorganized.

part-num is the number for the partition.

LOG <YES or NO>
This parameter specifies whether to log information during reorganization.

YES means to log information.

NO means not to log information.

UNLDDN <SYSUT1 or *ddname*>
This parameter specifies the DD name which is used in the DD statement and points to an unload dataset.

ddname is the name of the data definition used in the DD statement. The default is SYSREC.

WORKDDN <SYSUT1 or *ddname*>
This parameter specifies the name for the DD statement for a temporary work file.

ddname is the DD name; the default is SYSUT1.

SORTDEVT *device-type*
This parameter specifies the device type for temporary datasets.

device-type is the name of the device type.

SORTNUM *number*
This parameter specifies the number of temporary datasets to be dynamically allocated.

number is the number of datasets.

UNLOAD <CONTINUE or PAUSE or ONLY>
This parameter specifies whether to continue or to end processing after unloading is completed.

CONTINUE means to continue processing.

PAUSE means to end processing.

ONLY means to end processing and remove the status of the utility.

- **Authorization**

Action	Authority	Privilege
Use the REORG utility	SYSADM	REORG
	DBADM	
	DBMAINT	
	DBCTRL	

- **Usage**
The REORG utility can be used from DB2I, JCL batch, or CLIST.

◘ REPAIR—Repair DB2 data

- **General format**
```
REPAIR [OBJECT] [LOG <YES or NO>]
       <SET TABLESPACE [database].tablespace>
   [DSNUM number]
   [NOCOPYPEND]
```

- **Description**
The REPAIR utility changes data in table spaces, indexes, and system catalogs. This utility should be used with great care, usually by a person who has extensive knowledge of DB2.

OBJECT is an optional keyword used for clarity only.

LOG <YES or NO>
This parameter specifies whether to log information during the repair.

YES means to log information.

NO means not to log information.

TABLESPACE *database.tablespace*
This parameter specifies the table space to be repaired.

database is the name of the database. The default is DSNDB04.

tablespace is the name of the table space to be repaired.

DSNUM *number*
This parameter specifies the dataset to be repaired.

number is the number for the dataset.

NOCOPYPEND
This parameter resets the restriction for copy pending.

- **Authorization**

Action	Authority	Privilege
Use the REPAIR utility	SYSADM DBCTRL DBMAINT	REPAIR

- **Usage**
  The REPAIR utility can be used from DB2I, JCL batch, or CLIST.

◘ **RUNSTATS—Collect data to optimize access to DB2 tables**

- **General format**
Format 1:

```
RUNSTATS  <TABLESPACE [database].tablespace>
    [INDEX (ALL or index-name,...)]
    [SHRLEVEL <REFERENCE or CHANGE>]
```

Format 2:

```
RUNSTATS  <INDEX index-name,...>
    [SHRLEVEL <REFERENCE or CHANGE>]
```

- **Description**
  The RUNSTATS utility is used to gather information about table spaces and indexes, and to optimize the access to DB2 data. When this utility is run, the DB2 catalog is updated with the information, and during the bind process, it is used to build the access path. It is also used to determine whether to reorganize the table spaces and indexes.

TABLESPACE *database.tablespace*
This parameter specifies the table space for which information is to be collected.

database is the name of the database. The default is DSNDB04.

tablespace is the name of the table space.

INDEX (<u>ALL</u> or *index-name*)
This parameter specifies one or more indexes for which information is to be collected.

ALL means all table spaces. ALL is the default and is used only with TABLESPACE.

index-name is the name of an index.

SHRLEVEL <<u>REFERENCE</u> or CHANGE>
This parameter is used to specify how to allow other programs to access the table space while the RUNSTATS utility is running.

REFERENCE means read-only access.

CHANGE means read/write access.

- **Authorization**

Action	Authority	Privilege
Use the RUNSTATS utility	SYSADM	
	DBCTRL	STATS
	DBMAINT	

- **Usage**
The RUNSTATS utility can be used from DB2I, JCL batch, or CLIST.

◘ **STOSPACE—Tell storage space**

- **General format**
```
STOSPACE STOGROUP (* or group-name,...)
```

- **Description**
  The STOSPACE utility is used to write to a DB2 catalog the storage to allocate for table spaces and indexes belonging to a group.

  STOGROUP(* or *group-name*,...)
  This parameter is used to specify one or more groups for which storage information is to be written to the DB2 catalog.

  * means all storage groups.

  group-name is the name of one storage group.

- **Authorization**

Action	Authority	Privilege
Use the STOSPACE utility	SYSADM	STOSPACE

- **Usage**
  The STOSPACE utility can be used from DB2I, JCL batch, or CLIST.

5.3   SAMPLE JCL TO EXECUTE A DB2 COMMAND

A DB2 command is issued in batch mode by executing a DB2 program called IKJEFT01. The sample JCL shown below issues the RUN command in job step STEP1. The STEPLIB DD statement is used to enter the library from which this program is loaded and executed. Check with the system programmer to receive the library for your installation.

The RUN command is used to execute a program that has been precompiled, compiled, and link-edited, and has undergone the binding process. The program name, application plan, and load library are specified after the SYSTIN DD * statement. The PROGRAM parameter specifies execution of program SAABB020. The PLAN parameter is used to enter the application plan SAABBP20 for the program SAABB020. The LIB parameter specifies the library CANT.DB2.TBF0.PGMLOAD from which SAABB020 is loaded and executed.

```
//C840BGF2  JOB (acct-info),'DB2 COMMAND',
//              NOTIFY=C840BGF,MSGLEVEL=(2,0),
//              CLASS=X,MSGCLASS=X,REGION=6M
//*
//* THIS STEP ISSUES THE DB2 RUN COMMAND
//*
//STEP1           EXEC PGM=IKJEFT01
//STEPLIB         DD DISP=SHR,DSN=D2CS.DSNLOAD
//               DD DISP=SHR,DSN=D2CS.DSNEXIT
//SYSUDUMP        DD SYSOUT=*
//SYSPRINT        DD SYSOUT=*
//SYSTSPRT        DD SYSOUT=*
//SYSOUT          DD SYSOUT=*
//FILEO           DD SYSOUT=*
//SYSTSIN         DD *
DSN SYSTEM(D2CS)
RUN PROGRAM(SAABB020) +
    LIB   ('CANT.DB2.TBF0.PGMLOAD') +
    PLAN (SAABBP20)
  END
/*
```

5.4   SAMPLE JCL TO EXECUTE A DB2 UTILITY

A DB2 utility program is executed in batch mode by running a DB2 program called DSNUTILB. The sample JCL shown below executes the utility REPAIR in job step STEP1. The STEPLIB DD statement is used to enter the library from which this program is loaded and executed. Check with the system programmer to receive the library for your installation. The parameters for this utility are entered after the SYSIN DD * statement.

The REPAIR utility changes data in table spaces, indexes, and system catalogs. LOG NO specifies not to log information during repair. The TABLESPACE parameter specifies the database DCTSSALB and table space SCWSOB00 to be repaired. The NOCOPYPEND parameter resets the restriction for copy pending.

```
//C840BGF2  JOB (0999-001,008),'DB2-UTIL',
//              NOTIFY=C840BGF,MSGLEVEL=(2,0),
//              CLASS=X,MSGCLASS=X,REGION=6M
//*-------------------------------------------------
//*  THIS JOB STEP IS TO REPAIR A TABLESPACE
/*    TO NOCOPYPEND STATUS.
//*-------------------------------------------------
//REPAIRS   EXEC PGM=DSNUTILB,PARM='D2CS,C840BGF,',
//              REGION=4M
//STEPLIB         DD DISP=SHR,DSN=D2CS.DSNLOAD
//               DD DISP=SHR,DSN=D2CS.DSNEXIT
//SYSPRINT DD   SYSOUT=*
//SYSUDUMP DD   SYSOUT=*
```

```
//UTPRINT   DD   SYSOUT=*
//SORTWK01 DD   UNIT=VIO,SPACE=(CYL,(10,10),RLSE)
//SORTWK02 DD   UNIT=VIO,SPACE=(CYL,(10,10),RLSE)
//SORTWK03 DD   UNIT=VIO,SPACE=(CYL,(10,10),RLSE)
//SORTWK04 DD   UNIT=VIO,SPACE=(CYL,(10,10),RLSE)
//SYSUT1    DD   UNIT=VIO,SPACE=(CYL,(10,10),RLSE)
//SORTOUT   DD   UNIT=VIO,SPACE=(CYL,(10,10),RLSE)
//SYSIN     DD   *
REPAIR LOG NO SET
TABLESPACE DCTSSALB.SCWSOB00
NOCOPYPEND
/*
```

IMS

This chapter is a reference guide for programmers using IMS DB/DC and COBOL. It contains DL/I calls, return codes, and sample programs and JCLs. For each call, this chapter provides the syntax, a description of the function, and the parameters.

The subjects covered here can be grouped into these categories:

- Program entry and return conventions
- DL/I DB/DC calls
- DL/I system service calls
- DL/I status codes
- Sample COBOL program with DL/I calls
- Sample JCLs to compile, link-edit, and, run IMS COBOL program

Notational Convention: In the general format of the DL/I calls used in this chapter, there are a few symbols that are not part of the syntax; therefore they must not be included when you code your program. These symbols and their meanings are:

Symbol	Meaning
[]	The option enclosed by the brackets ([]) is not required but can be included.
<>	Only one of the alternatives enclosed by the angle brackets (<>) must be chosen.

or	The alternatives enclosed by the angle brackets (<>) are separated by "or."
____	The underlined word is the default value.
...	The horizontal or vertical ellipsis means that the preceding can be coded more than once.
Uppercase characters	All keywords of the command are written in uppercase characters; they must be coded as shown.
Lowercase characters	All strings in lowercase characters and italic are variables that can be changed to any other strings to suit your programming style. In your code they represent values that you supply to commands.

6.1 ENTRY AND RETURN CONVENTIONS

A program that uses DL/I functions must be coded with the ENTRY statement as the first statement in the PROCEDURE DIVISION. The program must also end with a GOBACK statement. The program is invoked by a DL/I batch initialization module, and after it is loaded, control is passed to it through an entry point called DLITCBL. DL/I also passes the address of each PCB (program communication block) defined in your COBOL program's PSB (program specification block). The definition is accomplished by a process called PSBGEN, which is done by a database administrator.

The general format of the entry and return points of a COBOL program is

```
LINKAGE SECTION.
01   pcb-name1
01   pcb-name2

PROCEDURE DIVISION.

    ENTRY 'DLITCBL' USING pcb-name1 [pcb-name2...].
    .
    .
    .
    GOBACK
```

The ENTRY statement specifies the entry point DLITCBL in your program.

The USING clause lists the names of one or more of the PCB

masks coded in the LINKAGE SECTION.

pcb-name1 and *pcb-name2* are PCB names. They should appear in the same order as in your program's PSBGEN.

The GOBACK statement returns control to DL/I so that it can deallocate resources and close datasets. If you use STOP RUN instead, control will return directly to the operating system, which you do not want to have happen without all the terminating functions having been performed.

6.2 DL/I DB Calls

In COBOL all IMS database calls are made using module CBLTDLI (COBOL to DLI), and in all cases the parameters passed are the same. The parameters *DLI-function*, *PCB-mask*, and *io-area* are required for each call; however *saa* is mandatory for function ISRT and optional for others.

The general format is

```
CALL 'CBLTDLI' USING DLI-function,
          PCB-mask,
          io-area,
          [saa,...].
```

DLI-function specifies one of the database functions. The functions are

GU	Get unique
GHU	Get hold unique
GN	Get next
GHN	Get hold next
GNP	Get next within parent
GHNP	Get hold next within parent
DLET	Delete
REPL	Replace
ISRT	Insert
FLD	Field
POS	Position

The following is a COBOL structure definition that assigns each DLI function code to a data name. It is a model that can be used to define a COPY member.

```
01    DLI-FUNCTIONS.
      05 DLI-GU          PIC (4)   VALUE 'GU  '.
      05 DLI-GHU         PIC (4)   VALUE 'GHU '.
      05 DLI-GN          PIC (4)   VALUE 'GN  '.
      05 DLI-GHN         PIC (4)   VALUE 'GHN '.
      05 DLI-GNP         PIC (4)   VALUE 'GNP '.
      05 DLI-GHNP        PIC (4)   VALUE 'GHNP'.
      05 DLI-ISRT        PIC (4)   VALUE 'ISRT'.
      05 DLI-DLET        PIC (4)   VALUE 'DLET'.
      05 DLI-REPL        PIC (4)   VALUE 'REPL'.
      05 DLI-CHKP        PIC (4)   VALUE 'CHKP'.
      05 DLI-XRST        PIC (4)   VALUE 'XRST'.
      05 DLI-PCB         PIC (4)   VALUE 'PCB '.
      05 DLI-POS         PIC (4)   VALUE 'POS '.
```

PCB-mask is the second parameter passed to DL/I and is the name of a PCB mask that is defined in the LINKAGE SECTION of the calling program. As mentioned earlier, the ENTRY statement establishes the correspondences between the PCB masks defined in the LINKAGE SECTION and the PCBs within the PSB of a program. Coding a PCB mask in a DL/I call involves specifying a database for which an operation is requested. In addition to identifying a database, a PCB mask is an area where DL/I stores status code to be used by calling programs. More information about *PCB-mask* is provided later in this chapter.

io-area is the third parameter passed to DL/I. It is the name of a data area defined in a program that is used to communicate data between the program and DL/I. For an insert or update operation, the data are written from this working storage area; similarly, retrieved data are placed in this area. More information about *io-area* is provided later in this chapter.

saa is the segment search argument, and it is optional. It specifies the segment occurrence upon which operations are performed. One or more *saa* can be entered in a DL/I call. There are two types of *saa*: qualified and unqualified. More information about *saa* is provided later in this chapter.

6.3 DB PCB Masks

As mentioned earlier, DL/I communicates with a program via a storage area called PCB (program communication block). This area must be defined in the LINKAGE SECTION, not the WORKING STORAGE SECTION of your program according to the format shown in Fig. 6.1. The name of this storage area is also specified in the ENTRY statement that is placed as the first statement in the PROCEDURE DIVISION. This area has two main purposes. First, it is used by your program to tell DL/I the name of a database to access. Second, DL/I places in it information related to the processing requested by the program.

Field Name	Length
Database name	8
Segment level number	2
Status code	2
Processing options	4
Reserved for DL/I	4
Segment name	8
Length of key feedback area	4
Number of sensitive segments	4
Key feedback area	Variable

Fig. 6.1 DB PCB mask format.

The following is the explanation of each field defined in the PCB mask.

Database name
    This is the name of the database. The DBA specifies the database name on the DBDNAME parameter of the PCB statement during the PSBGEN process.

Segment level number
    This field is for the current segment level in the database. After DL/I successfully processes a request, it places the current segment level in the range 01 to 15 in this field.

Status code
    DL/I places a 2-byte code after processing each request from your program. If the operation is successful, then spaces are moved into

this area. If a call results in any abnormal results or DL/I could not successfully complete it, then a 2-byte nonblank code is placed in this field. The list of status codes and an explanation of each is given later in this chapter. This code is used in a program to take appropriate action during successful or abnormal operation of DL/I.

Processing options
This field shows the processing options that a program is allowed to use. The value for this field is derived during the PSBGEN of your program.

Reserved for DL/I
This field is reserved for DL/I.

Segment name
This field is the segment name feedback area. DL/I places the name of the segment just processed in this area after each call. This field can be used to determine which part of the database is being accessed during unqualified calls.

Length of key feedback area
This binary field is used by DL/I. Its value is the length of the concatenated key of the lowest-level segment.

Number of sensitive segments
This binary field is determined by PSBGEN and is used by DL/I to report the number of SENSEG macros.

Key feedback area
This is a variable-length field; its length varies from one PCB to another. DL/I places in this field the key of the lowest-level segment.

The following is a model of a PCB mask that is defined in the LINKAGE SECTION of a program.

```
01    DB-PCB.
      05    DBD-NAME              PIC X(08).
      05    SEGMENT-LEVEL         PIC X(02).
      05    STATUS-CODE           PIC X(02).
      05    PROCESS-OPTION        PIC X(04).
      05    RESERVE-AREA          PIC S9(5) COMP.
```

```
05   SEGMENT-NAME              PIC X(08).
05   KEY-LENGTH                PIC S9(5) COMP.
05   NUMB-SENSIT-SEGMENT       PIC S9(5) COMP.
05   KEY-FEEDBACK-AREA         PIC X(11).
```

6.4 I/O AREA

As mentioned earlier, the I/O area within your program is used to send or receive data from the database using DL/I calls. This area is defined in the WORKING-STORAGE SECTION of the program. The following is an example of an I/O area called INPUT-OUTPUT-AREA, defined in the WORKING-STORAGE SECTION of this program fragment.

```
IDENTIFICATION DIVISION.
.
.
.
DATA DIVISION.
WORKING-STORAGE SECTION.
01   INPUT-OUTPUT-AREA.
     10 KEY-AREA          PIC X(10) VALUE SPACES.
     10 FIELD-AREA        PIC X(99) VALUE SPACES.
```

This storage area can be used, depending on your requirements, in DL/I calls.

6.5 SEGMENT SEARCH ARGUMENTS (SSAS)

The segment search argument (SAA) is an optional fourth element of a DL/I call. One or many SAAs can be part of a DL/I call. When specified, the SAA tells DL/I the segment occurrence upon which an operation is performed. There are two types of SAA: unqualified and qualified. To extend the function of a DL/I call, a qualified SAA can also include a command code.

6.5.1 Unqualified SSA

An unqualified SSA is a data storage area of 9 bytes. The format

is

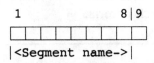

The first 8 bytes contain the segment name for which processing is requested, and the nineth byte must have a blank character. The name of the segment you specify must be defined in the DBD that the program is using. Fig. 6.2 shows an example of a COBOL storage definition for an unqualified SSA.

```
WORKING-STORAGE SECTION.
 .
 .
 .
01  UNQUALIFIED-SSA.
    10  U-SSA-SEGNAME-NAME PIC X(8) VALUE '........'.
    10  FILLER             PIC X    VALUE SPACE.
```

Fig. 6.2 COBOL storage definition for an Unqualified SSA.

6.5.2 Qualified SSA

A qualified SSA is more complicated than an unqualified call in the sense that you can specify the occurrence of a particular segment type. A qualified SAA is a storage area that has four fields: segment name, field name, relational operator, and search value. Fig. 6.3 shows the format for a qualified SAA.

segment-name is the segment name for which processing is requested. The name of the segment you specify must be defined in the DBD that the program is using.

field-name is the name of a field in a segment used during an operation.

relational-operator is a 2-byte operator in positions 18 and 19. This operator tells DL/I the kind of checking to be done on the field of a segment. Fig. 6.4 gives a list of operators which can be specified by either letters or symbols.

search-value is the value for the field name. The length of this field varies depending on the search criteria.

```
WORKING-STORAGE SECTION.
  .
  .
  .
01  UNQUALIFIED-SSA.
    10 U-SSA-SEGNAME-NAME PIC X(8)  VALUE '........'.
    10 FILLER             PIC X     VALUE SPACE.
```

segment-name(field-name
*   relational-operator*
*   search-value)*

COBOL storage area definition

```
WORKING-STORAGE SECTION.
  .
  .
  .
01  QUALIFIED-SSA.
    10 Q-SSA-SEGNAME-NAME PIC X(8) VALUE 'INVENSEG'.
    10 FILLER             PIC X VALUE '('.
    10 KEY-NAME           PIC X(8) VALUE 'INVENNUM'.
    10 OPERATOR           PIC X(2) VALUE ' ='.
    10 KEY-VALUE          PIC X(n) VALUE 'vv...v'.
    10 FILLER             PIC X VALUE ')'.
```

Fig. 6.3 Qualified SAA format.

Letters	Symbol	Description
EQ	=blank or blank=	Equal to
GE	>= or =>	Greater than or equal to
LE	<= or =<	Less than or equal to
GT	>blank or blank>	Greater than
LT	<blank or blank<	Less than
NE	¬= or =¬	Not equal to

Fig. 6.4 Relational operators for a qualified SAA.

Using SSA with command codes

The formats for unqualified and qualified SAAs can be expanded to add command codes. Command codes extend the functions of DL/I calls. Fig. 6.5 shows the format. Fig. 6.6 lists all the command codes that can be used with SAAs. After the segment name is a command code indicator (*), and following it is a 1-character command code.

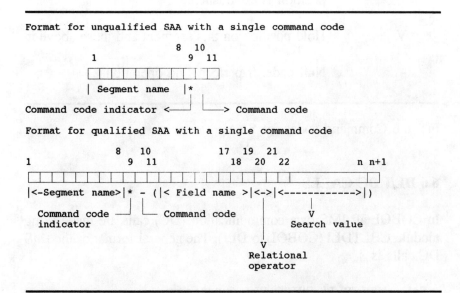

Fig. 6.5 Formats for SSAs with a single command code.

Command code	Description
C	Use the complete concatenated key to search a segment.
D	Path call.
F	Get the first occurrence of the segment under its parent.
L	Get the last occurrence of the segment under its parent.
N	Specify segments that are not to be replaced when segments are replaced after a get hold call.
P	Set parentage at this level.
Q	Enqueue a segment so that no one else can change it until you have finished processing it.
U	Limit the search for this segment on which position is established.
V	Hold position on this segment and those above it.
-	Null code. It performs no operation.

Fig. 6.6 Command codes for SAA.

6.6 DL/I DC CALLS

In COBOL all IMS data communication (DC) calls are made using module CBLTDLI (COBOL to DLI). The general format of the IMS DC calls is

```
CALL 'CBLTDLI' USING DLI-function,
          io-PCB or alternate-PCB,
          io-area,
          [,mod-name][,destination-name].
```

The parameters *DLI-function, io-PCB* or *alternate-PCB*, and *io-area* are required for each call; however, *mod-name* and *destination-name* are optional. In all cases the parameters passed to DL/I are not the same. Fig. 6.10 shows a list of functions and required parameters.

DLI-function is a function name placed in a 4-byte area. It can be one of the following values:

AUTH	Verify authorization
GU	Receive first segment of a message
GN	Receive next segment of a message
ISRT	Send a message
CHNG	Change destination
PURG	Purge a message
CMD	Enter an IMS command
GCMD	Receive a command

The following is a COBOL structure definition that assigns each DLI function code to a data area name. This model can be used to define a COPY member.

```
01    DLI-FUNCTIONS.
    *
    05 DLI-AUTH           PIC (4)   VALUE 'AUTH'.
    05 DLI-GU             PIC (4)   VALUE 'GU  '.
    05 DLI-GN             PIC (4)   VALUE 'GN  '.
    05 DLI-ISRT           PIX (4)   VALUE 'ISRT'.
    05 DLI-CHNG           PIX (4)   VALUE 'CHNG'.
    05 DLI-PURG           PIX (4)   VALUE 'PURG'.
    05 DLI-CMD            PIX (4)   VALUE 'CMD '.
    05 DLI-GCMD           PIX (4)   VALUE 'GCMD'.
```

io-PCB is a storage area used for communication between DL/I and a program. This area must be defined in the LINKAGE SECTION, not the WORKING STORAGE SECTION, of your program using the format shown in Fig. 6.7. The name of this storage area is also specified in the ENTRY statement that is placed as the first statement in the PROCEDURE DIVISION. After a call is completed, DL/I returns information regarding the results in this control block.

Field name	Length in bytes
Logical terminal name	8
Reserved	2
Status code	2
Current date	4
Current time	4
Sequence number	4
Descriptor name	8
User ID	8

Fig. 6.7 IO PCB mask format.

The following is the explanation of each field defined in the I/O PCB mask.

Logical terminal name
  When a program receives a message, DL/I places the name of the logical terminal in this 8-byte data area. And when a program sends a message, this area is the destination terminal to which data are transmitted.

Reserved
  This 2-byte data area is reserved for DL/I.

Status code
  DL/I places a 2-byte code after processing each request from your program. If the operation is successful, then spaces are moved into this area. If a call results in any abnormal results or DL/I could not successfully complete it, then a 2-byte nonblank code is placed in this field.

Current date
  This 4-byte data area holds the current Julian date in packed decimal and right-aligned. The format is YYDDD.

Current time
  This 4-byte data area holds the current time in packed decimal.

The format is HHMMSST.

Sequence number
DL/I assigns a sequence number to an input message; it is placed in this 4-byte field.

Descriptor name
DL/I stores the name of the message output descriptor (MOD) in this data area.

User ID
This field contains one of the following:

- Blanks if sign-on is not active
- User ID from the source terminal
- LTERM name of the source terminal
- PSBNAME of the source BMP

alternate-PCB is a data storage area in which a program can supply the destination where a message is to be sent. There are three fields in *alternate-PCB*. Fig. 6.8 lists the name and size of each field.

Field name	Length in bytes
Destination name	8
Reserved	2
Status code	2

Fig. 6.8 Alternate PCB mask format.

The following is the explanation of each field defined in the alternate PCB mask.

Destination name
This field holds the name of the logical terminal or the transaction code when a program is to send a message.

Reserved
   This 2-byte data area is reserved for DL/I.

Status code
   DL/I places a 2-byte code after processing each request from your
   program.

io-area is the name of a data area defined in a program that is used
to communicate data between the program and DL/I. It should be
large enough to hold the largest segment passed between the
program and DL/I. The I/O area has two formats: input and output.
Fig. 6.9 lists the name and size of each field.

Format for input I/O area

Field name	Length in bytes
LL	2
ZZ	2
TRANSCODE	1 to 8
TEXT	Variable

Format for output I/O area

Field name	Length in bytes
LL	2
Z1	1
Z2	1
TEXT	Variable

Fig. 6.9 I/O area format.

The following is the explanation of each field defined in the I/O area
format.

   LL
      This field contains the total length of the message in binary.

ZZ
> This 2-byte data area is reserved for DL/I.

TRANSCODE
> This data area contains the translation code which can be up to 8 bytes long.

TEXT
> This data area contains the message segment.

Z1
> This 1-byte data area is reserved for DL/I.

Z2
> This 1-byte data area contains device-dependent codes such as ring an alarm bell, connect a switch, and so on.

mod-name is the name of the MOD to which a program sends an output message.

destination-name is an 8-byte data area that contains the name of the logical terminal.

DC functions	Parameters
Verify authorization	*DLI-function, io-PCB, io-area*
Receive first segment	*DLI-function, io-PCB, io-area*
Receive next segment	*DLI-function, io-PCB, io-area*
Send a message	*DLI-function, io-PCB* or *alternate-PCB, io-area* [*,mod-name*]
Change destination	*DLI-function, alternate-PCB, destination-name*
Purge a message	*DLI-function, io-PCB* or *alternate-PCB* [*,io-area ,mod-name*]
Enter an IMS command	*DLI-function, io-PCB, io-area*
Receive a command	*DLI-function, io-PCB, io-area*

Fig. 6.10 List of DC calls and required parameters.

6.7 SYSTEM SERVICE CALLS

This section contains system service calls which can be called in an IMS application program. For each call, the syntax is given, followed by a description of parameters and a list of processing modes, such as BMP, MPP, IFP, and batch.

◘ CHKP—Basic checkpointing

- **General format**
  ```
  CALL 'CBLTDLI' USING DLI-function,io-PCB,io-area.
  ```

- **Description**
  DLI-function is the name of a data area containing 'CHKP'. This call is valid for batch, BMP, and MPP processing.

  io-PCB is the name of a 10-byte data area and is coded in the following way:

  ```
  01   IO-PCB.
       05   FILLER                PIC X(10).
       05   STATUS-CODE           PIC X(02).
  ```

  io-area is the name of a data area containing an 8-byte checkpoint identification. This checkpoint ID is used later in case of recovery of the database.

◘ CHKP and XRST—Symbolic checkpointing and restart

- **General format**
  ```
  CALL 'CBLTDLI' USING DLI-function,io-PCB,
          io-area-len,io-area,
          1st-area-len,1st-area,
          [...,7th-area-len,7th-area]
  ```

- **Description**
  DLI-function is the name of a data area containing 'CHKP' or 'XRST'. This call is valid for batch and BMP processing.

io-PCB is the name of a 10-byte data area and is coded in the following way:

```
01 IO-PCB.
   05    FILLER                    PIC X(10).
   05    STATUS-CODE               PIC X(02).
```

io-area-len is a data area containing the length in binary of the longest segment in PSB.

io-area is the name of a data area. For symbolic CHKP, it contains an 8-byte checkpoint identification. However, for XRST this area is 12 bytes long.

1st-area-len is the name of a 4-byte data area containing in binary the length of the first area to checkpoint.

1st-area is the name of the first data area to checkpoint.

7th-area-len is the name of a 4-byte data area containing in binary the length of the seventh area to checkpoint.

7th-area is the name of the seventh data area to checkpoint.

◘ DEQ—Dequeue segment

• General format
```
CALL 'CBLTDLI' USING DLI-function,io-PCB,io-area.
```

• Description
DLI-function is the name of a data area containing 'DEQ '. This call is valid for BMP and MPP processing.

io-PCB is the name of a data area for I/O PCB.

io-area is the name of a 4-byte data area containing one of the following characters: A, B, C, D, E, F, G, H, I, or J.

GSCD—Get address of system content directory

- **General format**

```
CALL 'CBLTDLI' USING DLI-function,io-PCB,io-area.
```

- **Description**

DLI-function is the name of a data area containing 'GSCD'. This call is valid for batch processing.

io-PCB is the name of a data area for I/O PCB.

io-area is the name of an 8-byte data area. The first 4 bytes are for the address of the system contents directory, and the next 4 bytes are for the program specification table.

INIT—Get data availability status code

- **General format**

```
CALL 'CBLTDLI' USING DLI-function,io-PCB,io-area.
```

- **Description**

DLI-function is the name of a data area containing 'INIT'. This call is valid for batch, BMP, IFP, and MPP processing.

io-PCB is the name of a data area for I/O PCB.

io-area is the name of a data area containing an INIT function. The length of this area depends on the INIT function requested. Fig. 6.11 shows the name and the length of each field.

Field name	Length in bytes
LL	2
ZZ	2
INIT function	Variable

Fig. 6.11 I/O area format for INIT function.

◘ LOG—Write record to system log

● **General format**
```
CALL 'CBLTDLI' USING DLI-function,io-PCB,io-area.
```

● **Description**
DLI-function is the name of a data area containing 'LOG '. This call is valid for batch, BMP, IFP, and MPP processing.

io-PCB is the name of a data area for I/O PCB.

io-area is the name of a data area containing the record to be written to the system log. Fig. 6.12 shows the name and the length of each field.

Field name	Length in bytes
LL	2
ZZ	2
C	1
TEXT	Variable

Fig. 6.12 I/O area format for LOG function.

◘ ROLB—Rollback

● **General format**
```
CALL 'CBLTDLI' USING DLI-function,io-PCB[,io-area].
```

● **Description**
DLI-function is the name of a data area containing 'ROLB'. This call is valid for batch, BMP, IFP, and MPP processing.

io-PCB is the name of a data area for I/O PCB.

io-area is the name of the data area where IMS stores the message segment.

◘ ROLL—Roll

- **General format**
  ```
  CALL 'CBLTDLI' USING DLI-function.
  ```

- **Description**

  DLI-function is the name of a data area containing 'ROLL'. This call is valid for batch, BMP, and MPP processing.

◘ ROLS—Back out database changes

- **General format**
  ```
  CALL 'CBLTDLI' USING DLI-function,io-PCB
                  [,io-area,token].
  ```

- **Description**

  DLI-function is the name of a data area containing 'ROLS'. This call is valid for batch, BMP and MPP processing.

  io-PCB is the name of a data area for I/O PCB.

  io-area is the name of a data area which has the same format as the I/O area in the SETS call.

  token is the name of a 4-byte data area containing an identifier.

◘ SETS—Set backout points

- **General format**
  ```
  CALL 'CBLTDLI' USING DLI-function,io-PCB
                  [,io-area,token].
  ```

- **Description**

  DLI-function is the name of a data area containing 'SETS'. This call is valid for batch, BMP, IFP, and MPP processing.

  io-PCB is the name of a data area for I/O PCB.

  io-area is the name of a data area which has the same format as the I/O area in the ROLS call.

token is the name of a 4-byte data area containing an identifier.

◘ STAT—Get IMS system statistical information

• General format

```
CALL 'CBLTDLI' USING DLI-function,io-PCB,io-area,
                     stat-function.
```

• Description

DLI-function is the name of a data area containing 'STAT'. This call is valid for batch, BMP, IFP, and MPP processing.

io-PCB is the name of a data area for I/O PCB.

io-area is the name of a data area large enough to hold the requested information.

stat-function is the name of a 9-byte data area containing the type and format of the statistical information. Fig. 6.13 lists the name and size of each field.

Field name	Length in bytes
STAT-FUNCTION	4
STAT-FORMAT	1
BLANKS	4

Fig. 6.13 I/O area format for STAT function.

STAT-FUNCTION must contain a valid type of statistics and must be one of the following:

    DBAS—Buffer pool statistics for ISAM database.
    VBAS—Buffer pool statistics for VSAM database.

STAT-FORMAT must contain one of the following format codes:

    F—Complete statistics formatted

U—Complete statistics unformatted
S—Summary of statistics

BLANKS must contain 4 blank characters.

◘ SYNC—Synchronization

- **General format**
CALL 'CBLTDLI' USING *DLI-function,io-PCB.*

- **Description**
DLI-function is the name of a data area containing 'SYNC'. This call is valid for BMP processing.

io-PCB is the name of a data area for I/O PCB.

6.8 DL/I STATUS CODES

This section contains the DL/I status codes. These codes are returned after DL/I processes a call against a database.

◘ AA

- **Description**
In a DL/I call with a ISRT or CHNG function, the response alternate PCB contains a transaction code instead of a logical terminal as a destination.

- **Action**
Change the response alternate PCB so that it contains a logical terminal as a destination.

◘ AB

- **Description**
The DL/I call requires a segment I/O area as one of its parameters but this is missing.

- **Action**

  Correct the call by including the name of a data area defined as the segment I/O area as one of the parameters.

◘ AC

- **Description**

  The SAA parameter for all get calls or ISRT calls is coded with a hierarchical error for one of the following reasons:
    - The specified segment is not defined in the DB PCB.
    - The hierarchic sequence is not correctly specified.
    - A STAT call contains an invalid function.

- **Action**

  Correct the call to specify a valid STAT function or segment name.

◘ AD

- **Description**

  The function argument for the call is not coded correctly. Some of the possible reasons for this error are:

    - The DB PCB or I/O PCB is not compatible with the function argument.
    - The function parameter has an invalid value.

- **Action**

  Check the PCB address and function parameter and make sure both have correct values.

◘ AF

- **Description**

  When using the GSAM access method, the size of a variable-length record is invalid when a GN, GHN, GHU, or GU was issued.

- **Action**
  Change the logic of the program so that the correct size for the record is set.

☐ AH

- **Description**
  An invalid SAA was encountered in an ISRT call. This condition also occurs when RSA is not coded in a GU call to a GSAM database.

- **Action**
  Correct the call by coding a correct SAA or adding an RSA.

☐ AI

- **Description**
  This condition occurs when opening a database set. One of the most common causes for this error is that JCL statements related to the database are not coded properly. This error can also occur when loading an existing database or executing processes other than load on an empty database.

- **Action**
  Check JCL for correct specification of the following: DDNAMES, dataset names, DCB, BLKSIZE, LRECL, and dataset organization. Or check PCB and make sure the correct operation is required.

☐ AJ

- **Description**
  The SSA specified for a call is invalid. The segment level field of the PCB contains the level number of the segment for which the SSA is incorrect. Some of the possible reasons for this condition are

  - An invalid command code is found in an SSA.
  - A relational operator found in an SSA is incorrect.
  - A call with a DLET function contains multiple or qualified

SSA's.
- A call with a REPL function contains qualified SSAs.
- A call with an ISRT function contains a last SSA as qualified.

- **Action**
Specify the correct SSA for a call with the DLET, REPL, or ISRT function.

◘ AK

- **Description**
A field name specified for a qualified SSA is not coded correctly. The segment-level field of the PCB contains the level number of the segment for which the SSA is incorrect.

- **Action**
Check the field name and correct the SSA.

◘ AL

- **Description**
This status code occurs when a program running in batch mode issues a message call. This condition also occurs if a ROLS, ROLB, or SETS function was issued in batch mode and one of the following condition occurs:

- The system log does not reside on DASD.
- The system log is on DASD, but dynamic backout is not specified.

- **Action**
Change the program so that a message call is not issued in batch mode or make corrections to calls related to the ROLS, ROLB, or SETS function.

◘ AM

- **Description**
The function specified on a call is not compatible with one or

more of the following: segment sensitivity, program type, transaction code, or PCB processing. The segment level field of the PCB contains the level number of the segment for which the SSA is incorrect.

● **Action**
Change the function of the call or PCB so that both are compatible.

◘ **AO**

● **Description**
This status code is returned when a physical I/O error occurred while processing a request.

● **Action**
Get help from the system programmer.

◘ **AP**

● **Description**
This status code is returned for the following reasons:

● A call with the CHKP function issued a transaction-oriented BMP.
● A message call has more than 4 parameters.

● **Action**
Correct the call in the program where this error occurred.

◘ **AT**

● **Description**
The length of the I/O area specified on a call is not large enough.

● **Action**
Check the call where the error occurred or the PSB definition and make the appropriate change.

◘ AU

● Description
The length for SSAs specified in a call is greater than the maximum length allowed in the definition of PSBGEN.

● Action
Check the PSB and program and make corrections.

◘ AY

● Description
The logical terminal name found in a response alternate PCB while making a call with the ISRT function has more than one physical terminal assigned to it.

● Action
The IMS master terminal operator must make the appropriate change to assign one physical terminal to this logical terminal.

◘ AZ

● Description
A call with the function PURG or ISRT was issued in a conversational program, and it was ignored.

● Action
Change the call where this error occurred.

◘ A1

● Description
On a call with the function CHNG, a logical terminal name was specified incorrectly in the I/O area.

● Action
Change the call where this error occurred.

◘ A2

- **Description**

  On a call with the function CHNG, a PCB was specified incorrectly.

- **Action**

  Change the call where this error occurred.

◘ A3

- **Description**

  On a call with the function ISRT or PURG, a PCB was specified incorrectly.

- **Action**

  Change the call where this error occurred.

◘ A4

- **Description**

  This status code is returned because a security violation occurred. This happens when a transaction code is entered at a terminal for which it is not authorized.

- **Action**

  Check with the security administrator or system programmer to gain access to this transaction code.

◘ A5

- **Description**

  On a call with the function ISRT or PURG, a parameter list was specified incorrectly.

- **Action**

  Change the call where this error occurred.

◘ A6

- **Description**

  On a call with the function ISRT, message processing was ignored. This happened because the length of the message is longer than the value specified in SEGSIZE of the TRANSACT macro.

- **Action**

  Correct the length of the output message.

◘ A7

- **Description**

  On a call with function ISRT, message processing was ignored. This happened because the number of message segments being added was larger than the value specified in SEGNO of the TRANSACT macro.

- **Action**

  Correct the number of segments in the output message.

◘ A8

- **Description**

  A call with the function ISRT was issued to a response alternate PCB, but this call followed a call with the function ISRT to the I/O PCB. This status code is returned when the reverse is true.

- **Action**

  Change the call where this error occurred.

◘ A9

- **Description**

  A call with the function ISRT for message processing was ignored. This happened when the function ISRT was issued to a response alternate PCB, but it specified SAMETRM=YES.

- **Action**

  Change the call where this error occurred.

■ BA

- **Description**

  The call was not completed because it required access to unavailable data. All update operations done by the current call up until this error have been backed out.

- **Action**

  No action can be taken by a programmer. This status code is for information purposes only.

■ BB

- **Description**

  The call was not completed because it required access to unavailable data. All update operations done since the last commit point have been backed out.

- **Action**

  No action can be taken by a programmer. This status code is for information purposes only.

■ CA

- **Description**

  On a call with the function CMD, a command verb was invalid.

- **Action**

  Change the call where this error occurred.

■ CB

- **Description**

  On a call with the function CMD, a command from an AOI program is not allowed.

- **Action**

  Change the call where this error occurred.

◘ CC

- **Description**

  After executing a command successfully, IMS returned one or more command responses.

- **Action**

  Issue GCMD calls to retrieve the command responses.

◘ CD

- **Description**

  The program does not have the authority to execute a command listed in a call with the function CMD.

- **Action**

  Contact the security administrator to get authorization.

◘ CE

- **Description**

  IMS rescheduled a message as a result of a call with the function GU since the last CMD call.

- **Action**

  None. The status code is for information only.

◘ CF

- **Description**

  A message was scheduled before IMS started.

- **Action**

  None. The status code is for information only.

◘ CG

• Description
A message was retrieved by a call with the function GU, which was originated from an AOI user exit.

• Action
None. The status code is for information only.

◘ CH

• Description
The Automated operator program interface (AOI) encountered a system error; the current command call was not ignored.

• Action
Execute the command again.

◘ CI

• Description
This status code is returned as a result of two status codes: CE and CF.

• Action
None. The status code is for information only.

◘ CJ

• Description
This status code is returned as a result of two status codes: CE and CG.

• Action
None. The status code is for information only.

◘ CK

- **Description**
  This status code is returned as a result of two status codes: CF and CG.

- **Action**
  None. The status code is for information only.

◘ CL

- **Description**
  This status code is returned as a result of three status codes: CE, CF, and CG.

- **Action**
  None. The status code is for information only.

◘ CM

- **Description**
  An exception response occurred when executing a command issued via a CMD call.

- **Action**
  Increase the size of WKAP.

◘ CN

- **Description**
  The value in the PSBIOAZ field is not correct.

- **Action**
  Change the program to provide the minimum required value (132 bytes).

■ **DA**

● **Description**
A call with function REPL or DLET attempted to change the key field in a segment.

● **Action**
Change the program to avoid this status code.

■ **DJ**

● **Description**
A call with a "get hold" function is issued after a REPL or DLET call. The call was not executed.

● **Action**
Change the call or the SSA.

■ **DX**

● **Description**
A call with the function DLET violated the delete rule for a segment.

● **Action**
Contact the database administrator (DBA) to determine the exact delete rule.

■ **FA**

● **Description**
This status code is returned when an arithmetic overflow occurs.

● **Action**
Change the program to avoid this status code.

☐ FC

● **Description**

The type of call and the segment type are not compatible.

● **Action**

Correct the call.

☐ FD

● **Description**

A deadlock happened when attempting to use resources.

● **Action**

Restart the process from the last commit point.

☐ FE

● **Description**

A call with the function FLD received a nonblank status code in the FSA. The codes are:

A—Operation is invalid.
B—The specified length is invalid.
C—The program attempted to change the key field.
D—The verify check was not successful.
E—The hex or packed decimal field is invalid.
F—The program attemped to change a segment that does not belong to it.
G—There was an arithmetic overflow error.

● **Action**

Make a program change based on the FSA status code.

☐ FF

● **Description**

The MSDB did not contain free space when a call with the ISRT function was issued.

- **Action**
Increase free space.

◻ FG

- **Description**
This status code is returned as a result of two status codes: FE and FW.

- **Action**
Make a program change based on the FSA status code.

◻ FH

- **Description**
The DEDB area was not accessible to the program when it issued a database call or reached a commit point.

- **Action**
Consult the database administrator to access the DEDB area.

◻ FI

- **Description**
The specified I/O area address is not accessible by the program.

- **Action**
Correct the portion of the program that caused this error.

◻ FM

- **Description**
The randomizer did not return a DMAC address. The return code from the randomizer is 4.

- **Action**

The program must take the logical processing step.

◘ FN

- **Description**

The field name of the FSA is undefined in the DBD and a call with the function FLD was issued.

- **Action**

To remove the effect of the bad FLD call, issue an ROLB call and correct the FLD call.

◘ FP

- **Description**

There is an invalid hexadecimal or packed-field value in the I/O area.

- **Action**

Correct the bad data.

◘ FS

- **Description**

The buffer limit for the region has been exceeded.

- **Action**

Restart the program in a larger buffer.

◘ FT

- **Description**

The number of SAAs in a fast path database call has exceeded the limit. Fifteen SAAs is the maximum limit for a DEBD call and one SAA is the maximum limit for MSDB.

- **Action**

Reduce the number of SAAs.

◼ FV

- **Description**

One or more verify operations failed at a commit point when a batch-oriented BMP issued an FLD call.

- **Action**

Change the program.

◼ FW

- **Description**

The program has used all the buffer pool or update data in all its buffers.

- **Action**

Change the program to issue CHKP and SYNC calls more often.

◼ GA

- **Description**

During a sequential retrieval of segments when a GNP or GN call was issued, a higher level was crossed.

- **Action**

This is not an error, and the response to this code depends on the programmer.

◼ GB

- **Description**

The end of the database was reached when processing a GN call.

- **Action**
  This is not an error, and the response to this code depends on the programmer.

■ GC

- **Description**
  While processing a request, IMS attemped to cross a unit-of-work (UOW) boundary.

- **Action**
  This is not an error, and the response to this code depends on the programmer.

■ GD

- **Description**
  Position was lost during a call request, and the reason for this condition is that a segment in the path was deleted through another PCB.

- **Action**
  This is not an error, and the response to this code depends on the programmer.

■ GE

- **Description**
  A segment occurrence was not found.

- **Action**
  This is not an error, and the response to this code depends on the programmer.

■ GG

- **Description**
  This status code is returned to a program that is active with a

processing option of GON and GOT, and that issued a call with a "get" function. While processing this call, IMS found an invalid pointer because concurrent update activities were happening in the database.

- **Action**
Reissue the call.

◘ GK

- **Description**
While processing an unqualified GN or GNP call, a different segment type, but at the same hierarchic level, was retrieved.

- **Action**
This is not an error, and the response to this code depends on the programmer.

◘ GL

- **Description**
A LOG request has an incorrect log code for user log records. The log code should be equal to or greater than X'A0'.

- **Action**
Correct the program.

◘ GP

- **Description**
A GNP call was issued without established parentage.

- **Action**
Change the program to establish the parentage before requesting a GNP call.

◻ II

● **Description**
The program issued a call to insert a segment that exists in the database.

● **Action**
This is not an error, and the response to this code depends on the programmer.

◻ IX

● **Description**
An ISRT call violated the insert rule for a segment.

● **Action**
Correct the program.

◻ LB

● **Description**
A program attempted to load a segment that already exists in the database.

● **Action**
Consult the database administrator (DBA) and then correct the program's load sequence or the ISRT call.

◻ LC

● **Description**
The program issued a request to load a segment for which the key field was out of sequence.

● **Action**
Correct the input data.

◘ **LD**

- **Description**
  The program issued a request to load a segment for which a parent does not exist in the database. This is an error in hierarchical sequence.

- **Action**
  Correct the program.

◘ **LE**

- **Description**
  The hierarchical sequence specified in the DBD is not the same as the sequence in the segment the program attempted to load.

- **Action**
  Correct the segment sequence.

◘ **MR**

- **Description**
  An ISRT call for a message segment was not processed by IMS because the terminal name was invalid.

- **Action**
  Specify the correct LTERM name in the message requeuer segment.

◘ **NA**

- **Description**
  One or more databases were not available when processing an INIT call with DBQUERY in the I/O area.

- **Action**
  This is not an error, and the response to this code depends on the programmer.

◘ NE

● **Description**
During indexing maintenance, a segment was not found.

● **Action**
Examine the indexing and recreate if required.

◘ NI

● **Description**
For a unique secondary index, a duplicate segment was encountered.

● **Action**
Determine whether the index should be unique and take appropriate action.

◘ NO

● **Description**
While a program was accessing a database, a physical I/O error occurred.

● **Action**
Consult the system programmer; this may be a hardware problem.

◘ NU

● **Description**
This status code is returned for your information only when IMS determines that a REPL, DLET, or ISRT call may return status code BA if an INIT STATUS GROUPA call has been requested.

● **Action**
None.

◘ QC

- **Description**
  A GU call failed; this call is a result of a CHKP issued by a BMP or MPP.

- **Action**
  This is for programmer information only.

◘ QD

- **Description**
  A message GN call was requested, but no more message segment is available.

- **Action**
  Process the message as it is.

◘ QE

- **Description**
  A message GN call was not followed by a GU call.

- **Action**
  Change the program so that calls are issued in proper sequence.

◘ QF

- **Description**
  The length of a message segment is less than 5. The minimum length should be the size of the message text plus 4 bytes.

- **Action**
  Change the program so that it builds a message segment of the proper size.

◘ QH

● Description
A terminal symbolic error is encountered; perhaps the output logical terminal name or a transaction code is unknown to IMS.

● Action
Correct the terminal name or transaction code, or define them in IMS.

◘ RA

● Description
A token does not match any token on an outstanding SETS call.

● Action
Look for a token usage error or cancelled SETS call.

◘ RC

● Description
The program issued a ROLS call and it was rejected by IMS.

● Action
Examine the PCB and see if it contains access to a GSAM, MSDB, or DEDB database.

◘ RX

● Description
The program issued a REPL call that violated the replace rule for a segment.

● Action
Change the REPL call.

■ SA

● **Description**
During processing of a SETS call, the storage space for the I/O area could not be obtained.

● **Action**
Increase the region size in the JOB statment of JCL and resubmit the job.

■ SB

● **Description**
A SETS call attempted to set a tenth level when only nine are allowed.

● **Action**
Change the program.

■ SC

● **Description**
The program issued a SETS call that was rejected by IMS.

● **Action**
Examine the PCB and see if it contains access to a GSAM, MSDB, or DEDB database.

■ TA

● **Description**
A CICS command level failed because the PSB is not defined in the PSB directory.

● **Action**
Specify a valid PSB.

◻ TC

• **Description**
The specified PSB is in use by a previous request.

• **Action**
Correct the program logic.

◻ TE

• **Description**
IMS is unable to initialize to the specified PSB.

• **Action**

Examine the PSB; a PSBGEN may be required.

◻ TG

• **Description**
There is no PSB scheduled for this program.

• **Action**
Examine the PSB; a PSBGEN may be required.

◻ TH

• **Description**
There is no PSB scheduled for this program.

• **Action**
Examine the PSB; a PSBGEN may be required.

◻ TI

• **Description**
The path to the segment is invalid.

- **Action**

  Check the logic of the program and correct any error.

◼ **TJ**

- **Description**

  DL/I is not active.

- **Action**

  Request the operator to start DL/I.

◼ **TL**

- **Description**

  A conflict in scheduling intent was encountered.

- **Action**

  Check the logic of the program and correct any error.

◼ **TN**

- **Description**

  An invalid system DIB was found.

- **Action**

  Request assistance from the system programmer.

◼ **TO**

- **Description**

  A path replace error was found.

- **Action**

  Request assistance from the system programmer.

◘ TP

• **Description**
The processing option or a number in the PCB is invalid.

• **Action**
Check the PCB and correct any error.

◘ TQ

• **Description**
An I/O PCB access is not allowed in a local DL/I call.

• **Action**
Check the PCB and correct any error.

◘ TR

• **Description**
The CICS XDLIPRE exit cancelled a request.

• **Action**
Request assistance from the system programmer.

◘ TY

• **Description**
The database is not open.

• **Action**
Make sure the database is open and reissue the transaction.

◘ TZ

• **Description**
The length of a segment was longer than the maximum 64 k bytes allowed.

- **Action**
  Correct the logic of the program.

◘ UC

- **Description**
  During batch processing of a program, a checkpoint record is written to the utility control facility (UCF) dataset.

- **Action**
  None.

◘ UR

- **Description**
  During batch processing of a program, an initial program load is restarted under the utility control facility (UCF).

- **Action**
  Change the program so that the PCB key feedback area and the I/O area restart the load process.

◘ US

- **Description**
  During batch processing of a program, an initial program load is halted.

- **Action**
  In this situation the program should issue a CHKP call.

◘ UX

- **Description**
  During batch processing of the program, both checkpoint processing and the program halted.

- **Action**
  Refer to the UC and US status codes.

◼ V1

- **Description**
  During an insert or update, the length of a variable-length segment is too long.

- **Action**
  Check the program and correct any error. The length of the segment must be equal to or less than the maximum length defined in the DBD.

6.9 SAMPLE COBOL PROGRAM WITH DL/I CALLS

Fig. 6.14 lists a program called SAIMS01. This program retrieves occurrences of two segments from an IMS database and then writes to two output files. The two segments are CF000100 and CF000500.

The following is an explanation of portions of the program that are directly related to DL/I calls. Later in this chapter there are two JCLs, one to compile and link-edit the program SAIMS01, and the other to execute the program SAIMS01 in batch mode.

1 The SELECT statements associate the file definition (FD) of the output files with external datasets.

2 This data area is for DL/I functions. Each element contains a function code which is used in the program when making DL/I calls.

3 This data area is used both for retrieving data and for writing to the output file. The element SEGMENT-AREA is used for storing the segment read from the database; it is also an entry making DL/I calls in the program. The program writes to the files from CF000100-SEGMENT-OUT and CF000500-SEGMENT-OUT.

4 As mentioned earlier, the storage area called DB-PCB is defined in the LINKAGE SECTION for communication between DL/I and the program.

5 This ENTRY statement is required in an IMS program. Note that its parameter is the storage area DB-PCB defined in the LINKAGE SECTION.

6 This is a DL/I call that is used to get the first occurrence of a segment. The arguments are GU-FUNC, DB-PCB, and SEGMENT-AREA, all previously explained and defined in the WORKING-STORAGE or LINKAGE SECTION. This call is part of the initialization of the program and is executed only once.

7 After a segment has been retrieved, DL/I places its name in an area called SEGM-NAME, an element of DB-PCB. This portion of the program separates the segments into three categories: CF000100, CF000500, and the rest.

8 This is another DL/I call of the program; it retrieves the next occurrences of the segments. Unlike the previous DL/I call, it is part of the main program and is executed many times. The arguments are GN-FUNC, DB-PCB, and SEGMENT-AREA.

```
        IDENTIFICATION DIVISION.
      *---------------------------*
        PROGRAM-ID.    SAIMS01.
        DATE-COMPILED.
      *----------------------------------------------------------------
      *    THIS BATCH IMS PROGRAM READS THE ACCOUNTS DATABASE SEGMENTS
      *    SEQUENTIALLY, ATTACHES THE TELEPHONE NUMBER FROM THE ROOT
      *    SEGMENT CF000100 TO SEGMENT CF000500, AND WRITES BOTH RECORDS
      *    TO DIFFERENT SEQUENTIAL FILES.
      *----------------------------------------------------------------


        ENVIRONMENT DIVISION.
      *---------------------------*
        CONFIGURATION SECTION.

        OBJECT-COMPUTER.    IBM-9000.

        INPUT-OUTPUT SECTION.

        FILE-CONTROL.
            SELECT CF000100 ASSIGN TO UT-S-CF000100.
            SELECT CF000500 ASSIGN TO UT-S-CF000500.


        DATA DIVISION.
      *---------------*
        FILE SECTION.

        FD    CF000100
              RECORD CONTAINS 300 CHARACTERS
              RECORDING MODE F
              BLOCK CONTAINS 0 RECORDS
              LABEL RECORD IS OMITTED.
        01    CF000100-REC              PIC  X(300).
```

```
FD    CF000500
      RECORD CONTAINS 610 CHARACTERS
      RECORDING MODE F
      BLOCK CONTAINS 0 RECORDS
      LABEL RECORD IS OMITTED.
01    CF000500-REC                      PIC  X(610).

WORKING-STORAGE SECTION.
*-----------------------*

*-----------------------------------------------------------------
01  FUNCTION-CODES.
*-----------------------------------------------------------------
      05  GU-FUNC                       PIC  X(04) VALUE 'GU  '.
      05  GN-FUNC                       PIC  X(04) VALUE 'GN  '.

*-----------------------------------------------------------------
01  INPUT-OUTPUT-REC.
*-----------------------------------------------------------------
      05  INPUT-OUTPUT-AREA.
          10  TELEPHONE-NO-OUT          PIC  X(010) VALUE SPACES.
          10  SEGMENT-AREA              PIC  X(600) VALUE SPACES.
      05  FILLER         REDEFINES INPUT-OUTPUT-AREA.
          10  FILLER                    PIC  X(010).
          10  CF000100-SEGMENT-OUT.
              15  FILLER                PIC  X(007).
              15  TELEPHONE-NO-IN       PIC  X(010).
              15  FILLER                PIC  X(283).
          10  FILLER                    PIC  X(300).
      05  FILLER         REDEFINES INPUT-OUTPUT-AREA.
          10  CF000500-SEGMENT-OUT.
              15  FILLER                PIC  X(010).
              15  SUB-ACCT-NO           PIC  X(020).
              15  FILLER                PIC  X(580).

LINKAGE SECTION.
*---------------*

01  DB-PCB.
      05  DBD-NAME                      PIC X(08).
      05  SEGM-LEVEL                    PIC X(02).
      05  STATUS-CODE                   PIC X(02).
          88  END-OF-DATABASE               VALUE 'GB'.
      05  PROCESS-OPTION                PIC X(04).
      05  RESERVE-AREA                  PIC S9(5) COMP.
      05  SEGM-NAME                     PIC X(08).
      05  KEY-LENGTH                    PIC S9(5) COMP.
      05  NO-SENSIT-SEGMENT             PIC S9(5) COMP.
      05  KEY-FEEDBACK-AREA             PIC X(200).


PROCEDURE DIVISION.
*------------------*

      ENTRY 'DLITCBL' USING DB-PCB.

0000-MAINLINE.
*-----------------------------------------------------------------
*   THIS IS THE MAIN LINE OF THE PROGRAM.
*-----------------------------------------------------------------
      PERFORM 1000-INIT.
      PERFORM 2000-PROC UNTIL END-OF-DATABASE.
      PERFORM 3000-TERM.

1000-INIT.
*-----------------------------------------------------------------
*   THIS PARAGRAPH OPENS THE FILES AND DOES THE INITIAL READ.
*-----------------------------------------------------------------
      OPEN  OUTPUT CF000100 CF000500

      CALL 'CBLTDLI' USING GU-FUNC, DB-PCB, SEGMENT-AREA.
```

```
        IF STATUS-CODE = SPACES
            NEXT SENTENCE
        ELSE
            DISPLAY 'STATUS CODE IS ' STATUS-CODE
            PERFORM 3000-TERM
        END-IF.

    2000-PROC.
    *----------------------------------------------------------------
    *  THIS PARAGRAPH CONTROLS THE PROCESSING OF THE PROGRAM.
    *----------------------------------------------------------------
        IF STATUS-CODE = 'GA'
        OR STATUS-CODE = 'GK'
        OR STATUS-CODE = SPACES
            NEXT SENTENCE
        ELSE
            DISPLAY 'STATUS CODE IS ' STATUS-CODE
            PERFORM 3000-TERM
        END-IF.
        EVALUATE SEGM-NAME
            WHEN 'CF000100'
                MOVE TELEPHONE-NO-IN TO TELEPHONE-NO-OUT
                    WRITE CF000100-REC FROM CF000100-SEGMENT-OUT
            WHEN 'CF000500'
                IF SUB-ACCT-NO < SPACES
                    WRITE CF000500-REC FROM CF000500-SEGMENT-OUT
                END-IF
            WHEN OTHER
                CONTINUE
        END-EVALUATE.

        MOVE SPACES TO SEGMENT-AREA.

        CALL 'CBLTDLI' USING GN-FUNC, DB-PCB, SEGMENT-AREA.

    3000-TERM.
        CLOSE           CF000100 CF000500.
        GOBACK.
```

Fig. 6.14 Sample COBOL program to access an IMS database.

6.10 SAMPLE JCL TO COMPILE AND LINK-EDIT A COBOL PROGRAM

Fig. 6.15 shows a job stream that is used to compile and link-edit the program SAIMS01, described earlier. It consists of a procedure called BCHTSIC2 which accomplishes these two processes. Such a procedure is available in all installations; check with your coworkers or supervisor to find out the name of the procedure to compile and link-edit an IMS batch program. Most likely it will be similar to the one listed in Fig. 6.15. One of the most important parts of this process is including linkage editor control statements in the job stream, which will be explained shortly.

1 This PROC statement defines BCHTSIC2 as a JCL procedure.

2 This EXEC statement calls the COBOL compiler IGYCRCTL.

3 This EXEC statement calls the linkage editor IEWL.

4 This EXEC statement executes the BCHTSIC2 procedure, previously defined.

5 There are three linkage editor control statements that must be entered after the LKED.SYSIN DD statement. They are INCLUDE RESLIB (CBLTDLI), ENTRY DLITCBL, and, NAME SAIMS01.

The second one specifies the entry point, which must be the same as the one specified in the program. The third control statement specifies the name of the program, SAIMS01 in this case.

```
        //IMSCOMP JOB (0200,200),'MITRA',CLASS=X,
        //           MSGCLASS=X,NOTIFY=C840BGF
        /*JOBPARM COPIES=1,LINES=100
        //*-------------------------------------
1 -->   //BCHTSIC2 PROC MEM='',
        // PGMSRC='TEST.IMS.PGMSRC',
        // COPYLIB='TEST.COB.CPYSRC',
        // PGMLOAD='TEST.IMS.PGMLOAD',
        // CBPARM='APOST',
        // LKPARM='XREF,LET,LIST',
        // REGN=1M
        //*
        //*
```

```
          //**********************************************
          //* EXEC COBOL COMPILER
          //**********************************************
          //*
2 -->     //COB EXEC PGM=IGYCRCTL,REGION=&REGN,
          // PARM=('SOURCE,XREF,RENT,RES,DATA(24)',
          // 'LIB,NOSEQ,MAP,NOLIST,OFFSET',
          // &CBPARM)
          //STEPLIB DD DSN=SYS1.COB2COMP,DISP=SHR
          //SYSLIB DD DISP=SHR,DSN=&COPYLIB
          //SYSPRINT DD SYSOUT=*
          //SYSIN DD DISP=SHR,DSN=&PGMSRC(&MEM)
          //SYSLIN DD DSN=&&LOADSET,DISP=(MOD,PASS),
          // DCB=(RECFM=FB,LRECL=80,BLKSIZE=3120),
          // UNIT=SYSDA,SPACE=(80,(250,100))
          //*
          //SYSUT1 DD UNIT=SYSDA,SPACE=(460,(350,100))
          //SYSUT2 DD UNIT=SYSDA,SPACE=(460,(350,100))
          //SYSUT3 DD UNIT=SYSDA,SPACE=(460,(350,100))
          //SYSUT4 DD UNIT=SYSDA,SPACE=(460,(350,100))
          //SYSUT5 DD UNIT=SYSDA,SPACE=(460,(350,100))
          //SYSUT6 DD UNIT=SYSDA,SPACE=(460,(350,100))
          //SYSUT7 DD UNIT=SYSDA,SPACE=(460,(350,100))
          //*
          //**********************************************
          //* LINK EDIT
          //**********************************************
          //*
3 -->     //LKED EXEC PGM=IEWL,REGION=&REGN,
          // PARM=('LIST,AMODE=24',
          //  &LKPARM),
          // COND=(4,LT,COB)
          //RESLIB DD DISP=SHR,DSN=SYS5.IMSSERV.RESLIB
          //SYSLIB DD DISP=SHR,DSN=SYS1.COB2LIB
          // DD DISP=SHR,DSN=&PGMLOAD
          //SYSLMOD DD DISP=SHR,DSN=&PGMLOAD(&MEM)
          //SYSUT1 DD UNIT=SYSDA,DCB=BLKSIZE=1024,
          // SPACE=(1024,(200,20))
          //SYSPRINT DD SYSOUT=*
          //SYSLIN DD DISP=(OLD,DELETE),DSN=&&LOADSET
          // DD DISP=SHR,DSN=TEST.SYS.PARMLIB(DFSLI000)
          //*------------------------------------------
          // PEND
          //*------------------------------------------
4 -->     //JS001 EXEC PROC=BCHTSIC2
          //COB.SYSIN DD *
              IDENTIFICATION DIVISION.
              *-----------------------*
              PROGRAM-ID.    SAIMS01.
              DATE-COMPILED.
              .
              .
              .
              GOBACK.
          //LKED.SYSIN DD *
5 -->         INCLUDE RESLIB(CBLTDLI)
              ENTRY DLITCBL
              NAME SAIMS01
          /*
```

Fig. 6.15 JCL to compile and link-edit a COBOL/IMS program.

6.11 RUNING A PROGRAM THAT USES DL/I

This section shows how to run a program that uses DL/I functions. Before going any further, there are two items that have to be considered before running any IMS programs. They are the DBD (database descriptor) and the PSB (program specification block). The DBD describes the structure of a database; there is one for each DL/I database. The program accesses a database according to a *view*. This view is defined by a PSB. Before a program can use a database, two processes must take place: generation of a DBD, called DBDGEN, and generation of the PSB, called PSBGEN. These two steps are accomplished by a database administrtor (DBA).

After an IMS batch program is compiled and link-edited without error, and the PSBGEN and DBDGEN processes are accomplished, the program is executed using a DL/I batch initialization module called DFSRRC00. Fig. 6.16 lists a job stream to invoke the program SAIMS01, previously discussed. The following is a brief discussion of the JCL in Fig. 6.16.

1 This portion of the JCL specifies the library where the load module SAIMS01 resides.

2 The EXEC statement calls the DL/I batch initialization module called DFSRRC00; one of its parameters is the name of the program, SAIMS01.

3 These DD statements specify IMS libraries.

4 This DD statement allocates the dataset to store the occurrences of segment CF000100.

5 This DD statement allocates the dataset to store the occurrences of segment CF000500.

6 These DD statements specify the IMS datasets.

```
        //IMSPROG   JOB (acct-info),'RUN IMS PROG',
        //           CLASS=X,MSGLEVEL=(1,1)
        //*-------------------------------------------------------
1 -->   //JOBLIB   DD  DISP=SHR,DSN=TEST.IMS.PGMLOAD
        //         DD  DISP=SHR,DSN=IMSSERV.APFLIB
        //*-------------------------------------------------------
2 -->   //STEP01   EXEC PGM=DFSRRC00,REGION=6M,
        //              PARM='DLI,SAIMS01,D401READ,10,00,,,,,,,,,,N,,,N'
        //DFSTROUT DD  SYSOUT=*
        //SYSOUT   DD  SYSOUT=*
        //SYSUDUMP DD  SYSOUT=*
        //IMSUDUMP DD  SYSOUT=*
        //SYSPRINT DD  SYSOUT=*
3 -->   //IMS      DD  DISP=SHR,DSN=TEMP.PSBLOAD
        //         DD  DISP=SHR,DSN=IMSSERV.PSBLIB
        //         DD  DISP=SHR,DSN=IMSSERV.DBDLIB
        //DFSRESLB DD  DISP=SHR,DSN=IMSSERV.RESLIB
        //DFSVSAMP DD  DISP=SHR,DSN=CBIS.PROD.PARMLIB(GS505CTL)
        //IEFRDER  DD  DUMMY
        //IMSMON   DD  DUMMY
4 -->   //CF000100 DD  DSN=TEMP.SAR01.CF000100,
        //             DISP=(,CATLG,CATLG),
        //             SPACE=(CYL,(250,50),RLSE),
        //             UNIT=SYSDA,
        //             DCB=(LRECL=300,BLKSIZE=3000,RECFM=FB)
5 -->   //CF000500 DD  DSN=TEMP.SAR01.CF000500,
        //             DISP=(,CATLG,CATLG),
        //             SPACE=(CYL,(400,50),RLSE),
        //             UNIT=SYSDA,
        //             DCB=(LRECL=610,BLKSIZE=6100,RECFM=FB)
        //***************** DATABASES ***************************
6 -->   //D400ID10 DD  DISP=SHR,DSN=RCIIV.D400ID10
        //D400ID1X DD  DISP=SHR,DSN=RCIIV.D400ID1X
        //D400SX11 DD  DISP=SHR,DSN=RCIIV.D400SX11
        //SYSIN    DD  DUMMY
```

Fig. 6.16 A JCL to execute a COBOL/IMS batch program.

MVS UTILITIES

This chapter is a reference guide for programmers using MVS utility programs. The utilities discussed here can be grouped into two types: those that manage data and files, and those that produce executable programs. In the data and file management category the utilities are:

IEBGENER	Transfers data, prints files, reorganizes files and changes file characteristics.
IEBPTPCH	Prints a sequential dataset or a member of a PDS.
IEBCOPY	Copies data and maintains partitioned datasets.
IEBUPDTE	Maintains source programs in batch mode.
IEBCOMPR	Compares two files.
IEHPROGM	Maintains catalogs and DASD VTOC.
SORT	Sorts, merges and copies files.

And the program utilities are:

IEWL	Creates an executable program from an object module.
IGYCRCTL	Creates an object module from a source program.

The chapter first describes the function of each utility, then provides information such as the following:

Return codes: When a utility ends execution, it returns a completion code to the calling program, such as JCL, REXX, or CLIST.

Job control statements: In this chapter, these statements are JCL

351

DD statements required to successfully complete the utility functions. Similar DD name definition can be accomplished through CLIST or REXX.

Utility control statements: These statements define the functions you want the utilities to perform. Each section contains a description of each statement and its parameters, followed by the syntax.

Compiler options: These options request the compiler program IGYCRCTL to perform optional processing.

Examples: These examples show how some of the utility functions can be executed through JCLs.

Notational Conventions: In the general format of the utility programs used in this chapter, there are a few symbols that are not part of the syntax; therefore they must not be included when you code JCL, CLIST, or REXX. These symbols and their meanings are:

Symbol	Meaning
[]	The option enclosed by the brackets ([]) is not required but can be included.
<>	Only one of the alternatives enclosed by the angle brackets (<>) must be chosen.
or	The alternatives enclosed by the angle brackets (<>) are separated by "or."
____	The underlined word is the default value.
...	The horizontal or vertical ellipsis means that the preceding can be coded more than once.
Uppercase characters	All keywords of the command are written in uppercase characters; they must be coded as shown.
Lowercase characters	All strings in lowercase characters and italic are variables that can be changed to any other strings to suit your programming style. In your code they represent values that you supply to commands.

7.1 IEBGENER

The IEBGENER program is perhaps the most frequently used program in data centers. This utility has many functions. They are:

TRANSFER DATA. IEBGENER can copy data from one kind of file to another.

- From a sequential dataset to a member of a partitioned dataset
- From a member of a partitioned dataset to a sequential dataset
- From a disk file to a tape file
- From a tape file to a disk file

PRINT A FILE. IEBGENER can send the contents of a sequential or PDS file to the printer.

REORGANIZE A FILE. IEBGENER can be used to expand a partitioned dataset. Also, it can be used to produce an "edited" sequential dataset or PDS member. Some of the editing functions are:

- Rearrange or omit data fields in a record.
- Replace data with literal values.
- Convert data from packed decimal to unpacked decimal and from unpacked decimal to packed decimal.

CHANGE FILE CHARACTERISTICS. IEBGENER can be used to "reblock" a file. For example, a file with LRECL=80, BLKSIZE=800 can be copied to a file with LRECL=80, BLKSIZE=8000.

- **Return code**

Code	Description
00	The processing is successfully completed.
04	The processing is completed but a warning message is issued.
08	The processing is terminated. Processing of header labels only is requested.
12	The program terminated; a fatal error occurred.
16	The program terminated; a user routine returned error code 16.

● Job control statements

The following is a sample JCL to run the IEBGENER program. Following the sample is the discussion of each DD statement required by IEBGENER.

```
//jobname  JOB (acct),'my name',MSGCLASS=C,NOTIFY=tsoid
//jobstep  EXEC PGM=IEBGENER
//SYSPRINT DD SYSOUT=*
//SYSUT1   DD DSN=dataset-name1,DISP=disposition1
//SYSUT2   DD DSN=dataset-name2,DISP=disposition2
//SYSIN    DD *
 control statements
/*
```

JOB   Initiates the job.

EXEC   Specifies execution of the program IEBGENER.

SYSPRINT DD   Specifies a message output dataset, which can be a system output device, tape, or disk.

SYSUT1 DD   Specifies the input dataset(s), which can be (a) sequential dataset(s) or (a) member(s) of a PDS.

SYSUT2 DD   Specifies the output dataset which can be a sequential dataset or a member of a PDS.

SYSIN DD   Specifies the control dataset.

● Utility control statements

IEBGENER has five control statements: GENERATE, EXITS, LABELS, MEMBER, and RECORD. The following describes each of the statements in turn:

The GENERATE statement is required when one of the following is specified:

● The output dataset is partitioned.
● Editing is requested.

- User routines are supplied.
- Label processing is requested.

The format for the GENERATE statement is

```
[label] GENERATE MAXNAME=n
     [,MAXFLDS=n]
     [,MAXGPS=n]
     [,MAXLITS=n]
```

where MAXNAME, MAXFLDS, MAXGPS, and MAXLITS specify limits for the numbers of member names, FIELDS, IDENTS, and character literals.

The EXITS statement specifies the names of user exit routines for processing user labels. The format is

```
[label] EXITS
     [INHDR=routine-name]      input header label
     [,OUTHDR=routine-name]    output header label
     [,INTLR=routine-name]     input trailer label
     [,OUTTLR=routine-name]    output trailer label
     [,KEY=routine-name]       output record key
     [,DATA=routine-name]      record change
     [,IOERROR=routine-name]   I/O error
     [,TOTAL=routine-name]     user total
```

The LABELS statement specifies whether IEBGENER should treat labels as data or not. It is required in cases where:

- User labels should not be copied to the output dataset.
- User labels are built from the records in the data portion of the SYSIN dataset.
- User labels are written to the output dataset after the exits routines have changed them.

The format is

```
[label] LABELS [DATA=YES or NO
          or ALL or ONLY or INPUT]
```

The MEMBER statement specifies a member of a PDS. The format is

```
[label] MEMBER NAME=(name[,alias]...)
```

The RECORD statement defines the record group and specifies editing directions to IEBGENER. The format is

```
[label] RECORD [IDENT=(length,name,input-location)]
    [,FIELD=([length]
                [,input-location or literal]
                [,conversion]
                [output-location])
    [,LABELS=n]
```

IDENT identifies a record group.
FIELD parameters describe editing directions for records in the record group.
LABELS specifies user label records.

● **Example**

In the following JCL example, IEBGENER is used to send the content of dataset C840BGF.SPUFI.OUTPUT to the system printer.

```
//PRINTGF JOB (Acct),'Laila',USER=C840BGF,CLASS=M
//*
//***************************************************
//* THIS JCL PRINTS A DATASET
//***************************************************
//*
//STEP01    EXEC PGM=IEBGENER
//*
//SYSPRINT DD SYSOUT=*
//SYSUT1   DD DSN=C840BGF.SPUFI.OUTPUT,DISP=SHR
//SYSUT2   DD SYSOUT=*
//SYSIN    DD DUMMY
/*
```

In the following JCL example, IEBGENER is used to copy the contents of dataset PROD.SUBSC.ACTV.FILE to dataset TEMP.SUBSC.ACTV.FILE. Before copying is done, the output file (defined by SYSUT2) is first allocated and cataloged.

```
//COPYBGF (Acct),'Sanjiv',USER=C840BGF,CLASS=M
//*
//*********************************************
//*
//* THIS JCL COPIES DATA FROM ONE DATASET
//* TO ANOTHER
//*
//*********************************************
```

```
//*
//STEP01   EXEC PGM=IEBGENER
//*
//SYSPRINT DD SYSOUT=*
//SYSUT1   DD DSN=PROD.SUBSC.ACTV.FILE,DISP=SHR
//SYSUT2   DD DSN=TEMP.SUBSC.ACTV.FILE,
//            DISP=(NEW,CATLG,DELETE),
//            UNIT=SYSDA,
//            DCB=(LRECL=204,BLKSIZE=20400,RECFM=FB),
//            SPACE=(CYL,(10,1),RLSE)
//SYSIN    DD DUMMY
/*
```

7.2   IEBPTPCH

The IEBPTPCH program performs the following functions:

- Printing a sequential dataset or a member of a PDS
- Punching a member of a PDS
- Formatting the output: repositioning data fields and unpacking decimal fields

● Return codes

Code	Description
00	The program is successfully completed.
04	A PDS member is not found or a sequential dataset is empty.
08	A PDS member does not exist. Processing continues with the next member.
12	The program terminated; a fatal error occurred or a user routine passed code 12 to IEBPTPCH.
16	The program terminated; a user routine returned error code 16.

● Job control statements

The following is a sample JCL to run the IEBPTPCH program. Following the sample is a discussion of each DD statement required by IEBPTPCH.

```
//jobname JOB (acct),'my name',MSGCLASS=C,NOTIFY=tsoid
//jobstep EXEC PGM=IEBPTPCH
```

```
//SYSPRINT DD SYSOUT=*
//SYSUT1   DD DSN=dataset-name,DISP=disposition
//SYSUT2   DD SYSOUT=*
//SYSIN    DD *
 control statements
/*
```

JOB   Initiates the job.

EXEC   Specifies execution of the program IEBPTPCH.

SYSPRINT DD   Specifies a message output dataset, which can be a system output device, tape, or disk.

SYSUT1 DD   Specifies the input dataset(s), which can be (a) sequential dataset(s) or (a) member(s) of a PDS.

SYSUT2 DD   Specifies the output (print or punch) dataset.

SYSIN DD   Specifies the control dataset.

● **Utility control statements**

IEBPTPCH has seven control statements: PRINT, PUNCH, TITLE, EXITS, LABELS, MEMBER, and RECORD. The following describes each of the statements.

The PRINT statement initiates a print operation; if used, it must be the first statement of the SYSIN stream. The format is

```
[label] PRINT [PREFORM=A or M]
              [,TYPORG=PS or PO]
              [,TOTCONV=XE or PZ]
              [,CNTRL=n or 1]
              [,STRTAFT=n]
              [,STOPAFT=n]
              [,SKIP=n]
              [,MAXNAME=n]
              [,MAXFLDS=n]
              [,MAXGPS=n]
              [,MAXLITS=n]
              [,INITPG=n]
              [,MAXLINE=n]
```

Keyword	Meaning
PREFORM	The first byte of the output record is an ANSI (A) or machine (M) control character.
TYPORG	The DSORD of the input file is sequential (PS) or PDS (PO).
TOTCONV	Convert input data to hexadecimal (XE) or unpacked zoned (PZ).
CNTRL	Spacing is 1, 2, or 3.
STRTAFT	Start *n* records after processing.
STOPAFT	Stop *n* records after processing.
SKIP	Print or punch every *n* records.
MAXNAME	Maximum number of member names.
MAXFLDS	Maximum number of field names.
MAXGPS	Maximum number of IDENT keywords.
MAXLITS	Maximum number of literals in an IDENT keyword.
INITPG	Starting page number.
MAXLINE	Maximum number of lines per page.

The PUNCH statement initiates a punch operation; if used, it must be the first statement of the SYSIN stream. The format is

```
[label] PUNCH [PREFORM=A or M]
            [,TYPORG=PS or PO]
            [,TOTCONV=XE or PZ]
            [,CNTRL=n or 1]
            [,STRTAFT=n]
            [,STOPAFT=n]
            [,SKIP=n]
            [,MAXNAME=n]
            [,MAXFLDS=n]
            [,MAXGPS=n]
```

```
[,MAXLITS=n]
[,INITPG=n]
[,CDSEQ=n]
[,CDINCR=n]
```

Keyword	Meaning
PREFORM	The first byte of the output record is an ANSI (A) or machine (M) control character.
TYPORG	The DSORD of the input file is sequential (PS) or PDS (PO).
TOTCONV	Convert input data to hexadecimal (XE) or unpacked zoned (PZ).
CNTRL	Stacker character is 1, 2, or 3.
STRTAFT	Start n records after processing.
STOPAFT	Stop n records after processing.
SKIP	Print or punch every n records.
MAXNAME	Maximum number of member names.
MAXFLDS	Maximum number of field names.
MAXGPS	Maximum number of IDENT keywords.
MAXLITS	Maximum number of literals in an IDENT keyword.
INITPG	Starting page number.
CDSEQ	Starting sequence number.
CDINCR	Increment number in generating sequence numbers.

The TITLE statement specifies a title or subtitle for the output.

The format is

```
[label] TITLE ITEM=('title',output-location)
```

The EXITS statement specifies the names of user exit routines for processing user labels. The format is

```
[label]  EXITS
    [INHDR=routine-name]        input header label
    [,INTLR=routine-name]       input trailer label
    [,INREC=routine-name]       input record
    [,OUTREC=routine-name]      output record
```

The LABELS statement specifies whether user labels are to be treated as data by IEBPTPCH. The format is

```
[label] LABELS [CONV=PZ or XE]
    [,DATA=YES or NO or ALL or ONLY]
```

The MEMBER statement specifies the names of members of an input PDS that is to be printed or punched. The format is

```
[label] MEMBER NAME=member-name
```

The RECORD statement specifies the group of records that is to be printed or punched. The format is

```
[label] RECORD [IDENT=(length,'name',input-location)]
    [,FIELD=(length
            [,input-location]
            [,conversion]
            [,output-location])]
```

where IDENT specifies a literal to be used to identify the last record in the record group and FIELD defines the length, input location, output location, and conversion factor.

● **Example**

In the following JCL example, IEBPTPCH prints the contents of SAABB020, a member of dataset TEST.COBOL.PGMSRC.

```
//PRINTGF JOB (Acct),'Natalia',USER=C840BGF,CLASS=M
//*
//****************************************************
//* THIS JCL PRINTS A PDS MEMBER
//****************************************************
//STEP01   EXEC PGM=IEBPTPCH
```

```
//SYSPRINT DD SYSOUT=*
//SYSUT1   DD DSN=TEST.COBOL.PGMSRC,DISP=SHR
//SYSUT2   DD SYSOUT=*
//SYSIN    DD *
  PRINT TYPORG=PO,MAXNAME=4,MAXFLDS=4
  MEMBER NAME=SAABB020
  RECORD FIELD=(80)
/*
```

7.3 IEBCOPY

The IEBCOPY utility program copies and maintains partitioned datasets. IEBCOPY has three main functions: compress datasets, copy members of PDS, and merge members of PDS.

COMPRESSION. When compressing a PDS, all the members are moved together, thus making contiguous unused space.

COPY. The program copies members from one PDS to another. Members can be copied selectively. It can also be used to rename a member.

MERGE. Two or more PDSs can be merged into one PDS.

● **Return codes**

Code   Description

00   The program is successfully completed.
04   An error condition has occurred from which recovery is possible.
08   The processing is terminated. Processing of header labels only is requested.

● **Job control statements**

The following is a sample JCL to run the IEBCOPY program. Following the sample is a discussion of each DD statement required by IEBCOPY.

```
//jobname JOB (acct),'my name',MSGCLASS=C,NOTIFY=tsoid
//jobstep  EXEC PGM=IEBCOPY,REGION=1024K,
//               PARM='SIZE=nnnnnnnnK'
//SYSPRINT DD SYSOUT=*
//ddname1  DD DSN=dataset-name,DISP=disposition
```

```
//ddname2   DD  DSN=dataset-name,DISP=disposition
//SYSUT3    DD  UNIT=SYSDA,SPACE=(TRK,(30,30),RLSE)
//SYSUT4    DD  UNIT=SYSDA,SPACE=(TRK,(30,30),RLSE)
//SYSIN     DD  *
 control statements
/*
//
```

JOB   Initiates the job.

EXEC   Specifies execution of the program IEBCOPY. The optional PARM value is the size of the buffer used for file input-output operation.

SYSPRINT DD   Specifies a message output dataset which can be a system output device, tape, or disk. It is also the output for the results of the comparison.

ddname1 DD   Specifies the input sequential or partitioned dataset.

ddname2 DD   Specifies the output dataset.

SYSUT3 DD   Specifies space in DASD as a work file.

SYSUT4 DD   Specifies space in DASD as a work file.

SYSIN DD   Specifies the control dataset.

● **Utility control statements**

IEBCOPY has five control statements: COPY, ALTERMOD, COPYMOD, SELECT, and EXCLUDE. The following describes each of the statements.

The COPY statement is the start of the copy operation and identifies the input and output DDNAMEs. The format is

```
[label] COPY OUTDD=ddname,
       INDD=(ddname1,ddname2,(ddname3,R),...)
       [,LIST=NO]
```

OUTDD specifies the DD name for the output file.
INDD specifies the DD name(s) for the input file(s).

LIST=NO means no member list of the PDS is required.

The ALTERMOD statement is used to insert RLD and segment text block counts into load modules. The format is

```
[label] ALTER OUTDD=ddname,
     [,LIST=NO]
```

The COPYMOD statement is used to copy load modules and repair damaged RLD and text records. The format is

```
[label] COPYMOD OUTDD=ddname,
    INDD=(ddname1,ddname2,(ddname3,R),...),
    [MAXBLK=<nnnnn or nnK>,]
    [MINBLK=<nnnnn or nnK>,]
    [,LIST=NO]
```

The SELECT statement specifies member names to be included in the copy operation. The format is

```
[label] SELECT MEMBER=(name1,name2,name3,...) or
[label] SELECT MEMBER=((name1,newname1),
                       (name2,newname2),...)
```

The EXCLUDE statement specifies member names to be excluded from the copy operation. The format is

```
[label] EXCLUDE MEMBER=(name1,name2,name3,...)
```

● **Example**

In the following JCL example, IEBCOPY compresses the dataset TEST.COBOL.PGMSRC.

```
//COMPRES (Acct),'Ming-Lam',USER=C840BGF,CLASS=M
//*
//**********************************************
//* THIS JCL COMPRESSES A DATASET
//**********************************************
//*
//STEP01   EXEC PGM=IEBCOPY,REGION=1024K
//SYSPRINT DD SYSOUT=*
//SYSUT1   DD DSN=TEST.COBOL.PGMSRC,DISP=OLD
//SYSUT3   DD UNIT=SYSDA,SPACE=(TRK,(30,30),RLSE)
//SYSUT4   DD UNIT=SYSDA,SPACE=(TRK,(30,30),RLSE)
//SYSIN    DD *
  COPY INDD=SYSUT1,OUTDD=SYSUT1
/*
```

In the following JCL example, IEBCOPY copies members from the input dataset TEST.COBOL.PGMSRC to the output dataset PROD.COBOL.PGMSRC. All copied members replace identically named members of the output PDS.

```
//COPY (Acct),'Mikhael',USER=C840BGF,CLASS=M
//*
//***********************************************
//* THIS JCL WILL COPY MEMERS OF A PDS
//***********************************************
//*
//STEP01    EXEC PGM=IEBCOPY,REGION=1024K
//*
//SYSPRINT DD SYSOUT=*
//INPUT1    DD DSN=TEST.COBOL.PGMSRC,DISP=OLD
//OUTPUT1   DD DSN=PROD.COBOL.PGMSRC,DISP=OLD
//SYSUT3    DD UNIT=SYSDA,SPACE=(TRK,(30,30),RLSE)
//SYSUT4    DD UNIT=SYSDA,SPACE=(TRK,(30,30),RLSE)
//SYSIN     DD *
  COPY INDD=INPUT1,OUTDD=((OUTPUT1,R))
/*
```

7.4 IEBUPDTE

The IEBUPDTE program is used to maintain source programs in batch mode. This program works on 80-byte logical records.

● **Return codes**

Code	Description
00	The program was successfully completed.
04	A control statement is coded incorrectly.
12	The program terminated; a fatal error occurred or a user routine passed code 12 to IEBUPDTE.
16	The program terminated; a user routine returned error code 16.

● **Job control statements**

The following is a sample JCL to run the IEBUPDTE program. Following the sample is a discussion of each DD statement required by IEBUPDTE.

```
//jobname JOB (acct),'my name',MSGCLASS=C,NOTIFY=tsoid
//jobstep EXEC PGM=IEBUPDTE,PARM='NEW or MOD'
//SYSPRINT DD SYSOUT=*
//SYSUT1   DD DSN=dataset-name1,DISP=disposition1
//SYSUT2   DD DSN=dataset-name2,DISP=disposition2
//SYSIN    DD *
 control statements
/*
```

JOB   Initiates the job.

EXEC   Specifies execution of the program IEBUPDTE. The PARM specifies the following values:

                     NEW—The input dataset does not exist. The source contains the control data set.

                     MOD—Both input and control datasets are used.

SYSPRINT DD   Specifies a message output dataset, which can be a system output device, tape, or disk.

SYSUT1   DD   Specifies the input dataset, which can be a sequential dataset or a member of a PDS.

SYSUT2   DD   Specifies the output dataset, which can be a sequential dataset or a member of a PDS.

SYSIN   DD   Specifies the control dataset.

• Utility control statements

IEBUPDTE has three types of control statements: function statements, detail statements, and data statements. Control statements of IEBUPDTE, with the exception of data statements, begin with a './' in columns 1 and 2.

Function statements start the IEBUPDTE operations. The function keywords are

ADD   Create a sequential dataset or member of PDS.

CHANGE   Update a PDS member or sequential file.
REPL   Replace a PDS member or sequential file entirely.
REPRO   Copy a PDS member or sequential file to the output
         file.

The format is

```
./[label] [ADD or CHANGE or REPL or REPRO]
   [LIST=ALL]
   [,SEQFLD=ddl or (ddl,ddl)]
   [,NEW=PO or PS]
   [,MEMBER=cccccccc]
   [,COLUMN=nn or 1]
   [,UPDATE=INPLACE]
   [,INHDR=cccccccc]
   [,INTLR=cccccccc]
   [,TOTAL=(routine-name,size)]
   [,NAME=cccccccc]
   [,LEVEL=hh]
   [,SOURCE=x]
   [,SSI=hhhhhhhh]
```

ADD, CHANGE, REPL, and REPRO are function keywords.

LIST=ALL specifies entire member.

SEQFLD specifies the location of the starting column and the length of the sequence numbers.

NEW specifies the file organization.

MEMBER specifies the member name.

COLUMN specifies the starting location of a record.

INHDR specifies the exit routine to handle header labels.

INTLR specifies the exit routine to handle trailer labels.

TOTAL specifies the installation exit routine to be executed before writing each logical record.

NAME specifies the alias name of a PDS member.

LEVEL specifies the change level in the directory entry.

SOURCE specifies the installation modification.

Detail statements provide additional information to the function statements. The format is

```
./[label] <NUMBER or DELETE>
    [SEQ1=cccccccc or ALL]
    [,SEQ2=cccccccc]
    [,NEW1=ccccccccc]
    [,INCR=ccccccccc]
    [,INSERT=YES]
```

NUMBER specifies a new sequence numbering scheme.

DELETE specifies the removal of logical records from a PDS member or sequential dataset.

SEQ1 specifies logical records.

SEQ2 specifies the last logical record.

NEW1 specifies the first sequence number.

INCR specifies the incremental value in assigning sequence numbers.

INSERT specifies insertion of a block of records.

Data statements supply the IEBUPDTE program with logical records to be added or replaced. There are three data statements: the LABEL statement, the ALIAS statement, and the ENDUP statement.

The LABEL statement specifies user labels for the output. The format is

```
./[name]   LABEL
UHL1 ...    user header label #1
UHL2 ...    user header label #2
    .
    .
    .
```

The ALIAS statement specifies an alias name to be created or retained in an output dataset directory. The format is

```
./[name]   ALIAS NAME=cccccccc
```

The ENDUP statement specifies the end of the control statements. The format is

```
./[label]  ENDUP
```

• Example

In the following JCL example, IEBUPDTE adds members SAABB010 and SAABB020 to PDS TEST.COBOL.PGMSRC. SAABB010 has sequence numbers in columns 73 through 80. SAABB020 does not have any sequence number; the detail statement NUMBER NEW1=5,INCR=10 instructs IEBUPDTE to generate the numbers. The generated numbers begin with 5 in increments of 10.

```
//IEBUPDTE JOB (Acct),'Amber',USER=C840BGF,CLASS=M
//*
//**************************************************
//* THIS JCL ADDS TWO MEMBERS TO A PDS
//**************************************************
//*
//STEP01   EXEC PGM=IEBUPDTE,PARM='NEW'
//*
//SYSPRINT DD SYSOUT=*
//SYSUT2   DD DSN=TEST.COBOL.PGMSRC,DISP=SHR
//SYSIN    DD *
./ ADD    NAME=SAABB010

  (data statements with sequence numbers in columns 73
through 80)
./ ADD    NAME=SAABB020
  (data statements without sequence numbers)
./ ENDUP
/*
```

7.5 IEBCOMPR

IEBCOMPR is a program to compare two files; the files can be sequential datasets or members of a PDS. All the logical records of both files are compared. The input files can be source files, JCLs, or data, but they cannot be load modules. One major propblem with IEBCOMPR is that if the records are not in sync, then all the remaining records of the compare process will be flagged as not equal. In other words, if a record is deleted from or added to a file, the rest of the records will not be equal.

● **Return codes**

Code   Description

00   The program was successfully completed.
08   The records are not equal; processing continues.
12   The program terminated; a fatal error occurred.
16   The program terminated; a user routine returned error code 16.

● **Job control statements**

The following is a sample JCL to run the IEBCOMPR program. Following the sample is a discussion of each DD statement required by IEBCOMPR.

```
//jobname JOB (acct),'my name',MSGCLASS=C,NOTIFY=tsoid
//jobstep  EXEC PGM=IEBCOMPR
//SYSPRINT DD SYSOUT=*
//SYSUT1   DD DSN=dataset-name,DISP=disposition
//SYSUT2   DD DSN=dataset-name,DISP=disposition
//SYSIN    DD *
 control statements
/*
```

JOB   Initiates the job.

EXEC   Specifies execution of the program IEBCOMPR.

SYSPRINT DD   Specifies a message output dataset, which can be a system output device, tape, or disk. It is also the output for the results of the comparison.

SYSUT1 DD   Specifies an input dataset to be compared.

SYSUT2 DD   Specifies an input dataset to be compared.

SYSIN   DD   Specifies the control dataset.

● **Utility control statements**

IEBCOMPR has three control statements: COMPARE, EXITS and LABELS. The following describes each of the statements.

COMPARE statement. The format is

```
[label] COMPARE TYPORG=<PS or PO>
```

The EXITS statement specifies the names of user exit routines for processing user labels. The format is

```
[label]  EXITS
          [INHDR=routine-name]      input header label
          [,INTLR=routine-name]     input trailer label
          [,ERROR=routine-name]     error
          [,PRECOMP=routine-name]   precompare
```

The LABELS statement specifies whether user labels are to be treated as data by IEBCOMPR. The format is

```
[label]  LABELS
          [DATA=YES or NO or ALL or ONLY or INPUT]
```

● **Example**

In the following JCL example, IEBCOMPR is used to comapre logical records of datasets PROD.SUBSC.ACTV.FILE and TEMP.SUBSC.ACTV.FILE.

```
//COMPARE (Acct),'Laila',USER=C840BGF,CLASS=M
//*
//**************************************
//* THIS JCL COMPARES TWO DATASETS
//**************************************
//*
//STEP01    EXEC PGM=IEBCOMPR
//*
//SYSPRINT DD SYSOUT=*
//SYSUT1   DD DSN=PROD.SUBSC.ACTV.FILE,DISP=SHR
//SYSUT2   DD DSN=TEMP.SUBSC.ACTV.FILE,DISP=SHR
//SYSIN    DD DUMMY
/*
```

7.6   IEHPROGM

The IEHPROGM program is used to maintain catalogs and DASD VTOC. With IEHPROGM, the following tasks can be accomplished:

- Scratch a sequential dataset or member of PDS.
- Rename a sequential dataset or member of PDS.
- Catalog and uncatalog non-VSAM dataset entries in an OS CVOL.
- Connect or release two OS CVOLs
- Create or maintain a generation data group (GDG).
- Add and delete passwords from the MVS PASSWORD dataset.

• Return codes

Code   Description

00	The program was successfully completed.
04	Syntax error.
08	Invalid control statement or invalid request.
12	The program terminated; an I/O error occurred.
16	The program terminated; an unrecoverable error occurred.

• Job control statements

The following is a sample JCL to run the IEHPROGM program. Following the sample is a discussion of each DD statement required by IEHPROGM.

```
//jobname JOB (acct),'my name',MSGCLASS=C,NOTIFY=tsoid
//jobstep  EXEC PGM=IEHPROGM,PARM=parm
//SYSPRINT DD SYSOUT=*
//ddname1  DD DSN=dataset-name1,DISP=disposition
//ddname2  DD DSN=dataset-name2,DISP=disposition
//SYSIN    DD *
 control statements
/*
//
```

JOB   Initiates the job.

EXEC   Specifies   execution   of   the   program

IEHPROGM. The optional PARM value is 'LINECNT=*xx*', where *xx* is the number of lines per page.

SYSPRINT DD   Specifies a message output dataset, which can be a system output device, tape, or disk.

ddname1 DD   Specifies a permanently mounted volume.

ddname2 DD   Specifies a mountable volume.

SYSIN DD   Specifies the control dataset.

● **Utility control statements**

IEHPROGM has the following control statements:

SCRATCH Delete a sequential dataset or member of a PDS. The format is

```
[label] SCRATCH [VTOC or DSNAME=name],
        VOL=device=(volume-list)
        [,PURGE]
        [,MEMBER=member-name]
        [,SYS]
```

DSNAME specifies a fully qualified dataset name to be scratched.

VOL specifies a device type and volume serial number.

PURGE means to scratch all.

MEMBER specifies a PDS member to be scratched.

SYS specifies to erase system dataset(s) only and it is valid when used with VTOC.

RENAME Change the name of a dataset or PDS member. The format is

```
[label] RENAME DSNAME=oldname,
        VOL=device=(volume-list),
```

```
          NEWNAME=newname
          [ ,MEMBER=member-name]
```

DSNAME specifies a fully qualified dataset name to be renamed.

VOL specifies the device type and volume serial number.

NEWNAME specifies a fully qualified dataset name which is the new name.

MEMBER specifies a PDS member to be renamed.

CATLG   Make an entry for a non-VSAM dataset in an OS CVOL catalog. The format is

```
[label]    CATLG DSNAME=name,
            VOL=device=(volume-list) or
                  (volser,seq#)
          [ ,CVOL=device=cvolser]
```

DSNAME specifies a fully qualified dataset name to be cataloged.

VOL specifies the DASD volume or the volume serial number and the dataset sequence number.

CVOL specifies the name of the OS CVOL catalog.

UNCATLG Remove an entry for a non-VSAM dataset from an OS CVOL catalog. The format is

```
[label]    UNCATLG DSNAME=name,
          [ ,CVOL=device=cvolser]
```

DSNAME specifies a fully qualified dataset name to be uncataloged.

CVOL specifies the name of the OS CVOL catalog.

BLDX   Build a new index in an OS CVOL catalog. The format is

```
[label] BLDX INDEX=name,
          [ ,CVOL=device=cvolser]
```

INDEX specifies the index name to be built.

CVOL specifies the name of the OS CVOL catalog.

DLTX   Delete an empty index from an OS CVOL catalog. The format is

```
[label] DLTX INDEX=name,
      [,CVOL=device=cvolser]
```

INDEX specifies the index name to be deleted.

CVOL specifies the name of the OS CVOL catalog.

BLDA   Build an index alias in an OS CVOL catalog. The format is:

```
[label] BLDA INDEX=name,
      ALIAS=alias-name
      [,CVOL=device=cvolser]
```

INDEX specifies the index name to be built.

ALIAS specifies the alias name, which must be 8 characters or less.

CVOL specifies the name of the OS CVOL catalog.

DLTA   Delete an index alias in an OS CVOL catalog. The format is:

```
[label] DLTA INDEX=name,
        [,CVOL=device=cvolser]
```

INDEX specifies the index name to be built.

CVOL specifies the name of the OS CVOL catalog.

CONNECT Connect two OS CVOLs with a high-level index name. The format is

```
[label] CONNECT INDEX=name,
```

```
            VOL=device=volser
              [,CVOL=device=cvolser]
```

INDEX specifies the index name that connects two CVOLs.

VOL specifies the OS CVOL catalog.

CVOL specifies the master catalog.

RELEASE Disconnect two OS CVOLs. The format is

```
[label] RELEASE INDEX=name,
               [,CVOL=device=cvolser]
```

INDEX specifies the index name.

CVOL specifies the master catalog.

BLDG   Build an index for a generation data group (GDG):
          the format is

```
[label] BLDG INDEX=name,
          ENTRIES=n
          [,CVOL=device=cvolser]
          [,EMPTY]
          [,DELETE]
```

INDEX specifies the GDG index name to be built.

ENTRIES specifies the number of GDG entries.

CVOL specifies the name of the OS CVOL catalog.

EMPTY means to uncatalog all the GDG entries when the GDG index is full.

DELETE means to delete GDG entries when they are replaced by new entries.

ADD   Add a password entry to the PASSWORD dataset.
          The format is

```
[label]   ADD DSNAME=dsn
            [,PASWORD2=new-password]
```

```
[,CPASWORD=control-password]
[,TYPE=code]
[,VOL=device=list]
[,DATA='user-data']
```

DSNAME specifies the dataset where password entry is to be added.

PASWORD2 specifies the password to be added.

CPASWORD specifies the control password.

TYPE specifies the protection code of the password.

VOL specifies the device type and serial number(s) of the volume(s).

DATA specifies the data to be added in the password entry.

REPLACE   Replace a password entry in the PASSWORD dataset. The format is

```
[label]   REPLACE DSNAME=dsn
          [,PASWORD1=current-password]
          [,PASWORD2=new-password]
          [,CPASWORD=control-password]
          [,TYPE=code]
          [,VOL=device=list]
          [,DATA='user-data']
```

DSNAME specifies the dataset where password entry is to be replaced.

PASWORD1 specifies the current password.

PASWORD2 specifies the password to be replaced.

CPASWORD specifies the control password.

TYPE specifies the protection code of the password.

VOL specifies the device type and serial number(s) of the volume(s).

DATA specifies the data to be replaced in the password entry.

DELETEP   Remove a password entry from the PASSWORD dataset. The format is

```
[label]   DELETEP DSNAME=dsn
          [,PASSWORD1=current-password]
          [,CPASWORD=control-password]
          [,VOL=device=list]
```

DSNAME specifies the dataset where password entry is to be deleted.

PASWORD1 specifies the current password.

CPASWORD specifies the control password.

VOL specifies the device type and serial number(s) of the volume(s).

LIST   List password entries. The format is

```
[label]   LIST DSNAME=dsn
          [,PASSWORD1=current-password]
```

DSNAME specifies the dataset where password entry is to be listed.

PASWORD1 specifies the current password.

● **Example**

In the following JCL example, IEHPROGM is used to scratch all datasets from the directory of a mountable volume.

```
//SCRATCH (Acct),'Jane',USER=C840BGF,CLASS=M
//*
//*****************************************************
//* THIS JCL WILL SCRATCH ALL DIRECTORY ENTRIES FROM A
//* MOUNTABLE VOLUME
//*****************************************************
//*
//STEP01    EXEC PGM=IEHPROGM
//SYSPRINT DD SYSOUT=*
//DD2       DD UNIT=DISK,VOLUME=SER=102230,DISP=OLD
//SYSIN     DD *
```

```
SCATCH VTOC,VOL=DISK=102230,SYS
/*
```

7.7   IEWL

IEWL is a linkage editor program that converts an object module to an executable load module. The object module is created when a source program is compiled or assembled. The linkage editor resolves external symbols, and, with options specified through JCL or control statements, it constructs the final form of the load module.

● Job control statements

The following is a sample JCL to run the IEWL program. Following the sample is a discussion of each DD statement required by IEWL.

```
//LNKEDIT  JOB (acct),'my name',MSGCLASS=C,NOTIFY=tsoid
//jobstep  EXEC PGM=IEWL,REGION=1024K,
//              PARM='parameters...'
//SYSPRINT DD SYSOUT=*
//SYSTERM  DD SYSOUT=*
//SYSLIN   DD DSN=object-library-name,DISP=SHR,
//         DD DDNAME=SYSIN
//SYSLMOD  DD DSN=load-library-name,DISP=SHR
//SYSLIB   DD DSN=auto-call-library-name,DISP=SHR
//ddname   DD DSN=input-library-name,DISP=SHR
//SYSUT1   DD UNIT=SYSDA,DISP=SHR,SPACE=(TRK,(30))
//SYSIN    DD *
 control statements
/*
//
```

JOB   Initiates the job.

EXEC   Specifies execution of the program IEWL. The PARM can be used to pass values of the linkage editor. The following is a list of PARM option values.

> AC=n   Set authorization code.

> DC   Set downward compatible attribute.

> SCTR   Use "scatter" load module format.

NE	Set not-editable attribute.
OL	Set only-loadable attribute.
OVLY	Set overlay attribute.
RENT	Set reentrant attribute.
REUS	Set serially reusable attribute.
REFR	Set refreshable attribute.

AMODE=31 or 24 or ANY
> Set the addressing mode.

RMODE=24 or ANY
> Set the residency mode.

LET or NOLET
> Produce or do not produce a load module.

MAP or NOMAP
> Produce or do not produce a map.

XREF	Produce a cross-reference.
NCAL	Do not search SYSLIB to resolve external references.

PRINT or NOPRINT
> Print or do not print messages to SYSLOUT DD.

TERM	Send error messages to SYSTERM.

SIZE=(v1,v2)
> Specify the size of the region and buffer.

SYSPRINT DD   Specifies the output dataset for the linkage editor. It can be a system output device, tape, or disk.

SYSTERM DD	Specifies a secondary output dataset for diagnostic messages; this is needed only if the TERM link-edit option is used.
SYSLIN DD	Specifies the input for the linkage editor.
SYSLMOD DD	Specifies the output dataset where the load module is produced.
SYSLIB DD	Specifies the "auto call" library.
ddname DD	Is any additional DD statements added to the linkage editor JCL.
SYSUT1 DD	Specifies the work file.
SYSIN DD	Specifies the control dataset.

● **Control statements**

IEWL has the following control statements:

The ALIAS statement assigns an alias for a load module. The format is

```
ALIAS [external-name or symbol]
      [,external-name or symbol]...
```

The CHANGE statement changes the name of an entry point, external, or CSECT name in a load module. The format is

```
CHANGE external-name(newname)
  [,external-name(newname)]...
```

The ENTRY statement assigns an entry point for a program. The format is

```
ENTRY entry-name
```

The EXPAND statement directs the linkage editor to add one or more binary zero bytes to one or more CSECTS of a load module. The format is

```
EXPAND csect-name(nnnn)
  [,csect-name(nnnn)]...
```

where *nnnn* is the number of bytes to add.

The IDENTIFY statement directs the linkage editor to add information, up to 40 characters, to the identification record (IDR) of one or more specified CSECTs. The format is

```
IDENTIFY csect-name('data-value')
  [,csect-name('data-value')]...
```

The INCLUDE statement directs the linkage editor to read additional sequential datasets or PDS members. The format is

```
INCLUDE ddname[(member1)],
  [ddname[(member1,member2,member3)]...]
```

The INSERT statement directs the linkage editor to move a CSECT from an input stream to a segment in the overlay structure. The format is

```
INSERT csect1
```

The LIBRARY statement specifies libraries, in addition to SYSLIB, to be searched to resolve external references. The format is

```
LIBRARY [ddname(member1,member2,...)],
  (external-name1,*(external-name2))
```

The MODE statement changes an addressing and/or residency mode of a load module. The format is

```
MODE mode[,mode]
```

where *mode* is AMODE(24), AMODE(31) or AMODE(ANY).

The NAME statement specifies the name of the load module that is being link-edited. The format is

```
NAME memname[(R)]
```

The ORDER statement specifies the sequential order in which CSECT should be arranged in a load module. The format is

```
ORDER csect-name1[(P)],csect-name2,...
```

The OVERLAY statement identifies the start of an overlay segment or region. The format is

```
OVERLAY symbol[(REGION)]
```

The PAGE statement link-edits and aligns a CSECT of a load module on a 4K page boundary. The format is

```
PAGE csect-name1[,csect-name2]...
```

The REPLACE statement renames or deletes a CSECT in a load module. The format is

```
REPLACE oldcsect-name[(newcsect-name)],...
```

The SETCODE statement sets the APF (Authorization Program Facility) code for a load module. The format is

```
SETCODE AC(n)
```

where *n* is 1, 2, or 3.

The SETSSI statement sets the System Status Information (SSI) for a local module. The format is

```
SETSSI xxxxxxxx
```

where *xxxxxxxx* is an 8-hex-digit value.

● **Example**

In the following JCL example, IEWL is used to link-edit an object module (contained in &&OBJMOD, for example SAAAB010) and produce the load module in PDS

TEST.COBOL.PGMLOAD(SAAAB010). The object module is generated by a compiler or assembler program.

```
//LNKEDIT (Acct),'Michelle',USER=C840BGF,CLASS=M
//STEP01   EXEC PGM=IEWL,REGION=1M,
//             PARM=(LET,NOMAP,NOXREF,LIST)
//SYSLIB    DD DSN=SYS1.COB2LIB,DISP=SHR
//             DSN=TEST.COBOL.PGMLOAD,DISP=SHR
//SYSPRINT DD SYSOUT=*
//SYSLIN    DD DSN=&&OBJMOD,DISP=(OLD,DELETE)
//SYSLMOD DD DSN=TEST.COBOL.PGMLOAD(SAAAB010),DISP=SHE
//SYSUT1    DD UNIT=SYSDA,DCB=BLKSIZE=1024,
//             SPACE=(1024,(200,20))
//
```

7.8   IGYCRCTL—COBOL II COMPILER

The IGYCRCTL program is the compiler for the language VS COBOL II. It takes a source program and produces a machine-language object module. After the source code is compiled without any errors, it is then link-edited with a linkage editor (IEWL utility) to produce an executable program. VS COBOL II allows the user to supply options during compilation which provide additional services in addition to compilation. Some of these services are

- Produce a listing of the source program.
- Produce a listing of machine-language instructions.
- Produce cross references
- Set literal delimiters.
- Process COPY, BASIS, and REPLACE statements.
- Produce debugging information during execution time.

• Job control statements

The following is a sample JCL to run the IGYCRCTL program. Following the sample is a discussion of each DD statement required by IGYCRCTL.

```
//COMPILE  JOB (acct),'my name',MSGCLASS=C,NOTIFY=tsoid
//jobstep  EXEC PGM=IGYCRCTL,REGION=1024K,
//             PARM=(options)
//STEPLIB   DD DSN=SYS1.COB2COMP,DISP=SHR
//SYSLIB    DD DSN=copy-member-library,DISP=SHR
//SYSPRINT DD SYSOUT=*
//SYSTERM   DD SYSOUT=*
//SYSUT1    DD UNIT=SYSDA,DISP=SHR,SPACE=(subparms)
//SYSUT2    DD UNIT=SYSDA,DISP=SHR,SPACE=(subparms)
```

```
//SYSUT3   DD UNIT=SYSDA,DISP=SHR,SPACE=(subparms)
//SYSUT4   DD UNIT=SYSDA,DISP=SHR,SPACE=(subparms)
//SYSUT5   DD UNIT=SYSDA,DISP=SHR,SPACE=(subparms)
//SYSUT6   DD UNIT=SYSDA,DISP=SHR,SPACE=(subparms)
//SYSUT7   DD UNIT=SYSDA,DISP=SHR,SPACE=(subparms)
//SYSLIN   DD DSN=&&OBJMOD,DISP=(MOD,PASS),
//            UNIT=SYSDA,SPACE=(subparms)
//SYSIN    DD *
 source program
/*
//
```

JOB	Initiates the job.
EXEC	Specifies execution of the program IGYCRCTL. The PARM can be used to pass values of compilation options to the IGYCRCTL program. The compiler options are listed later in this chapter.
STEPLIB DD	Specifies the partitioned dataset that contains the load modules of the compiler.
SYSLIB DD	Specifies the partitioned dataset that contains copy members. It is required if COPY or BASIS statements are found in the source program.
SYSPRINT DD	Specifies the output dataset, which can be a system output device, tape, or disk. The output from the compiler includes program listing, diagnostic messages, etc.
SYSTERM DD	Specifies a secondary output dataset for diagnostic messages; it is needed only if the TERMINAL compiler option is used.
SYSUT1 DD - SYSUT7 DD	Specify working files for the compiler. These files must reside on DASD, with LRECL=80 and RECFM=F or FB.
SYSLIN DD	Specifies the output dataset for the object module, with LRECL=80 and RECFM=F or FB.

SYSIN   DD   Specifies the input dataset containing the source program, with LRECL=80 and RECFM=F or FB.

● **Compiler options**

The compiler options can be set in the following ways:

- As fixed installation defaults
- As changeable installation defaults
- Using PROCESS (or CBL) statements in the source code
- As JCL parameters

Fixed installation defaults cannot be overridden.

Changeable installation defaults can be overridden by PROCESS/CBL statements and/or parameters in the EXEC statement of JCL. If any conflict arises between these specifications or they are mutually exclusive, then the PROCESS/CBL statements take precedence over parameters.

The PROCESS statements must be coded before the IDENTIFICATION DIVISION header in the program. The format is

```
PROCESS optionall,option2...

  IDENTIFICATION DIVISION.
```

The following is a list of options and their abbreviations. The default values are underlined. Each has been described in more detail in Chap. 4.

Option	Abbreviation and default
ADV	<ADV or NOADV>
APOST	<APOST or Quote>
BUFSIZE	<BUF(nnnnn or nnnK) or BUF(4096)>
COMPILE	<Compile or NOCompile(W or E or S) or NOC(S) >
DATA	<DATA(24) or DATA(31)>

DECK	<Deck or NODeck>
DUMP	<DUmp or NODUmp>
DYNAM	<DYNam or NODYNam>
FASTSRT	<FaStsRT or NOFaStsoRT>
FDUMP	<FDUmp or NOFDUmp>
FLAG	<Flag(x, [y]) or NOFlag or Flag(I)>
	where x and y are I, W, E, S, or U
LIB	<LIB or NOLIB>
LINECOUNT	<LineCount or LC(60)>
LIST	<LIST or NOLIST>
MAP	<MAP or NOMAP>
NUMBER	<NUMber or NONUMBer>
OBJECT	<OBJect or NOOBject>
OFFSET	<OFFset or NOOFFset>
OPTIMIZE	<OPTimize or NOOPTimize>
OUTDD	<OUTdd(ddname) or OUTDD(SYSOUT)>
PFDSGN	<PFDsgn or NOPFDsgn>
RENT	<RENT or NORENT>
RESIDENT	<RESident or NOREsident>
SEQUENCE	<SEQuence or NOSEQuence>
SIZE	<SiZe(nnnnn or nnnK or MAX) or Sz(MAX)>
SOURCE	<NOSource or Source>
SPACE	<SPACE(1 or 2 or 3) or SPACE(1)>
SSRANGE	<SSRange or NOSSRange>
TERMINAL	<TERMinal or NOTERMinal>
TEST	<TESt or NOTEst>
TRUNC	<TRUnc or NOTRUnc>
VBREF	<VBREF or NOVBREF>
WORD	<WorD(xxx) or NOWorD>
XREF	<Xref or NOXref>
ZWB	<NOZWB or ZWB>

● **Example**

In the following JCL example, IGYCRCTL is used to compile a program in PDS TEST.COBOL.PGMSRC(SAAAB010). The object output is placed on disk file &&OBJMOD, which is usually passed to a linkage edit program. The copy members are in dataset TEST.COBOL.CPYSRC. The compiler load modules are in SYS1.COB2COMP. Finally, the listing and message go to SYSPRINT DDNAME.

```
//COMPILE (Acct),'Michelle',USER=C840BGF,CLASS=M
//*
//*************************************************
//* THIS JCL COMPILES A COBOL PROGRAM
//*************************************************
//*
//STEP01    EXEC PGM=IGYCRCTL,REGION=1024K,
//             PARM=('SOURCE,XREF,MAP,NOLIST,OFFSET')
//STEPLIB  DD DSN=SYS1.COB2COMP,DISP=SHR
//SYSLIB   DD DSN=TEST.COBOL.CPYSRC,DISP=SHR
//SYSPRINT DD SYSOUT=*
//SYSTERM  DD SYSOUT=*
//SYSUT1   DD UNIT=SYSDA,DISP=SHR,SPACE=(460,(350,100))
//SYSUT2   DD UNIT=SYSDA,DISP=SHR,SPACE=(460,(350,100))
//SYSUT3   DD UNIT=SYSDA,DISP=SHR,SPACE=(460,(350,100))
//SYSUT4   DD UNIT=SYSDA,DISP=SHR,SPACE=(460,(350,100))
//SYSUT5   DD UNIT=SYSDA,DISP=SHR,SPACE=(460,(350,100))
//SYSUT6   DD UNIT=SYSDA,DISP=SHR,SPACE=(460,(350,100))
//SYSUT7   DD UNIT=SYSDA,DISP=SHR,SPACE=(460,(350,100))
//SYSLIN    DD DSN=&&OBJMOD,DISP=(MOD,PASS),
//             DCB=(RECFM=FB,LRECL=80,BLKSIZE=3120),
//             UNIT=SYSDA,SPACE=(80,(250,100))
//SYSIN    DD DSN=TEST.COBOL.PGMSRC(SAAAB010),DISP=SHR
//
```

7.9 SORT

The SORT program is used to sort, copy and merge input file(s). The results can be placed in a specified output file, or the input file can also be the output file.

● **Job control statements**

The following is a sample JCL to run the SORT program. Following the sample is a discussion of each DD statement required by SORT.

```
//jobname JOB (acct),'my name',MSGCLASS=C,NOTIFY=tsoid
//jobstep  EXEC PGM=SORT,REGION=1024K,
//              PARM=parameters
//SORTLIB  DD DSN=dataset-name,DISP=SHR
//SYSPRINT DD SYSOUT=*
//SORTIN   DD DSN=dataset-name,DISP=SHR
//SORTINnn DD DSN=dataset-name,DISP=SHR
//SORTOUT  DD DSN=dataset-name,DISP=SHR
//SORTWKnn DD UNIT=SYSDA,DISP=SHR,SPACE=(CYL,(5,2))
//SORTCKPT DD DSN=dataset-name,DISP=SHR
//SYSOUT   DD SYSOUT=*
//$ORTPARM DD DSN=dataset-name,DISP=SHR
//SYSIN    DD *
 control statements
/*
```

JOB   Initiates the job.

EXEC   Specifies execution of the program SORT. Similarly, other program names such as ICEMAN, IERRCO00, IGHRCO00, and SYNCSORT can also be invoked. The optional PARM can be used to pass values to the SORT program. Some of the PARM values are:

BMSG
Turn on 'B'-level information messages.

CMP=[CPD or CLC]
Comparison of packed decimal (CPD) or zoned decimal (CLC) fields.

COMMAREA(n,x) or NOCOMMAREA
Common area, where n is the size and x is the initial values.

CORE=n or nK or MAX or MAX-n or MAX-nK
Amount of core to be used by the SORT program, where n is the number of bytes, nK is the number of 'K' (1024-byte units) and MAX is the maximum available.

DEBUG
Produce a SNAP dump if a fatal error occurs.

DIAG
Enable the IOERR=ABE or RC16=ABE parameter.

DYNALLPC=d or (d) or (d,n) or OFF
Control dynamic allocation of work files, where d is for disk, n is the number of SORTWKnn DDs to allocate and OFF disables work file allocation.

E15=COB or E35=COB
E15 and E35 exits are COBOL.

EQUAL or NOEQUALS
Preserve order of records for same fields.

FILSZ=n or En
Estimate of the number of records in the input file.

FLAG(I) or FLAG(U) or NOFLAG
Message routing flags. FLAG(I) routes critical messages to the console, and FLAG(U) routes them to the console and SYSOUT.

SORTLIB DD	Specifies the SORT program library name.
SORTIN DD	Specifies the input dataset for a sort operation, which can be a sequential dataset, a member of a PDS or VSAM file.
SORTIN*nn* DD	Specifies the input files for a merge operation.
SORTOUT DD	Specifies the output dataset for a sort or merge operation.
SORTWK*nn* DD	Specifies the sort work files to be used by the SORT program. Up to 32 files can be allocated.
SYSOUT DD	Specifies the message dataset.
$ORTPARM DD	Specifies overriding parameters and control statements for the sort operation.
SYSIN DD	Specifies the control dataset.

● **Control statements**

The SORT utility has the following control statements:

The SORT statement sorts or copies input files. The formats are

```
SORT FIELDS=(pos1,len1,type1,opt1,
                    pos2,len2,type2,opt2,...)
    [,SIZE=n or En]
    [,FILSZ=n or En]
    [,DYNALLOC=(d,n) or (OFF)]
    [,SKIPREC=n]
    [,EQUALS or CHKPT]

SORT FIELDS=COPY
    [,SKIPREC=n]
    [,STOPAFT=n]
    [,CKPT or CHKPT]
```

The MERGE statement merges or copies input files. The formats are

```
MERGE FIELDS=(pos1,len1,type1,opt1,
                     pos2,len2,type2,opt2,...)
    [,FILES=n]
    [,EQUALS or NOEQUALS]
    [,CKPT or CHKPT]

MERGE FIELDS=COPY
    [,SKIPREC=n]
    [,STOPAFT=n]
    [,CKPT or CHKPT]
```

where FIELDS identifies the fields for a sort or merge operation. Each field is described with four values: the position (*pos1*) of the field in the record, the length (*len1*) of the field, the type (*type1*) of the field, and the sort order (*opt1*). One or more fields' decriptions can be entered. The types of data are

AC	EBCDIC converted to ASCII before a merge or sort operation.
AQ	Collating sequence
ASL	Leading ASCII separate sign (+ or -)
AST	Trailing ASCII separate sign (+ or -)
BI	Binary
CH	Character
CLO or OL	Leading overpunch
CSL or OL	Leading EBCDIC separate sign (+ or -)

CST or TS	Trailing EBCDIC separate sign (+ or -)
FL	Floating-point binary
FI	Fixed-point binary
PD	Packed signed decimal
ZD or CTO	Zoned decimal

The RECORD statement is needed when an E15 or E35 exit routine changes the length in the input record. The format is

```
RECORD TYPE=[F or V]
     [,LENGTH=(leng1,leng2,leng3,
          leng4,leng5,leng6,leng7)]
```

TYPE specifies the input record format (F for fixed format and V for variable format).

LENGTH specifies the record length. The various length values are as follows:

leng1	Maximum input record length
leng2	Maximum record length after E15 exit processing of data
leng3	Maximum record length after E35 exit processing of data
leng4	Minimum input record length
leng5	Most frequent record length used as input
leng6 and *leng7*	Lengths used with the SORT HISTOGRM program

The INCLUDE statement establishes selection criteria for the records that are to be included in the output dataset. The format is

```
INCLUDE COND=([expression,
          [AND or OR],expression],...)
          [,FORMAT=x]
```

OMIT statement establishes selection criteria for the records that are to be excluded from the output dataset. The format is

```
OMIT COND=([expression,[AND or OR],expression],...)
     [,FORMAT=x]
```

where *expression* is
   field1,length1,type1,
   [EQ or NE or GT or LT or LE],
   [*field2,length2,type2* or *constant-value*]

field1	Relative byte number of a field
length1	Length in bytes of *field1*
type1	Data type of *field1*
field2	Relative byte number of a field.
length2	Length in bytes of *field2*
type2	Data type of *field2*
constant	A constant specified as a decimal number.

FORMAT specifies the type of field format.

● **Example**

In the following JCL example, SORT is used to sort the data
TEMP.SAR.CF01200 and place the result in
TEMP.SAR.CF01200.SORTED. In this job, space for three sort
work files (SORTWK01, SORTWK02, and SORTWK03) has been
allocated. The control statement specifies two fields as sort keys.
The first field is at position 1 of the record, it is 27 bytes in
length, and its data type is character. The sort order is ascending.
The second field is at position 48, it is 10 bytes in length, and its
data type is character. The sort order is again ascending. The SIZE
is specified as E2000.

```
//SORT (Acct),'Mauricio',USER=C840BGF,CLASS=M
//*
//**********************************************
//* THIS JCL SORTS A FILE
//**********************************************
//STEP01    EXEC PGM=SORT,TIME=60,PARM='CORE=MAX'
//SORTLIB   DD DSN=SYS.SOFT.SORTLIB,DISP=SHR
//SYSDUMP   DD SYSOUT=*
//SYSOUT    DD SYSOUT=*
//SORTWK01 DD UNIT=SYSDA,SPACE=(CYL,(5,2),RLSE)
//SORTWK02 DD UNIT=SYSDA,SPACE=(CYL,(5,2),RLSE)
//SORTWK03 DD UNIT=SYSDA,SPACE=(CYL,(5,2),RLSE)
//SORTIN    DD DSN=TEMP.SAR.CF01200,DISP=SHR
//SORTIN    DD DSN=TEMP.SAR.CF01200.SORTED,DISP=SHR
//SYSIN     DD *
 SORT FIELDS=(1,27,CH,A,48,10,CH,A),SIZE=E2000
/*
```

OS JCL AND JES2

This chapter is a reference guide for programmers using OS JCL and JES2. It contains statements and parameters that are used to perform a task in batch mode under MVS/OS. The statements covered here are:

- Comment statement
- JOB statement
- EXEC statement
- DD statement
- OUTPUT statement
- JES2 control statement
- Other control statements

Each section consists of a description of the statement and its parameters, the general formats, and examples.

Notational Convention: In the general format of the JCL or JES2 statements used in this chapter, there are a few symbols that are not part of the syntax, therefore they must not be included when coding your JCL. These symbols and their meanings are:

Symbol   **Meaning**

[]   The option enclosed by the brackets ([]) is not required but can be included.

<>   Only one of the alternatives enclosed by the angle brackets (<>) must be chosen.

or	The alternatives enclosed by the angle brackets (<>) are separated by "or."
____	The underlined word is the default value.
...	The vertical or horizontal ellipsis means that the preceding can be coded more than once.
Uppercase characters	All keywords of the command are written in uppercase characters; they must be coded as shown.
Lowercase characters	All strings in lowercase characters and italic are variables that can be changed to any other strings to suit your programming style. In your code they represent values that you supply to commands.

8.1 COMMENT STATEMENT

A comment statement is used to document a job. Such a statement is not executed; it appears on the output listing. In the first three positions are the characters //*, followed by a character string. The general format is

```
//*comment
```

In the following JCL example, the second line is a comment statement with the string "EXECUTE PROGRAM TO UPDATE DATABASE."

```
//C840BGFI JOB (0200,200),'Joanne Peters',CLASS=L,
//          MSGCLASS=X
//*  EXECUTE PROGRAM TO UPDATE DATABASE
//STEP01    EXEC PGM=SAAAB010
//STEPLIB   DD DSN=TEST.COBOL.PGMLOAD,DISP=SHR
//CWSD01    DD DSN=TEST.CF010100.SORTED,DISP=SHR
//CWSD20    DD DSN=TEST.CF012000.SORTED,DISP=SHR
```

8.2 JOB STATEMENT

The JOB statement tells the system that a batch job is to be executed. It is placed in the first line of a job, which marks the start of the job in the stream of many jobs. Following this statement are other JCL statements. In the first two positions are the characters //, followed by a job name, the keyword JOB, accounting information, and other parameters. The general format of the JOB statement is

```
//job-name JOB (accounting-info) other-parameters
```

This section explains all the parameters for the JOB statement. They are Accounting information, ADDRSPC, CLASS, COND, GROUP, MSGCLASS, MSGLEVEL, NOTIFY, PASSWORD, PERFORM, programmer's name, REGION, RESTART, SECLABEL, TIME, TYPRUN, and USER.

In the following example, the JOB statement gives the job name as C840BGFI, accounting information as (0200,200), the programmer's name as 'Dave Smith', the user as C840BGF, and the job class as T.

```
//C840BGFI JOB (0200,200),'Dave Smith',USER=C840BGF,
//        CLASS=T
```

◻ Accounting information parameter

● General format
```
//jobname (pano,room,time,lines,cards,
//                    forms,copies,log,linect)
```

● Description
This parameter specifies the account number for a job execution and any other accounting information required by your installation. It is placed after the JOB keyword. There are several subparameters, each separated from the next with a comma. If a subparameter is omitted, place a comma in its position only if other parameters follow. The subparameters are as follows:

pano	Specifies the job account number, up to 4 alphanumeric characters.
room	Specifies the room number, up to 4 alphanumeric characters.
time	Specifies the estimated execution time in minutes, up to 4 decimal numbers.
lines	Specifies the estimated line count in thousands, up to 4 decimal numbers.
cards	Specifies the estimated number of cards to punch from the job's sysout datasets, up to 4 decimal numbers.
forms	Specifies the form to be used during printing of this

	job's sysout dataset, up to 4 alphanumeric characters.
copies	Specifies the number of copies to print or punch of this job's sysout dataset.
log	Specifies whether or not to print the job log. The character N means not to print the job log. If this subparameter is omitted or is any other character, then the job log is printed.
linect	Specifies the number of lines per page.

● Example

In the following example, the JOB statement specifies that the account number is 0200, the room number is 200, the time is 30 minutes, the line number is omitted and the estimated number of cards is 1000.

```
//C840BGFI JOB (0200,200,30,,1000),'Mitra',CLASS=L
```

◘ ADDRSPC parameter

● General format
```
ADDRSPC=VIRT or REAL
```

● Description

The ADDRSPC parameter directs the MVS to use virtual storage (pageable) or real storage (nonpageable) during the execution of your job.

● Example

In the following example, the JOB statement specifies that the system is to allocate to this job 1 Mbyte of real storage.

```
//C840BGFI JOB(0200,200,30,,1000),'Mitra',ADDRSPC=REAL
```

◘ CLASS parameter

● General format
```
CLASS=jobclass
```

● Description

The CLASS parameter assigns a class to your job during processing. The class for a job depends on the characteristics of the job and the rules established by the installation. A list of job classes can be obtained from the system programmer or operations staff.

jobclass is an alphanumeric character in the range A through Z or 0 through 9.

● **Example**
In the following example, the JOB statement assigns class L to job C840BGFI.

```
//C840BGFI JOB (0200,200,30,,1000),'Mitra',CLASS=L
```

◘ COND parameter

● **General format**
```
COND=(code,operator)
    or
COND=((code,operator)[,(code,operator)]...)
```

● **Description**
The COND parameter specifies a condition that the system should check before executing each step of the job. If the condition is satisfied, all the remaining steps are skipped and the job terminates. It is a global test for the whole job. The condition is made up of a code and a comparison operator. The code is tested againt the return code of a step before the step is executed. More than one condition can be entered with the COND statement.

code is the code tested against the return code for each step; it is in the range 0 through 4095.

operator is the operator used to make the comparison with the return code. The operators are

Code	Description
GT	Greater than
GE	Greater than or equal to
EQ	Equal to
NE	Not equal to
LT	Less than

LE   Less than or equal to

- **Example**
In the following example, the JOB statement includes a COND
parameter which specifies that if 5 is greater than or equal to the
return code of any step or 10 is less than the return code, the
system must terminate the rest of the job.

```
//C840BGFI JOB (0200,200),'Mitra',
//            COND=((05,GE),(10,LT))
```

◻ GROUP parameter

- **General format**
GROUP=group-name

- **Description**
The GROUP parameter specifies an RACF group to which a
RACF user is to be connected.

group-name is a group name up to 8 alphanumeric or national ($,
#, and @) characters.

- **Example**
In the following example, the JOB statement includes the GROUP
parameter to specify a group name C840$.

```
//C840BGFI JOB (0200,200),'Mitra',GROUP=C840$,CLASS=A
```

◻ MSGCLASS parameter

- **General format**
MSGCLASS=class

- **Description**
The MSGCLASS parameter assigns the job log to a specified
sysout output class. If this parameter is omitted in a JOB
statement, then the sysout output class defaults to the installation
class. The job log consists of

- JCL statements of the job

- JES2 or JES3 messages
- MVS operator messages
- In-stream procedure statements
- Cataloged procedure statements

class is a valid class of 1 character, A through Z or 0 through 9.

- **Example**

In the following JOB statement, the MSGCLASS parameter specifies X as the sysout output class.

```
//C840BGFI JOB (0200,200),'Mitra',CLASS=L,MSGCLASS=X
```

☐ **MSGLEVEL parameter**

- **General format**

```
MSGLEVEL=([statement][,message])
```

- **Description**

The MSGLEVEL parameter controls the content of the job log. The listing of the log depends on the subparameters *statement* and *message*.

statement specifies which JCL and JES statements are to be printed; its values are

 0 Print JOB statement only.
 1 Print all JCL statments, JES statements, and messages.
 2 Print JCL and JES statements.

message specifies the messages to be printed; its values are

 0 Print JCL messages; in case of an ABEND, print JES messages.
 1 Print JCL and JES messages.

If the MSGLEVEL parameter is omitted, the installation default values are assigned to the *statement* and *message* subparamters.

- **Example**

In the following JOB statement, the MSGLEVEL parameter

assigns 1 to the *statement* and *message* subparameters. As a result, everything is printed in the job log.

```
//C840BGFI JOB (0200,200),'Mitra',
//           CLASS=L,MSGLEVEL=(1,1)
```

◻ NOTIFY parameter

● General format
```
NOTIFY=userid
```

● Description

The NOTIFY parameter requests the system to send a message to your TSO session when the job ends, normally or abnormally. If you are not logged on and the job you submitted terminates, the message is kept in the system until you log on to that system. At that moment, the message is broadcast to your TSO session.

userid is a TSO userid up to 8 characters in length.

● Example
In the following JOB statement, the NOTIFY parameter requests that user C840BGF be notified when job C840BGFI ends.

```
//C840BGFI JOB (0200,200),'Mitra',
//           CLASS=L,NOTIFY=C840BGF
```

◻ PASSWORD parameter

● General format
```
PASSWORD=[password][,new-password]
```

● Description

The PASSWORD parameter specifies your current or new password to RACF or another security system.

password and *new-password* are valid RACF passwords.

● Example
In the following JOB statement, the PASSWORD parameter

specifies BLUEJAYS as the current password for job C840BGFI.

```
//C840BGFI JOB (0200,200),'Mitra',
//             CLASS=L,PASSWORD=BLUEJAYS
```

◘ PERFORM parameter

● **General format**
```
PERFORM=n
```

● **Description**
The PERFORM parameter specifies a performance group number for a job. A performance group determines how jobs are allowed to use CPU, storage, and channels.

n is a number in the range 1 through 9999; it is obtained from the system programmer.

● Example
In the following JOB statement, the PERFORM parameter specifies 25 as the performance group number.

```
//C840BGFI JOB (0200,200),'Mitra',CLASS=L,PERFORM=25
```

◘ Programmer's name parameter

● **General format**
```
'programmer-name'
```

● **Description**
The programmer's name identifies the job owner. It is placed after the accounting information in the JOB statement.

programmer-name can include any alphanumeric or special character, and is up to 20 characters in length.

● **Example**
In the following three JOB statements, the programmer's names are J.R.Dallas, 'JCL TEST', and 'MY-PROGRAM #2'. Note that the programmer's name may or not be enclosed with quotes.

```
//C840BGFI JOB (0200,200),J.R.Dallas,CLASS=L,MSGCLASS=X

//C840BGFI JOB (0200,200),'JCL TEST',CLASS=L,MSGCLASS=X

//C840BGFI JOB (0200,200),'MY-PROGRAM #2',MSGCLASS=X
```

◘ REGION parameter

● General format
```
REGION=nnnnK or nnnnM
```

● Description
The REGION parameter specifies the maximum number of bytes of virtual storage that the system must obtain for the execution of any step of the job. The REGION parameter of the JOB statement overrides the REGION parameter of the EXEC statement.

nnnn is the number of k bytes (1024-byte blocks) or Mbytes (1 megabyte blocks). If *nnnn* is 0, then the system requests the largest region size.

● Example
In the following JOB statement, the REGION parameter requests 1 Mbyte of storage for any step of job C840BGFI.

```
//C840BGFI JOB (0200,200),J.R.Dallas,CLASS=L,REGION=1M
```

◘ RESTART parameter

● General format
```
RESTART=*                                    or
        stepname                             or
        stepname.procstepname                or
        stepname.procstepname,checkid
```

● Description
The RESTART parameter tells the system to restart a job at a specific job step or at a specific checkpoint number in a job step.

* means to start at the first job step.

stepname is the name of the step where the job should restart.

procstepname is the name of the procedure step where the restart should occur.

checkid is the number of the checkpoint where the restart should occur.

● **Example**
In the following JOB statement, the RESTART parameter specifies restarting the job at SAABB020.SS02.

```
//C840BGFI JOB (0200,200),J.R.Dallas,CLASS=L,
//          RESTART=SAABB020.SS02
```

◘ **SECLABEL parameter**

● **General format**
```
SECLABEL=x
```

● **Description**
The SECLABEL parameter specifies the security level at which a job should be executed. If SECLABEL is omitted, the default value for your security system will be used.

x is a security label of up to 8 alphanumeric characters, with the first being nonnumeric. This label is obtained from your system security administrator.

● **Example**
In the following JOB statement, the SECLABEL parameter specifies SA020 as a security label.

```
//C840BGFI JOB (0200,200),J.R.Dallas,CLASS=L,
//          SECLABEL=SA020
```

◘ **TIME parameter**

● **General format**
```
TIME=([minutes][,seconds] or
       1440                 or
       NOLIMIT              or
       MAXIMUM)
```

● **Description**

The TIME parameter specifies a limit on the amount of CPU time a job can use. As a job step ends, the CPU time it consumed is subtracted from the time limit specified for the job. At any time before the job ends, if the time limit specified by the TIME parameter is consumed, the job will be terminated by the system with an S322 abend, even though a particular step has not been completed. This parameter overrides any TIME parameter of the EXEC statement in the job.

minutes is the number of CPU minutes.

seconds is the number of CPU seconds.

1440 means an unlimited amount of CPU time.

NOLIMIT is the same as 1440 for MVS/ESA Version 4 or above.

MAXIMUM means up to 357,912 minutes of CPU time, which is about 248.5 days of continuous CPU use.

● **Example**

In the following JOB statement, the TIME parameter specifies 10 minutes and 30 seconds as the limit on the CPU time job C840BGFI can consume.

```
//C840BGFI JOB (0200,200),'JCL TEST',
//             CLASS=L,TIME(10,30)
```

◻ **TYPRUN parameter**

● **General format**

```
TYPRUN=COPY    or
       HOLD    or
       JCLHOLD or
       SCAN
```

● **Description**

The TYPRUN parameter specifies special processing of the job.

COPY means to copy the input stream of the job directly to SYSOUT, without executing the job.

HOLD means to hold the job in a waiting mode until it is released for execution by the user or operator.

JCLHOLD means to hold the job without any JCL processing until it is released for execution by the user or operator.

SCAN means to perform JCL syntax checking; the job is not executed.

● **Example**

In the following JOB statement, the TYPRUN parameter specifies scanning the job for any syntax error. The job is not executed.

```
//C840BGFI JOB (0200,200),'JCL TEST',
//              CLASS=L,TYPRUN=SCAN
```

◻ **USER parameter**

● **General format**

```
USER=user-name
```

● **Description**

The USER parameter specifies your RACF userid. This parameter is optional, and it is used in the following situations:

● A job is submitted to be executed in the network node where the security check is done.

● A job is submitted by a TSO user on behalf of another TSO user.

● A job needs access to RACF-protected resources.

user-name is a user identification defined in RACF; it is up to 7 alphanumeric or national characters.

● **Example**

In the following JOB statement, the USER parameter specifies C840BGF as a userid.

```
//C840BGFI JOB (0200,200),'JCL TEST',
//              CLASS=L,USER=C840BGF
```

8.3 EXEC STATEMENT

The EXEC statement identifies to the system a step of a job. A job step consists of an EXEC statement followed by one or more DD statements. In the first two positions of the EXEC statement are the characters //, followed by a step name, the keyword EXEC, one or more optional parameters, and an optional comment.

The general format is

```
//[stepname] EXEC parameter... [comment]
```

stepname is the optional name of the job. It starts in column 2 of the EXEC statement and consists of 1 to 8 alphanumeric or national characters.

parameter is the name of an EXEC statement. You can specify one or more parameters. Below, they are explained in detail. They are ADDRSPC, COND, DPRTY, DYNAMNBR, PARM, PERFORM, PGM, PROC, RD, REGION, and TIME. The EXEC keyword must be followed by either PGM or PROC but never both.

comment is the comment, which is placed one blank character after the last parameter.

In the following EXEC statement, the step name is SAAS01 and the parameters are PGM, ADDRSPC, and REGION.

```
//SAAS01 EXEC PGM=SAABB020,ADDRSPC=REAL,
//            REGION=1M
```

◘ ADDRSPC parameter

- **General format**
  ADDRSPC=<u>VIRT</u> or REAL

- **Description**
  The ADDRSPC parameter directs the MVS to use virtual storage (pageable) or real storage (nonpageable) during the execution of the job step. An ADDRSPC parameter of a JOB statement overrides an EXEC ADDRSPC parameter.

● **Example**

The following EXEC statement requests the system to allocate 1 Mbyte of real storage during the execution of the job step SAAS01.

```
//SAAS01 EXEC PGM=SAABB020,ADDRSPC=REAL,REGION=1M
```

◘ **COND parameter**

● **General format**

```
COND[.procstepname]=
   (code,operator[,stepname][.procstepname])
```

       or

```
COND[.procstepname]=
   ((code,operator[,stepname][.procstepname]),
      (code,operator[,stepname][.procstepname]),...)
```

       or

```
COND=EVEN or ONLY
```

● **Description**

The COND parameter determines whether a job step is to be skipped or executed. If coded with an EXEC statement, it tells the system to test the return codes of all prior job steps against a specified condition. If the test is satisfied, then the job step where the COND= is found is skipped; otherwise the job step is executed. Up to eight tests can be requested.

code is the code tested against the return code from each step, which is in the range 0 through 4095.

operator is the operator used to make the comparison with the return code. The operators are:

Code	Description
GT	Greater than
GE	Greater than or equal to
EQ	Equal to
NE	Not equal to
LT	Less than
LE	Less than or equal to

stepname is the name of a step for which the return code is to be tested.

procstepname is the name of a step of a JCL procedure for which the return code is to be tested.

- **Example**
  In the following EXEC statement, COND=(8,LE,COB) specifies that the LINK step is to be skipped if the previous step COB returns a condition code higher than 8.

  ```
  //LINK EXEC PGM=IEWL,PARM='LET,LIST',COND=(8,LE,COB)
  ```

☐ DPRTY parameter

- **General format**
  ```
  DPRTY[.procstepname]=([value1][,value2])
  ```

- **Description**
  The DPRTY parameter assigns a dispatching priority to a job step. Using this priority, the system resource manager (SRM) determines how often to execute the step task. If installation control specification (ICS) is in use, the DPRTY may be ignored by your installation. The dispatching priority is determined by the formula

  Dispatching priority = (*value1**16) + *value2*

  If the DPRTY parameter is not used in a job step, JES2 will assign a priority to the job step; otherwise this parameter overrrides the priority assigned by JES2 to a job step.

  procstepname is the name of a step of a JCL procedure.

  value1 is the first value, in the range 0 to 15.

  value2 is the second value.

- **Example**
  In the following EXEC statement, DPRTY=(15,10) is evaluated to a dispatch priority of 250 and assigned to the step STEP01.

```
//STEP01 EXEC PGM=IDCAMS,DPRTY=(15,10)
```

◘ DYNAMNBR parameter

• General format
```
DYNAMNBR=n
```

• Description
The DYNAMNBR parameter specifies the number of task I/O
table (TIOT) slots to reserve. The TIOT slots are used for datasets
that are dynamically allocated during the execution of the job step.

n is a number in the range $0 < n < (1635 - dd)$, where dd is the
number of DD statements in the job step.

• Example
In the following EXEC statement, DYNAMNBR=12 specifies that
slots equal to 12 plus the number of DD statements after this
EXEC statement are to be held for reuse.

```
//STEP01 EXEC PGM=IDCAMS,DYNAMNBR=12
```

◘ PARM parameter

• General format
```
PARM[.procstepname]=information
```

• Description
The PARM parameter is used to pass information to a program
being executed in this job step. The running program must be
coded to receive the information. The information is enclosed in
parentheses or apostrophes. The information may consist of one or
more expressions, separated by commas.

procstepname is the name of a step of a JCL procedure.

information can be up to 100 characters, including commas but
excluding the parentheses and apostrophes. The commas are
passed to the program, but the parentheses and apostrophes are
withheld.

● **Example**

In the following EXEC statement, through the PARM parameter the information 'LET,LIST' is passed to the program IEWL.

```
//LINK EXEC PGM=IEWL,PARM='LET,LIST',COND=(8,LE,COB)
```

◻ PERFORM parameter

● **General format**
```
PERFORM[.procstepname]=n
```

● **Description**

The PERFORM parameter specifies a performance group number for a job step. A performance group determines how the job step is allowed to use CPU, storage, and channels. It is an optional parameter; if it is omitted, a default value is assigned to the job step.

procstepname is the name of a step of a JCL procedure.

n is a number in the range 1 through 9999; it is obtained from the system programmer.

● **Example**

In the following EXEC statement, the PERFORM parameter specifies 12 as the performance group number.

```
//SAAS01 EXEC PGM=SAABB020,PERFORM=12,REGION=1M
```

◻ PGM parameter

● **General format**
```
PGM=program-name                  or
   *.stepname.ddname               or
   *.stepname.procstepname.ddname
```

● **Description**

The PGM parameter specifies the program to be executed for a particular job step. It can be entered directly or refer back to a previous step.

program-name is a program name to be executed for the job step and is also a member of a PDS. The name consists of alphanumeric or national (\$, #, and @) characters, but the first character must be alphanumeric. The PDS is referred by a JOBLIB DD statement or a STEPLIB DD statement or is a system library.

.stepname.ddname refers to a DD statement defined in an earlier job step, where *stepname* is a job name associated with an EXEC statement and *ddname* refers to a member of a PDS.

.stepname.procstepname.ddname refers to a member of a PDS in a JCL procedure.

- **Example**
In the following EXEC statement, the PGM parameter specifies to execution of the program SAABB020, found in the PDS TEST.COBOL.PGMLOAD.

```
//C840BGFI JOB (0200,200),'TEST PROGRAM',CLASS=L
//SAAS01 EXEC PGM=SAABB020,REGION=1M
//STEPLIB DD DSN=TEST.COBOL.PGMLOAD
```

In the EXEC statement of the GO step, the PGM parameter refers back to a member of a PDS defined in the previous step LINK. The *ddname* is SYSLMOD, again found in the step LINK.

```
//C840BGFI JOB (0200,200),'LINK & GO',CLASS=L
//LINK     EXEC PGM=IEWL
//SYSKMOD  DD  DSN=&&LOADMOD(SAABB020),UNIT=3350,
//             DISP=(MOD,PASS),
//             SPACE=(1024,(50,20,1))
//GO       EXEC PGM=*.LINK.SYSLMOD
```

☐ **PROC parameter**

- **General format**
```
PROC=procedure-name or
     procedure-name
```

- **Description**
The PROC parameter specifies the JCL procedure to be executed. The parameter is entered after the EXEC keyword; if the keyword PROC is omitted, it is assumed to be a procedure name.

procedure-name is a name of a cataloged or in-stream JCL procedure.

● **Example**

In the following example, the procedure name is specified with and without the keyword PROC.

```
//STEP01   EXEC MYPROC

   or

//STEP01   EXEC PROC=MYPROC
```

◻ **RD parameter**

● **General format**

```
RD[.procstepname]=    R       or
                      RNC     or
                      NR      or
                      NC
```

● **Description**

The RD (restart definition) parameter instructs the system to restart the job in case of failure or not to use checkpoint restart facilities in the program being executed or on the DD statement.

procstepname is the name of a step of a JCL procedure.

R means to restart automatically.

RNC means to restart automatically with no checkpoints allowed.

NR means no automatic restart, but checkpoints are allowed.

NC means no automatic restart and no checkpoints allowed.

● **Example**

In the following EXEC statement, the RD parameter is used to instruct the operator to restart the job step if it fails.

```
//SAAS01 EXEC PGM=SAABB020,RD=R,REGION=1M
```

◘ REGION parameter

● General format
```
REGION=nnnnK or nnnnM
```

● Description
The REGION parameter specifies the maximum number of bytes
of virtual storage that the system must obtain for the execution of
the job step. The REGION parameter of the JOB statement
overrides the REGION parameter of the EXEC statement.

nnnn is the number of kbytes (1024-byte blocks) or Mbytes (1-
megabyte blocks). If *nnnn* is 0, then the system requests the
largest region size.

● Example
In the following EXEC statement, the REGION parameter requests
the system for the largest available region size to execute the
program SAABB020.

```
//SAAS01 EXEC PGM=SAABB020,REGION=0M
```

◘ TIME parameter

● General format
```
TIME=([minutes][,seconds] or
          1440            or
          NOLIMIT         or
          MAXIMUM)
```

● Description
The TIME parameter specifies a limit on the amount of CPU time
a job step can use. When the time limit specified by the TIME
parameter is consumed, the job will be terminated by the system
with an S322 abend. The TIME parameter of the JOB statement
overrides any TIME parameter of the EXEC statement in the job.

minutes is the number of CPU minutes.

seconds is the number of CPU seconds.

1440 means an unlimited amount of CPU time.

NOLIMIT is the same as 1440 for MVS/ESA Version 4 or above.

MAXIMUM means up to 357,912 minutes of CPU time, which is about 248.5 days of continuous CPU use.

● **Example**
In the following EXEC statement, the TIME parameter allows a maximum of 1 CPU minute to execute the program SAABB020.

```
//SAAS01 EXEC PGM=SAABB020,REGION=1M,TIME=1
```

8.4 DD STATEMENT

A DD statement describes a dataset or any other resource as input or output to a program in the job step. It can be used to allocate a dataset or any other resource. In the first two positions are the characters //, followed by a DD name, a DD keyword, one or more optional parameters, and an optional comment.

The general format is

```
//[ddname]  DD parameter,...  comment
```

ddname is the name of the job step and it must be unique within a job step. *ddname* must start in column three of the DD statement. It is a mandatory field; if *ddname* is omitted, then the dataset is concatenated to a dataset previously defined by another DD statement. *ddname* may consist of alphanumeric or national characters, and is up to 8 characters in length. There are some special DD names, each of which represents a facility. They are used when these facilities are needed. These DD names are described in detail later in this chapter. They are

JOBCAT	JOBLIB	STEPCAT	STEPLIB
SYSABEND	SYSCHK	SYSCKEOV	SYSIN
SYSMDUMP	SYSUDUMP		

Also, there are other DD names that are special to JES3. They should not be used on a DD statement in a JES3 system. They are:

JCBIN	JCBLOCK	JCBTAB	JCLIN

JESI*nnnn*	JESJCL	JESMSG	JOURNAL
JST	SYSMSG	JS3CATLG	J3JBINFO
J3SCINFO			

DD is the keyword that identifies a DD statement. It is placed after the DD name, separated by a blank. Following the DD keyword is a blank and any parameters.

parameter can be of two kinds: positional and keyword. The positional parameters are

    * DATA   DUMMY DYNAM

The keyword parameters are optional; they are

ACCODE	AMP	AVGREC	BURST
CHARS	CHKPT	CNTL	COPIES
DATACLAS	DCB	DDNAME	DEST
DISP	DLM	DSNAME	EXPDT
FCB	FLASH	FREE	HOLD
KEYLEN	KEYOFF	LABEL	LIKE
LRECL	MGMTCLAS	MODIFY	OUTLIM
OUTPUT	PROTECT	RECFM	RECORG
REFDD	RETPD	SECMODEL	SEGMENT
SPACE	SPIN	STORCLAS	SUBSYS
SYSOUT	TERM	UCS	UNIT
VOLUME			

comment can be placed after any parameter.

● **Example**

In the following job step STEP01, there are six DD statements. The DD names STEPLIB, SYSOUT, and SYSIN are for the system, while CWSD01, CWSD20, and SAASO are DD names specific to this job step. Note that the lines following the DD name SAASO do not have DD names. This means that they are part of the DD name SAASO. In each of the DD statements various parameters, such as DSN, DISP, and so on, have been used. All the parameters are described later in this chapter.

```
//C840BGFI JOB (0200,200),'Joanne Peters',CLASS=L
//STEP01    EXEC PGM=SAAAB010
//STEPLIB   DD DSN=TEST.COBOL.PGMLOAD,DISP=SHR
```

```
//CWSD01    DD  DSN=TEST.CF010100.SORTED,DISP=SHR
//CWSD20    DD  DSN=TEST.CF012000.SORTED,DISP=SHR
//SAASO     DD  DSN=TEST.JUN0992.CWSO,
//              DISP=(,CATLG,DELETE),
//              SPACE=(CYL,(1,1),RLSE),
//              UNIT=SYSDA,
//              DCB=(LRECL=130,BLKSIZE=13000,RECFM=FB)
//SYSOUT    DD  SYSOUT=*
//SYSIN     DD  *
920601
/*
```

◘ ACCODE parameter

• General format
```
ACCODE=access-code
```

• Description
The ACCODE parameter specifies a new accessibility code or changes an old one for an ISO/ANSI/FIPS version 3 tape to write to a dataset. An exit routine, written for your installation, verifies the code after it is written to the dataset. If your job is authorized to use the code, then the job step can access the dataset; otherwise, the system abends the job with an error message.

access-code is the accessibility code, consisting of 1 to 8 characters. The first character must be an uppercase alphabetic character (A to Z). The default is a blank (X'40).

• Example
In the following DD statement, the ACCODE parameter specifies M as the accessibility code.

```
//TAPE   DD  UNIT=3400,VOL=SER=T12090,DSNAME=TAPEFILE,
//              LABEL=(1,AL),ACCODE=M
```

◘ AMP parameter

• General format
```
AMP=['subparameter,...']
```

where *subparameter* is one of the following:

```
AMORG
BUFND=n
BUFNI=n
```

```
BUFSP=n
CROPS=NCK or
      NRC or
      NRE or
      RCK
OPTCD=I   or
      L   or
      IL
RECFM=F   or
      FB  or
      V   or
      VB
STRNO=n
SYNAD=module
TRACE=(subparameter,...)
```

• Description

The AMP parameter adds information to an access method control block (ACB) for a VSAM dataset. The VSAM dataset can be a key-sequenced (KSDS) file, an entry-sequenced (ESDS) file, or a relative record (RRDS) file. AMP has many subparameters and you can enter one or more of the following subparameters separated by commas:

AMORG indicates that the dataset specified in the DD statement is a VSAM file.

BUFND specifies the number of buffers for data.

BUFNI specifies the number of buffers for indexes.

BUFSP specifies the maximum size of data and index buffers in number of bytes.

CROPS specifies the checkpoints.

OPTCD specifies the sequential dataset interface options.

RECFM specifies the record format of a sequential dataset.

STRNO indicates the number of request parameter lists.

SYNAD specifies the exit routine to be loaded by the sequential dataset interface.

TRACE indicates that trace records are to be written.

- **Example**
In the following DD statement, the AMP parameter specifies a buffer size of 2000 bytes, 3 data buffers, 4 index buffers, and 3 request parameter lists.

```
//VSAMDS01 DD DSN=TEST.DATA.JUN08,DISP=SHR,
//         AMP=('BUFSP=2000,BUFND=3,BUFNI=4,STRNO=3')
```

◘ **AVGREC parameter**

- **General format**
```
AVGREC=<U or K or M>
```

- **Description**
The AVGREC parameter specifies the unit of storage space for dataset allocation. It refers to the primary and secondary quantities of the SPACE= parameter of a DD statement. It is used by the system if SMS (System Managed Storage) is used.

U means number of records.

K means multiples of 1024 records.

M means multiples of 1,048,576 records.

- **Example**
In the following DD statement, AVGREC=U specifies that the primary and secondary quantities specified in the SPACE= parameter represent the number of records for which space is to be allocated.

```
//SAASO   DD DSN=TEST.JUN0992.CWSO,DATACLAS=SYSC,
//           DISP=(,CATLG,DELETE),
//           SPACE=(6160,(50,2)),AVGREC=U
```

◘ **BURST parameter**

- **General format**
```
BURST=<YES or Y or NO or N>
```

- **Description**
The BURST parameter specifies whether to burst, trim and stack

the printed pages coming out of the 3800 printer or leave them in continuous fanfold. The default is not to burst.

YES or Y means to burst.

NO or N means to leave the pages in continuous fanfold.

- **Example**

In the following DD statement, BURST=Y specifies bursting, triming and stacking the printed pages.

```
//REPORT   DD SYSOUT=A,BURST=Y
```

◼ **CHARS parameter**

- **General format**

```
CHARS=table-name                          or
      (table-name1,table-name2,...)        or
         DUMP
```

- **Description**

The CHARS parameter specifies one or more character arrangement tables for data printed on a 3800 printer.

table-name, *table-name1*, and *table-name2* are names of character arrangement tables. The name should be 1 to 4 characters. The tables are built using the IEBIMAGE utility, which resides in SYS1.IMAGELIB. The first 3 characters of the member name of this library are 'XTB'. The last 4 characters of the member name are used with the CHARS parameter.

DUMP specifies a 204-character-per-line special character set for dump printing.

- **Example**

In the following DD statement, CHARS=GT51 specifies printing using landscape characters.

```
//OUT1   DD SYSOUT=V,CHARS=GT51,PAGEDEF=V06483
```

◻ CHKPT parameter

• General format
```
CHKPT=EOV
```

• Description
The CHKPT parameter requests the system to write a checkpoint for every end-of-volume reached in a multivolume dataset. The checkpoint for the last end-of-volume is not written.

EOV means end-of-volume.

• Example
In the following DD statement, the CHKPT=EOV parameter specifies writing a checkpoint for every end-of-volume reached when writing data to dataset TEST.CUSTOMER.INFO.

```
//SAAOUT DD DSN=TEST.CUSTOMER.INFO,DISP=(NEW,KEEP)
//           CHKPT=EOV,UNIT=SYSDA,VOLUME=(,,,8)
```

◻ CNTL parameter

• General format
```
CNTL=*.label              or
     *.stepname.label     or
     *.stepname.procstepname.label
```

• Description
The CNTL parameter refers to a CNTL statement found in the earlier part of the job. A label specified in the CNTL parameter is used to search for the earlier CNTL statement.

label is the label name of an earlier CNTL statment.

stepname.label specifies a label in a job step.

stepname.procstepname.label specifies a label in a JCL procedure.

• Example
In the following DD statement, the CNTL=*.STEP03.DDSA refers to label STEP03 in job step DDSA.

```
//STEP02 DD CNTL=*.STEP03.DDSA
```

◘ COPIES parameter

• General format
```
COPIES=nnn                                    or
       (nnn,(group-value,group-value,...)) or
       (,(group-value,group-value,...))
```

• Description
The COPIES parameter specifies the number of copies of the sysout data to print.

nnn is the number of copies: from 1 through 255 for JES2 and from 1 through 254 for JES3.

group-value is the number of copies of each page to print.

• Example
In the following DD statement, the COPIES=3 parameter specifies printing 3 copies of the sysout data.

//SYSUT2 DD SYSOUT=V,OUTPUT=*.OUT1,**COPIES=3**

◘ DATA or * parameter

• General format
```
<DATA or *>
```

• Description
THe DATA or * parameter is used when the in-stream dataset in the job has the characters // in columns 1 and 2. The data are placed following the DD statement with the DATA or * parameter. You use * for data without JCL and DATA with JCL. The end of the in-stream data is marked in the following ways:

- The characters '/*' are found in columns 1 and 2.
- The delimiter character specified with a DLM keyword is found in columns 1 and 2.
- There are no more in-stream data.

• Example
In the following example, the first line is a DD statement with the

DATA parameter. Every thing following this statement is accepted by the system as in-stream data until the '/*' is found in columns 1 and 2.

```
//SYSUT1 DD DATA
//C840BGFI JOB (0200,200),'Joanne Peters',CLASS=L
//STEP01   EXEC PGM=SAAAB010
//STEPLIB  DD DSN=TEST.COBOL.PGMLOAD,DISP=SHR
//CWSD01   DD DSN=TEST.CF010100.SORTED,DISP=SHR
/*
```

◘ DATACLAS parameter

• General format
```
DATACLAS=data-class-name
```

• Description
The DATACLAS parameter specifies the data class and is used by the system only when System Managed Storage (SMS) is installed. The data class is used during the creation of a sequential dataset, PDS, or VSAM dataset.

data-class-name is a data class name defined by the storage administrator for the system you are using.

• Example
In the following DD statement, the DATACLAS parameter specifies SYSSC as the data class during the allocation of dataset TEST.JUN0992.CWSO.

```
//SAASO    DD DSN=TEST.JUN0992.CWSO,DATACLAS=SYSC,
//            DISP=(,CATLG,DELETE),
//            SPACE=(6160,(50,2)),AVGREC=U
```

◘ DCB parameter

• General format
```
DCB=(subparameter,...)   or
    dsname                or
    *.ddname              or
    *.stepname.ddname     or
    *.stepname.procstepname.ddname
```

● **Description**

The DCB parameter specifies file characteristics that are used to complete the data control block (DCB) information for file operations.

subparameter is one of the following DCB subparameters:

Parameter	Description
BFALN=[F or D]	Fullword or doubleword boundary
BFTEK=R	Specifies variable-length records
BFTEK=D	Specifies dynamic buffering
BFTEK=S	Specifies simple mode logical records
BFTEK=E	Specifies exchange mode logical records
BFTEK=A	Specifies locate mode logical records
BLKSIZE=*n-bytes*	Block size in number of bytes
BUFIN=*buffers*	Number of buffers for input
BUFL=*bytes*	Buffer length
BUFMAX=*buffers*	Maximum number of buffers
BUFNO=*buffers*	Number of buffers for DCB
BUFOFF=*n* or L	Specifies the size of the block prefix used with an ASCII tape dataset, where *n* is number of bytes and L means 4 bytes
BUFOUT=*buffers*	Number of buffers for output
BUFSIZE=*bytes*	Size of buffer
CPRI=R or E or S	Transmission priority
CYLOFL=*tracks*	Number of tracks per cylinder
DEN=1 or 2 or 3 or 4	Magnetic density
DIAGNS=TRACE	Trace option
DSORG=*organization*	Dataset organization
EROPT=*x*	Error option
FUNC=I or R or P or W or D or X or T	Type of dataset to be opened
GNCP=*n*	Maximum number of I/O macro instructions
INTVL=*n* or 0	Interval
IPLTXID=*member*	Member of PDS
KEYLEN=*bytes*	Length of key
LIMCT=*blocks* or *tracks*	Number of block or tracks to search

LRECL=*bytes*	Record length
MODE=C or E or O or R	Mode of operation with card reader or card punch
NCP=*n*	Number of READ or WRITE macro instructions before CHECK macro instructions
NTM=*tracks*	Tracks per cylinder
OPTCD=A or R or E or F or W	Optional services to be performed by control program
PCI=N or R or A or X	Program-controlled interruptions
PRTSP=0 or 1 or 2 or 3	Spacing for online printer
RECFM=*format*	Record format
RESERVE= (*byte1,byte2*)	Number of bytes to reserve
RKP=*number*	Position of the first byte of the key
STACK=1 or 2	Stacker bin to receive a card
THRESH=*nn*	Percentage of the nonreusable disk messsage
TRTCH=C or E or T or ET	Recording technique for 7-track tape

dsname is a cataloged dataset name.

*.ddname, **.stepname.ddname*, and **.stepname.procstepname.ddname* refer back to an earlier DD statement.

● **Example**
In the following DD statement, DCB specifies the characteristics of dataset TEST.JUN0992.CWSO. The dataset record length is 130, the block size is 13000, and the record format is fixed block.

```
//SAASO     DD DSN=TEST.JUN0992.CWSO,
//             DISP=(,CATLG,DELETE),
//             SPACE=(CYL,(1,1),RLSE),
//             UNIT=SYSDA,
//             DCB=(LRECL=130,BLKSIZE=13000,RECFM=FB)
```

◘ DDNAME parameter

● General format
```
DDNAME=ddname
```

● Description
The DDNAME parameter is used to defer definition of a dataset until later in the same job step.

ddname is the name of a DD statement later in the job step.

◘ DEST parameter

● General format
```
DEST=destination
```

● Description
The DEST parameter specifies the destination for a sysout dataset.

destination can be a local or remote terminal, a TSO ID, a node in the network, a printer, or a workstation. In JES2 it is one of the following:

LOCAL
name
N*nnnn*
N*nn*R*mmmm*
N*nnn*R*mmm*
N*nnnn*R*mm*
R*nnnn*
RM*nnnn*
RMT*nnnn*
U*nnnn*
(*node,userid*)

In JES3 it is one of the following:
ANYLOCAL
device-name
device-number
group-name
node-name
(*node,userid*)

● **Example**

In the following DD statement, the DEST parameter specifies U1214 as the destination for the sysout dataset.

```
//SYSUT2 DD SYSOUT=V,DEST=U1214
```

◻ **DISP parameter**

● **General format**
```
DISP=[status] or
     ([status] [,normal-termination-disp] [,abend-disp])

       [NEW] [,DELETE    ] [,DELETE   ]
       [OLD] [,KEEP      ] [,KEEP     ]
DISP=  [SHR] [,PASS      ] [,CATLG    ]
       [MOD] [,CATLG     ] [,UNCATLG  ]
       [,  ] [,          ]
```

● **Description**

The DISP parameter provides the disposition of a dataset to the system. There are three subparameters: status, disposition for normal termination of the job step, and disposition for an abnormal termination of the job step.

status may be one of the following: NEW, OLD, SHR, MOD, or blank.

normal-termination-disp may be one of the following: DELETE, KEEP, PASS, CATLG, or blank.

abend-disp may be one of the following: DELETE, KEEP, CATLG, or UNCATLG.

● **Example**

In the following DD statement, DISP specifies the normal termination disposition as CATLG and the abnormal disposition as DELETE for dataset TEST.JUN0992.CWSO. Note that the status is not specified; therefore a comma is coded in its absence.

```
//SAASO     DD DSN=TEST.JUN0992.CWSO,
//              DISP=(,CATLG,DELETE),
//              SPACE=(CYL,(1,1),RLSE),
//              UNIT=SYSDA,
//              DCB=(LRECL=130,BLKSIZE=13000,RECFM=FB)
```

▢ DLM parameter

● General format
```
DLM=delimiter
```

● Description
The DLM parameter specifies a delimiter to mark the end of in-stream data. With the delimiter the in-stream data can have characters // or /* in columns 1 and 2.

delimiter can be any two characters. If special characters ($, #, or @) are used, then the delimiter must be enclosed in apostrophes.

● Example
In the following example, the first line is a DD statement with the DLM parameter which specifies WW as a delimiter. The information following this statement is accepted by the system as in-stream data until the WW is found in columns 1 and 2.

```
//SYSUT1 DD *,DLM=WW
//C840BGFI JOB (0200,200),'Joanne Peters',CLASS=L
//STEP01    EXEC PGM=SAAAB010
//STEPLIB   DD DSN=TEST.COBOL.PGMLOAD,DISP=SHR
//CWSD01    DD DSN=TEST.CF010100.SORTED,DISP=SHR
WW
```

▢ DSNAME parameter

● General format
```
DSNAME or DSN = data-set-name or refer-back
```

● Description
The DSNAME or DSN parameter specifies a temporary or permanent dataset name to be associated with a DD statement.

data-set-name is the name of the dataset. If it is a temporary file, it is prefixed with two ampersand characters (&&). The dataset name must follow the MVS naming convention. It can be a sequential file, a partitioned dataset member, a GDG number, or an ISAM file area. The following shows the different categories of datasets:

Permanent datasets:

> *dsname*
> *dsname*(*member*)   Partitioned dataset member
> *dsname*(*gdg-number*)   Generation data group number
> *dsname*(*area*)   ISAM file area

Temporary datasets:

> *&&dsname*
> *&&dsname*(*member*)   Partitioned dataset member
> *&&dsname*(*area*)   ISAM file area

refer-back points to a DD name which refers to a dataset in an earlier DD statement. There are three formats for *refer-back*:

> **.ddname* refers to a DD name in an earlier DD statement of the same job step.

> **.stepname.ddname* refers to a DD name in an earlier job step.

> **.stepname.procstepname.ddname* refers to a DD name in a JCL procedure.

● Example

In the following DD statement, the DSN parameter specifies the dataset name TEST.JUN0992.CWSO. It is associated with the DD name SAASO.

```
//SAASO      DD  DSN=TEST.JUN0992.CWSO,
//               DISP=(,CATLG,DELETE),
//               SPACE=(CYL,(1,1),RLSE),
//               UNIT=SYSDA,
//               DCB=(LRECL=130,BLKSIZE=13000,RECFM=FB)
```

◘ DUMMY parameter

● **General format**
```
//ddname DD DUMMY
```

● **Description**
The DUMMY parameter allocates no device to a DD statement, therefore, no disposition and I/O processing are performed. If you have to use other parameters, they must have correct syntax.

● **Example**
In the following DD statements, the DUMMY parameter is used to allocate no device to DD statements SAASO and SYSIN.

```
//SAASO    DD DUMMY,DSN=TEST.JUN0992.CWSO,DISP=SHR
//SYSIN    DD DUMMY
```

◘ DYNAM parameter

● **General format**
```
//ddname DD DYNAM
```

● **Description**
The DYNAM parameter reserves a TIOT slot that is used for dynamically allocated resources and is held for later use.

● **Example**
In the following DD statement, the DYNAM parameter is used.

```
//SAAHOLD  DD DYNAM
```

◘ EXPDT parameter

● **General format**
```
EXPDT=yyddd or yyyy/ddd
```

● **Description**
The EXPDT parameter specifies an expiry date for a dataset. This date is used by the system during the creation of the dataset. When the expiry date is reached, the dataset can be deleted. This parameter is supported only by MVS/ESA and System Managed Storage (SMS).

yyddd is the Julian date, where *yy* is in the range 00 to 99 and *ddd* is in the range 001 to 366.

yyyy/ddd is the year and number of days within the year, where *yyyy* is in the range 0000 to 9999 and *ddd* is in the range 001 to 366.

If the following dates are specified, it means never delete the dataset:

99365, 99366, 1999/365 and 1999/366.

● **Example**
In the following DD statement, the expiry date for dataset TEST.JUN0992.CWSO is set to the year 2000 and day 120 of that year.

```
//SAASO    DD EXPDT=2000/120,DSN=TEST.JUN0992.CWSO,
//            DISP=(,CATLG)
```

◘ **FCB parameter**

● **General format**
```
FCB=fcb-name or
       (fcb-name,[,ALIGN][,VERIFY])
```

● **Description**
The FCB parameter specifies the form to use when printing the sysout dataset.

fcb-name is a standard FCB or an FCB name in SYS1.IMAGELIB. The names have the following forms:

FCB2*xxxx*—3211, 3203 Model 5 or SNA printer
FCB3*xxxx*—3800 printer
FCB4*xxxx*—4248 printer
STD1—6 lines per inch on 8.5-inch-long paper
STD2—6 lines per inch on 11-inch-long paper
STD3—8 lines per inch

ALIGN means to request the operator to align the form before printing starts.

VERIFY means to request the operator to check whether the spcified form is appropriate for printing the data.

● **Example**
In the following DD statement, the FCB parameter specifies STD2 as the form for printing the sysout dataset.

```
//SAARPT   DD SYSOUT=*,FCB=STD2
```

◻ FLASH parameter

● **General format**
```
FLASH=overlay-name          or
   (overlay-name[,count])   or
   NONE
```

● **Description**
The FLASH parameter specifies the forms overlay and number of copies when the sysout dataset is printed on a 3800 printer.

overlay-name is the name of the forms overlay.

count is the number of copies of the dataset to print, in the range 1 to 255.

NONE means that no forms overlay flashing is to be done.

● **Example**
In the following DD statement, the FLASH parameter specifies LOG01 as the forms overlay and 10 as the number of copies to print.

```
//SAARPT   DD SYSOUT=*,FLASH=(LOG01,10)
```

◻ FREE parameter

● **General format**
```
FREE=END or CLOSE
```

● **Description**
The FREE parameter specifies when to release the resources allocated to a DD statement.

END means to release (deallocate) the resources at the end of the job step. This is the default value.

CLOSE means to release (deallocate) the resources when the dataset is closed.

- **Example**
  In the following DD statement, FREE specifies deallocating dataset TEST.JUN0992.CWSO when it is closed.

```
//SAASO    DD FREE=CLOSE,DSN=TEST.JUN0992.CWSO,
//            DISP=SHR
```

☐ HOLD parameter

- **General format**
  ```
  HOLD=<YES or Y or NO or N>
  ```

- **Description**
  The HOLD parameter specifies whether to hold or print a sysout dataset.

  YES or Y means to hold the sysout dataset until the operator or a TSO user releases it to be printed.

  NO or N means to print the sysout dataset as soon as it is available.

- **Example**
  In the following DD statement, the HOLD parameter specifies to holding the sysout dataset until the operator or a TSO user releases it for printing.

  ```
  //SAARPT   DD SYSOUT=*,HOLD=Y
  ```

☐ JOBCAT DD statement

- **General format**
  ```
  //JOBCAT   DD DISP=SHR,DSN=catalog-name
  ```

- **Description**

  The JOBCAT DD statement specifies an ICF or VSAM catalog to be searched when locating cataloged datasets while a job is being executed. JOBCAT must be positioned after the JOB statement and before the first EXEC statement of the job. JOBCAT must always follow a JOBLIB DD statement if there is one.

- **Example**

  In the following job, the JOBCAT DD statement is used to specify the catalog JOANNE. Note that it is placed after the JOB statement and before the first EXEC statement.

```
//C840BGFI JOB (0200,200),'Joanne Peters',CLASS=L
//JOBLIB    DD DSN=TEST.COBOL.PGMLOAD,DISP=SHR
//JOBCAT    DD DISP=SHR,DSN=JOANNE
//STEP01    EXEC PGM=SAAAB010
//CWSD01    DD DSN=TEST.CF010100.SORTED,DISP=SHR
```

◘ JOBLIB DD statement

- **General format**

```
//JOBLIB   DD  DSN=program-library,DISP=SHR
```

- **Description**

  The JOBLIB DD statement specifies the library where the program load module resides. In one statement, you may enter one or more dataset names, using concatenation, and the system will search all of them for the programs that are used in the job. The JOBLIB DD statement must be placed after the JOB statement and before the first EXEC statement of the job. If a STEPLIB DD statement is used in a job step, it takes precedence over the JOBLIB DD statement.

- **Example**

  In the following job, the JOBLIB DD statement is used to specify the program load library TEST.COBOL.PGMLOAD.

```
//C840BGFI JOB (0200,200),'Joanne Peters',CLASS=L
//JOBLIB    DD DSN=TEST.COBOL.PGMLOAD,DISP=SHR
//STEP01    EXEC PGM=SAAAB010
//CWSD01    DD DSN=TEST.CF010100.SORTED,DISP=SHR
```

◘ KEYLEN parameter

• General format
KEYLEN=n

• Description
The KEYLEN parameter specifies the length of the key for the dataset found in the DD statement. It is used only in the MVS/ESA system.

n is a number in bytes in the range 0 to 255 for non-VSAM files and 1 to 255 for VSAM files.

• Example
In the following DD statement, KEYLEN specifies 24 as the key length for the VSAM file TEST.CF010100.VSAM.

```
//CWSD01  DD DSN=TEST.CF010100.VSAM,DISP=SHR,KEYLEN=24
```

◘ KEYOFF parameter

• General format
KEYOFF=n

• Description
The KEYOFF parameter specifies a relative offset in bytes of the key in a VSAM KSDS record, when it is created. It is effective only if System Managed Storage (SMS) is used. This parameter can be used to override the key offset for a DATACLAS.

n is a number in the range 0 to the logical record length minus the key length.

• Example
In the following DD statement, KEYOFF specifies 24 as the key offset for each record of the VSAM file TEST.CF010100.VSAM.

```
//CWSD01  DD DSN=TEST.CF010100.VSAM,DISP=SHR,KEYOFF=24
```

◘ LABEL parameter

• General format
```
LABEL=[data-set-seq]
     [,or ,label]
     [, or ,PASSWORD or ,NOPWREAD]
     [,IN or ,OUT]
     [,RETPD=nnnn or ,EXPDT=<yyddd or yyyy/ddd>]
```

• Description
The LABEL parameter specifies the label information, access password, availability for input-output operation, and retention or expiration date for tape or DASD datasets.

data-set-seq is a sequence number, in the range of 1 to 4 decimal digits, for a tape dataset. The sequence number can be omitted for the following reason:

- The dataset is cataloged.
- All members of a GDG dataset are requested.
- A dataset is passed from a previous job step.

label is the label type of a dataset. It is not retained for a cataloged dataset; if it is not specified in the LABEL parameter, the system assumes subparameter SL. The following is a list of subparameters for the LABEL parameter:

SL   The dataset has a standard label. This is the default value.

SUL   The dataset has both a standard label and a user-defined label.

AL   The dataset on tape has an ISO/ANSI Version 1 label or an ISO/ANSI/FIPS Version 3 label.

AUL   The dataset on tape has a user-defined label and an ISO/ANSI Version 1 label or an ISO/ANSI/FIPS Version 3 label.

NSL   The dataset on tape has a nonstandard label.

NL   The dataset on tape has no label.

BLP   The system is requested to bypass the label processing.

LTM   The dataset has a leading tapemark.

PASSWORD specifies that the dataset is protected; therefore, a password is required to perform read or write operations.

NOPWREAD specifies that the dataset is not protected; therefore, a password is not required to perform read or write operations.

IN specifies that the system must open the dataset for reading from the file only.

OUT specifies that the system must open the dataset for writing to the file only.

RETPD specifies the retention period for a dataset.

nnnn is the number of days until the dataset can be deleted; it can be from 1 to 4 decimal digits.

EXPDT specifies the expiry date of a dataset.

yyddd is a Julian date; *yy* is the year and *ddd* is the number of days of the same year.

yyyy/ddd is a Julian date in an MVS/ESA system, where *yyyy* is a four-digit year and *ddd* is the number of days of the same year.

- **Example**
The following DD statement, which allocates a new generation of a GDG dataset, uses the LABEL parameter. The LABEL parameter specifies the dataset sequence as 2, the label as standards, and the expiry date as year 93 and day 300 of the same year.

```
//SYSUT2  DD DSN=MY.TAPE.DATA(+1),DISP=(NEW,CATLG),
//           UNIT=TAPE,LABEL=(2,SL,EXPDT=93300)
```

◘ LIKE parameter

● **General format**
```
LIKE=dataset-name
```

● **Description**
The LIKE parameter tells the system to use all the file attributes from an existing dataset for a new dataset. It is effective only if System Managed Storage (SMS) is installed.

dataset-name is the name of an existing dataset whose attributes are used for creating a new dataset.

● **Example**
In the following DD statement, the LIKE parameter tells the system to use all the attributes of dataset PROD.CWSO.FILE when allocating dataset TEST.JUN0992.CWSO.

```
//SAASO    DD EXPDT=2000/120,DSN=TEST.JUN0992.CWSO,
//            DISP=(,CATLG),LIKE=PROD.CWSO.FILE
```

◘ LRECL parameter

● **General format**
```
LRECL=n or X or nnnnnK
```

● **Description**
The LRECL parameter specifies the length of the logical records of a dataset. This parameter is equivalent to the LRECL= subparameter of the DCB parameter.

n is the number of bytes in each record of the dataset. The length is in the range 1 to 32,760 for a non-VSAM dataset or 1 to 32,761 for a VSAM dataset (except a VSAM linear space dataset).

X is a flag to indicate that the dataset is a QSAM with record format VBS and that some of the records may be longer than 32,760 bytes.

nnnnnK is the number of K units in each record for an ISO/ANSI/FIPS Version 3 file, where K is 1024 bytes and *nnnnn* is in the range 1 to 16,383.

● **Example**

In the following DD statement, the LRECL parameter specifies 400 bytes as the record length of dataset TEST.JUN0992.CWSO.

```
//SAASO     DD EXPDT=2000/120,DSN=TEST.JUN0992.CWSO,
//             DISP=(,CATLG),LRECL=400
```

◘ **MGMTCLAS parameter**

● **General format**
```
MGMTCLAS=class-name
```

● **Description**

The MGMTCLAS parameter specifies the management class. It is effective only if System Managed Storage (SMS) is used and when creating a sequential dataset, a partitioned dataset, or a VSAM dataset.

class-name is the management class, obtained from the storage management administrator.

● **Example**

In the following DD statement, the MGMTCLAS parameter specifies TEST as the management class name when creating dataset TEST.JUN0992.CWSO.

```
//SAASO     DD EXPDT=2000/120,DSN=TEST.JUN0992.CWSO,
//             DISP=(,CATLG),MGMTCLAS=TEST
```

◘ **MODIFY parameter**

● **General format**
```
MODIFY=module-name or
         (module-name,trc)
```

● **Description**

The MODIFY parameter specifies a copy-modification module which is used by JES2 when printing a sysout dataset on a 3800 printer.

module-name is a module name residing in PDS SYS1.IMAGELIB, created by the IEBIMAGE utility.

trc is a number from 0 to 3 which specifies a tablename in the CHARS parameter. The number 0 references the first table in the CHARS parameter, 1 references the second table, 2 references the third table and 3 references the fourth table.

- **Example**

In the following DD statement, the MODIFY parameter specifies a copy-modification module A and 0 to refer to GS15 in the CHARS parameter.

```
//SAAST0    DD UNIT=3800,MODIFY=(A,0),CHARS=(GS15,GS10)
```

◻ OUTLIM parameter

- **General format**
```
OUTLIM=number
```

- **Description**

The OUTLIM parameter specifies the maximum number of records of sysout data to be written. If the limit is reached, the job may be aborted with an S722 abend, depending on whether the SYSOUT limit exit routine allows an exemption.

number is the maximum number of records of sysout data written; it is in the range 1 to 16,777,215.

- **Example**

In the following DD statement, the limit on the number of records written is 10,000.

```
//SAARPT    DD SYSOUT=V,OUTLIM=10000
```

◻ OUTPUT parameter

- **General format**
```
OUTPUT=reference or
          (reference[,reference]...)

   where reference is
     *.name
     *.stepname.name
     *.stepname.procstepname.name
```

- **Description**

The OUTPUT parameter is used to refer to an OUTPUT DD statement in a DD statement.

reference is a DD name. The DD name is either in the same job step, in another job step, or in a job step in a JCL procedure.

- **Example**

In the following job, the OUTPUT parameter is used in the SYSUT2 DD statement to refer back to an OUTPUT statement called OUT1.

```
//C840BQBI JOB (0200,200),'M. Arbelaez',CLASS=L
//PRINT1   EXEC PGM=IEBGENER,COND=EVEN
//OUT1     OUTPUT CHARS=GT51,PAGEDEF=V06483
//SYSPRINT DD SYSOUT=*,CHARS=GT51
//SYSUT1   DD DSN=TEMP.REPORT.SAA,DISP=OLD
//SYSUT2   DD SYSOUT=V,OUTPUT=*.OUT1,COPIES=2
//SYSIN    DD DUMMY
```

◻ PROTECT parameter

- **General format**

```
PROTECT= YES or Y
```

- **Description**

The PROTECT parameter requests RACF to protect a dataset. The request is made when the dataset is created.

YES or Y means to protect the dataset on DASD, tape dataset, or tape volume.

- **Example**

In the following DD statement, the PROTECT parameter requests RACF to protect the dataset TEST.JUN0992.CWSO.

```
//SAASO    DD EXPDT=2000/120,DSN=TEST.JUN0992.CWSO,
//            DISP=(NEW,CATLG,DELETE),
//            SPACE=(CYL,(1,1),RLSE),
//            UNIT=SYSDA,
//            DCB=(LRECL=130,BLKSIZE=13000,RECFM=FB),
//            PROTECT=Y
```

◘ RECFM parameter

● General format
```
RECFM=rec-format
```

● Description
The RECFM parameter specifies the record format for a dataset. It is equivalent to the RECFM= subparameter of the DCB parameter.

rec-format is the record format; it is one of the following:

Format   Description

Format	Description
F	Fixed-length
FB	Fixed-length and blocked
FBS	Fixed-length, blocked, and spanned
FS	Fixed-length and spanned
V	Variable-length
VB	Variable-length and blocked
VBS	Variable-length, blocked, and spanned
VS	Variable-length and spanned
U	Undefined length
A	Records contain ISO/ANSI characters
M	Records contain machine code control characters

● Example
In the following DD statement, the LRECL parameter specifies a fixed-length record format for dataset TEST.JUN0992.CWSO.

```
//SAASO     DD DSN=TEST.JUN0992.CWSO,
//             DISP=SHR,
//             LRECL=130,RECFM=F
```

◘ RECORG parameter

● General format
```
RECORG= KS or ES or RR or LS
```

● Description
The RECORG parameter, effective only if System Managed

Storage (SMS) is installed, specifies a file organization when a VSAM dataset is created. The following is a list of file organizations:

KS—key sequenced dataset (KSDS)
ES—entry sequenced dataset (ESDS)
RR—relative record dataset (RRDS)
LS—linear spaces dataset (ESDS)

● **Example**
In the following DD statement, the RECORG parameter specifies relative record dataset as the file organization of the VSAM file TEST.CF010100.VSAM.

```
//CWSD01  DD DSN=TEST.CF010100.VSAM,DISP=SHR,RECORG=RR
```

◘ **REFDD parameter**

● **General format**
```
REFDD=*.ddname
      *.jobstepname.ddname
      *.jobstepname.procstepname.ddname
```

● **Description**
The REFDD parameter, effective only if System Managed Storage (SMS) is installed, copies the attributes of a dataset to the dataset where this parameter is used. The dataset from which the attributes are being copied must have been previously described in the same job. The REFDD parameter has some limitations on what it can copy:

● It cannot copy the EXPDT or RETPD values for the dataset.
● It cannot refer back in the job to a GDG dataset, a temporary dataset, or a coded member of a PDS.
● It cannot refer back to DD statements having a * or DATA parameter.

.ddname refers back to a DD name in the job step.

.jobstepname.ddname refers back to a DD name in another job step.

.jobstepname.procstepname.ddname refers back to a job step in a JCL procedure.

- **Example**

In the following DD statement SAAS02, the REFDD parameter is used to refer back to DD statement SAAS01. This refer-back parameter copies the attributes of dataset PROD.JUN0992.CWSO and applies them to the dataset TEST.JUN0992.CWSO.

```
//SAAS01    DD DSN=PROD.JUN0992.CWSO,
//             DISP=SHR
//SAAS02    DD DSN=TEST.JUN0992.CWSO,
//             DISP=(,PASS),REFDD=*.SAAS01
```

◻ RETPD parameter

- **General format**
RETPD=*nnnn*

- **Description**

The RETPD parameter, effective only if System Managed Storage (SMS) is installed, specifies a retention period for a newly created dataset. After this period expires, the dataset can be deleted or written over by another dataset. This parameter is supported only by MVS/ESA and System Managed Storage (SMS).

nnnn is the number of days after which the dataset is either deleted or overwritten. The range of this number is 0000 to 9999. The actual expiry date is calculated by adding *nnnn* to the current date.

- **Example**

In the following DD statement, the expiry date for the dataset TEST.JUN0992.CWSO is the current date plus 120 days.

```
//SAASO     DD RETPD=120,DSN=TEST.JUN0992.CWSO,
//             DISP=(,CATLG)
```

◻ SECMODEL parameter

- **General format**
SECMODEL=(*RACF-profile-name*[,GENERIC])

- **Description**
  The SECMODEL parameter, effective only if System Managed Storage (SMS) is installed, copies security information from an existing RACF-protected dataset when creating a new dataset. The SECMODEL parameter copies the following information from the RACF dataset profile:

  AUDIT/GLOBALAUDIT OWNER   ID
  DATA   UACC
  ERASE   WARNING
  LEVEL   SECLEVEL

  RACF-profile-name is the profile of an existing RACF-protected dataset that is to be copied.

  GENERIC means that *RACF-profile-name* is a generic RACF profile.

- **Example**
  In the following DD statement SAASO2, the SECMODEL parameter tells the system to copy security information from dataset PROD.JUN0992.CWSO when creating dataset TEST.JUN0992.CWSO.

```
//SAASO1    DD DSN=PROD.JUN0992.CWSO,
//          DISP=SHR
//SAASO2    DD DSN=TEST.JUN0992.CWSO,SPACE=(,,31),
// DISP=(,CATLG),SECMODEL=(PROD.JUN0992.CWSO,GENERIC)
```

◻ SEGMENT parameter

- **General format**
  SEGMENT=*n*

- **Description**
  The SEGMENT parameter splits a sysout dataset into different segments that can be printed concurrently on different printers. With this parameter it is also possible to start the printing of the sysout dataset before the execution of the job ends.

  n is the number of pages of sysout data that form a segment to be printed or processed.

● **Example**

In the following DD statement, the SEGMENT parameter tells the system to group the sysout data into 1000-page segments, and print each segment as it is ready.

```
//SYSOUT    DD SYSOUT=A,CHARS=GT51,SEGMENT=1000
```

◻ **SPACE parameter**

● **General format**

General request:

```
SPACE =    ( <TRK or CYL or blk or reclen>
           ,(primary[,secondary][,dir-blocks or index])
           [,RLSE]
              [,CONTIG or MXIG or ALX]
           [,ROUND]
```

Request specific tracks:

```
SPACE=(ABSTR,(primary[,address][,dir-blocks or index]))
```

Request directory space:

```
SPACE=(,(,,dir-blocks))
```

● **Description**

The SPACE parameter specifies the space to allocate on a DASD volume when creating a new dataset. You can request the DASD space by tracks, cylinders, blocks, or record length. The record length specification is valid only when SMS is installed.

TRK means that a track is the space allocation unit.

CYL means that a cylinder is the space allocation unit.

blk is the length of the block, which is also the space allocation unit if the AVGREC parameter is not used.

reclen is the average record length, which is also the space allocation unit if the AVGREC parameter is used. *reclen* is in the range 1 to 65,535.

primary is the number of allocation units (TRK, CYL, *blk*, or *reclen*) the system acquires as the initial space for the dataset. Up to five extents of the primary quantity can be obtained on the first volume used for allocation.

secondary is the number of allocation units (TRK, CYL, *blk*, or *reclen*) the system acquires as additional space if required. Up to sixteen extents can be obtained.

dir-blocks is the number of directory blocks to reserve for a partitioned dataset (PDS). Each directory block is 256 bytes long.

index is the number of allocation units (TRK or CYL) to be reserved for the index of an ISAM dataset.

RLSE specifies the release of any allocated space that is not used. The release occurs when the file is closed.

CONTIG means that contiguous space must be allocated for the primary quantity; if it is not available the job is terminated with a "Space requested not available" message.

MXIG means to allocate the largest contiguous space that is equal to or greater than the specified primary quantity.

ALX mean to find five separate contiguous spaces for the specified primary quantity.

ROUND means that when *blk* is the allocation unit, the space allocated must be rounded up to a cylinder boundary.

ABSTR specifies obtaining space at the absolute track address.

address is the track number, specified when the ABSTR subparameter is used.

● **Example**
In the following DD statement, the SPACE parameter requests space for a new dataset TEST.JUN0992.CWSO. It specifies obtaining 3 cylinders as the primary quantity and 2 cylinders as the secondary quantity. It also specifies that if any allocated space is not used, it must be released after the dataset is closed.

```
//SAASO     DD DSN=TEST.JUN0992.CWSO,
//             DISP=(NEW,CATLG,DELETE),
//             SPACE=(CYL,(3,2),RLSE),
//             UNIT=SYSDA,
//             DCB=(LRECL=130,BLKSIZE=13000,RECFM=FB)
```

◻ SPIN parameter

● General format
```
SPIN=UNALLOC or NO
```

● Description
The SPIN parameter specifies that the sysout data are printed when the DD name is unallocated or when the job terminates.

UNALLOC means to print the sysout data when the dataset is closed.

NO means to print the sysout data when the job ends.

● Example
In the following DD statement, the SPIN parameter tells the system to print the sysout data when the dataset is closed and not to wait until the job ends.

```
//SYSOUT   DD SYSOUT=A,CHARS=GT51,COPIES=3,SPIN=UNALLOC
```

◻ STEPCAT DD statement

● General format
```
//STEPCAT DD DSN=catalog-name,DISP=SHR
```

● Description
The STEPCAT DD statement specifies an ICF or VSAM catalog. This catalog is searched by the system when locating cataloged datasets during the execution of a job step. STEPCAT takes precedence over a JOBCAT DD statement.

● Example
In the following job, the STEPCAT DD statement is used to specify the catalog JOANNE.

```
//C840BGFI JOB (0200,200),'Joanne Peters',CLASS=L
//JOBLIB   DD DSN=TEST.COBOL.PGMLOAD,DISP=SHR
//STEP01   EXEC PGM=SAAAB010
//STEPCAT  DD DISP=SHR,DSN=JOANNE
//CWSD01   DD DSN=TEST.CF010100.SORTED,DISP=SHR
```

◘ STEPLIB DD statement

• General format
```
//STEPLIB  DD  DSN=program-library,DISP=SHR
```

• Description
The STEPLIB DD statement specifies the library where a program
load module resides for a job step. In one statement, you may
enter one or more dataset names, using concatenation, and the
system will search all of them for the program. The STEPLIB DD
statement must be placed after the JOB statement and before the
first EXEC statement of the job. The STEPLIB DD statement for
a job step takes precedence over the JOBLIB DD statement, if it
is included.

• Example
In the following job, the STEPLIB DD statement is used to
specify the program load library TEST.COBOL2.PGMLOAD. It
takes precedence over the library specified by the JOBLIB DD
statement.

```
//C840BGFI JOB (0200,200),'Joanne Peters',CLASS=L
//JOBLIB   DD DSN=TEST.COBOL.PGMLOAD,DISP=SHR
//STEP01   EXEC PGM=SAAAB010
//STEPLIB  DD DSN=TEST.COBOL2.PGMLOAD,DISP=SHR
//CWSD01   DD DSN=TEST.CF010100.SORTED,DISP=SHR
```

◘ STORCLAS parameter

• General format
```
STORCLAS=storage-name
```

• Description
The STORCLAS parameter, which is effective only if System
Managed Storage (SMS) is installed, specifies the storage class to
be used during the creation of a sequential dataset, PDS, or VSAM
dataset.

storage-name is a storage class name defined by the storage administrator for the system you are using.

● **Example**
In the following DD statement, the STORCLAS parameter specifies SEQ01 as the storage class during the creation of dataset TEST.JUN0992.CWSO.

```
//SAASO     DD DSN=TEST.JUN0992.CWSO,STORCLAS=SEQ01,
//             DISP=(,CATLG,DELETE),
//             SPACE=(6160,(50,2)),AVGREC=U
```

◘ **SUBSYS parameter**

● **General format**
```
SUBSYS=subsystem-name[,subsystem-parameter]
```

● **Description**
The SUBSYS parameter specifies a subsystem that is to process the dataset of the DD statement.

subsystem-name is the name of a subsystem; it can be up to 4 alphanumeric and national characters.

subsystem-parameter is the parameter, if any, passed to the subsystem.

● **Example**
In the following DD statement, the SUBSYS parameter specifies R34$ as the name of the subsystem that is to process dataset TEST.JUN0992.CWSO.

```
//SUBR34$    DD DSN=TEST.JUN0992.CWSO,SUBSYS=R34$
```

◘ **SYSABEND DD statement**

● **General format**
```
//SYSABEND DD output
```

● **Description**
The SYSABEND DD statement is used to output a formatted dump of the work area of the user's program and task control

blocks. This request also outputs the system LSQA storage area.

output can be SYSOUT, DASD, or tape.

- **Example**
In the following job step, the SYSABEND DD statement is used
to output the work area of the program SAACB000 and the task
control block to SYSOUT.

```
//STEP1      EXEC PGM=SAACB000
//STEPLIB    DD DISP=SHR,DSN=TEST.COBOL.PGMLOAD
//SYSABEND   DD SYSOUT=*
//SYSABOUT   DD SYSOUT=*
//SYSPRINT   DD SYSOUT=*
//SYSIN      DD *
1992-06-01
/*
```

◘ SYSCHK DD statement

- **General format**
```
//SYSCHK    DD DSN=checkpoint-dsn,DISP=(,CATLG),
//          UNIT=TAPE
```

- **Description**
The SYSCHK DD statement describes a checkpoint dataset if a
checkpoint is being written or read.

checkpoint-dsn is a checkpoint dataset name on tape. It can also
be on a DASD volume, if the volume is not being shared.

- **Example**
In the following SYSCHK DD statement, the dataset
TEST.MY.CKPT.FILE is specified as a checkpoint dataset.

//SYSCHK DD DSN=TEST.MY.CKPT.FILE,
//   DISP=(,CATLG),UNIT=TAPE

◘ SYSCKEOV DD statement

- **General format**
```
//SYSCKEOV DD DSN=checkpoint-dsn,DISP=(,CATLG),
//            UNIT=TAPE
```

• Description
The SYSCKEOV DD statement describes a checkpoint dataset when the checkpoint is being written at the end of a volume and the CHKPT parameter of the DD statement is used.

checkpoint-dsn is a checkpoint dataset name on tape. It can also be on a DASD volume, if the volume is not being shared.

• Example
In the following SYSCKEOV DD statement, the dataset TEST.MY.CKPT.FILE is specified as a checkpoint dataset for a checkpoint written at the end of a volume.

```
//SYSCKEOV  DD DSN=TEST.MY.CKPT.FILE,
//               DISP=(,CATLG),UNIT=TAPE
```

◻ SYSIN DD statement

• General format
```
//SYSIN DD parameter
```

• Description
The SYSIN DD statement specifies the start of an in-stream dataset.

parameter is either * or DATA, and immediately following it are the in-stream data.

• Example
In the following job step, the SYSIN DD statement is used to input data to SAACB000. In this case the in-stream data are 1992-06-01.

```
//STEP1     EXEC PGM=SAACB000
//STEPLIB   DD DISP=SHR,DSN=TEST.COBOL.PGMLOAD
//SYSABOUT  DD SYSOUT=*
//SYSPRINT  DD SYSOUT=*
//SYSIN     DD *
1992-06-01
/*
```

◻ SYSMDUMP DD statement

● **General format**
```
//SYSMDUMP DD output
```

● **Description**
The SYSMDUMP DD statement is used to output a formatted dump of the work area of the user's program and task control blocks. This request also outputs the system LSQA storage area.

output can be SYSOUT, DASD, or tape.

● **Example**
In the following job step, the SYSMDUMP DD statement is used to output the work area of the program SAACB000 and the task control block to SYSOUT.

```
//STEP1      EXEC PGM=SAACB000
//STEPLIB    DD DISP=SHR,DSN=TEST.COBOL.PGMLOAD
//SYSMDUMP   DD SYSOUT=*
//SYSABOUT   DD SYSOUT=*
//SYSPRINT   DD SYSOUT=*
//SYSIN      DD *
1992-06-01
/*
```

◻ SYSOUT parameter

● **General format**
```
SYSOUT=class                               or
       (class,[INTRDR][,form-name])        or
       (class,[writer-name][,form-name]) or
       (,)

//SYSOUT DD output
```

● **Description**
The SYSOUT parameter classifies data to be printed or punched as a "SYStem OUTput" dataset. These output data are handled by JES2 or JES3, which is associated with an output class.

class is an output class to which the output data belong. *class* can be any character from A to Z or 0 to 9. If *class* is the character '*' or '$', this means that the output class is the same as the class specified in the MSGCLASS parameter of the JOB statement.

INTRDR requests the system to read the data going to this DD statement back to a JES2 internal reader. This allows a JCL to be written to a SYSOUT DD statement.

form-name is the name of the form that is to be mounted in the printer before printing the sysout dataset.

writer-name is the name of a JES external writer that is to process the data written to this DD statement.

output can be SYSOUT, DASD, or tape.

• **Example**
In the following job, there are three DD statements with the SYSOUT parameter and one SYSOUT DD statement. The SYSOUT with SYSPRINT DD statement specifies *, which assigns the same class as the MSGCLASS parameter of the JOB DD statement. Next is a SYSOUT DD statement with a SYSOUT parameter which specifies class A for this sysout dataset. Finally, the REPORT DD statement specifies class V for the sysout dataset.

```
//C840BGFI JOB (0200,200),'Joanne Peters',CLASS=L
//JOBLIB    DD DSN=TEST.COBOL.PGMLOAD,DISP=SHR
//STEP01    EXEC PGM=SAAAB010
//STEPLIB   DD DSN=TEST.COBOL2.PGMLOAD,DISP=SHR
//CWSD01    DD DSN=TEST.CF010100.SORTED,DISP=SHR
//SYSPRINT  DD SYSOUT=*
//SYSOUT    DD SYSOUT=A,CHARS=GT51
//REPORT    DD SYSOUT=V,CHARS=GT51
```

◘ **SYSUDUMP DD statement**

• **General format**
```
//SYSUDUMP DD output
```

• **Description**
The SYSUDUMP DD statement is used to output a formatted dump of the work area of the user's program and task control blocks. This request also outputs the system LSQA storage area.

output can be SYSOUT, DASD, or tape.

● **Example**

In the following job step, the SYSUDUMP DD statement is used to output the work area of the program SAACB000 and the task control block to SYSOUT.

```
//STEP1      EXEC PGM=SAACB000
//STEPLIB    DD DISP=SHR,DSN=TEST.COBOL.PGMLOAD
//SYSUDUMP   DD SYSOUT=*
//SYSABOUT   DD SYSOUT=*
//SYSPRINT   DD SYSOUT=*
//SYSIN      DD *
1992-06-01
/*
```

◘ **TERM parameter**

● **General format**
```
TERM=TS
```

● **Description**

The TERM parameter tells the system that the dataset is received from or transmitted to a TSO terminal.

In foreground mode, TS means that the dataset comes from or goes to a TSO terminal. In batch mode, TERM=TS is the same as SYSOUT=*.

● **Example**

In the following DD statement, the TERM parameter specifies that input or output data are from or for a TSO terminal.

```
//DATA1    DD TERM=TS
```

◘ **UCS parameter**

● **General format**
```
UCS=character-set-code
       (character-set-code[,FOLD][,VERIFY])
```

● **Description**

The UCS parameter specifies the following:

● Use the universal character set (UCS) when printing this

sysout dataset.
- Use the print train when printing this sysout dataset on an impact printer.
- Use a character arrangement for printing this sysout dataset on a 3800 printer.

character-set-code is the name of a universal character set; it can be up to 4 alphanumeric or national characters national characters.

FOLD means to load the chain or train for the universal character set in fold mode.

VERIFY means that the operator must check, before printing of the dataset starts, whether the character set image is correct for the chain or train.

- **Example**
In the following DD statement, UCS specifies character set code YN and requests the operator to check the character set image before printing starts.

```
//PRINT  DD UNIT=1403,UCS=(YN,,VERIFY)
```

◘ UNIT parameter

- **General format**
```
UNIT=([device-number][,unit-count][,DEFER])     or
      ([device-type][,P][,DEFER])               or
      ([group-name][,][,DEFER])                 or
      AFF=ddname
```

- **Description**
The UNIT parameter specifies the physical device where a dataset is to be found or created. It also instructs the system as to the number of devices to assign and defers mounting of a device until the dataset is opened for processing.

device-number is the number, of up to 3 characters, of a device. This number should be used only when it is absolutely necessary; incorrect coding of this subparameter may delay processing.

device-type is a device name and is one of the following:

Code	Device
3330	3330 Model 1
3330-1	3330 Model 11
3350	3350 DASD
3375	3375 DASD
3380	3380 DASD
3400-6	3420 tape drive (reel type)
3400-9	3480 tape cartridge

group-name is the name of a group of devices, for example, TAPE, SYSDA, or SYSALLDA. Group names vary from one installation to another.

unit-count is the number of devices for a dataset, in the range 1 to 59.

DEFER means to defer mounting of a device until the dataset is opened for processing.

P means to mount all the volumes for the dataset at the same time.

AFF tells the system to allocate datasets on the different removable volumes to the same device.

ddname is a previous DD name in the same job step.

- **Example**
In the following DD statement, the UNIT parameter specifies the group name as SYSDA for a new dataset TEST.JUN0992.CWSO.

```
//SAASO    DD DSN=TEST.JUN0992.CWSO,
//            DISP=(NEW,CATLG,DELETE),
//            SPACE=(CYL,(3,2),RLSE),
//            UNIT=SYSDA,
//            DCB=(LRECL=130,BLKSIZE=13000,RECFM=FB)
```

◻ **VOLUME parameter**

- **General format**
```
VOLUME=([PRIVATE][,RETAIN][,vol-seq][,vol-count]) or
VOL=SER=volser                                    or
```

```
VOL=SER=(volser1,volser2,...)                    or
VOL=REF=dsname                                   or
VOL=REF=*.dsname                                 or
VOL=REF=*.stepname.dsname                        or
VOL=REF=*.stepname.procstepname.ddname
```

- **Description**

The VOLUME parameter specifies the volume serial number where a dataset is to be found or created.

PRIVATE means that the request is for a private volume.

RETAIN means that the volume should not be demounted or rewound after the dataset is closed. It is valid with the PRIVATE subparameter.

vol-seq is the volume number for a dataset which resides in multiple volumes. This number is in the range 1 to 255.

vol-count is the maximum number of volumes required for an OUTPUT dataset. This number is in the range 1 to 255.

volser, *volser1*, and *volser2* are volume serial numbers where a dataset is to be found or created. One or more volume serial numbers can be specified.

dsname is the dataset name from which the volume serial information is taken.

*.dsname refers back to a DD name in the same job step.

*.stepname.dsname refers back to a DD name in another job step.

*.stepname.procstepname.ddname refers to a DD name in a JCL procedure.

- **Example**

In the following DD statement, the VOL=SER parameter specifies the volume serial number CEL112 where a new dataset TEST.JUN0992.CWSO is to be created.

```
//SAASO     DD DSN=TEST.JUN0992.CWSO,
//               DISP=(NEW,CATLG,DELETE),
//               SPACE=(CYL,(3,2),RLSE),
```

```
//                UNIT=SYSDA,VOL=SER=CEL112,
//                DCB=(LRECL=130,BLKSIZE=13000,RECFM=FB)
```

8.5   OUTPUT STATEMENT

The OUTPUT statement specifies options for processing a sysout dataset. The OUTPUT statement is effective only if it is explicitly or implicitly referenced in a DD statement. In the first two positions are the characters //, followed by a name field, a blank, the OUTPUT keyword, a blank, one or more optional parameters, and an optional comment.

The general format is

```
//name   OUTPUT parameter,... comment
```

name is the name of the OUTPUT statement. This name, which can include alphanumeric or national characters, can be up to 8 characters in length and is unique within a job.

parameter is optional; one or more of the following can be specified:

ADDRESS	BUILDING	BURST	CHARS
CKPTLINE	CKPTPAGE	CKPTSEC	CLASS
COMPACT	CONTROL	COPIES	DATACK
DEFAULT	DEPT	DEST	DPAGELBL
FCB	FLASH	FORMDEF	FORMS
GROUPID	INDEX	JESDS	LINDEX
LINECT	MODIFY	NAME	OUTDISP
PAGEDEF	PIMSG	PRMODE	PRTY
ROOM	SYSAREA	THRESHLD	TITLE
TRC	UCS	WRITER	

These parameters are described in detail in the following section.

comment is placed after a parameter with a blank in between.

In the following job, the OUTPUT parameter is used in a SYSUT2 DD statement to refer back to an OUTPUT statement called OUT1. In the OUTPUT statement, processing options CHARS and PAGEDEF are specified.

```
//C840BQBI JOB (0200,200),'M. Arbelaez',CLASS=L
//PRINT1   EXEC PGM=IEBGENER,COND=EVEN
//OUT1      OUTPUT CHARS=GT51,PAGEDEF=V06483
//SYSPRINT DD SYSOUT=*,CHARS=GT51
//SYSUT1    DD DSN=TEMP.REPORT.SAA,DISP=OLD
//SYSUT2    DD SYSOUT=V,OUTPUT=*.OUT1,COPIES=2
//SYSIN     DD DUMMY
```

◘ ADDRESS parameter

● General format
```
ADDRESS=[destination,...]
```

● Description
The ADDRESS parameter specifies an address or destination which is to appear on separator pages of sysout data printed for this job. The destination indicates where printed data are to be delivered.

destination is the address which is to appear on separator pages of a printed sysout dataset. It can be up to 60 characters long and include the following:

- Periods
- Alphanumeric characters
- National characters
- Parentheses, plus signs, hyphens, backslashes, asterisks, and ampersands

A destination with blanks must be enclosed in apostrophes.

● Example
In the following OUTPUT statement, the ADDRESS parameter specifies 'DEPT # 10 - ACCOUNT PROCESSING.' as the destination value.

```
//OUT1      OUTPUT CHARS=GT12,BURST=Y,
//              ADDRESS='DEPT # 10 - ACCOUNT PROCESSING.'
```

◘ BUILDING parameter

● General format
```
BUILDING=name
```

- **Description**

The BUILDING parameter specifies a name of a building which is to appear on separator pages of sysout data printed for this job. The building name indicates where printed data are to be delivered.

name is the building name which is to appear on separator pages of a printed sysout dataset. The name can be up to 60 characters long and include the following:

- Periods
- Alphanumeric characters
- National characters
- Parentheses, plus signs, hyphens, backslashes, asterisks, and ampersands

A name with blanks must be enclosed in apostrophes.

- **Example**

In the following OUTPUT statement, the BUILDING parameter specifies 'VICTORIA BLDG - #S1210' as the building name.

```
//OUT1      OUTPUT CHARS=GT12,BURST=Y,
//             BUILDING='VICTORIA BLDG - #S1210'
```

◻ BURST parameter

- **General format**

```
BURST=YES or Y or NO or N
```

- **Description**

The BURST parameter indicates whether to burst, trim, and stack the printed pages coming out of the 3800 printer, or to leave them in continuous fanfold. The default is not to burst. If both the DD and OUTPUT statements have the BURST parameter, the parameter on the DD statement overrides the one on the OUTPUT statement.

YES or Y means to burst.

NO or N means to leave the pages in continuous fanfold.

● **Example**

In the following OUTPUT statement, BURST=Y specifies bursting, trimming, and stacking the printed pages of the sysout dataset.

```
//OUT2   OUTPUT CHARS=GT12,BURST=Y
```

■ **CHARS parameter**

● **General format**
```
CHARS=table-name                      or
      (table-name1,table-name2,...)   or
         DUMP                         or
      STD     (JES3 only)
```

● **Description**

The CHARS parameter specifies one or more character arrangement tables for data printed on a 3800 printer.

table-name, *table-name1*, and *table-name2* are names of character arrangement tables. The name should be 1 to 4 characters. The tables are built using the IEBIMAGE utility, which reside in SYS1.IMAGELIB. The first 3 characters of the member name of this library are 'XTB'. The last four characters of the member name are used with the CHARS parameter.

DUMP specifies a 204-character per line special character set for dump printing.

STD means to use the standard character arrangement for a JES3 installation only.

● **Example**

In the following OUTPUT statement, CHARS=GT51 specifies printing using landscape characters.

```
//OUT1   OUTPUT CHARS=GT51,PAGEDEF=V06483
```

■ **CKPTLINE parameter**

● **General format**
```
CKPTLINE=nnnnn
```

- **Description**

The CKPTLINE parameter specifies the maximum number of lines per page when printing a sysout dataset. Along with this parameter, JES uses the CKPTPAGE parameter as a guide to how often to transmit across an SNA network. The CKPTLINE parameter is effective only for 3800 printer models 3 and 8 and is supported only by JES3.

nnnnn is the number of lines per page, in the range from 0 to 32,767.

- **Example**

In the following OUTPUT statement, the CKPTLINE parameter specifies 2000 as the maximum number of lines per logical page.

```
//OUT3   OUTPUT CKPTLINE=2000,CKPTPAGE=5
```

◻ CKPTPAGE parameter

- **General format**
```
CKPTPAGE=nnnnn
```

- **Description**

The CKPTPAGE parameter specifies the maximum number of pages of data to print between JES checkpoints. CKPTSEC takes precedence over CKPTPAGE if both parameters are specified.

nnnnn is the number of pages in the range from 1 to 32,767.

- **Example**

In the following OUTPUT statement, the CKPTPAGE parameter specifies 10 as the maximum number of pages.

```
//OUT3   OUTPUT CKPTLINE=2000,CKPTPAGE=10
```

◻ CKPTSEC parameter

- **General format**
```
CKPTSEC=nnnnn
```

● Description

The CKPTSEC parameter specifies the maximum number of seconds to wait between JES checkpoints during printing of sysout data for a job. CKPTSEC takes precedence over CKPTPAGE if both parameters are specified.

nnnnn is the number of seconds in the range from 1 to 32,767.

● Example

In the following OUTPUT statement, the CKPTSEC parameter specifies 100 as the maximum number of seconds to wait between JES checkpoints.

```
//OUT3   OUTPUT CKPTLINE=2000,CKPTSEC=100
```

◘ CLASS parameter

● General format
```
CLASS=c or *
```

● Description

The CLASS parameter specifies an output class that is to be assigned to the sysout data of an OUTPUT statement. The output classes differ from one installation to another.

c is the output class assigned to sysout data. The output classes differ from one installation to another. It can be any character from A to Z or 0 to 9.

* means to assign to the sysout data the output class specified in the MSGCLASS parameter of the JOB statement.

● Example

In the following OUTPUT statement, the CLASS parameter sets the value V as the class for the sysout data to be printed.

```
//OUT1      OUTPUT CLASS=V,CHARS=GT51,PAGEDEF=V06483
```

◘ COMPACT parameter

● General format
COMPACT=*name*

● Description
The COMPACT parameter specifies a compaction name that is used by JES when transmitting sysout data across an SNA network.

name is the name of a compaction table, which is a load module. The name is up to 8 characters long.

● Example
In the following OUTPUT statement, the COMPACT parameter specifies CAR5 as the load module for the compaction table. JES will use this table when sending data to terminal 222 at node 333.

```
//OUT1     OUTPUT CLASS=V,COMPACT=CAR5,DEST=N222R333
```

◘ CONTROL parameter

● General format
CONTROL=[PROGRAM or SINGLE or DOUBLE or TRIPLE]

● Description
The CONTROL parameter specifies one of the following:

● The carriage control characters are produced by a program.
● Single, double, or triple spacing is used for sysout data.

PROGRAM means that the first character of every record of the sysout data for this OUTPUT statement is a carriage control character.

SINGLE means that the sysout data of this OUTPUT statement must be single spaced.

DOUBLE means that the sysout data of this OUTPUT statement must be double spaced.

TRIPLE means that the sysout data of this OUTPUT statement must be triple spaced.

- **Example**

In the following OUTPUT statement, the CONTROL parameter specifies that the first character of every record of the sysout data for this statement is a carriage control character.

```
//OUT1     OUTPUT CLASS=V,CONTROL=PROGRAM
```

◼ COPIES parameter

- **General format**

```
COPIES=nnn                                       or
       (nnn,(group-value,group-value,...)) or
       (,(group-value,group-value,...))
```

- **Description**

The COPIES parameter specifies the number of copies of the sysout data to print. The number is discarded for the 3800 printer if a group value is also used.

nnn is the number of copies, ranging from 1 to 255 for JES2 and from 1 to 254 for JES3.

group-value is the number of copies of each page to print.

- **Example**

In the following OUTPUT statement, the COPIES parameter specifies printing 10 copies of the sysout data for this statement.

```
//OUT1     OUTPUT CLASS=V,COPIES=10
```

◼ DATACK parameter

- **General format**

```
DATACK=[BLOCK or UNBLOCK or BLKPOS or BLKCHAR]
```

- **Description**

The DATACK parameter specifies whether or not data check errors are to be blocked when sysout data are printed using the Print Services Facility (PSF). The errors occur either when invalid characters are sent to the printer or when the character position is incorrect.

BLOCK means to block errors caused by both invalid characters and incorrect character positioning.

UNBLOCK means not to block errors caused by invalid character or incorrect characters positioning.

BLKPOS means to block errors caused by character positioning only.

BLKCHAR means to block errors caused by invalid characters only.

● **Example**
In the following OUTPUT statement, the DATACK parameter specifies blocking errors caused by character positioning using PSF.

```
//OUT1      OUTPUT DATACK=BLKPOS
```

◘ DEFAULT parameter

● **General format**
DEFAULT = Y or YES or N or NO

● **Description**
The DEFAULT parameter specifies whether this OUTPUT statement is the default for the sysout data. If it is the default, then the OUTPUT statement is implicitly referenced in a sysout DD statement; otherwise the OUTPUT statement must be explicitly referenced for it to be effective.

Y or YES means to make this OUTPUT statement the default for the DD statement.

N or NO means not to make this OUTPUT statement the default for the DD statement. In other words, it must be explicitly referenced in a SYSOUT DD statement.

● **Example**
In the following job, there are two OUTPUT statements named
OUT1 and OUT2. OUT2 is specified with DEFAULT to be the
default for the SYSOUT DD statement. OUT1 is not the default;
therefore it is referenced explicitly by a DD statement named
SYSUT2. The DD statement named SYSPRINT does not have an
OUTPUT parameter; therefore, to print its sysout data, the system
will use the OUTPUT statement called OUT2.

```
//C840BQBI JOB (0200,200),'M. Arbelaez',CLASS=L
//PRINT1   EXEC PGM=IEBGENER,COND=EVEN
//OUT1     OUTPUT CHARS=GT51,DEST=U1214
//OUT2     OUTPUT DEFAULT=YES,GT51,DEST=U1299
//SYSPRINT DD SYSOUT=V
//SYSUT1   DD DSN=TEMP.REPORT.SAA,DISP=OLD
//SYSUT2   DD SYSOUT=V,OUTPUT=*.OUT1,COPIES=2
//SYSIN    DD DUMMY
```

◘ **DEPT parameter**

● **General format**
DEPT=*name*

● **Description**
The DEPT parameter specifies a name of a department which is
to appears on separator pages of sysout data printed for this
OUTPUT statement. The department name indicates where printed
data are to be delivered.

name is the department name which is to appear on separator
pages of a printed sysout dataset. The name can be up to 60
characters long and include the following:

● Periods
● Alphanumeric characters
● National characters
● Parentheses, plus signs, hyphens, backslashes, asterisks, and
  ampersands

A name with blanks must be enclosed in apostrophes.

● **Example**
In the following OUTPUT statement, the DEPT parameter

specifies 'Human Resources - #HU10' as the department name.

```
//OUT1      OUTPUT CHARS=GT12,BURST=Y,
//             DEPT='Human Resources - #HU10'
```

◻ DEST parameter

- **General format**
  DEST=*destination*

- **Description**
  The DEST parameter specifies the destination for a sysout dataset
  for an OUTPUT statement.

  destination can be a local or remote terminal, a TSO ID, a node
  in the network, a printer, or a workstation. In JES2 it is one of the
  following:

  > LOCAL
  > *name*
  > N*nnnn*
  > N*nn*R*mmmm*
  > N*nnn*R*mmm*
  > N*nnnn*R*mm*
  > R*nnnn*
  > RM*nnnn*
  > RMT*nnnn*
  > U*nnnn*
  > (*node,userid*)

  In JES3 it is one of the following:
  > ANYLOCAL
  > *device-name*
  > *device-number*
  > *group-name*
  > *node-name*
  > (*node,userid*)

- **Example**
  In the following job step called PRINT1, there is an OUTPUT
  statement named OUT1. OUT1 has the DEST parameter
  specifying U1214 as the destination for the sysout dataset and is

referenced in a DD statement called SYSUT2. Therefore the sysout data for OUT1 will be printed at destination U1214.

```
//PRINT1    EXEC PGM=IEBGENER,COND=EVEN
//OUT1      OUTPUT CHARS=GT51,DEST=U1214
//SYSPRINT  DD SYSOUT=V
//SYSUT1    DD DSN=TEMP.REPORT.SAA,DISP=OLD
//SYSUT2    DD SYSOUT=V,OUTPUT=*.OUT1,COPIES=2
```

◘ DPAGELBL parameter

• General format
```
DPAGELBL=[YES or Y or NO or N]
```

• Description
The DPAGELBL parameter specifies whether or not to print the security label of a job on each page of output data as a result of this OUTPUT statement. The security label is defined by the system security administrator.

YES or Y means to print the security label.

NO or N means not to print the security label.

• Example
In the following job, the OUTPUT statement called OUT1 specifies that the security label be printed. In this case, the label SYSTEMS will be printed on each page of the output.

```
//C840BQBI JOB (0200,200),'M. Lim',CLASS=L,MSGCLASS=X,
//               SECLABEL=SYSTEMS
//OUT1      OUTPUT DPAGELBL=Y,SYSAREA=Y,DEST=U1214
//PRINT1    EXEC PGM=IEBGENER,REGION=1M
//SYSPRINT  DD SYSOUT=V
//SYSUT1    DD DSN=TEMP.REPORT.SAA,DISP=OLD
//SYSUT2    DD SYSOUT=V,OUTPUT=*.OUT1,COPIES=2
```

◘ FCB parameter

• General format
```
FCB=fcb-name or
   (fcb-name[,ALIGN][,VERIFY])
```

• Description
The FCB parameter specifies the form to use when printing the

sysout dataset in this OUTPUT statement. The FCB in the DD statatment overrides the one in the OUTPUT statement if both are specified.

fcb-name is a standard FCB or an FCB name in SYS1.IMAGELIB. The names are in the following forms:

FCB2*xxxx* - 3211, 3203 Model 5, or SNA printer
FCB3*xxxx* - 3800 printer
FCB4*xxxx* - 4248 printer
STD1   - 6 lines per inch on 8.5-inch-long paper
STD2   - 6 lines per inch on 11-inch-long paper
STD3   - 8 lines per inch

ALIGN means to request the operator to align the form before printing starts.

VERIFY means to request the operator to check whether the spcified form is appropriate for printing the data.

- **Example**
In the following OUTPUT statement, the FCB parameter specifies STD2 as the form for printing the sysout dataset.

```
//OUT1   OUTPUT FCB=STD2
```

◘ FLASH parameter

- **General format**
```
FLASH=overlay-name            or
   (overlay-name[,count])     or
   NONE
```

- **Description**
The FLASH parameter specifies the forms overlay and number of copies when the sysout dataset for this OUTPUT statement is printed on a 3800 printer.

overlay-name is the name of the forms overlay.

count is the number of copies of the dataset to print, in the range 1 to 255.

NONE means that no forms overlay flashing is to be done.

● **Example**

In the following OUTPUT statement, the FLASH parameter specifies LOG01 as the forms overlay and 10 as the number of copies to print.

```
//OUT3 OUTPUT    FLASH=(LOG01,10)
```

◘ **FORMDEF parameter**

● **General format**
FORMDEF=*name*

● **Description**

The FORMDEF parameter specifies a library member which is used by the Print Services Facility (PSF) and has PSF control statements. The control statements inform PSF how to print the sysout dataset for this OUTPUT statement. This parameter is effective only for 3800 Model 3 printers.

name is a name of a PSF library member.

● **Example**

In the following OUTPUT statement, the FORMDEF parameter specifies TESTFORM as the member name which contains control statements for printing the sysout data.

```
//OUT3 OUTPUT    FORMDEF=TESTFORM
```

◘ **FORMS parameter**

● **General format**
FORMS=*formname* or
     STD

● **Description**

The FORMS parameter specifies a form to be used for printing the sysout data for this OUTPUT statement.

formname is the name of the form; it is inserted before printing the sysout data. The name can be up to 8 characters long.

STD means to use standard form (JES3 only).

- **Example**
In the following OUTPUT statement, the FORMS parameter specifies NEWFORM as the form to be used for printing the sysout data.

```
//OUT3 OUTPUT    FORMS=NEWFORM
```

◘ GROUPID parameter

- **General format**
GROUPID=*groupname*

- **Description**
The GROUPID parameter identifies a group to which the sysout data for this OUTPUT statement belong.

groupname is the group identification. It is up to 8 characters in length.

- **Example**
In the following job, the OUTPUT statement called OUT1 specifies that the group identification for the sysout data is to be SASRPT.

```
//C840BQBI JOB (0200,200),'SAS Reports',CLASS=L
//OUT1     OUTPUT GROUPID=SASRPT,DEST=U1214
//PRINT1   EXEC PGM=IEBGENER,REGION=1M
//SYSPRINT DD SYSOUT=V
//SYSUT1   DD DSN=TEMP.REPORT.SAA,DISP=OLD
//SYSUT2   DD SYSOUT=V,OUTPUT=*.OUT1,COPIES=2
```

◘ INDEX parameter

- **General format**
INDEX=*nn*

- **Description**

  The INDEX parameter specifies the size of the left margin when printing sysout data for this OUTPUT statement on a 3211 impact printer.

  nn is the number of character positions in the left margin. This number is in the range 1 to 31.

- **Example**

  In the following OUTPUT statement, the INDEX parameter specifies the size of the left margin as 8 character positions. This is for a 3211 impact printer.

  ```
  //P3211 OUTPUT    INDEX=8
  ```

▣ JESDS parameter

- **General format**
  ```
  JESDS=[ALL or JCL or LOG or MSG]
  ```

- **Description**

  The JESDS parameter specifies how to print a job's JCL, job log, and message dataset. What the sysout dataset contains is controlled by the MSGCLASS and MSGLEVEL parameters of the JOB statement. The OUTPUT statement with the JESDS parameter should be placed after the JOB statement and the first EXEC statement of the job. The JES2 /*JOBPARM parameter overrides the JESDS parameter if both are specified in the job.

  ALL means to print the job's JCL, job log, and messages according to the options of the OUTPUT statement.

  JCL means to print the job's JCL and JES control statements according to the options of the OUTPUT statement.

  LOG means to print the job log according to the options of the OUTPUT statement.

  MSG means to print the messages according to the options of the OUTPUT statement.

- **Example**

In the following job, the OUTPUT statement called OUT1 specifies printing of the job's JCL, job log, and messages at destination U1214.

```
//C840BQBI JOB (0200,200),'SAS Reports',MSGCLASS=X
//OUT1     OUTPUT JESDS=ALL,DEST=U1214
//PRINT1   EXEC PGM=IEBGENER,REGION=1M
```

◘ LINDEX parameter

- **General format**
  LINDEX=nn

- **Description**

The LINDEX parameter specifies the size of the right margin when printing sysout data for this OUTPUT statement on a 3211 impact printer.

nn is the number of character positions in the right margin. This number is in the range 1 to 31.

- **Example**

In the following OUTPUT statement, the LINDEX parameter specifies the size of the right margin as 8 character positions. This is for a 3211 impact printer.

```
//P3211 OUTPUT   LINDEX=8,INDEX=8
```

◘ LINECT parameter

- **General format**
  LINECT=nnn

- **Description**

The LINECT parameter specifies the maximum number of lines per page to print for the sysout data. When this limit is reached, the system automatically starts a new page. Of course, a carriage control character can start a new page before the maximum number of lines has been printed on a page.

nnn is the maximum number of lines per page for the sysout dataset printed. The range of this number is from 0 to 255.

● **Example**

In the following OUTPUT statement, the LINECT parameter specifies 55 as the maximum number of lines per page to print.

```
//P3211 OUTPUT    LINECT=55,INDEX=8
```

◘ **MODIFY parameter**

● **General format**
```
MODIFY=module-name or
       (module-name,trc)
```

● **Description**

The MODIFY parameter specifies a copy-modification module which is used by JES2 when printing a sysout dataset on a 3800 printer.

module-name is a module name residing in PDS SYS1.IMAGELIB, created by the IEBIMAGE utility.

trc is a number from 0 to 3 which specifies a tablename in the CHARS parameter. The number 0 references the first table in the CHARS parameter, 1 references the second table, 2 references the third table, and 3 references the fourth table.

● **Example**

In the following OUTPUT statement, the MODIFY parameter specifies a copy-modification module CHECK101 and 0 to refer to GS15 in the CHARS parameter.

```
//OUT2    OUTPUT MODIFY=(CHECK101,0),CHARS=(GS15,GS16)
```

◘ **NAME parameter**

● **General format**
```
NAME=name
```

● **Description**

The NAME parameter specifies a preferred name to appear on each separator page of sysout data printed with this OUTPUT statement.

name is the preferred name which is to appear on separator pages of a printed sysout dataset. The name can be up to 60 characters long and include the following:

- Periods
- Alphanumeric characters
- National characters
- Parentheses, plus signs, hyphens, backslashes, asterisks, and ampersands

A name with blanks must be enclosed in apostrophes.

- **Example**

In the following OUTPUT statement, the NAME parameter specifies DJONES as the preferred name to appear on each separator page when printing this sysout dataset.

```
//OUT1      OUTPUT CHARS=GT12,BURST=Y,
//          DEPT='Human Resources - #HU10',NAME=DJONES
```

◘ OUTDISP parameter

- **General format**

OUTDISP = ([WRITE or HOLD or KEEP or PURGE],
        [WRITE or HOLD or KEEP or PURGE])

- **Description**

The OUTDISP parameter specifies the disposition of a sysout dataset of an OUTPUT statement. Two different subparameters can be included. The first one is for a job that ends successfully, and the second is for a job that abends. If a HOLD parameter of the DD statement is used, the OUTDISP parameter is rendered ineffective.

WRITE means to print the dataset; unless held by the operator, it is deleted when the job terminates.

HOLD means to hold the dataset until released. When it is released, the disposition changes to WRITE.

KEEP means to print the dataset and keep it in the spool. The operator or job owner can subsequently delete it from the spool.

PURGE means to delete the dataset before it is printed.

● **Example**
In the following OUTPUT statement, the OUTDISP parameter specifies printing the sysout dataset if the step job is successful, and otherwise deleting it.

```
//OUT2  OUTPUT OUTDISP=(WRITE,PURGE),CHARS=(GS15,GS16)
```

◘ PAGEDEF parameter

● **General format**
```
PAGEDEF=name
```

● **Description**
The PAGEDEF parameter specifies a library member which is used by the Print Services Facility (PSF). The member contains page definitions, such as page size and carriage control characters, for sysout data to be printed.

name is a name of a PSF library member that contains control statements.

● **Example**
In the following OUTPUT statement, the PAGEDEF parameter specifies AB2ZE as the name of the member which contains control statements to determine page definitions for the sysout data to be printed.

```
//OUT3 OUTPUT    PAGEDEF=AB2ZE
```

◘ PIMSG parameter

● **General format**
```
PIMSG=[YES or Y]
      [NO  or N]
```

● **Description**

The PIMSG parameter specifies whether or not the Print Services Facility (PSF) should print error messages.

YES or Y means that error messages should be printed at the end of the printed sysout dataset.

NO or N means that error messages should not be printed.

● **Example**

In the following OUTPUT statement, the PIMSG parameter specifies printing of error messages issued by PSF.

```
//OUT3 OUTPUT   PAGEDEF=AB2ZE,PIMSG=Y
```

◘ PRMODE parameter

● **General format**
```
PRMODE=[PAGE or LINE or mode]
```

● **Description**

The PRMODE parameter specifies the process mode required to print the sysout data of this OUTPUT statement.

PAGE means that a page-mode printer is to be used to print data.

LINE means that a line-mode printer is to be used to print data.

mode is a process mode defined by the system program of your installation. The process name is up to 8 characters long.

● **Example**

In the following OUTPUT statement, the PRMODE parameter specifies that a page-mode printer is to be used to print the sysout dataset of this statement.

```
//OUT3 OUTPUT   PAGEDEF=AB2ZE,PRMODE=PAGE
```

◻ PRTY parameter

● General format
PRTY=*nnn*

● Description
The PRTY parameter sets the priority for printing a sysout dataset.

nnn is a number in the range 0 to 255. A higher number means that the dataset is printed sooner.

● Example
In the following OUTPUT statement, the PRTY parameter specifies the highest priority (255) for printing this sysout dataset.

```
//OUT3 OUTPUT    PAGEDEF=AB2ZE,PRTY=255
```

◻ ROOM parameter

● General format
ROOM=*name*

● Description
The ROOM parameter specifies a name of a room which is to appear on separator pages of sysout data printed for this OUTPUT statement. The room name indicates where printed data are to be delivered.

name is the room name which is to appear on separator pages of a printed sysout dataset. The name can be up to 60 characters long and include the following:

- Periods
- Alphanumeric characters
- National characters
- Parentheses, plus signs, hyphens, backslashes, asterisks, and ampersands

A name with blanks must be enclosed in apostrophes.

● Example
In the following OUTPUT statement, the ROOM parameter

specifies 'Operations - Room S400' as the room name.

```
//OUT1      OUTPUT CHARS=GT12,BURST=Y,
//                 ROOM='Operations - Room S400'
```

◼ SYSAREA parameter

● **General format**
```
SYSAREA=[YES or Y or NO or N]
```

● **Description**
The SYSAREA parameter specifies whether or not to print the security level at which this job is executed in the reserved area of the page.

YES or Y means to print the security level.

NO or N means not to print the security level.

● **Example**
In the following job, the OUTPUT statement called OUT1 specifies that the security label is to be printed in the reserved area of each page.

```
//C840BQBI JOB (0200,200),'M. Lim',CLASS=L,MSGCLASS=X,
//                 SECLABEL=SYSTEMS
//OUT1      OUTPUT  DPAGELBL=Y,SYSAREA=Y,DEST=U1214
//PRINT1    EXEC PGM=IEBGENER,REGION=1M
//SYSPRINT  DD SYSOUT=V
//SYSUT1    DD DSN=TEMP.REPORT.SAA,DISP=OLD
//SYSUT2    DD SYSOUT=V,OUTPUT=*.OUT1,COPIES=2
```

◼ THRESHLD parameter

● **General format**
```
THRESHLD=nnnnnnnn
```

● **Description**
The THRESHLD parameter, effective for JES3 only, sets the maximum number of lines to print for this sysout dataset.

nnnnnnnn is a number in the range 1 to 99,999,999.

● **Example**
In the following OUTPUT statement, THRESHLD specifies
20,000 as the maximum number of lines to print for the sysout
dataset.

```
//OUT1     OUTPUT CHARS=GT12,BURST=Y,THRESHLD=20000
```

◼ **TITLE parameter**

● **General format**
```
TITLE=name
```

● **Description**
The TITLE parameter specifies a title which is to appear on
separator pages of sysout data printed for this OUTPUT statement.

name is the title which is to appear on separator pages of a printed
sysout dataset. The title can be up to 60 characters long and
include the following:

● Periods
● Alphanumeric characters
● National characters
● Parentheses, plus signs, hyphens, backslashes, asterisks, and
  ampersands

A title with blanks must be enclosed in apostrophes.

● **Example**
In the following OUTPUT statement, the TITLE parameter
specifies 'SAS REPORT' as the title for this printed sysout
dataset.

```
//OUT1     OUTPUT CHARS=GT12,BURST=Y,
//                 TITLE='SAS REPORT'
```

◼ **TRC parameter**

● **General format**
```
TRC=[YES or Y or NO or N]
```

- **Description**

The TRC parameter specifies whether or not the sysout data contain table reference character codes.

YES or Y means that the dataset contains table reference character codes in position 2 if the carriage control character is used in position 1, or in position 1 if the carriage control character is not used.

NO or N means that the dataset does not contain reference character codes.

- **Example**

In the following OUTPUT statement, the TRC parameter specifies that column 2 of each line contains a table reference character code.

```
//OUT1     OUTPUT CHARS=GT12,BURST=Y,TRC=Y
```

◻ UCS parameter

- **General format**

```
UCS=character-set-code
```

- **Description**

The UCS parameter specifies use of the universal character set (UCS) when printing this sysout dataset.

character-set-code is the name of a universal character set; it can be up to 4 alphanumeric or national characters.

- **Example**

In the following OUTPUT statement, UCS specifies that the character set with code A11 be used to print the sysout dataset.

```
//PRINT   OUTPUT UCS=A11
```

◻ WRITER parameter

- **General format**

```
WRITER=name
```

● **Description**

The WRITER parameter specifies an external program that is to process the sysout dataset instead of JES.

name is the name of the writer program that is to process the sysout dataset. This program must be started by the operator before it will be available to process the dataset.

● **Example**

In the following OUTPUT statement, WRITER specifies SYS45SA as the external writer program to process the sysout dataset.

```
//PRINT   OUTPUT WRITER=SYS45SA
```

8.6   JES2 CONTROL STATEMENTS

The JES2 control statements are used with JCL statements to control the input and output processing of a job. Each statement has the characters /* in columns 1 and 2, followed by a JES2 verb and any parameters. A JES2 control statement must be placed after a JOB statement in a job but should never be part of an in-stream or cataloged procedure.

The general format is

```
/*jes2-verb parameter
```

jes2-verb is a keyword that specifies a particular type of JES2 control statement. The keywords are:

JOBPARM MESSAGE   NETACCT   NOTIFY OUTPUT
PRIORITY ROUTE   SETUP   SIGNOFF SIGNON
XEQ   XMIT

The control statements associated with each of these verbs are discussed later in this section.

parameter specifies an option of a JES2 control statement.

In the following job, the JES2 control statement is /*ROUTE PRINT

U1214. The statement keyword is ROUTE, and the parameter is PRINT.

```
//C840BQBI JOB (0200,200),'Laila G.',CLASS=L,MSGCLASS=X
/*ROUTE PRINT U1214
//PRINT1    EXEC PGM=IEBGENER,COND=EVEN
//SYSPRINT DD SYSOUT=*,CHARS=GT51
//SYSUT1    DD DSN=TEMP.REPORT.SAA,DISP=OLD
//SYSUT2    DD SYSOUT=V,COPIES=2
//SYSIN     DD DUMMY
```

◘ /*JOBPARM statement

• General format
```
/*JOBPARM [BURST=[Y or N] or B=[Y or N]]
      [BYTES=nnnnnn or M=nnnnnn]
   [CARDS=nnnnnnn or C=nnnnnnn]
   [COPIES=nnn or N=nnn]
   [FORMS=[xxxxxxxx or STD] or F=[xxxxxxxx or STD]]
   [LINECT=nnn or K=nnn]
   [LINES=nnnn or L=nnnn]
   [NOLOG or J]
   [PAGES=nnnnn or G=nnnnn]
   [PROCLIB=ddname or P=ddname]
   [RESTART=[Y or N] or E=[Y or N]]
   [ROOM=xxxx or R=xxxx]
   [[[S= or SYSAFF]* or
         (*,IND) or ANY or
         (ANY,IND) or (ssss) or
            (ssss,IND) or (ssss,ssss,ssss,...) or
         (ssss,ssss,...,IND)
   ]
   [TIME=nnnn or T=nnnn]
```

• Description
The /*JOBPARM statement passes options to JES2 to process a job. It is used to override installation values of JES2.

BURST or B specifies whether to burst, trim, and stack a printed data or to print them on a continuous sheet of paper.

BYTES or M specifies the limit on the number of bytes of data to be printed for this job. When this limit is reached, a local JES2 exit routine decides whether to continue or to terminate the job.

CARDS or C specifies the maximum number of cards to punch as output of this job. When this limit is reached, a local JES2 exit routine decides whether to continue or to terminate the job.

COPIES or N specifies the number of copies of the data to print. The number ranges from 1 to 255, inclusive.

FORMS or F specifies the form to use to print the sysout data.

LINECT or K specifies the maximum number of lines to print on a page. This number ranges from 1 to 255, inclusive.

LINES or L specifies the maximum number of lines to print for this job. The number is in thousands and ranges from 0 to 9999. When this limit is reached, a local JES2 exit routine decides whether to continue or to terminate the job.

NOLOG or J instructs JES2 not to print the job log. If this parameter is not coded, the job log is printed.

PAGES or G specifies the maximum number of pages to print for this job. This number ranges from 0 to 99,999. When this limit is reached, a local JES2 exit routine decides whether to continue or to terminate the job.

PROCLIB or P specifies a DD name of a DD statement of the JES2 start-up JCL that allocates the JCL procedure libraries. These libraries are used to interpret the JCL for this job. The default DD name is PROC00.

RESTART or E specifies the step to take if an IPL and subsequent JES2 warm start occur while your job is executing. Y means to reexecute the job from the start. N means not to restart the job.

ROOM or R specifies a room number; it is used to distribute the printed sysout data of this job. The room number is a value of up to 4 alphanumeric characters.

S or SYSAFF specifies the 'SYSTEM AFFINITY' for a job.

TIME specifies an estimated time of execution for this job in wall-clock minutes. The value is an integer in the range 0 to 9999, inclusive.

● **Example**
In the following job, the /*JOBPARM control statement specifies

that 2 copies of the sysout data are to be printed and that the maximum number of lines for this job is 50,000.

```
//C840BQBI JOB (0200,200),'Sanjiv G.',MSGCLASS=X
/*JOBPARM COPIES=2,LINES=50
//PRINT1   EXEC PGM=IEBGENER,COND=EVEN
//SYSPRINT DD SYSOUT=*,CHARS=GT51
//SYSUT1   DD DSN=TEMP.REPORT.SAA,DISP=OLD
//SYSUT2   DD SYSOUT=V
//SYSIN    DD DUMMY
```

◘ /*MESSAGE statement

- **General format**
  /*MESSAGE text

- **Description**
  The /*MESSAGE statement is used to communicate a message to the MVS console operator. As soon as the /*MESSAGE statement is encountered by JES2, the message is sent.

  text is the message that is sent to the operator. It must be placed between columns 11 and 71. It should not exceed 61 characters.

- **Example**
  The following /*MESSAGE statement specifies that the message 'CALL AT EXT. 4803 IF THIS JOB ABENDS. THANKS.' is to be sent to the operator.

  ```
  /*MESSAGE CALL AT EXT. 4803 IF THIS JOB ABENDS. THANKS.
  ```

◘ /*NETACCT statement

- **General format**
  /*NETACCT accounting-information

- **Description**
  The /*NETACCT statement specifies accounting information that can be used at network level.

  accounting-information consist of up to 8 alphanumeric characters.

- **Example**
The following /*NETACCT statement specifies C84023F as the accounting information which is transmitted to the destination node with the job.

```
/*NETACCT C84023F
```

◘ /*NOTIFY statement

- **General format**
```
/*NOTIFY   [nodename.userid  or
            nodename:userid  or
            nodename/userid  or
            nodename(userid) or
            userid
            ]
```

- **Description**
The /*NOTIFY statement specifies a network node and a user identification to which JES2 should send notification messages for this job.

nodename is the name of the network node where the user is to be found.

userid is the user identification of a TSO or VM user.

- **Example**
The following /*NOTIFY statement specifies the destination where notification messages are to be sent. The network node is RBSDFA, and the userid is Z1335MG.

```
/*NOTIFY RBSDFA.Z1335MG
```

◘ /*OUTPUT statement

- **General format**
```
/*OUTPUT code
      [<BURST or B> = <Y or N>]
      [<X or CHARS> = <xxx or (xxxx[,xxxx] ...)>]
      [<CKPTLNS or E> = nnnnn]
      [<CKPTPPGS or P> = nnnnn]
      [<COMPACT or Z> = nn]
      [<N or COPIES> = <nnn or (nnn,(group-val,...))>]
```

```
[<G or COPYG> = <group-val or (group-val,...)>]
[<D or DEST> = <destination or
                (destination1,...)>]
[<C or FCB> = xxxx]
[<O or FLASH> = <overlay or (overlay,count) or
                NONE>]
[<Q or FLASHC> = count]
[<F or FORMS> = <xxxx or STD>]
[<INDEX or I> = nn]
[<LINDEX or L> = nn]
[<LINECT or K> = nnn]
[<M or MODIFY> = <module-name or
                (module-name,trc)>]
[<MODTRC or M> = trc]
[<UCS or T> = xxxx]
```

where *destination* is one of the following:

LOCAL	*nodename.userid*	R*nnnn*
name	*nodename:userid*	RM*nnnn*
N*nnnn*	*nodename/userid*	RMT*nnnn*
N*nn*R*mmmm*	*nodename(userid)*	U*nnnn*
N*nnn*R*mmm*		
N*nnnn*R*mm*		

● **Description**

The /*OUTPUT statement specifies the characteristics of one or more sysout datasets for this job.

code is a code of up to 4 characters that uniquely identifies this /*OUTPUT statement.

BURST or B specifies whether to burst, trim, and stack printed data or to print them on a continuous sheet of paper.

X or CHARS specifies a character-arranged table to be used when JES2 prints sysout data on a 3800 printer.

CKPTLNS or E specifies the number of lines per page of output. The number is in the range 0 to 32,767.

CKPTPPGS or P specifies the number of pages to transmit between printing checkpoints. The number is in the range 0 through 32,767.

COMPACT or Z specifies the compaction table to be used when

transmitting the sysout data.

N or COPIES specifies the number of copies of the data to print. The number ranges from 1 to 255, inclusive.

G or COPYG specifies the number of copies of the data to print on a 3800 printer only. The number ranges from 1 to 255, inclusive.

D or DEST specifies up to 4 different network destinations for the sysout data for this /*OUTPUT statement.

C or FCB specifies the name of the forms control buffer (FCB) that JES2 is to use when printing the sysout dataset.

O or FLASH specifies a form overlay to be used when printing the output dataset on a 3800 printer.

Q or FLASHC specifies the number of copies to flash with the forms overlay.

FORMS or F specifies the form to use to print the sysout data.

INDEX or I specifies the size of the left margin when printing the sysout dataset on a 3211 printer.

LINDEX or L specifies the size of the right margin when printing the sysout dataset on a 3211 printer.

LINECT or K specifies the maximum number of lines to print on a page. This number ranges from 1 to 255, inclusive.

Y or MODIFY specifies the name of a copy-modification module. This name is a member of PDS SYS1.IMAGELIB.

M or MODTRC specifies the table name in the CHARS parameter.

UCS or T specifies the name of the universal character set (UCS) to use.

● **Example**
The following /*OUTPUT statement specifies the following:

● The code for this /*OUTPUT statement is RPT1.
● The COPIES parameter specifies printing of 3 copies of the sysout dataset.
● The destination is RBSDFA.Z1335MG.

```
/*OUTPUT RPT1 COPIES=3,DEST=RBSDFA.Z1335MG
```

◘ **/*PRIORITY statement**

● **General format**
```
/*PRIORITY n
```

● **Description**
The /*PRIORITY statement sets the priority at which this job will be executed and for all its output.

n is a number from 0 to 15, where 15 has the highest priority.

● **Example**
The following /*PRIORITY statement specifies 10 as the priority level for this job and its output.

```
/*PRIORITY 10
```

◘ **/*ROUTE statement**

● **General format**
```
/*ROUTE [PRINT or PUNCH] destination
```

● **Description**
The /*ROUTE statement specifies either sending a job's output to a specific network node or requesting execution of a job at a specific network node. This statement must be placed after the JOB statement and before the first EXEC statement.

PRINT means to route a printed dataset to a destination.

PUNCH means to route a punched dataset to a destination.

destination is one of the following:

LOCAL	*nodename.userid*	R*nnnn*
name	*nodename.userid*	RM*nnnn*
N*nnnn*	*nodename/userid*	RMT*nnnn*
N*nn*R*mmmm*	*nodename(userid)*	U*nnnn*
N*nnn*R*mmm*		
N*nnnn*R*mm*		

● **Example**

The following /*ROUTE statement specifies that the printed sysout dataset is to be routed to the destination RBSDFA.Z1335MG.

```
/*ROUTE PRINT DEST=RBSDFA.Z1335MG
```

◘ **/*SETUP statement**

● **General format**
```
/*SETUP  [volser,...] or text
```

● **Description**

The /*SETUP statement requests the operator to mount a tape or DASD volume.

volser is a mountable DASD or tape volume serial number required during the execution of this job.

text is a message to the operator regarding this request.

● **Example**

The following /*SETUP statement requests the operator to mount volumes TAPE10 and TAPE12.

```
/*SETUP TAPE10,TAPE12
```

◘ **/*SIGNOFF statement**

● **General format**
```
/*SIGNOFF
```

- **Description**
  The /*SIGNOFF statement ends the processing of a remote job session.

- **Example**
  The following /*SIGNOFF statement requests JES2 to stop the processing of a remote job stream session.

  ```
  /*SIGNOFF
  ```

◘ /*SIGNON statement

- **General format**
  ```
  /*SIGNON [REMOTEnnn or RMTnnnn] [password1] [password2]
  ```

- **Description**
  The /*SIGNON statement starts the processing of a remote job session.

- **Example**
  The following /*SIGNON statement requests JES2 to start the processing of a remote job stream session.

  ```
  /*SIGNON REMOTE234 MONDAY
  ```

◘ /*XEQ statement

- **General format**
  ```
  /*XEQ [Nnnnn or nodename[.vmguestid]]
  ```

- **Description**
  The /*XEQ statement specifies the node of the JES network where this job is to be executed.

  Nnnnn is the node number, where nnnn is between 1 and 1000.

  nodename is a node of a network defined locally.

  vmguestid is the name of a guest system running under a VM system.

- **Example**

The following /*XEQ statement specifies NEWYORK as the network node where this job is to be executed.

```
/*XEQ NEWYORK
```

▣ /*XMIT statement

- **General format**

```
/*XMIT [Nnnnn or
       nodename or
       nodename.userid or
       nodename:userid or
       nodename/userid or
       nodename(userid) or
       nodename.vmguestid or
       nodename:vmguestid or
       nodename/vmguestid or
       nodename(vmguestid)
   ] [DLM=xx]
```

- **Description**

The /*XMIT statement transmits a record from a JES2 network node to another network node. The destination network node need not be a JES2 node.

N*nnnn* is the node number, where *nnnn* is between 1 and 1000.

nodename is a node of a network defined locally.

vmguestid is the name of a guest system running under a VM system.

DLM specifies a two-character delimiter that is used by JES2 when transmitting the data.

- **Example**

In the following job, the /*XMIT control statement makes JES2 transmit the lines following it to network node NEWYORK. At NEWYORK the transmitted data, which make up a job, are executed.

```
//C840BQBI JOB (0200,200),'XMIT to NEW YORK '
/*XMIT NEWYORK DLM='$$'
//C840BQBI JOB (0200,200),'Sanjiv G.',MSGCLASS=X
```

```
/*JOBPARM COPIES=2,LINES=50
//PRINT1   EXEC PGM=IEBGENER,COND=EVEN
//SYSPRINT DD SYSOUT=*,CHARS=GT51
//SYSUT1   DD DSN=TEMP.REPORT.SAA,DISP=OLD
//SYSUT2   DD SYSOUT=V
//SYSIN    DD DUMMY
$$
```

8.7   OTHER STATEMENTS

◘ IF/THEN/ELSE/ENDIF statement

● **General format**

```
//[name] IF [()relational-expression[)] [comments] THEN
    JCL-statement
    .
    .
    .
//[name] ELSE   [comments]
    JCL-statement
    .
    .
    .
//[name] ENDIF
```

● **Description**

The IF/THEN/ELSE/ENDIF statement allows one or more steps of a job to be executed conditionally depending on a result. The result is an evaluation of a relational expression. The statement associated with the keyword IF contains the relational expression. After the expression is evaluated, if the result is TRUE, the JCL statements following the IF clause are executed. If the result is FALSE, then the JCL statements after the ELSE clause are executed. The ENDIF clause marks the end of the IF/THEN/ELSE/ENDIF statement.

The IF/THEN/ELSE/ENDIF statement can be nested up to 15 levels.

The IF/THEN/ELSE/ENDIF statement can be placed anywhere after the JOB statement of the job. It must not include the following statements: JOB, JCLLIB, JOBCAT, STEPCAT, and XMIT.

The following statements are executed regardless of their place within the IF/THEN/ELSE/ENDIF statement: PROC, PEND, INCLUDE, SET, /*, ??, //*, JES2 control statements, JES3 control statements, and JCL command statements.

name is an optional name of a IF, ELSE, or ENDIF statement starting in column 3.

comments is the comment field.

relational-expression is made up of operators and operands. Operators are

GT or >	Greater than
LT or <	Less than
NG or |>	Not greater than
NL or |<	Not less than
EQ or =	Equal to
NE or |=	Not equal to
GE or >=	Greater than or equal to
LE or <=	Less than or equal to
NOT or |	Logical NOT
AND or &	Logical AND
OR or |	Logical OR

The order of evaluation is NOT, GT, LT, NG, NL, EQ, NE, GE, LE, AND, and OR.

Operands are

RC	The highest return value from a previously executed job step
stepname.RC	The return value from a job step
stepname.procstepname.RC	The return value from a step of a JCL procedure

ABEND=TRUE or ABEND	An abend condition from a previous job step
stepname.ABEND or *stepname*.ABEND=TRUE	An abend condition from a job step
stepname.procstepname.ABEND or *stepname.procstepname*.ABEND=TRUE	
	An abend condition from a step of a JCL procedure
ABEND=FALSE or |ABEND	
	A lack of an abend condition from a previously executed job step
|*stepname*.ABEND or *stepname*.ABEND=FALSE	A lack of an abend condition from a job step
|*stepname.procstepname*.ABEND or *stepname.procstepname*.ABEND=FALSE	
	A lack of an abend condition from a step of a JCL procedure
ABEND=S*xxx* or ABEND=U*nnnn*	A specific system abend code or user abend code in hexadecimal value from a previously executed job step
stepname.ABEDCC=S*xxx* or *stepname*.ABENDCC=U*nnnn*	
	A system or user abend code from a specific job step
stepname.procstepname.ABEDCC=S*xxx* or *stepname.procstepname*.ABENDCC=U*nnnn*	
	A system or user abend code from a specific step of a JCL procedure
stepname.RUN	A test of whether a specific job step was executed

*stepname.procstepname.*RUN

> A test of whether a specific step of a JCL procedure was executed

*stepname.*RUN=FALSE

> A test of whether a specific job step was not executed

*stepname.procstepname.*RUN=FALSE

> A test of whether a specific step of a JCL procedure was not executed

JCL-statement is any valid JCL statement.

● **Example**

The following job contains an example of how to use an IF/THEN/ELSE/ENDIF statement. In the line with the IF clause the relational expression is (STEP01.RC = 0). The expression, which refers to the return code of job step STEP01 being 0, is evaluated. If the result of this evaluation is TRUE—in other words, if the return code from the previous step is 0—then the job step PRINT1 is executed. If the result of the evaluation is FALSE—in other words, if the return code from the previous job is not 0—the job step BACKUP is executed.

```
//C840BQBI JOB (0200,200),'FANCY JCL CODING',MSGCLASS=X
//*
//STEP01   EXEC PGM=SAABB010
//INFILE   DD DSN=TEMP.SAS.FILE,DISP=SHR
//REPORT   DD DSN=TEMP.REPORT.SAS,DISP=SHR
//    IF ( STEP01.RC = 0 ) THEN
//PRINT1   EXEC PGM=IEBGENER
//SYSPRINT DD SYSOUT=*,CHARS=GT51
//SYSUT1   DD DSN=TEMP.REPORT.SAS,DISP=OLD
//SYSUT2   DD SYSOUT=V,CHARS=GT51
//SYSIN    DD DUMMY
//    ELSE
//BACKUP   EXEC PGM=IEBGENER
//SYSPRINT DD SYSOUT=*,CHARS=GT51
//SYSUT1   DD DSN=TEMP.SAS.FILE,DISP=OLD
//SYSUT2   DD DSN=TEMP.SAS.BACKUP.FILE,DISP=SHR
//SYSIN    DD DUMMY
//    ENDIF
```

■ INCLUDE statement

● General format
```
//name   INCLUDE MEMBER=member-name [comments]
```

● Description
The INCLUDE statement is replaced with one or more valid JCL statements found in dataset specified by a JCLLIB statement or in a system procedure library. The JCL statement(s) read from the library become(s) part of the job during execution.

name is an optional name of the INCLUDE statement; it starts in column 3.

member-name is a member of the library; its entire content replaces the INCLUDE statement.

comments is the comment field.

● Example
Let us say that the following statements are stored in SYS2.USER.PROCLIB in a member called SORTS01.

```
//SYSUDUMP   DD SYSOUT=J,
//              DCB=(RECFM=VA,LRECL=121,BLKSIZE=121)
//SORTLIB    DD DSN=SYS.SOFT.SORTLIB,DISP=SHR
//SYSSORT    DD SYSOUT=J
//SORTWK01   DD UNIT=SYSDA,SPACE=(CYL,(2,2),RLSE)
//SORTWK02   DD UNIT=SYSDA,SPACE=(CYL,(2,2),RLSE)
//SORTWK03   DD UNIT=SYSDA,SPACE=(CYL,(2,2),RLSE)
//SORTWK04   DD UNIT=SYSDA,SPACE=(CYL,(2,2),RLSE)
```

The following is a job with an INCLUDE statement called S01INCL.

```
//C840BGFI JOB (0200,200),'ABBY M.',CLASS=L,MSGCLASS=X
//SAAB0S01   EXEC PGM=SORT,TIME=60,PARM='CORE=MAX-32K'
//S01INCL    INCLUDE MEMBER=SORTS01
//SYSIN    DD *
  SORT FIELDS=(1,10,CH,A),SIZE=E2000
//SORTIN   DD DSN=TEMP.SAR01.CF012000,DISP=SHR
//SORTOUT  DD DSN=TEMP.CF012000.SORTED,DISP=SHR
```

During the execution of the job C840BGFI, the INCLUDE statement will be replaced by the content of PDS member SORTS01 and the job will look like this:

```
//C840BGFI JOB (0200,200),'ABBY M.',CLASS=L,MSGCLASS=X
//SAAB0S01  EXEC PGM=SORT,TIME=60,PARM='CORE=MAX-32K'
//SYSUDUMP  DD SYSOUT=J,
//             DCB=(RECFM=VA,LRECL=121,BLKSIZE=121)
//SORTLIB   DD DSN=SYS.SOFT.SORTLIB,DISP=SHR
//SYSSORT   DD SYSOUT=J
//SORTWK01  DD UNIT=SYSDA,SPACE=(CYL,(2,2),RLSE)
//SORTWK02  DD UNIT=SYSDA,SPACE=(CYL,(2,2),RLSE)
//SORTWK03  DD UNIT=SYSDA,SPACE=(CYL,(2,2),RLSE)
//SORTWK04  DD UNIT=SYSDA,SPACE=(CYL,(2,2),RLSE)
//SYSIN     DD *
  SORT FIELDS=(1,10,CH,A),SIZE=E2000
//SORTIN    DD DSN=TEMP.SAR01.CF012000,DISP=SHR
//SORTOUT   DD DSN=TEMP.CF012000.SORTED,DISP=SHR
```

◻ JCLLIB statement

● General format
```
//name JCLLIB ORDER=(dsn1[,dsn2][,dsn3]...)[comments]
```

● Description
The JCLLIB statement specifies private or system libraries that are to be searched when looking for a member specified in an INCLUDE statement.

ORDER is a required keyword that specifies that the order of the search is the same as the order in which the libraries are listed as part of the JCLIB statement.

name is an optional name of a JCLLIB statement; it starts in column 3.

dsn1, *dsn2*, and *dsn3* are fully qualified dataset names where private or system JCL procedures are referenced in INCLUDE statement(s).

comments is the comment field.

● **Example**

In the following JCLLIB statement, three libraries where JCL procedures are to be found are specified. These libraries are searched for a member specified in an INCLUDE statement in the same order as they are listed.

```
//SASLIBS    JCLLIB ORDER=(SYS1.PROCLIB,
//                SYS2.USER.PROCLIB,
//                SAS940.JCLLIB)
```

◘ **PROC and PEND statements**

● **General format**

```
//[proc-name] PROC [parameter] [comments]
    ·
    ·
    ·
//[pend-name] PEND [comments]
```

● **Description**

The PROC statement is the beginning of a JCL procedure. The PEND statement marks the end of a JCL procedure. JCL procedures can be in-stream or stored in a library.

proc-name is the name of the procedure.

parameter is a value passed to the JCL procedure during execution.

comments is the comment field.

pend-name is the name of the PEND statement.

● **Example**

In the following job, an in-stream JCL procedure called LOAD is defined. It has two parameters: DATE and TABLE. The procedure ends with a PEND statement called LEND. After this, the EXEC statement JES001 uses this procedure and passes the value for TABLE as CWSO. Since no value for DATE is specified, the default value JUL1092 is used during the execution of this job.

```
//C840BGFL JOB (0200,200),'Frances Gabe',MSGCLASS=X
//JOBLIB   DD DISP=SHR,DSN=D2CS.DSNLOAD
//*------------------------------------------------
//* THIS IN-STREAM PROC LOADS A DB2 TABLE FROM A
//* SEQUENTIAL FILE.
//*------------------------------------------------
//LOAD    PROC DATE=JUL1092,TABLE=
//LOADTL EXEC PGM=DSNUTILB,PARM='D2CS,C840BGF,'
//SYSPRINT DD SYSOUT=*

//SYSUDUMP DD SYSOUT=*
//UTPRINT  DD SYSOUT=*
//SORTWK01 DD UNIT=VIO,SPACE=(CYL,(100,100),RLSE)
//SORTWK02 DD UNIT=VIO,SPACE=(CYL,(100,100),RLSE)
//SORTWK03 DD UNIT=VIO,SPACE=(CYL,(100,100),RLSE)
//SORTWK04 DD UNIT=VIO,SPACE=(CYL,(100,100),RLSE)
//SYSUT1   DD UNIT=VIO,SPACE=(CYL,(100,100),RLSE)
//SORTOUT  DD UNIT=VIO,SPACE=(CYL,(100,100),RLSE)
//SYSREC00 DD DISP=OLD,DSN=TEMP.PS00.TSA0.&DATE..&TABLE
//SYSIN    DD DISP=SHR,DSN=C840BGF.PARM(L&TABLE)
//LEND      PEND
//*----------------------------------------------------
//* EXECUTE THE PROC LOAD
//----------------------------------------------------
//JES001    EXEC LOAD,TABLE=CWSO
//
```

◻ SET Statement

● General format
```
//name SET symbolic=value[,symbolic=value][comments]
```

● Description
The SET parameter assigns values to symbolic parameters.

symbolic is the name of the parameter to which a value is assigned.

value is the value assigned to the symbolic parameter.

name is an optional name of a SET statement; it starts in column 3.

comments is the comment field.

● **Example**

The following SET statement called APCD01 assigns the value 'PS00.TSA0' to the symbolic parameter APCODE. The DD statement has the symbolic parameter APCODE and the previously assigned value is used, giving the dataset name as PS00.TSA0.REPORT.

```
//APCD01   SET APCODE='PS00.TSA0'
//REPORT DD DSN=&APCODE.REPORT,DISP=SHR
```

This chapter is a reference guide for programmers using REXX in both CMS and TSO environments. It contains statements that make up an exec. The types of statements covered here are

- REXX instructions
- Host REXX commands
- Host environment command functions

This chapter also provides information on REXX built-in functions that can be used by statements.

REXX supports free-format statements, which can appear anywhere between columns 1 and 72. A statement can have any number of embedded blanks and can be terminated with either an end-of-line character or a semicolon (;).

More than one statement can appear on one line, separated from each other with semicolons. Also, one statement can span more than one line, in which case a comma at the end of the line indicates a continuation of the statement.

Comments appear between the delimiters /* and */ and can span one or more lines.

This chapter also includes other useful information, such as

- Arithmetic operators

- Concatenation operators
- Operator precedence
- Logical operators
- Comparison operators
- Variable names

General Format: The general form of a REXX statement is

```
[label:] term... [;]
```

where *term* is either a comment enclosed by the delimiters /* and */ or an expression. An expression can be one of the following: a character expression, a numeric expression, a comparison expression, or a logical expression.

Notational Convention: In the general format of the REXX statements used in this chapter, there are a few symbols that are not part of the syntax, therefore they must not be included when you code your program. These symbols and their meanings are:

Symbol	Meaning
[]	The option enclosed by the brackets ([]) is not required but can be included.
<>	Only one of the alternatives enclosed by the angle brackets (<>) must be chosen.
or	The alternatives enclosed by the angle brackets (<>) are separated by "or."
____	The underlined word is the default value.
...	The vertical or horizontal ellipsis means that the preceding can be coded more than once.
Uppercase characters	All keywords of the command are written in uppercase characters; they must be coded as shown.
Lowercase characters	All strings in lowercase characters and italic are variables that can be changed to any other strings to suit your programming style. In your code they represent values that you supply to commands.

9.1   ARITHMETIC OPERATORS

The arithmetic operators used in REXX numeric expressions are as follows:

Operator	Operation
+	Addition
-	Subtraction
*	Multiplication
/	Division, returning decimal quotient
%	Division, returning integer quotient
//	Division, returning remainder
**	Exponential
-n	Negation
+n	Addition

9.2   CONCATENATION OPERATORS

The following concatenation operators are supported by REXX.

Operator	Operation
blank	Concatenate two strings with a blank character in between.
||	Concatenate two strings without a blank character in between.

9.3   OPERATOR PRECEDENCE

In REXX, if there is more than one operator in an expression, then operations are performed according to the following order of precedence:

Order	Operation	Operators
1	Expressions in parentheses	()
2	Prefix operators	- + \
3	Exponential operator	**
4	Multiplication and division	* / % //

5	Addition and subtraction	+ -
6	Concatenation	‖
7	Comparison	== = \== \= > <
		>< >= <= \< \>
8	Logical AND	&
9	Logical OR and EXCLUSIVE OR	| &&

9.4   LOGICAL OPERATORS

A logical operator is used when a Boolean operation is peformed on two binary operands. The following is a list of logical operators, including the operation and return code.

Operator	Operation	Returns
&	AND	1 if both comparisons are true; otherwise 0.
|	OR	1 if one of several comparisons is true; otherwise 0.
&&	XOR	1 if only one of a group of comparisons is true; otherwise 0.
\	NOT	The reverse of the logical value of the expression.

9.5   COMPARISON OPERATORS

A comparison operator is used when two operands are compared with each other. After a comparison expression is processed, from left to right, it yields 1 if the comparison condition is true and 0 if the comparison condition is false. The following is a list of REXX comparison operators.

Operator	Operation
==	Strictly equal
=	Equal
\==	Not strictly equal
\=	Not equal
>	Greater than
<	Less than

><	Greater than or less than
>=	Greater than or equal to
<=	Less than or equal to
\<	Not less than
\>	Not greater than
>>=	Strickly greater than or equal to
<<=	Strickly less than or equal to
<>	Less or greater than
>>	Strickly greater than
<<	Strickly less than

9.6   VARIABLE NAMES

In REXX variable names can be up to 250 characters long. A variable may consist of the following characters:

Uppercase characters A to Z
Lowercase characters a to z
Numbers 0 to 9
Special characters   @ # $! ? . — and '4A'x

9.7   FUNCTIONS, COMMANDS AND INSTRUCTIONS

For each instruction, command, or function, this section provides a description of its functionality and parameters. In addition, there is a list of return codes and practical examples.

◻ ABBREV function

● **General format**
ABBREV(*string, prefix*[*,length*])

● **Description**
The ABBREV function checks for a prefix in a character string.

string is a character string to be checked for a prefix.

prefix is a character string.

length is the maximum number of prefix characters that should match the leading characters of the string.

- **Return**

The ABBREV function returns 1 (TRUE) if *prefix* is found in *string*; otherwise it returns 0 (FALSE). The function returns a TRUE or FALSE code according to the following conditions:

Return Code	Condition
1	*prefix* is equal to the leading characters of *string* and the number of characters matched is less than *length*.
0	*prefix* is not equal to the leading characters of *string*.
0	The number of characters matched is greater than *length*.

- **Example**

```
ABBREV('Profile','Pro')          returns 1 (TRUE)
ABBREV('SUN','')                 returns 1 (TRUE)
ABBREV('SUNDAY','SUN',3)         returns 1 (TRUE)
ABBREV('Monday','day')            returns 0 (FALSE)
ABBREV('JOHN',Jo)                returns 0 (FALSE)
```

◘ ABS function

- **General format**

```
ABS(number)
```

- **Description**

The ABS function calculates the absolute value of a number.

number is a number for which the absolute value is returned.

- **Return**

The function returns the value of *number* without consideration of the sign. The number of digits returned is determined by the current value of the NUMERIC DIGITS variable.

- **Example**

```
ABS('34.56')    returns the value 34.56.
ABS(' -3.476')  returns the value 3.476.
```

◻ ADDRESS instruction

● General format

```
ADDRESS host-environment [expression] or
     [VALUE] expression ;
```

● Description

The ADDRESS instruction specifies the host environment where non-REXX commands are to be executed. The host environment can be set temporarily or permanently depending on whether the expression is coded or not. The setting of the host environment is checked with the ADDRESS function.

host-environment is a character string constant; it is one of the following:

ISPEXEC	Routes commands to SPFF/PDF.
ISREDIT	Routes commands to a PDF edit macro processor.
TSO	Routes commands to TSO.
MVS	Invokes a program using the normal MVS program search.
LINK	Issues an MVS LINK macro to the routine being invoked.
ATTACH	Issues an MVS ATTACH macro to the routine being invoked.
CMS	Routes commands to CMS.
DOS	Routes commands to DOS/VSE.
XEDIT	Routes commands to XEDIT.

expression is first evaluated by REXX; the result is sent to the host environment as a command to be executed. If *expression* is not specified then the destination is set permanently until the next ADDRESS instruction is issued. Subsequent non-EXEC commands will be sent to this new host environment. If *expression* is specified, then the host environment is effective during the execution of this ADDRESS instruction.

VALUE is used if the first character of *expression* is a special character.

● **Return**
The return code from the host environment, after the command is executed, is placed in the special variable RC.

● **Example**
The following ADDRESS instruction sends the command FREE DATASET("TEST.COBOL.PGMLOAD") to TSO to be executed.

```
ADDRESS TSO 'FREE DATASET("TEST.COBOL.PGMLOAD")'
```

In the next example, the command 'STATE PROFILE EXEC' is sent to CMS to be executed.

```
ADDRESS CMS 'STATE PROFILE EXEC'
```

▣ ADDRESS function

● **General format**
```
ADDRESS
```

● **Description**
The ADDRESS function returns the name of the host environment to which non-REXX commands are currently routed.

● **Return**
The function returns the current name of the host environment. It is one of the following:

ISPEXEC   ISREDIT TSO   MVS   LINK
ATTACH   CMS   DOS   XEDIT

● **Example**
```
ADDRESS()   /* returns the current destination of the
               host environment */
```

■ ARG function

• General format
```
ARG([n][,option])
```

• Description
The ARG function either returns an argument string or tests the existence of an argument passed to a previously called function or routine.

n is an argument number. If it is specified, the *n*th argument is returned.

option is a character string whose first character is an E or an O. If it is specified, the ARG function checks for the presence of the *n*th argument string.

• Return
The function returns the following:

- If *n* and *option* are not specified, it returns the number of arguments passed to the function.

- If *option* is E, it returns 1 if argument *n* exists; otherwise it returns 0.

- If *option* is O, it returns 1 if argument *n* is omitted; otherwise it returns 0.

• Example
```
ARG()           /* returns the number of arguments */
                /* passed to the function */
ARG(3)          /* returns the third argument */
ARG(2,'Omitted')   /* checks whether the 2nd
                      argument has been omitted */
```

■ ARG instruction

• General format
```
ARG template;
```

• Description
The ARG instruction parses the arguments passed to a program or

subroutine and places them in variables. The parsing is done according to parsing rules of REXX.

template consists of symbols, separated by blanks.

- **Return**
  The function returns parsed arguments.

- **Example**
  Let's say the following function is called by

      MYWORK('DATA 3', 30, 50).

  Mywork: Arg string, num1, num2

  After parsing, the symbols will have the following values:

      STRING has 'DATA 3'.
      NUM1 has '30'.
      NUM2 has '50'.

◘ BITAND function

- **General format**
  BITAND(*string1*[,[*string2*][,*pad*]])

- **Description**
  The BITAND function performs an AND operation on two strings bit by bit. The number of bits on which the operation is performed is determined by the longest string. If padding is supplied, the AND operation of the shorter input string is extended. If padding is not supplied, the AND operation stops when the bits of the shorter string have been exhausted; the remaining bits of the longer string are added to the result.

  string1, *string2*, and *pad* are input strings used for the AND operation. *string1* is required; *string2* and *pad* are optional.

- **Return**
  The function returns a string which is the result of an AND operation on *string1*, *string2*, and *pad*.

● Example

```
BITAND('63'x,'33'x)    /* returns  '23'x */
BITAND('43'x,'4444'x) /* returns  '4044'x */
BITAND('43'x,'4444'x,'70'x)    /*returns  '4440'x */
```

◙ BITOR function

● General format

```
BITOR(string1[,[string2][,pad]])
```

● Description

The BITOR function performs an OR operation on two strings bit
by bit. The number of bits on which the operation is performed is
determined by the longest string. If padding is supplied, the OR
operation on the shorter input string is extended. If padding is not
supplied, the OR operation stops when the bits of the shorter string
have been exhausted; the remaining bits of the longer string are
added to the result.

string1, *string2*, and *pad* are input strings used for the OR
operation. *string1* is required; *string2* and *pad* are optional.

● Return

The function returns a string which is the result of an OR
operation on *string1*, *string2*, and *pad*.

● Example

```
BITOR('63'x,'33'x)     /* returns  '73'x */
BITOR('63'x,'3333'x)  /* returns  '7333'x */
BITOR('63'x,'3333'x,'77'x)   /* returns  '7377'x */
```

◙ BITXOR function

● General format

```
BITXOR(string1[,[string2][,pad]])
```

● Description

The BITXOR function performs an XOR operation on two strings
bit by bit. The number of bits on which the operation is performed
is determined by the longest string. If padding is supplied, the
XOR operation of the shorter input string is extended. If padding
is not supplied, the XOR operation stops when the bits of the

shorter string have been exhausted; the remaining bits of the longer string are added to the result.

string1, *string2*, and *pad* are input strings used for the XOR operation. *string1* is required; *string2* and *pad* are optional.

● **Return**
The function returns a string which is the result of an XOR operation of *string1*, *string2*, and *pad*.

● **Example**
```
BITXOR('63'x,'33'x)    /* returns  '40'x */
BITXOR('63'x,'3333'x)  /* returns  '4033'x */
BITXOR('63'x,'3333'x,'77'x)  /* returns  '4040'x */
```

◘ **CALL instruction**

● **General format**
```
CALL name [expression,...];
```

● **Description**
The CALL instruction executes a subroutine, a program, a built-in function, or an external routine. Control is passed to the called routine, and after its execution is completed, control is returned to the statement following the CALL statement in the calling routine.

name is the name of the subroutine, program, or function to be invoked.

expression is first evaluated and resolved into parameters to be passed to the invoked routine. The entry of an expression is optional.

● **Return**
After completion of the called routine, any return value is placed in the variable *return*. If no value is returned by the invoked routine, then *return* is initialized to null.

● **Example**
In the following program fragment a subroutine *square* is called, which calculates the square root of an expression *y*.

```
arg  y            /* parse y */
call square y     /* call the routine to calculate */
                  /* the square root of y */
say 'square root of 'y ' is ' result

square: procedure    /* procedure called square */
   arg n             /* parse y */
   return n*n        /* calculate and return square */
                     /* root */
```

◻ CENTER function

• General format
CENTER(*string,length*[,*pad*])

• Description
The CENTER function centers a string within a given area.

string is the string to be centered. If *string* is longer than the specified area, it is truncated on both sides.

length is the number of characters within which *string* is to be centered.

pad is the character to use for padding on both the right and left sides of the centered *string*. If *pad* is not entered, then spaces are used.

• Return
The function returns the centered *string*.

• Example
```
CENTER(ABCD,8,'.')     returns '..ABCD..'
CENTER(ABCD,8)         returns '  ABCD  '
```

◻ COMPARE function

• General format
COMPARE(*string1,string2*[,*pad*])

• Description
The COMPARE function compares two strings.

string1 and *string2* are the strings being compared.

pad is an optional padding character; if it is not specified, the default character is blank (x'40').

● **Return**

The function returns:

● Zero if both input strings are the same.
● A nonzero value if the input strings are not the same; this value is also the position of the first mismatched characters.

● **Example**
```
COMPARE('345','345')        returns 0 (exact match)
COMPARE('MOO%% ','MOO','%') returns 6 (1st mismatch
                            after padding character
COMPARE('daa','do')         returns 1 (1st mismatched
                            character.
```

◘ CONDITION function

● **General format**
```
CONDITION([option])
```

● **Description**

The CONDITION function gets the information for the currently trapped REXX condition.

option is one of the following: C, D, I, or S. Their meanings are as follows:

C   causes the name of the current trapped condition to be returned.

D   causes the description of the string to be returned.

I   causes the name of the actual instruction that was being executed when the condition was trapped to be returned.

S   causes the status of the condition trapped to be returned.

● **Return**

The function returns the information related to the currently trapped condition depending on the option. A null string is returned if no condition trap is in effect.

- **Example**
  ```
  CONDITION(I) returns the instruction that caused the
  trap.
  ```

◘ COPIES function

- **General format**
  ```
  COPIES(string,n)
  ```

- **Description**

  The COPIES function concatenates or appends a string to itself a
  certain number of times.

  string is the string concatenated to itself.

  n is the number of times to concatenate *string* to itself.

- **Return**

  The function returns a concatenated string, or a null string if *n* is
  zero.

- **Example**
  ```
  COPIES('Hi',2)      returns   'HiHi'
  COPIES('Hi',0)      returns   '' (null string)
  ```

◘ C2D function

- **General format**
  ```
  C2D(string[,n])
  ```

- **Description**

  The C2D function converts a string into a decimal number.

  string is a string that is 0 to 250 characters in length.

  n is the number of bytes where the signed fixed-number part of
  string is to be stored.

- **Return**

  The function returns a decimal number.

● **Example**
```
C2D('08'x)              returns decimal 9
C2D('E4',2)             returns  decimal  288  (positive
                        number in two bytes)
```

◘ C2X function

● **General format**
```
C2X(string)
```

● **Description**
The C2X function converts a string into its equivalent EBCDIC hexadecimal numbers.

string is a character string to be converted to its equivalent EBCDIC numbers.

● **Return**
The function returns EBCDIC numbers.

● **Example**
```
C2X('123ABC')          returns 'F1F2F3C1C2C3'
```

◘ DATATYPE function

● **General format**
```
DATATYPE(string[,type])
```

● **Description**
The DATATYPE function tests the data type of a string.

string is a character string whose data type is to be tested.

type is the type to be tested for. If *type* is not specified, the default data type to be tested for is NUM, if it is numeric; the default type is CHAR for all other cases.

● **Return**
The function returns 1 (TRUE) if *string* is of the specified or default data type; otherwise it returns 0 (FALSE). The following list gives the relationship between the return values and *type*.

Type	Return code
A—Alphanumeric	1 if *string* contains only characters in the range a to z, A to Z, and 0 to 9
N—Numeric	1 if *string* is a valid REXX number
W—Whole number	1 if *string* is a valid REXX whole number
L—Lower case	1 if *string* contains only characters in the range a to z
U—Upper case	1 if *string* contains only characters in the range A to Z
M—Mixed case	1 if *string* contains only characters in the range a to z and A to Z
S—Symbol	1 if *string* contains only valid REXX symbols
B—Bit	1 if *string* contains only 1s and 0s
X—Hexadecimal	1 if *string* contains characters in the range a to f, A to F, 0 to 9, or blank

● **Example**

```
DATATYPE(' 55 ')            returns NUM (numeric)
DATATYPE('&e55 ')           returns CHAR (character string)
DATATYPE('Bob','M')         returns 1 (mixed case)
DATATYPE('67.89','N')       returns 1 (numeric)
DATATYPE('67.89','X')       returns 0 (not hexadecimal
                            numbers)
DATATYPE('')                returns CHAR (null string)
```

◼ **DATE function**

● **General format**

```
DATE([option])
```

● **Description**

The DATE function gets the current date.

option is a code specifying the format of the date. The default format is '*dd mmm yyyy*', as in 21 Jul 1992.

- **Return**

The function returns the current date in a format specified by one of the following options:

Option	Returns date in format
C—Century	Number of days into the current century in the form '*ddddd*'
D—Days	Number of days into the current year in the form '*ddd*'
U—USA	Date in the form '*mm/dd/yy*'
E—European	Date in the form '*dd/mm/yy*'
J—Julian	Date in the form '*yyddd*'
M—Month	Full name of current month
O—Ordered	Date in the form '*yy/mm/dd*'
S—Sort	Date in the form '*yyyymmdd*'
W—Week	Day of the week (e.g., Monday, Tuesday, etc.)

- **Example**

```
DATE()        returns the current date ('23 July
              1992')
DATE(J)       returns the date in Julian format
              (92205)
DATE(D)       returns the number of days into this
              year (205)
```

◘ **DELSTACK host REXX command**

- **General format**

DELSTACK

- **Description**

  The DELSTACK command removes the data stack and deletes all elements from it.

- **Return**

  None.

- **Example**

  ```
  "DELSTACK"    /* removes stack */
  ```

◘ DELSTR function

- **General format**

  ```
  DELSTR(string,n[,length])
  ```

- **Description**

  The DELSTR function deletes a certain number of characters from a string.

  string is the string from which characters are deleted.

  n is the starting position from which characters are deleted in *string*.

  length is the number of characters to delete. If *length* is greater than the total number of characters in *string*, then no action is taken. If *length* is not specified, then all characters from position *n* on are deleted.

- **Return**

  The function returns the changed string.

- **Example**

  ```
  DELSTR('ABCDEF',2,1)    deletes 'B', leaving 'ACDEF'
  DELSTR('ABCDEF',3,2)    deletes 'CD', leaving 'ABEF'
  DELSTR('ABCDEF',9)      no change
  ```

◘ DELWORD function

- **General format**

  ```
  DELWORD(string,n[,length])
  ```

● **Description**

The DELWORD function deletes a certain number of words from a string.

string is the string from which words are deleted.

n is the starting position from which words are deleted in *string*.

length is the number of words to delete. If *length* is greater than the total number of words in *string*, then no action is taken. If *length* is not specified, then all the words from position *n* on are deleted.

● **Return**

The function returns the changed string.

● **Example**
```
DELSTR('Ten days, two hours, and five minutes',3,2)

        returns  'Ten days, and five minutes'

DELSTR('Ten days, two hours, and five minutes',8)

        returns   'Ten days, two hours, and five
        minutes'
```

◘ DIGITS function

● **General format**
```
DIGITS()
```

● **Description**

The DIGITS function retrieves the current setting of the NUMERIC DIGITS option.

● **Return**

The function returns the current setting of NUMERIC DIGITS.

● **Example**
```
DIGITS()  /* get the current NUMERIC DIGITS */
```

◘ DO instruction

● General format

```
DO [expression or variable=start]
   [TO limit][BY increment];
   [FOR expression];
   [WHILE expression];
   [UNTIL expression];
   statement
      .
      .
      .
END [symbol];
```

Simple DO

```
DO
   statement
      .
      .
      .
END;
```

Controlled Repetitive DO

```
DO variable=start [TO end];
   statement
      .
      .
      .
END;
```

DO-WHILE loop

```
DO variable=start [TO end] WHILE expression;
   statement
      .
      .
      .
END;
```

DO-FOR loop

```
DO variable=start [TO end] FOR expression;
   statement
      .
      .
      .
END;
```

DO-UNTIL loop

```
DO variable=start [TO end] UNTIL expression;
   statement
      .
      .
      .
```

```
END;
```

DO-FOREVER loop

```
DO FOREVER ;
   statement
      .
      .
      .
END;
```

• Description

The DO instruction executes a group of REXX statements a
number of times depending on an expression. The expression is
evaluated every time the DO loop is executed. The DO instruction
can be divided into the following categories:

- Simple DO
- Controlled repetitive DO
- DO-WHILE loop
- DO-FOR loop
- DO-UNTIL loop
- DO-FOREVER loop

expression is any valid REXX expression.

variable is any valid REXX variable name.

start is the value to which *variable* is initialized before the start of
the DO loop.

end is the limit; when *variable* passes this value, the loop
terminates.

increment is the value by which *variable* is incremented.

statement is a valid REXX statement which is executed with the
DO loop.

The END clause marks the end of the DO instruction.

• Return
None.

● **Example**

In the following program fragment, the variable *start* is initialized to 3. In the DO instruction, the variable is *x* and its starting value is 3. The variable *x* is incremented by 2 during every iteration of the DO loop. The loop stops when *x* is 40. During every loop, the statement 'say x' is executed.

```
start=3;                 /* initialize start to 3 */
Do x=start to 40 by 2;   /* starting value of x is 3 */
   say x                  /* statement to be executed */
End;                     /* in the DO loop */
```

◘ DROP instruction

● **General format**
```
DROP name...
```

● **Description**

The DROP instruction restores one or more variables to their uninitialized state. In other words, such variables no longer have any values.

name is a valid variable name to be freed.

● **Return**
None.

● **Example**
```
fruit = 'apple'  /* initialize the variable fruit to */
                 /* 'apple'    */
DROP fruit       /* free the variable fruit   */
```

◘ DROPBUF host REXX command

● **General format**
```
DROPBUF [n]
```

● **Description**

The DROPBUF host REXX command removes a specified buffer and its elements from the data stack.

n is the buffer number to be deleted.

- **Return**

  After completion of DROPBUF, the command variable RC is set to one of the following codes:

  0—Completion was successful.
  1—The buffer number is invalid
  2—The buffer number does not exist.

- **Example**
  ```
  "DROPBUF 2"   /* drop buffer 2 and all its elements */
                /* from the stack */
  ```

◘ D2C function—Convert decimal to character

- **General format**
  ```
  D2C(number[,n])
  ```

- **Description**

  The D2C function converts a decimal number to a character string in binary representation.

  number is a whole number to be converted.

  n is the number of characters in the result.

- **Return**

  The function returns the binary representation of a decimal number.

- **Example**
  ```
  D2C(8)          returns '08'x
  D2C(-127,2)     returns 'FF81'x (-127 = FF81 hex)
  ```

◘ D2X function—Convert decimal to hexadecimal

- **General format**
  ```
  D2X(number[,n])
  ```

- **Description**

  The D2X function converts a decimal number to a character string in hexadecimal representation.

number is a whole number to be converted.

n is the number of characters in the result.

● Return
The function returns the hexadecimal representation of a decimal number.

● Example
```
D2C(8)            returns '08'
D2C(-127,4)       returns 'FF81' (-127 = FF81 hex)
```

◘ ERRORTEXT function—Return message text

● General format
```
ERRORTEXT(n)
```

● Description
The ERRORTEXT function returns a message text associated with an error number.

n is the error number; it is in the range 0 to 99.

● Return
The function returns the message text or a null string if the error number or message is not defined.

● Example
```
ERRORTEXT(16) returns 'Label not found'
```

◘ EXECIO command—Read and write data

● General format
```
Read operation:

  EXECIO [lines or *] [DISKR or DISKRU] ddname
                  [linenum or 1]
      [ ( [[FINIS] [LIFO or FIFO or SKIP]] or
                [STEM var [FINIS]] [)]
      ]

Write operation:

  EXECIO [lines or *] DISKW ddname
        [ ([STEM var] [FINIS] [)] ]
```

- **Description**

The EXECIO REXX command is used to read or write data to or from datasets and PDS members. It performs the following operations:

- Read data from file and place in data stack.
- Read data from file and place in variables.
- Read data from data stack and write to file.
- Read data from variables and write to file.

lines is the number of lines to read or write.

DISKR means a read operation.

DISKRU means a read operation for update.

DISKW means a write operation.

linenum is the record number for a read operation.

FINIS means to close the file after a read or write operation.

LIFO means to write to the data stack in last-in first-out sequence.

FIFO means to write to the data stack in first-in first-out sequence.

SKIP means to only read the number of records contained in lines, and not to write them to the data stack.

STEM specifies the names of variables to which data are written or from which data are read.

- **Return**

After completion of EXECIO, command variable RC is set to the following codes:

0—Successful completion
1—Data truncated during a write operation
2—End of file reached
20—Fatal error

● **Example**
```
"ALLOC F(TEMP) DA('TEMP.SAA.FILE') SHR" /* allocate */
                                         /* file*/
'EXECIO 3 DISKR TEMP (FINIS' /* read 3 records and */
                              /* place them into stack*/
```

◘ **EXECUTIL command—Control REXX processing**

● **General format**
```
EXECUTIL [EXECDD(CLOSE or NOCLOSE)]
         [TS] [TE] [HT] [RT] [HI]
         [RENAME NAME (function) [SYSNAME(sysname)]
                 [DD(sysdd)]]
         [ SEARCHDD(NO or YES)]
```

● **Description**
The EXECUTIL command is used to control processing. This command can perform the following:

● Halt execution of an EXEC.
● Start or stop tracing.
● Start or stop input and output.
● Allow SYSEXEC to search for EXECs.

EXECDD specifies whether to close a system exec library or leave it open after an exec is fetched.

CLOSE means to close the system exec library.

NOCLOSE means to leave the system exec library open.

TS means to turn on the tracing of the exec being executed.

TE means to turn off the tracing of the exec being executed.

HT means not to send output to a terminal.

RT means to send output to a terminal that was stopped previously.

HI means to halt interpretation and execution of all current execs that are being executed.

RENAME is used to rename functions.

◘ EXIT instruction—Terminate exec

● General format
```
EXIT [expression];
```

● Description
The EXIT instruction ends the execution of a REXX exec and returns control to the calling program.

expression is optional; its value is evaluated before termination of the exec.

● Return
A value is returned to the calling program depending on whether *expression* is part of the EXIT instruction.

● Example
In the following program fragment, the exec will terminate returning the value '12'.

```
x = 4
EXIT x*3 /* terminate exec */
```

◘ EXTERNALS function

● General format
```
EXTERNALS()
```

● Description
The EXTERNALS function gets the number of elements in the terminal input buffer. This does not apply to TSO, as there is no equivalent terminal buffer.

● Return
The function returns the number of elements for CMS and always 0 for TSO.

● Example
```
EXTERNALS() returns 0 in TSO
```

▣ FIND function

- **General format**
  FIND(*string*,*phrase*)

- **Description**
  The FIND function finds the first occurrence of a phrase in a string of words. FIND compresses blanks into a single blank.

  string is a string of words to be searched from left to right for a specified phrase.

  phrase is a string of one or more words that is searched for in *string*.

- **Return**
  The function returns the first position of the phrase if it is found; otherwise it returns 0.

- **Example**
  ```
  FIND('All dogs go to Heaven','go  to') returns 3
  FIND('Honey they shrunk my pay','my pay') returns 4
  FIND('Honey they shrunk my pay','the baby') returns 0
  ```

▣ FORM function—Get the NUMERIC FORM setting

- **General format**
  FORM()

- **Description**
  The FORM function returns the current setting of NUMERIC FORM.

- **Return**
  The function returns 'SCIENTIFIC' or 'ENGINEERING'.

- **Example**
  ```
  NUMERIC FORM ENGINEERING
  x = FORM()            /* returns ENGINEERING */
  ```

◘ FORMAT function—Format numeric values

● **General format**
```
FORMAT(number[,before][,after])
```

● **Description**

The FORMAT function formats a numeric value; otherwise default formatting is done.

number is the numeric value to be formatted. If only *number* is entered, it is formatted and rounded using the standard REXX rules.

before is the number of digits allowed to the left of the decimal point.

after is the number of digits allowed to the right of the decimal point.

● **Return**

The function returns the formatted numeric value.

● **Example**
```
x = FORMAT("13.2",3,2)    returns ' 13.20'
```

◘ FUZZ function—Get the NUMERIC FUZZ setting

● **General format**
```
FUZZ()
```

● **Description**

The FUZZ function returns the current setting of NUMERIC FUZZ. The default REXX setting is 0.

● **Example**
```
NUMERIC FUZZ 1
x = FUZZ()              returns 1
```

◘ HI host REXX command—Halt interpretation

● **General format**
```
HI
```

● **Description**
The HI host REXX command halts the execution of all currently running execs.

● **Example**
```
"HI"        /* terminate all currently running execs */
```

◘ HT host REXX command—Halt typing

● **General format**
```
HT
```

● **Description**
The HT host REXX command suppresses SAY output.

● **Example**
```
HT              /* halt output */
Say '%%%%'      /* output is suppressed */
```

◘ IF instruction

● **General format**
```
IF expression [;] THEN [;] statement
             [ELSE [;] statement]
```

● **Description**
The IF instruction executes one or many REXX statements based on the result of evaluating an expression.

expression is a valid REXX expression; after its evaluation, the result is either 1 (TRUE) or 0 (FALSE).

THEN is a keyword that marks the statement(s) to be executed if *expression* evaluates to 1 (TRUE).

statement is a valid REXX statement.

ELSE is the keyword that marks the statement(s) to be executed if *expression* evaluates to 0 (FALSE).

Note: The statement of either THEN or ELSE is executed, never both.

● **Example**
In the following program fragment, the expression in the IF instruction is x < 3. After the expression is evaluated, depending on whether the result is 1 or 0, the NOP or SAY instruction is executed.

```
IF x < 3
   THEN NOP
   ELSE
    SAY "x is greater than or equal to 3"
```

■ **INDEX function—Search for substring**

● **General format**
```
INDEX(string,substring[,start-position])
```

● **Description**
The INDEX function searches for a substring in a string and returns the position of the first occurrence of the substring.

string is the string to be searched.

substring is the string to be searched for.

start-position is the starting position in *string*; its default value is 1.

● **Return**
The function returns

- 0 if *substring* is not found in *string*
- A numeric value which is relative to 1 if the substring is found

● **Example**
```
INDEX('Hi mom','mom')          returns 4
INDEX('Hi mom','dad')          returns 0
INDEX('Hi mom','mam')          returns 0
```

```
INDEX('Hi mom','mom',3)        returns 4
```

◻ INSERT function—Insert string

• General format
```
INSERT(ins-string,string[,[n][,[length][,pad]]])
```

• Description
The INSERT function inserts a string into another string at a specified position. Padding is done if required.

ins-string is the string inserted into *string*.

string is the string in which *ins-string* is inserted.

n is the character position after which *ins-string* is inserted in *string*. The value of *n* must be nonnegative, and its default value is 0.

length is the length of *ins-string*.

pad is the character for padding if *length* is greater than the length of *ins-string*.

• Return
The function returns *string* with *ins-string* inserted.

• Example
```
INSERT(' ','GOODBOY',4)      returns 'GOOD BOY'
INSERT('ABC','abc',5,6,'%')  returns 'abc%%ABC%%%'
```

◻ INTERPRET instruction—Interpret a statement

• General format
INTERPRET *expression* ;

• Description
The INTERPRET instruction interprets and executes an expression.

expression contains one or many valid REXX statements. It is first evaluated and then executed by the REXX interpreter as if it were a REXX statement.

● **Example**
```
ohmy = "SAY 'ohmy'"

INTERPRET ohmy            /* interpret and execute */
```

◘ **ITERATE instruction—End current iteration of DO loop**

● **General format**
```
ITERATE[name];
```

● **Description**
The ITERATE instruction stops the current iteration of a DO loop and transfers control to the END statement. The DO loop continues after testing any expression associated with the loop.

name is a control variable for the DO loop.

● **Example**
The following DO loop will display 1, 3, and 4; it skips the display of 2 because of the ITERATE instruction with the loop.

```
DO j = 1 TO 4
   IF j = 2 THEN ITERATE
   SAY j
END
```

◘ **JUSTIFY function—Right- and left-justify text**

● **General format**
```
JUSTIFY(string,length[,pad])
```

● **Description**
The JUSTIFY function does right and left justification of a text. Blanks are added in between words if required.

string is the text to be justified.

length is the length of the justified text.

pad is the padding character.

- **Return**

  The function returns the justified text.

- **Example**

  ```
  JUSTIFY("All dogs go to heaven",23) returns
    "All  dogs  go to heaven".
  ```

◻ LASTPOS function—Find the last position of a sub-string

- **General format**

  ```
  LASTPOS(substring,string[,start])
  ```

- **Description**

  The LASTPOS function finds the last occurrence, starting from position 1, of a substring within a string.

  substring is the string searched for in *string*.

  string is the string searched for in *substring*.

  start is the starting position for the search.

- **Return**

  The function returns the position of the last occurrence if *substring* is found in *string*; otherwise it yields 0.

- **Example**

  ```
  LASTPOS("dogs","All dogs go to heaven") returns 5
  LASTPOS("hogs","All dogs go to heaven") returns 0
  ```

◻ LEAVE instruction—Terminate a DO loop

- **General format**

  ```
  LEAVE[name];
  ```

- **Description**

  The LEAVE instruction stops a DO loop and transfers control to the statement following the END statement.

  name is a control variable for the DO loop.

- **Example**

The following DO loop will display 1 and stop when the value of j is 2.

```
DO j = 1 TO 4
   IF j = 2 THEN LEAVE
   SAY j
END
```

◘ LEFT function—Left justify text

- **General format**
```
LEFT(string,length[,pad])
```

- **Description**

The LEFT function left-justifies a text.

string is the text to be justified.

length is the length of the justified text.

pad is the padding character.

- **Return**

The function returns the left-justified text.

- **Example**
```
LEFT("All dogs go to heaven",23) returns
   "All dogs go to heaven  ".
```

◘ LENGTH function—Get the length of a string

- **General format**
```
LENGTH(string)
```

- **Description**

The LENGTH function determines the number of characters in a string.

string is the string for which the length is to be determined.

- **Return**

The function returns the length of *string*.

- **Example**

```
LENGTH("All dogs go to heaven") returns 21.
```

◻ LINESIZE function—Get the line length of the terminal

- **General format**

```
LINESIZE()
```

- **Description**

The LINESIZE function gets the current setting for the line length of the TSO terminal.

- **Return**

The function returns the current terminal line length minus 1.

◻ LISTDSI function— Get dataset information

- **General format**

```
LISTDSI( dataset-name [VOLUME(vol-ser) or PREALLOC]
             [DIRECTORY or NODIRECTORY]
             [RECALL or NORECALL]

        or

LISTDSI( filename FILE )
```

- **Description**

The LISTDSI function retrieves characteristic information from an existing MVS file and stores it in special REXX variables.

dataset-name is the name of a file conforming to TSO conventions.

VOLUME(*vol-ser*) is the volume specification if the dataset is not cataloged.

PREALLOC specifies that allocation is extracting the dataset information.

DIRECTORY specifies that the directory of a PDS is to be read in order to get the information.

NODIRECTORY means that no directory information is to be read.

RECALL specifies recall of a dataset migrated by HSM.

NORECALL specifies that no recall of the dataset is required.

filename is the DD name of an allocated dataset.

FILE is a keyword which is assocated with *filename*.

The following is a list of special REXX variables:

Variable Name	Describtion
SYSDSNAME	Dataset name
SYSVOLUME	Volume serial number
SYSUNIT	Device type for volume
SYSDSORG	Dataset organization
SYSRECFM	Record format
SYSLRECL	Logical record length
SYSBLKSIZE	Block size
SYSKEYLEN	Key length
SYSALLOC	Space allocation quantity
SYSUSED	Quantity of space used
SYSPRIMARY	Primary allocation quantity
SYSSECONDS	Secondary allocation quantity
SYSUNITS	Space units (CYLINDER, TRACK, or BLOCK)
SYSEXTENTS	Number of DASD extents already used
SYSCREATE	Creation date (*yyyy*/*ddd*) of dataset
SYSREFDATE	Last reference date (*yyyy*/*ddd*) of dataset
SYSEXDATE	Expiration date (*yyyy*/*ddd*) of dataset
SYSPASSWORD	Password status: NONE, READ, or WRITE
SYSRACFA	RACF indication (NONE, GENERIC, or DISCRETE)
SYSUPDATED	Change indicator (YES or NO)
SYSTRKSCYL	Number of tracks per cylinder
SYSBLKSTRK	Number of directory blocks per track

SYSADIRBLK	Directory blocks allocated (for PDS only)
SYSUDIRBLK	Directory blocks used (for PDS only)
SYSMEMBERS	Number of PDS members
SYSMSGLVL1	1st-level message
SYSMSGLVL2	2nd-level message
SYSREASON	Reason code upon error

● **Return**

The function returns one of the following codes:

0   Normal completion of function.
4   Some directory information for dataset not obtained.
16   Severe error; no variables were properly set.

● **Example**

In the following statements, the LISTDSI function retrieves information from the partitioned dataset TEST.COB.PGMSRC and displays the number of members in the PDS.

```
x = LISTDSI('TEST.COB.PGMSRC' 'DIRECTORY')
SAY "Number of members in PDS: SYSMEMBERS
```

◼ **MAKEBUF command—Add a buffer to the data stack**

● **General format**
```
MAKEBUF
```

● **Description**

The MAKEBUF command adds a new buffer to the current data stack.

● **Return**

The command returns the number of the new buffer in variable RC.

● **Example**

In the following example, the NEWSTACK command creates a new stack, and the MAKEBUF command adds a new buffer to the stack just created. Then the SAY instruction prints the number assigned to the new buffer.

```
"NEWSTACK"
"MAKEBUF"
SAY "Buffer number: " RC
```

◘ MAX function—Determine the maximum value

- **General format**
  ```
  MAX(number,...)
  ```

- **Description**
  The MAX function returns the maximum numeric value from a list
  of numeric values. Up to 20 numbers are allowed.

  number is a numeric value.

- **Return**
  The function returns the maximum value. The size of the returned
  value depends on the current setting of NUMERIC DIGITS.

- **Example**
  ```
  MAX(22,34,67,100,1,4)    returns 100.
  ```

◘ MIN function—Determine the minimum value

- **General format**
  ```
  MIN(number,...)
  ```

- **Description**
  The MIN function returns the minimum numeric value from a list
  of numeric values. Up to 20 numbers are allowed.

  number is a numeric value.

- **Return**
  The function returns the minimum value. The size of the returned
  value depends on the current setting of NUMERIC DIGITS.

- **Example**
  ```
  MIN(22,34,67,100,1,4)    returns 1.
  ```

◘ MSG function—Set CLIST CONTROL MSG option

- **General format**

```
MSG( 'OFF' or 'ON' )
```

- **Description**

The MSG function returns the current setting and sets the CONTROL MSG option.

OFF means to suppress messages issued by a TSO command.

ON means to display messages issued by a TSO command.

- **Example**

The following statement sets the CLIST CONTROL MSG status to OFF and returns the current MSG setting.

```
x = MSG('OFF')
```

◘ NEWSTACK command—Create a new data stack

- **General format**

```
NEWSTACK
```

- **Description**

The NEWSTACK command creates a new data stack which becomes the current stack.

- **Example**

In the following example, the NEWSTACK command creates a new stack, and the MAKEBUF command adds a new buffer to the stack just created. Then the SAY instruction prints the number assigned to the new buffer.

```
"NEWSTACK"
"MAKEBUF"
SAY "Buffer number: " RC
```

◘ NOP instruction—No operation

- **General format**

```
NOP
```

- **Description**

  The NOP instruction does nothing.

- **Example**

  In the following program fragment, the expression in the IF instruction is x < 3. After the expression is evaluated, depending on whether the result is 1 or 0, the NOP or the SAY instruction is executed. The NOP instruction does not produce any result, but the SAY instruction does.

```
IF x < 3
   THEN NOP
   ELSE
     SAY "x is greater or equal to 3"
```

◻ NUMERIC instruction—Set numeric formats

- **General format**
```
NUMERIC < DIGITS [expression or 9] > or
       < FORM [SCIENTIFIC or ENGINEERING] > or
       < FUZZ [expression or 0] >;
```

- **Description**

  The NUMERIC instruction sets the format for evaluating and reporting arithmetic operations.

  DIGITS specifies the number of significant digits to use in calculations and reporting. The *expression* after DIGITS must resolve to a positive number. The default number is 9.

  FORM specifies the expression of arithmetic values in exponential notation. There are two kinds: SCIENTIFIC and ENGINEERING.

  SCIENTIFIC means that only one nonzero digit appears before the decimal point of the mantissa, e.g., 3.5E+5.

  ENGINEERING means that the exponent is a power of three, e.g., 23E+3.

  FUZZ specifies the number of digits to ignore during a numeric comparison. The *expression* after FUZZ must resolve to a positive number. The default is 0.

◘ OPTIONS instruction—Pass options to the REXX language processor

● General format
```
OPTIONS expression;
```

● Description
The OPTIONS instruction passes special parameters to the REXX language processor in an MVS-TSO installation to set the DBCS environment. This instruction should appear at the beginning of an EXEC.

expression must have only the following words; any other word is ignored.

ETMODE	Enable support for DBCS characters in strings.
NOETMODE	Disable support for DBCS characters in strings.
EXMODE	Enable support for DBCS data operations.
NOEXMODE	Disable support for DBCS data operations.

◘ OUTTRAP function—Trap TSO output

● General format
```
OUTTRAP( 'OFF' or
    <variable,[max or '*' or BLANK]
        [,'CONCAT' or 'NOCONCAT']
    >)
```

● Description
The OUTTRAP function traps the output issued from a TSO/E command. Only output going to the terminal with the PULINE macro is trapped.

OFF means to disable trapping of TSO output to the terminal.

variable is a stem variable.

max is the maximum number of lines to be trapped, which must be in the range 1 to 999,999,999. Any number of lines beyound this specification is not trapped and displayed on the terminal.

* or BLANK means to trap all TSO output lines.

CONCAT means to append to previously trapped output lines.

NOCONCAT means to overwrite previously trapped output lines.

● **Return**
The function returns the name of the stem variable that is specified to collect TSO output lines.

● **Example**
```
x = OUTTRAP('OFF')   /* turn trapping off */
y = OUTTRAP()        /* returns stem variable */
```

◘ OVERLAY function—Overlay a string

● **General format**
```
OVERLAY(new-string,string[,[n][,length][,pad]])
```

● **Description**
The OVERLAY function overlays a string with a new string starting at a given position in the target string. Padding is done if either of the strings is to be extended.

new-string is the string that is to overlay the target *string*.

string is the string to be overlaid by *new-string*.

n is the position of the character in *string* from which the overlay is to start. *n* must be a positive number.

length is the length of *new-string*.

pad is the padding character.

● **Return**
```
The function returns the overlaid string.
```

- **Example**
  ```
  x = OVERLAY('123','1yzv3',2,4.'.'      returns '1123.3'
  ```

■ **PARSE instruction—Assign data**

- **General format**
  ```
  PARSE [UPPER] <ARG or
                 EXTERNAL or
                 NUMERIC or
                 PULL or
                 SOURCE or
                 VALUE [expression] WITH or
                 VAR name or
                 VERSION>
        [template];
  ```

- **Description**

  The PARSE instruction places data into one or more variables. The source of the data can be a terminal, a data stack, or arguments passed to a function or subroutine.

  UPPER means to convert assigned data to uppercase. The case of the source data remains unchanged.

  ARG means that the source of the data is arguments passed to a REXX exec or routine.

  template consists of alternating patterns and variable names.

  EXTERNAL means that the input data are from a terminal.

  NUMERIC specifies returning the current settings for NUMERIC options.

  PULL means that the source data is REXX data stacks.

  SOURCE means that the source of the data is the program.

  VALUE specifies evaluation of *expression*.

  WITH is a keyword in context of *expression*.

  VAR specifies that *name* contains the source data.

VERSION specifies returning the current version of REXX.

- **Example**

```
CALL Mywork('DATA 3', 30, 50).
EXIT
Mywork: Arg string, num1, num2
    SAY string          /* displays 'DATA 3' */
    SAY num1            /* displays 30 */
    SAY num2            /* displays 50 */
    Return
```

◻ POS function—Search for a substring

- **General format**

```
POS(substring,string[,start-pos])
```

- **Description**

The POS function searches a string for the first occurrence of a substring.

substring is the string to be searched for.

string is the string to search for the *substring*.

start-pos is the starting position.

- **Return**

The function returns the character position, relative to 1, if *substring* is found; otherwise a zero is returned.

- **Example**

```
POS("to","All dogs go to heaven") returns 13.
```

◻ PROCEDURE instruction—Define a procedure

- **General format**

```
PROCEDURE [EXPOSE name,...];
```

- **Description**

The PROCEDURE instruction defines a procedure.

EXPOSE is the keyword used to define one or more global

variables that are used within the procedure.

name is a global variable name.

- **Example**
```
x = "Birds"
CALL proc
EXIT
proc: PROCEDURE EXPOSE x
   SAY x          /* displays "Birds" */
   Return
```

◘ PROMPT function—Set CLIST CONTROL PROMPT option

- **General format**
```
PROMPT('OFF' or 'ON')
```

- **Description**

The PROMPT function sets the CLIST CONTROL PROMPT to on or off status.

OFF means that a TSO command cannot prompt the user for additional information. A command with missing information will fail.

ON means that a TSO command can prompt the user for additional information.

- **Return**

The function returns the current CONTROL PROMPT status.

- **Example**
```
x = PROMPT('ON')   /* set CONTROL PROMPT to on*/
SAY x              /* display previous status */
```

◘ PULL instruction—Get an element from the top of the data stack

- **General format**
```
PULL [template];
```

● **Description**

The PULL instruction reads the top element of a data stack and uses it as source data. If the data stack is empty, then PULL will read from the terminal. The PULL instruction is the same as the REXX instruction PARSE UPPER PULL [*template*].

template consists of alternating patterns and variable names.

● **Example**
```
SAY 'Please enter your first name:'
PULL name
```

◘ **PUSH instruction—Put an element at the top of the data stack**

● **General format**
```
PUSH [expression];
```

● **Description**

The PUSH instruction places a new element at the top of the data stack.

expression is the data element to be placed in the data stack.

● **Example**
```
line = "WallyMagoo"
PUSH line      /* place line at the top of the stack */
```

◘ **QBUF command—Get the number of buffers in the stack**

● **General format**
```
QBUF
```

● **Description**

The QBUF command gets the number of buffers created by MAKEBUF command in the current stack, .

● **Return**

The command places the number in buffers in the stack in the special variable RC.

● **Example**
```
"QBUF"      /* query number of buffers */
SAY RC      /* display number of buffers */
```

◻ **QELEM command—Get the number of elements in the buffer**

● **General format**
```
QELEM
```

● **Description**
The QELEM command gets the number of elements in the current buffer.

● **Return**
The command places the number of elements in the buffer in the special variable RC.

● **Example**
```
"QELEM"     /* query number of elements */
SAY RC      /* display number of elements */
```

◻ **QSTACK command—Get the number of stacks**

● **General format**
```
QSTACK
```

● **Description**
The QSTACK command gets the number of current stacks.

● **Return**
The command places the number of current stacks in the special variable RC.

● **Example**
```
"QSTACK"    /* query number of stacks */
SAY RC      /* display number of stacks */
```

◻ **QUEUE instruction—Put an element at the bottom of the data stack**

● **General format**
```
QUEUE [expression];
```

- **Description**

  The QUEUE instruction places a new element at the bottom of the data stack.

  expression is the data element to be placed in the data stack.

- **Example**
  ```
  line = "WallyMagoo"
  QUEUE line /* place line at the bottom of the stack */
  ```

◻ QUEUED function—Get the number of elements in the queue

- **General format**
  ```
  QUEUED()
  ```

- **Description**

  The QUEUED function returns the number of elements remaining in the data stack.

- **Return**

  The function returns the number of elements in the stack.

- **Example**
  ```
  x = QUEUED()     /* query number of elements in queue */
  SAY x            /* display number of elements */
  ```

◻ RANDOM function—Generate a random number

- **General format**
  ```
  RANDOM([min][,[max][,seed]])
  ```

- **Description**

  The RANDOM function generates a pseudo-random number with a specified or default minimum and maximum range.

  min is the minimum value above which the pseudo-random number is generated. The default is zero.

  max is the maximum value below which the pseudo-random number is generated. The default is 999.

seed is a positive value used to start the random number generation process.

• Return
The function returns a positive number as the pseudo-random number.

• Example
The following statement will generate a pseudo-random number in the range 10 to 1000 using the value 3 as the seed.

```
y = RANDOM(10,1000,3)
```

◘ RETURN instruction—Return from routine

• General format
```
RETURN [expression];
```

• Description
The RETURN instruction passes control back to the calling function or subroutine. Control goes to the statement following the CALL statement.

expression is first evaluated and the result returned to the calling function or subroutine.

• Example
```
    CALL Mywork(30, 50)
    EXIT
Mywork: Arg num1, num2
    y = num1 * num2 /* calculate sum */
    RETURN y;       /* return sum to caller */
```

◘ REVERSE function—Reverse the order of characters in a string

• General format
```
REVERSE(string)
```

• Description
The REVERSE function reverses the order of all characters in a string, i.e., the first character is placed in the last position.

string is a string whose characters are reversed.

- **Return**

The function returns the reversed string.

- **Example**

```
REVERSE('abcde') returns 'edcba'.
```

■ **RIGHT function—Right-justify text**

- **General format**

```
RIGHT(string,length[,pad])
```

- **Description**

The RIGHT function right-justifies a text, using padding characters if necessary.

string is the text to be justified.

length is the length of the justified text.

pad is the padding character.

- **Return**

The function returns the right-justified text.

- **Example**

```
RIGHT("All dogs go to heaven",23) returns
   "  All dogs go to heaven".
```

■ **RT command—Resume typing**

- **General format**

```
RT
```

- **Description**

The RT command resumes sending output from a SAY instruction to the terminal after it has previously been stopped with an HT (halt typing) command.

- **Example**
```
"RT"            /* resume output of SAY instruction */
SAY 'Resume output'
```

◻ SAY instruction—Display data

- **General format**
```
SAY [expression] ;
```

- **Description**

The SAY instruction sends a line of data to a terminal or SYSTSPRT DD statement in batch mode.

expression is a valid REXX expression which is first resolved and then displayed by the SAY instruction.

- **Example**
```
SAY 'SAY what?'
name = 'Joe'
year = 10
SAY name ' is ' year 'old.'
```

◻ SELECT instruction—Conditional execution of statements

- **General format**
```
SELECT
   WHEN expression[;] THEN[;] statement
   [WHEN expression[;] THEN[;] statement]
   [WHEN expression[;] THEN[;] statement]
      .
      .
      .
   [OTHERWISE[;] statement]
END;
```

- **Description**

The SELECT instruction executes only one statement from a group of statements. The selection depends on the result of evaluating an expression placed after the WHEN clause. If the result of the evaluation is 1 (TRUE), then the statement associated with this expression, that is placed after the THEN clause, is executed. If the result is 0 (FALSE), then the next expression with the SELECT instruction is evaluated. This continues until all the expressions with the WHEN clause have been evaluated and the associated statements executed if necessary. If none of the expressions with the WHEN clause yields 1 and an OTHERWISE clause exists, then the statement specified with that clause is executed. There must be at least one expression and statement with the WHEN and THEN clauses.

WHEN starts the condition clause.

expression is a valid REXX expression which is tested; the associated statement is executed if the result is 1.

The THEN clause specifies the statement to be executed.

statement is a valid REXX statement.

OTHERWISE specifies the statement to be executed when none of the above statements are performed.

END indicates the end of the SELECT instruction.

- **Example**
```
SELECT
    WHEN y = 0 THEN SAY 'Y is 0'
    WHEN y = 1 THEN SAY 'Y is 1'
    WHEN y = 2 THEN SAY 'Y is 2'
    OTHERWISE SAY 'Y < 0 or > 2'
END
```

◘ **SIGN function—Determine the sign of a number**

- **General format**
```
SIGN(number)
```

- **Description**
The SIGN function determines the sign of a number.

number is the value whose sign is to be determined.

- **Return**
The function returns the following:

    -1 if *number* is negative
    0 if *number* is equal to zero
    +1 if *number* is positive

● Example

```
SIGN('-2.38')      returns -1
SIGN(0.0)          returns 0
SIGN('2.4')        returns +1
```

◼ SIGNAL instruction—Exception condition handler

● General format

```
SIGNAL label
   or
SIGNAL [VALUE] expression
   or
SIGNAL OFF [ERROR or FAILURE or HALT
          or NOVALUE or SYNTAX] NAME label
   or
SIGNAL ON [ERROR or FAILURE or HALT
          or NOVALUE or SYNTAX] NAME label
```

● Description

The SIGNAL instruction can be used in one of the following ways:

- To pass program control to a label or routine
- To enable exception condition processing
- To disable exception condition processing

label is the name of a label to which control is passed.

VALUE specifies the expression which is evaluated.

OFF specifies disabling the conditions that follow.

ON specifies enabling the conditions that follow.

ERROR means that there was a nonzero return code after a host command was executed.

HALT means that the terminal attention key has been pressed and an HT command entered.

NOVALUE means that a variable that is not initialized has been used in a statement.

SYNTAX means that the REXX interpreter found a syntax error.

FAILURE means that a negative code was returned after an MVS command was executed.

- **Example**

```
SIGNAL ON NOVALUE novalue /* goto novalue */
      .
      .
      .
Attention: SAY 'Variable not initialized'
      EXIT
```

◘ SOURCELINE function—Get a program line

- **General format**

```
SOURCELINE([line-number])
```

- **Description**

The SOURCELINE function retrieves the relative line number of a REXX exec line.

line-number is optional; when it is specified, the program line of the exec is returned. If *line-number* is not specified, then the function returns the line number of the last line.

◘ SPACE function—Insert characters between words

- **General format**

```
SPACE(string[,[n][,pad]])
```

- **Description**

The SPACE function either inserts or removes padding characters between words in a string.

string is the string which padding characters are added to or removed from.

n is the number of padding characters to insert between words of *string*.

pad is the padding character.

- **Return**
  The function returns the changed string.

- **Example**
  ```
  SPACE("All dogs go to heaven",2,'.')
      returns'All..dogs..go..to..heaven".

  SPACE('A B C D      E',0)    returns 'ABCDE'.
  ```

◻ **STORAGE function—Access and store data in MVS main storage**

- **General format**
  ```
  STORAGE([address[,[length][,data]]])
  ```

- **Description**
  The STORAGE function is a TSO/E external function that is used to read data from a specified address and optionally change its content.

  address is a hexadecimal address for accessing and storing data.

  length is the number of bytes to retrieve from *address*.

  data is the data to overwrite at *address*.

- **Return**
  The function returns the data read from main storage.

- **Example**
  The following statement will return 10 bytes read from address 40E20 and overwrite 'DOGCATCHER' at the same location.

  ```
  STORAGE(40E20,10,'DOGCATCHER')
  ```

◻ **STRIP function—Remove leading/trailing characters**

- **General format**
  ```
  STRIP(string[,[Both or Leading or Trailing][,char]])
  ```

- **Description**
  The STRIP function removes any leading and trailing characters from a string.

string is the data from which characters are removed.

Both means to remove both leading and trailing characters from *string*.

Leading means to remove leading characters from *string*.

Trailing means to remove trailing characters from *string*.

char is the character to be removed from *string*; the default is a blank.

● **Return**
The function returns the stripped string.

● **Example**
```
STRIP(' Heavenly ',L)        returns 'Heavenly '.
STRIP('.Heavenly.',B,'.')    returns 'Heavenly'.
```

◻ **SUBCOM command—Check a host environment**

● **General format**
```
SUBCOM environment
```

● **Description**
The SUBCOM command checks a specified environment.

environment is one of the following:
```
TSO       MVS     LINK
ATTACH    ISPEXEC ISREDIT
```

● **Return**
The following code is placed in special variable RC:

   0 if the specified environment is valid
   1 if the specified environment is not valid

● **Example**
```
"SUBCOM TSO"
if RC = 0 THEN SAY 'TSO is active'
ELSE           SAY 'TSO is not active'
```

◘ SUBSTR function—Extract a substring

● General format
SUBSTR(*string*,*position*[,[*length*][,*pad*]])

● Description
The SUBSTR function extracts a substring from a string starting at a specified character position.

string is the string from which a portion is extracted.

position is the character position in *string* at which the substring is extracted; it is also the first character of the extracted substring.

length is the number of bytes of the substring.

pad is the padding character.

● Return
The function returns the substring.

● Example
SUBSTR('Hot dog',4) returns ' dog'

◘ SUBWORD function—Extract a word from a string

● General format
SUBWORD(*string*,*word-position*[,*word-count*])

● Description
The SUBWORD function extracts one or more words from a string starting at a specified word position.

string is the string from which one or more words are extracted.

word-position is a word position in *string* relative to 1; it is also the first position from which words are extracted.

word-count is the number of words to be extracted. The default is all remaining words.

- **Return**

The function returns the extracted words.

- **Example**

```
SUBWORD('Hot dog',2) returns 'dog'
```

SYMBOL function—Get the status of a variable name

- **General format**

SYMBOL(*name*)

- **Description**

The SYMBOL function returns the status of a variable name.

name is a valid REXX variable name.

- **Return**

The function returns:

VAR	If the variable name has been assigned a value and has not been deleted with a DROP function
LIT	If the variable name has not been assigned a value or if it has been deleted with a DROP function
BAD	If the variable name is not valid

- **Example**

```
d = "horses"
x = SYMBOL("d")          /* returns VAR */
y = SYMBOL("f")          /* returns LIT */
```

SYSDSN function—Check dataset status

- **General format**

SYSDSN(*dsname* or '*dsname*(*member*)')

- **Description**

SYSDSN is a TSO function that checks the status of a dataset.

dsname is the dataset name for which the status is requested.

member is the member of the partitioned dataset for which the status is requested.

● **Return**

The function returns the following information about the dataset or member:

    OK
    MEMBER NOT FOUND
    MEMBER SPECIFIED, BUT DATA SET IS NOT PARTITIONED
    DATA SET NOT FOUND
    ERROR PROCESSING REQUESTED DATA SET
    PROTECTED DATA SET
    VOLUME NOT IN THE SYSTEM
    INVALID DATA SET NAME
    UNAVAILABLE DATA SET

● **Example**
```
dsn = SYSDSN("'SYS1.PROCLIB'")
if dsn = 'OK' SAY 'SYS1.PROCLIB exists'
```

◻ **SYSVAR function—Get a TSO system variable**

● **General format**
```
SYSVAR(sysvarname)
```

● **Description**

The SYSVAR function retrieves the content of a TSO system variable.

sysvarname is one of the following TSO system variables:

SYSPREF	SYSPROC	SYSUID	SYSLTERM
SYSWTERM	SYSENV	SYSICMD	SYSISPF
SYSNEST	SYSPCMD	SYSCPU	SYSHSM
SYSLRACF	SYSRACF	SYSSRV	SYSTSOE

● **Return**

The function returns the content of a specified system variable.

- **Example**

The following will display the current TSO user identification after
'USER ID is '.

```
SAY 'USER ID is ' SYSVAR(SYSUID)
```

◻ **TE command—Trace end**

- **General format**

```
TE
```

- **Description**

The TE command terminates tracing.

- **Example**

```
"TE"   /* terminate tracing*/
```

◻ **TIME function—Get the current time of day**

- **General format**

```
TIME('Civil' or 'Elapse' or 'Hours' or 'Long' or
   'Minutes' or 'Normal' or 'Reset' or 'Seconds')
```

- **Description**

The TIME function returns the current time of day in different
formats.

- **Return**

The function returns the time in the following formats:

Code	Returns	Format
Civil	Time of day	*hh:mmxx*
Elapse	Elapsed time	*sssssss.uuuuuuu*
Hours	Hours since midnight	*hh*
Long	Time of day in the long form	*hh:mm:ss.uuuuuuu*
Minutes	Minutes since midnight	*mmmm*
Normal	Time of day	*hh:mm:ss*
Reset	Time elapsed since the elapsed clock was set or reset; the clock is reset	
Seconds	Seconds since midnight	*sssss*

- **Example**
```
x = TIME('H') /* return hours since midnight */
```

◻ TRACE instruction—Set REXX debugging options

- **General format**
```
TRACE [number];
     or
TRACE   [ [? or !] ['All' or
              'Commands' or
              'Error'    or
              'Failure'  or
              'Intermediates' or
              'Labels'   or
              'Normal'   or
              'Off'  or
              'Results'  or
              'Scan' ]];
```

- **Description**

The TRACE instruction enables and disables tracing of execution of REXX statements.

If *number* has a positive value, it is the number of trace pauses to skip over. If *number* is negative, it is the number of trace outputs to suppress.

? is a prefix which means to enable interactive debugging.

! is a prefix which means to turn off execution of host commands.

All means to display all expressions before execution.

Commands means to display the host command before execution.

Error means to display a host command returning a nonzero code.

Failure means to display a host command returning a negative code.

Intermediates means to display all expressions before execution and all intermediate results.

Labels means to display labels when they are encountered.

Normal means to display a host command returning a negative code.

Off means to end tracing.

Results means to display all expressions before execution and the results.

Scan means to check the syntax of REXX statements but not to execute them.

- **Example**
```
TRACE '?C' /* turn on host command tracing */
```

■ **TRACE function—Set or return current trace setting**

- **General format**
```
TRACE    ( [? or !] ['All' or
              'Commands' or
              'Error'    or
              'Failure'  or
              'Intermediates' or
              'Labels'   or
              'Normal'   or
              'Off'      or
              'Results'  or
              'Scan' )
```

- **Description**
  The TRACE function either sets or returns the current REXX trace setting. The following options are used: All, Commands, Error, Failure, Intermediates, Labels, Normal, Off, Results, and Scan. These options were previously described with the TRACE instruction. If the option is omitted, then the function returns the current setting.

- **Return**
  The function returns the current setting.

- **Example**
```
y = TRACE()        /* return the current setting */
x = TRACE('?C')    /* turn on tracing for host
                      commands */
```

◻ TRANSLATE function—Translate and reorder characters in a string

● **General format**

```
TRANSLATE(string[,[outtab][,intab][,pad]])
```

● **Description**

The TRANSLATE function translates and reorders the content of a string depending on input and output translation tables. If the first character of the input table is found in the string, then this matching character in the string is replaced with the first character in the output table. The characters in the input table map to characters in the output table. If only the string is specified, with all other arguments omitted, then TRANSLATE converts all characters to uppercase.

string is the string to be translated and reordered.

outtab is the output translation table.

intab is the input translation table.

pad is the padding character used to extend the length of *outtab* if required.

● **Example**

```
TRANSLATE('abcdef')  returns 'ABCDEF'
TRANSLATE('abcdef','1','abcdef','1') returns '111111'
```

◻ TRUNC function—Truncate a number

● **General format**

```
TRUNC(number[,decimal-places])
```

● **Description**

The TRUNC function formats a number to a specified number of decimal places.

number is the numeric value to be formatted.

decimal-places is the number of decimal places. The default value is 0.

- **Return**

  The function returns the formatted numeric value.

- **Example**
  ```
  TRUNC("1222.6757") returns '1222'
  TRUNC("1222.6757",2) returns '1222.67'
  ```

◻ **TS command—Trace start**

- **General format**
  ```
  TS
  ```

- **Description**

  The TS command starts REXX interactive tracing of the exec.

- **Example**
  ```
  "TS"   /* start tracing */
  ```

◻ **UPPER instruction—Translate to uppercase characters**

- **General format**
  ```
  UPPER variable,...;
  ```

- **Description**

  The UPPER instruction converts the content of one or more variables from lowercase characters to uppercase. This instruction is equivalent to PARSE UPPER and is available only in an MVS-TSO environment.

  variable is the name of the variable which is to be converted.

- **Example**
  ```
  x = "A new race of humanity"
  UPPER x

  SAY x     /* displays  'A NEW RACE OF HUMANITY'*/
  ```

◻ **USERID function—Return USERID**

- **General format**
  ```
  USERID()
  ```

- **Description**

  The USERID function returns user identification.

◘ VALUE function—Get the content of a symbol

- **General format**
  ```
  VALUE(name)
  ```

- **Description**

  The VALUE function returns the content of a symbol.

  name is a valid REXX symbol or variable name.

- **Example**
  ```
  x = 'My oh my'
  y = VALUE(x)
  SAY y        /* displays 'My oh my'*/
  ```

◘ VERIFY function—Compare two strings

- **General format**
  ```
  VERIFY(string1,string2
      [,'Match' or 'Nomatch'][,position])
  ```

- **Description**

  The VERIFY function compares two strings and determines the position of the first matching character in both strings or the position of the first character that does not match in both strings.

  string1 is one of the strings.

  string2 is the other string.

  Match is the option to check for a matching character in both *string1* and *string2*.

  Nomatch is the option to check for the first character in *string1* that does not match *string2*.

  position is the starting position of the comparison.

- **Return**

  The function returns the first position in *string1* that has a matching or not matching character. It returns zero if the option is 'Match' and all characters in *string1* and *string2* match. It also returns zero if none of the characters in *string1* and *string2* match, if the option is 'Nomatch'.

- **Example**
  ```
  VERIFY("abcd","ccc",'M')    returns 3
  VERIFY("abdc","2",'N')      returns 0
  ```

◘ WORD function—Get a word

- **General format**
  ```
  WORD(string,word-num)
  ```

- **Description**

  The WORD function extracts a word from a string at a give word position.

  string is the string the word is extracted from.

  word-num is the word position relative to 1 in *string*.

- **Return**

  The function returns the word extracted.

- **Example**
  ```
  WORD("The world is but one country",2) returns 'world'
  ```

◘ WORDINDX function—Get a word position in a string

- **General format**
  ```
  WORDINDEX(string,word-num)
  ```

- **Description**

  The WORDINDEX function returns the character position of a word in a string. It returns zero if the word is not found.

  string is the string that is searched for the character position of a word.

word-num is the position relative to 1 in *string* of the word whose character position is determined.

- **Example**

```
WORDINDEX("The world is but one country",2) returns 5
```

◘ WORDLENGTH function—Get a word length in a string

- **General format**

```
WORDLENGTH(string,word-num)
```

- **Description**

The WORDLENGTH function returns the length of a word in a string. It returns zero if the word is not found.

string is the string that is searched for the word.

word-num is the position relative to 1 in *string* of the word whose length is determined.

- **Example**

```
WORDLENGTH("The world is but one country",2) returns 5
```

◘ WORDPOS function—Get a word position in a string

- **General format**

```
WORDPOS(string-to-find,string-to-search[,word-num])
```

- **Description**

The WORDPOS function returns the position of a specified word in a string. It returns zero if the word is not found.

string-to-find is the word searched for in a string.

string-to-search is the string that is searched.

word-num is the number of the word at which the search starts and a word position relative to 1 in *string-to-search*.

- **Example**

```
WORDPOS("The world is but one country","is") returns 3
```

◘ WORDS function—Get the number of words in a string

- **General format**
  WORDS(*string*)

- **Description**

  The WORDS function returns the number of words in a string.

  string is the string whose words are counted.

- **Example**
  WORDS("The world is but one country") returns 6

◘ XRANGE function—Get a range of hexadecimal numbers

- **General format**
  XRANGE([*start*][,*end*])

- **Description**

  The XRANGE function returns a range of hexadecimal numbers given lower and upper limits.

  start is the lower limit of the range.

  end is the upper limit of the range.

- **Example**
  XRANGE('0','3') returns 'F0F1F2F3'x (EBCDIC)

◘ X2C function—Convert hexadecimal to character

- **General format**
  X2C(*hex-string*)

- **Description**

  The X2C function converts a string of hexadecimal values into a character string.

  hex-string is one or more hexadecimal digits to be converted.

- **Return**

  The function returns the converted character string.

- **Example**

  ```
  X2C('F0F1F2')    returns 012
  ```

◘ X2D function—Convert hexadecimal to decimal

- **General format**

  ```
  X2D(hex-string)
  ```

- **Description**

  The X2D function converts a string of hexadecimal values into a decimal string.

  hex-string is one or more hexadecimal digits to be converted.

- **Return**

  The function returns the converted decimal string.

- **Example**

  ```
  X2C('F0F0')    returns 61680
  ```

This chapter is a reference for programmers using SQL (Structured Query Language). SQL is a language for managing data in a relational database such as DB2 or SQL/DS. SQL statements can be used with an interactive facility like SPUFI or CMS. Alternatively, they can be embedded in an application program written in another language, such as C, COBOL, or PL/I.

Notational Conventions: In the general format of the SQL statements or built-in functions used in this chapter, there are a few symbols that are not part of the syntax; therefore they must not be included when you code your program. These symbols and their meanings are:

Symbol	Meaning
[]	The option enclosed by the brackets ([]) is not required but can be included.
<>	Only one of the alternatives enclosed by the angle brackets (<>) must be chosen.
or	The alternatives enclosed by the angle brackets (<>) are separated by "or."
____	The underlined word is the default value.
...	The vertical or horizontal ellipsis means that the preceding can be coded more than once.
Uppercase characters	All keywords of the command are written in uppercase characters; they must be coded as shown.

Lowercase
characters

All strings in lowercase characters and italic are variables that can be changed to any other strings to suit your programming style. In your code they represent values that you supply to commands.

10.1 SQL STATEMENTS

This section contains all the SQL statements. For each statement, it gives the syntax, followed by an explanation of the statement and its parameters. Also, there is a brief note indicating whether the statement can be used interactively, embedded in a program, or both. The examples will help you understand how the SQL statement is used.

◘ ALTER INDEX—Change attributes of an index

● General format

```
ALTER INDEX index-name
            [PART part-num]
            [BUFFERPOOL<BP0 or BP1 or BP2>]
            [CLOSE <YES or NO>]
            [DSETPASS password]
            [FREEPAGE page-num]
            [PCTFREE percent]
```

● Description
The ALTER INDEX statement is used to change the attributes of the index space that contains the index.

index-name is the name of the index, defined by the user and part of the DB2 catalog, that you want to modify.

PART *part-num*
This specifies the partition of an index to which the change is to apply.

part-num is the number of a partition.

BUFFERPOOL <BP0 or BP1 or BP2>
This specifies the name of the buffer pool of the index.
There are three buffer pools: BP0, BP1, and BP2.

CLOSE <YES or NO>
This specifies whether or not to close datasets associated with the
index to be altered, if they are not being used.
YES means to close the datasets.
NO means not to close the datasets.

DSETPASS *password*
This specifies the password to be passed to VSAM to access
datasets.

password is a string of characters acceptable to VSAM.

FREEPAGE *page-num*
This specifies leaving a free page after *page-num* pages.

page-num is any number between 0 and 255.

PCTFREE *percent*
This specifies the percentage of each page to leave free.

percent is any number between 0 and 99.

- **Usage**: SPUFI and application programs.

- **Example**
  The following example changes the index RBA.CLIENTS. Also,
  it specifies closing all datasets associated with the index if they are
  not being used.

```
ALTER INDEX RBA.CLIENTS
    CLOSE YES;
```

◘ **ALTER STOGROUP—Change the attributes of a storage
group**

- **General format**
```
ALTER STOGROUP stogroup-name
        [PASSWORD password]
        [ADD VOLUMES (vol-id,...)]
        [REMOVE VOLUMES (vol-id,...)]
```

- **Description**
The ALTER STOGROUP statement is used to change the attributes of a storage group.

stogroup-name is the name of the storage group that you want to modify.

PASSWORD *password*
This specifies the password to be passed to VSAM to access datasets.

password is a string of characters acceptable to VSAM.

ADD VOLUMES(*vol-id,...*)
This specifies one or more volumes to add to the storage group.

vol-id is the volume serial number.

REMOVE VOLUMES(*vol-id,...*)
This specifies one or more volumes to remove from the storage group.

vol-id is the volume serial number.

- **Usage**: SPUFI and application programs.

- **Example**
The following example changes the storage group DSN8G200. It passes the password PGLNEW to access VSAM datasets and adds volumes DSNV50 and DSNV40.

```
ALTER STOGROUP DSN8G200
   PASSWORD PGLNEW
   ADD VOLUMES(DSNV50,DSNV40);
```

◻ **ALTER TABLE—Add a column to a table and maintain keys**

- **General format**
```
ALTER TABLE table-name
   [ADD col-name data-type
```

```
            <NOT NULL WITH DEFAULT or
               FIELDPROC proc-name (parm-list)>]
         [VALIDPROC <prog-name or NULL>]
```

● **Description**

The ALTER TABLE statement is primarily used to add a column to a table.

table-name is the name of the table you want to change. It must exist in the DB2 catalog.

ADD *col-name data-type*
This specifies the name of the column that you want to add to the table and its data type.

col-name is a unique name for the column.

data-type is one of the data types found in the following list:

INTEGER   SMALLINT   FLOAT
DECIMAL   CHAR   VARCHAR
GRAPHIC   VARGRAPHIC   LONG VARGRAPHIC
LONG VARCHAR

NOT NULL WITH DEFAULT
This allows default values but not null values.

FIELDPROC *proc-name(parm-list)*
This specifies a field procedure for column.

proc-name is a name of a procedure; it is supplied by the systems programmer.

parm-list is one or more parameters that are passed to the procedure.

VALIDPROC *prog-name* or NULL
This specifies whether to run a validation program or not.

prog-name is the name of the program that is run during the update or insertion of a row to validate a range of values. It is supplied by systems programmer to validate the range of values for a table. There is one such program for each table.

NULL means not to run a validation program.

- **Usage:** SPUFI and application programs.

- **Example**
  The following example adds the column CONTACT_2 to the table RBA.CLIENTS.

```
ALTER TABLE RBA.CLIENTS
   ADD CONTACT_2 CHAR(20);
```

◻ ALTER TABLESPACE—Change a tablespace

- **General format**
```
ALTER TABLESPACE [database-name.]tablespace-name
               [PART <part-num]
               [BUFFERPOOL<BP0 or BP1 or BP2>]
               [LOCKSIZE <ANY or PAGE or TABLESPACE>]
               [CLOSE <YES or NO>]
               [DSETPASS password]
               [FREEPAGE page-num]
               [PCTFREE percent]
```

- **Description**
  The ALTER Table space statement is used to change the attributes of the table space of a DB2 database.

  database-name is the name of the the database where the table space is to be modified. The default is DSNDB04.

  tablespace-name is the name of the table space you want to change.

  PART *part-num*
  This specifies the partition of a partitioned table space to which the change is to apply.

  part-num is the number of a partition.

  BUFFERPOOL <BP0 or BP1 or BP2>
  This specifies the names of the buffer pool of the table space.

There are three buffer pools: BP0, BP1 and BP2.

LOCKSIZE <ANY or PAGE or TABLESPACE>
This specifies the lock level for the table space.

ANY means to allow DB2 to determine the locking level.

PAGE means to set locks at page level.

TABLESPACE means to set locks at table-space level.

CLOSE <YES or NO>
This specifies whether or not to close datasets associated with the table space to be altered, if they are not being used.

YES means to close the datasets.

NO means not to close the datasets.

DSETPASS *password*
This specifies the password to be passed to VSAM to accessed datasets.

password is a string of characters acceptable to VSAM.

FREEPAGE *page-num*
This specifies leaving a free page after *page-num* pages.

page-num is any number between 0 and 255.

PCTFREE *percent*
This specifies the percentage of each page to leave free.

percent is any number between 0 and 99.

• **Usage:** SPUFI and application programs.

• **Example**
The following example changes the table space RBA.CLIENTS. Also, it specifies closing all datasets associated with the table space if they are not being used.

```
ALTER Table space RBA.CLIENTS
   CLOSE YES;
```

◘ CLOSE—Close a cursor

● **General format**
```
CLOSE cursor-name
```

● **Description**

A cursor is a pointer to the current row of a result table. After you have completed processing a result table, the cursor must be CLOSEd. But a cursor must first be DECLAREd and OPENed before it is used or closed. A COMMIT statement automatically closes all cursors.

cursor-name is the name of a cursor that was previously used in the DECLARE CURSOR statement.

● **Usage**: Application programs.

● **Example**

In the following SQL statement, the cursor BRANCH_C is closed.

```
EXEC SQL
   CLOSE BRANCH_C
END-EXEC
```

◘ COMMENT ON—Add or replace comments on tables, views, or columns

● **General format**
```
COMMENT ON
   <TABLE <table-name or view-name>
         IS comment-string>            or
   <COLUMN <table-name.column-name    or
         view-name.column-name>
         IS comment-string>            or
   <table-name or view-name>
         (column-name IS comment-string,...) >
```

● **Description**

The COMMENT ON statement adds or replaces comments in the catalogs of DB2.

TABLE <*table-name* or *view-name*>
This specifies what to comment on: a table or view.

table-name is the name of a table already in
SYSIBM.SYSTABLES.

view-name is the name of a view already in
SYSIBM.SYSTABLES.

COLUMN <*table-name.column-name* or
       view-name.column-name>
This specifies commenting on a column.

column-name is the name of the column that already exists in a
table or view.

IS *comment-string*
This is a keyword which precedes the comment you want to
specify.

comment-string can be any SQL string constant, up to 254 bytes.

- **Usage**: SPUFI and application programs.

- **Example**
  The following example updates a comment on the table
  RBA.CLIENTS.

```
COMMENT ON TABLE RBA.CLIENTS
    IS 'LAST BACKUP Jan 17, 1992'
```

◼ COMMIT—Make a change permanent

- **General format**
  ```
  COMMIT [WORK]
  ```

- **Description**
  The COMMIT statement is used to make changes in data
  permanent after they have been successfully completed. If you do
  not use COMMIT within your program and the execution of the

program ends successfully, then DB2 will issue a COMMIT. It is highly recommended that you use COMMIT in your program, say every 100 updates of rows. COMMIT frees resources, allowing other programs to use them. Also, it saves you from having to rerun the whole job when only part of it failed.

- **Usage**: Interactive and application programs.

- **Example**
The following command issues a COMMIT statement:

```
EXEC SQL COMMIT END-EXEC
```

◘ CREATE DATABASE—Define a database

- **General format**
```
CREATE DATABASE database-name
       [STOGROUP stogroup-name]
          [BUFFERPOOL<BP0 or BP1 or BP2 or BP32K>]
```

- **Description**
The CREATE DATABASE statement creates a DB2 database, which consists of many objects. The objects are tables, indexes, table spaces, and index spaces which are logically related to one another.

database-name must be a database name that does not already exist in a DB2 database.

STOGROUP *stogroup-name*
This specifies the storage group that is to be used for the table spaces and index spaces.

stogroup-name is the name of the storage group that you want to use. The default is SYSDEFLT.

BUFFERPOOL <BP0 or BP1 or BP2 or BP32K>
This specifies the name of the buffer pool of the table space and indexes. There are four buffer pools: BP0, BP1, BP2, and BP32k.

- **Usage**: SPUFI and application programs.

- **Example**

The following example creates database RBA001, using the storage group RBAST01. Also, it specifies BP2 as the default buffer pool.

```
CREATE DATABASE RBA001
    STOGROUP RBAST01
    BUFFERPOOL BP2;
```

◻ CREATE INDEX—Create an index on a table

- **General format**

```
CREATE [UNIQUE] INDEX index-name ON table-name
    [(column-name <ASC or DESC>,...)]
    [CLUSTER [(PART part-num VALUES (constant,...))]]
    [SUBPAGES <1 or 2 or 4 or 8 or 16>]
    [BUFFERPOOL <BP0 or BP1 or BP2>]
        [CLOSE <YES or NO>]
        [DSETPASS password]
    USING VCAT <catalog-name or STOGROUP stogroup-name>
        [FREEPAGE page-num]
        [PCTFREE percent]
```

- **Description**

The CREATE INDEX statement creates an index on an existing table of the DB2 database.

UNIQUE

This optional keyword is used to create only unique index keys.

INDEX *index-name*

This specifies the name of an index for which an index space is created.

index-name is the name of the index, which does not exist in the DB2 catalog.

ON *table-name*

This specifies the name of the table on which the index is to be created.

table-name is the name of a table already described in the DB2 catalog.

column-name is the name of a column that is to be part of the index key. You can enter one or more column names that are part of a table definition. The maximum number of columns you can enter in this statement is 16. Following each name you can specify the order of index entries.

ASC means ascending order. ASC is the default.

DESC means descending order.

CLUSTER
This makes an index a cluster index.

PART *part-num*
This specifies the highest number of the index key in one partition of a partitioned index.

part-num is the highest number in the sorting sequences of the index column.

VALUES (*constant,...*)
This specifies one or more contant values for each partition number associated with the PART clause.

constant is a string constant, enclosed in apostrophes, that is part of the index.

SUBPAGES <1 or 2 or 4 or 8 or 16>
This specifies the number of subpages for each physical page. The default is 4.

BUFFERPOOL <BP0 or BP1 or BP2>
This specifies the name of the buffer pool of the index.
There are three buffer pools: BP0, BP1, and BP2.

CLOSE <YES or NO>
This specifies whether or not to close datasets associated with the index, if they are not being used.
YES means to close the datasets. This is the default.
NO means not to close the datasets.

DSETPASS *password*
This specifies the password to be passed to VSAM to access datasets.

password is a string of characters acceptable to VSAM.

USING VCAT *catalog-name*
This specifies the datasets for the index.

catalog-name is the VSAM catalog name and is the first dataset entry for the index.

STOGROUP *stogroup-name*
This specifies the storage group that is to be used for the index spaces.

stogroup-name is the name of the storage group that you want to use.

FREEPAGE *page-num*
This specifies leaving a free page after *page-num* pages.
page-num is any number between 0 and 255. The default value is 0.

PCTFREE *percent*
This specifies the percentage of each page to leave free.

percent is any number between 0 and 99. The default value is 10.

- **Usage**: SPUFI and application programs.

- **Example**
The following example creates an index IXCLIENTS on the table CLIENTS. Also, it specifies having only unique index keys and using storage group RBAST01. The CLUSTER parameter defines IXCLIENTS as the clustering index for table CLIENTS.

```
CREATE UNIQUE INDEX IXCLIENTS
    ON CLIENTS
        (CLIENTID DESC)
    USING STOGROUP RBAST01
    SUBPAGES 8
    CLUSTER
```

◘ CREATE STOGROUP—Define a storage group

● **General format**
```
CREATE STOGROUP stogroup-name
    VOLUMES (vol-id,...)
    VCAT catalog-name
    [PASSWORD password]
```

● **Description**
The CREATE STOGROUP statement assigns one or more DASD volumes to a storage group. The VSAM datasets associated with a storage group are allocated in these volumes.

stogroup-name is the name of the storage group that you want to define. It should be a name that has not been used in the DB2 catalog.

VOLUMES(*vol-id,...*)
This specifies one or more volumes that are assigned to the storage group.

vol-id is the volume serial number.

VCAT *catalog-name*
This specifies the name of a VSAM catalog.

catalog-name is the VSAM catalog name.

PASSWORD *password*
This specifies the password to be passed to VSAM to access datasets.

password is a string of characters acceptable to VSAM.

● **Usage**: SPUFI and application programs.

● **Example**
The following example defines the storage group RBAST01. It passes the password PGLNEW to access VSAM datasets and assigns volumes VOL1 and VOL2 to the storage group. The VCAT parameter specifies the highest-level qualifier as BBB.

```
CREATE STOGROUP RBAST01
   PASSWORD PGLNEW
   VOLUMES(VOL1,VOL2)
   VCAT BBB
```

◻ CREATE SYNONYN—Give an alternative name to a table or view

● General format
```
CREATE SYNONYM synonym
   FOR <table-name or view-name>
```

● Description
The CREATE SYNONYM statement gives a table or view an alternative name. The synonyms' definitions are kept in the DB2 catalog and can be used in SQL statements; DB2 will do the translation.

synonym is the alternative name you want to give to a table or view.

FOR *table-name* or *view-name*
This specifies the table or view for which the synonym is defined.

table-name is the name of an existing table.

view-name is the name of an existing view.

● Usage: Interactive and application programs.

● Example
In the following example, a synonym CLT is created and associated with the fully qualified table RBA.CLIENTS.

```
CREATE SYNONYM CLT
         FOR RBA.CLIENTS
```

◻ CREATE TABLE—Create a table for a database

● General format
```
CREATE TABLE table-name
    col-name data-type
         [NOT NULL FIELDPROC proc-name(parm-list) or
```

```
            NOT NULL WITH DEFAULT],...
   [IN [database-name.]tablespace-name or
       IN DATABASE database-name]
   [EDITPROC prog-name ]
   [VALIDPROC prog-name]
```

● **Description**

The CREATE TABLE statement creates a table within a DB2 database. Also, this statement lets you create columns and specify programs for editing and validation.

table-name is the name of the table you want to create. It must exist in the DB2 catalog. The creator of the table has all the privileges.

col-name is a unique name for a column.

data-type is one of the data types found in the following list:

INTEGER   SMALLINT   FLOAT
DECIMAL   CHAR   VARCHAR
 GRAPHIC   VARGRAPHIC LONG VARGRAPHIC
 LONG VARCHAR

NOT NULL
This prevents columns from having null values but does not specify a default.

FIELDPROC *proc-name* (*parm-list*)
This specifies a field procedure.

proc-name is a name of a procedure; it is supplied by the systems programmer.

parm-list is one or more parameters that are passed to the procedure.

NOT NULL WITH DEFAULT
This allows columns to have default values instead of null values. The DB2 default values for data types are as follows:

Data Type	Default Value
Numeric	0
Fixed length character string	Blanks
Variable length character string	A string of length 0
Date	Current date
Time	Current time
Timestamp	Current timestamp

IN *database-name.tablespace-name* or
IN DATABASE *database-name*
This specifies the database and the table space where the table is to be created.

database-name is the name of a database that has already been created. If you choose not to specify the database explicitly, then the default is DSNBD04.

tablespace-name is the name of a table space that has already been created. If you choose to omit the table space name, then a table space is created with a name derived from the table name and default values for attributes.

EDITPROC *prog-name*
This specifies whether to run a editing program or not.

prog-name is the name of the program that is run during the update or insertion of a row.

VALIDPROC *prog-name*
This specifies whether to run a validation program or not.

prog-name is the name of the program that is run during the update or insertion of a row to validate the range of values.

- **Usage**: SPUFI and application programs.

- **Example**
The following creates a table of CLIENTS. The table will have four columns: CLIENTS_ID, CLIENTS_ADDR, CLIENTS_CITY, and CLIENTS_C. It will reside in database RBA and table space RBATS01.

```
CREATE TABLE CLIENTS
   (CLIENTS_ID   SMALLINT     NOT NULL WITH DEFAULT,
   (CLIENTS_ADDR CHAR (20)    NOT NULL WITH DEFAULT,
   (CLIENTS_CITY CHAR (25)    NOT NULL WITH DEFAULT,
   (CLIENTS_C    VARCHAR (25) NOT NULL WITH DEFAULT )
IN RBA.RBATS01
```

◘ CREATE TABLESPACE—Allocate and a format table space

● General format

```
CREATE TABLESPACE table space-name [IN database-name]
     USING VCAT <catalog-name or
             STOGROUP stogroup-name >
        [NUMPARTS number ]
        [BUFFERPOOL <BP0 or BP1 or BP2 or BP32K>]
     [LOCKSIZE <ANY or PAGE or TABLESPACE>]
        [CLOSE <YES or NO>]
        [DSETPASS password]
        [FREEPAGE page-num]
        [PCTFREE percent]
```

● Description

The CREATE Table space statement allocates a space where one or more tables are created later.

tablespace-name is the name of the table space you want to create.

database-name is the name of the the database where the table space is to be allocated. The default is DSNDB04.

NUMPARTS *number*
This specifies partitioning of the table space.

number is the number of partitions, ranging from 1 to 64.

BUFFERPOOL <BP0 or BP1 or BP2 or BP32K>
This specifies the name of the buffer pool of the table space. There are three buffer pools: BP0, BP1, BP2, and BP32K.

LOCKSIZE <ANY or PAGE or TABLESPACE>
This specifies the lock level for the table space.

ANY means to allow DB2 to determine the locking level.

PAGE means to set locks at page level.

TABLESPACE means to set locks at table space level.

CLOSE <YES or NO>
This specifies whether or not to close datasets associated with the table space, if they are not being used.

YES means to close the datasets.

NO means not to close the datasets.

DSETPASS *password*
This specifies the password to be passed to VSAM to access datasets.

password is a string of characters acceptable to VSAM.

USING VCAT *catalog-name*
This specifies the datasets for the table space.

catalog-name is the VSAM catalog name.

STOGROUP *stogroup-name*
This specifies the storage group that is to be used for the table space.

stogroup-name is the name of the storage group that you want to use.

FREEPAGE *page-num*
This specifies leaving a free page after *page-num* pages.

page-num is any number between 0 and 255. Page 0 is the default.

PCTFREE *percent*
This specifies the percentage of each page to leave free.

percent is any number between 0 and 99.

- **Usage**: SPUFI and application programs.

● **Example**

The following example creates a table space called RBATS001 in database RBA. Also, it specifies the storage group as RBASG001 and the buffer pool as BP0.

```
CREATE TABLESPACE RBATS001
    IN RBA
    USING STOGROUP RBASG001
    BUFFERPOOL BP0
```

◘ **CREATE VIEW—Create a view from a table or view**

● **General format**
```
CREATE VIEW view-name [(column-name,...)]
    AS subselect-statement
    [WITH-CHECK-OPTION]
```

● **Description**

The CREATE VIEW statement derives a virtual table from one or more tables or views.

view-name is the view you want to create.

column-name is a unique name of a column already defined in a table. You can have one or more columns in this statement.

AS *subselect-statement*
This defines the view in association with the SELECT statement.

subselect-statement is a SELECT statement. This statement is described in more detail later in this chapter.

WITH CHECK OPTION
This option checks all inserts and updates against view definitions.

● **Usage**: Interactive and application programs.

● **Example**

The following example creates a view called CUSTNAME through a SELECT statement. The view consists of two columns, SOC_SEC and FIRST_AND_LAST, from the CUSTOMER table. The WITH CHECK OPTION verifies all inserts and updates against view definitions.

```
CREATE VIEW CUSTNAME
  (SOC_SEC,FIRST_AND_LAST)
  AS SELECT CUST_SOC_SEC, CUST_NAME
    FROM CUSTOMER
    WHERE CUST_SOC_SEC < 7000000
  WITH CHECK OPTION
```

◘ DECLARE CURSOR—Define a cursor

• General format

```
DECLARE cursor-name CURSOR FOR select-statement
```

• Description

The DECLARE CURSOR statement defines a cursor, which points to a row of a table. It consists of a cursor name and a SELECT statement. Subsequently, the declared cursor can be OPENed, FETCHed, or CLOSEd.

cursor-name is the name of the cursor you want to define.

select-statement is a SELECT statement; this statement is described in detail later in this chapter.

• Usage: Application programs.

• Example

In the following example, a cursor called CLIENTS_C is defined. It will point to each row in the table CLIENTS that is returned as a result of the SELECT statement.

```
EXEC SQL
  DECLARE CLIENT_C CURSOR FOR
  SELECT CLIENTS_ID, CLIENTS_ADDR, CLIENTS_CITY
    FROM CLIENTS
    WHERE CLIENTS_ID = :TRANS-BRANCH-ID
END-EXEC
```

◘ DECLARE TABLE—Declare a table in a program

• General format

```
DECLARE <table-name or view-name> TABLE
      (column-name data-type
       [NOT NULL FIELDPROC  or
        NOT NULL WITH DEFAULT],...)
```

• Description

The DECLARE TABLE statement is mainly used to document your program. It is also used by the precompiler to verify the information in the DECLARE TABLE statement against SQL statements in the program. The table declaration can be generated with the DCLGEN command.

table-name is the name of a table you want to document.

view-name is the name of a view you want to document.

column-name is a name of a column of the table or view.

data-type is one of the data types found in the following list:

INTEGER	SMALLINT	FLOAT
DECIMAL	CHAR	VARCHAR
GRAPHIC	VARGRAPHIC	LONG VARGRAPHIC
LONG VARCHAR		

NOT NULL
This prevents columns from having null values but does not specify a default.

NOT NULL WITH DEFAULT
This allows columns to have default values instead of null values. The DB2 default values for data types are:

Data Type	Default Value
Numeric	0
Fixed length character string	Blanks
Variable length character string	A string of length 0
Date	Current date
Time	Current time
Timestamp	Current timestamp

• Usage: Application programs.

• Example

In the following example, the table CLIENTS is declared.

```
EXEC SQL DECLARE CLIENTS TABLE
( CL_CL_NAME                CHAR(25) NOT NULL,
  CL_CITY                   CHAR(15),
  CL_LANG                   CHAR(1),
  CL_P_CDE                  CHAR(7),
  CL_PROV                   CHAR(15),
  CL_SITE                   CHAR(4),
  CL_COMPANY_NO             CHAR(10),
  CL_SERV_NAME              CHAR(25),
  CL_NODE_ID                CHAR(8),
  CL_STUB_NO                CHAR(4)
) END-EXEC.
```

◘ DELETE—Delete rows from a table or view

● General format

Not using cursor:

```
DELETE FROM <table-name or view-name>
   WHERE search-condition
```

Using cursor:

```
DELETE FROM <table-name or view-name>
   WHERE CURRENT OF cursor-name
```

● Description

The DELETE statement removes a varying number of rows from a table or view depending on the search condition. The deletion of rows can be done with or without the cursor.

FROM *table-name* or *view-name*
This specifies the table or view from which the rows are to be removed.

table-name is the name of a table already defined in a DB2 catalog.

view-name is the name of a view already defined in a DB2 catalog.

WHERE *search-condition*
This clause determines how many rows will be deleted. If it is omitted, then all the rows will be removed.

search-condition is the same as the search condition used in the WHERE clause of the SELECT statement. Depending on the condition, many rows or no rows may be deleted.

WHERE CURRENT OF *cursor-name*
This clause determines how many rows will be deleted using a cursor.

cursor-name is the name of a cursor, defined previous to using it in the DELETE statement. The DECLARE CURSOR statement defines the cursor. When this statement is executed, it deletes the row where the cursor is positioned. After the deletion, the cursor points to before the next row.

● **Usage**: Interactive and application programs.

● **Example**
The following example deletes all rows from the table CLIENTS where the column CL_CL_NAME is 'SMITH'.

```
DELETE
   FROM CLIENTS
   WHERE CL_CL_NAME = 'SMITH';
```

◻ DROP—Remove an object

● **General format**
```
DROP <DATABASE database-name       or
      INDEX index-name             or
      STOGROUP stogroup-name       or
      SYNONYM synonym-name         or
      TABLESPACE[database-name.]tablespace-name or
      VIEW view-name
```

● **Description**
The DROP statement deletes a specific DB2 object, such as a particular view, index, database, and so on. It removes from the DB2 catalog the named object entry and any associated objects below it.

DATABASE *database-name*
This specifies the database to be deleted.

database-name is the name of a database already defined in the DB2 catalog. It must not be DSNDB04 or DSNDB06.

INDEX *index-name*
This specifies the index to be deleted.

index-name is a name of an unpartitioned and user-created index already defined in the DB2 catalog.

STOGROUP *stogroup-name*
This specifies the storage group to be deleted.

stogroup-name is the name of a storage group already defined in the DB2 catalog. Here, the storage group name should be used with care; that is, it must not be used by any table space or index space.

SYNONYM *synonym-name*
This specifies a synonym to be deleted.

synonym-name is the name of a synonym that you created.

TABLESPACE *database-name.tablespace-name*
This specifies the table space to be deleted.

database-name is the name of a database already created. If you choose not to specify the database explicitly, then the default is DSNDB04.

tablespace-name is the name of a table space already created.

VIEW *view-name*
This specifies the view to be deleted.

view-name is the name of a view already defined.

- **Usage:** Interactive and application programs.

- **Example**
The following example drops table RBA.CLIENTS.

```
DROP TABLE RBA.CLIENTS;
```

◻ EXPLAIN—Get information on execution of an SQL statement

- **General format**

  EXPLAIN <PLAN or ALL>
      [SET QUERYNO = *number*]
      FOR *explanable-statement*

- **Description**

  The EXPLAIN statement gives information about the access plan of DB2. This information is valuable in fine tuning your SQL code to improve performance. This facility is also available through the BIND and REBIND commands. The difference is that the SQL EXPLAIN statement explains a single statement, whereas BIND explains every SELECT, INSERT, UPDATE, and DELETE statement of an application plan. (BIND and REBINDS commands are discussed in detail in Chapter 5).

  PLAN means to store the output in a table called *userid*.PLAN_TABLE, where *userid* is your DB2 authorization ID.

  ALL has the same effect as PLAN.

  SET QUERYNO = *number*
  This clause is useful in that it associates *number* with a SQL statement. This number will appear in the PLAN_TABLE in the QUERYNO column. The default is 1.

  FOR *explanable-statement*
  This clause specifies the SQL statement for which you want an explanation.

  explanable-statement can be any SELECT, INSERT, UPDATE, or DELETE statement.

- **Usage**: Interactive and application programs.

- **Example**

  The following example explains a SQL SELECT statement. The QUERYNO is set to 5.

  ```
  EXPLAIN PLAN SET QUERYNO = 5 FOR
  ```

```
SELECT CLIENTS_ID, CLIENTS_CITY
  FROM CLIENTS
  WHERE CLIENTS_ID > 50000
```

◘ FETCH—Get a row using the cursor

● General format
```
FETCH cursor-name INTO host-variable,...
```

● Description
The FETCH statement positions the cursor on the next row of its results table and assigns the column values to variables of your program.

cursor-name is the name of the cursor, which must be DECLAREd and OPENed before use.

INTO *host-variable*
This specifies the variables of your program. The INTO clause follows the same rules as the INTO clause of the SELECT statement. You can have one or more variables. The first value of the row is placed in the first variable, the second value of the row in the second variable, and so on.

host-variable is the name of a structure or variable.

● Usage: Interactive and application programs.

● Example
The following example fetches the cursor into variable DCLTRANSACTION.

```
EXEC SQL
  FETCH CURSOR_TXN
    INTO :DCLTRANSACTION
END-EXEC
```

◘ GRANT—Grant database privileges

● General format
```
GRANT database-privilege,...
  ON DATABASE database-name,...
  TO <PUBLIC or auth-id,...>
  [WITH GRANT OPTION]
```

- **Description**

  This GRANT statement gives one or more users privileges to use a resource at the database level of DB2. With this statement you can specify one or more privileges or databases.

  database-privilege is one of the following keywords:

Keyword	Privilege
DBADM	Administer a database
DBCTRL	Control a database
DBMAINT	Maintain a database
CREATETAB	Create table
CREATETS	Create a table space
DISPLAYDB	Issue the -DISPLAY DATABASE command
DROP	Drop a database
IMAGCOPY	Run the COPY and MERGECOPY utilities
LOAD	Run the LOAD utility
RECOVERDB	Run the RECOVER utility
REORG	Run the REORG utility
REPAIR	Run the REPAIR utility
STARTDB	Issue the -START DATABASE command
STATS	Run the RUNSTART and CHECK utilities
STOPDB	Issue the -STOP DATABASE command

ON DATABASE *database-name,...*
This specifies one or more databases for which privileges are to be given with the GRANT statement.

database-name is the name of a database already described in the DB2 catalog.

TO <PUBLIC or *auth-id,...*>
This specifies who gets the priviledge: individual users or all users.

PUBLIC means all users.

auth-id is an authorization ID. One or more IDs can be entered with the TO clause.

WITH GRANT OPTION
This clause allows users with the authorization IDs named in the
prior clause to grant the same privileges to others.

- **Usage:** Interactive and application programs.

- **Example**
The following example grants the REPAIR privilege on database
RBA001 to users LAILA and SANJIV. It also allows LAILA and
SANJIV to grant the privilege to others.

```
GRANT REPAIR
    ON DATABASE RBA001
    TO LAILA, SANJIV
    WITH GRANT OPTION;
```

◻ GRANT—Grant plan privileges

- **General format**
```
GRANT plan-privilege,...
    ON PLAN plan-name,...
    TO <PUBLIC or auth-id,...>
    [WITH GRANT OPTION]
```

- **Description**
This GRANT statement gives one or more users privileges to use
a resource at the application plan level of DB2. With this
statement you can specify one or more privileges or plans.

plan-privilege is one of the following keywords:

Keyword	Privilege
BIND	Issue the BIND, REBIND, and FREE commands against the plans named in this statement
EXECUTE	Run programs belonging to the plan named in this statement

ON PLAN *plan-name,...*
This specifies one or more application plans for which privileges
are to be given with the GRANT statement.

plan-name is the name of an application plan.

TO <PUBLIC or *auth-id,...*>
This specifies who gets the privilege: individual users or all users.

PUBLIC means all users.

auth-id is an authorization ID. One or more IDs can be entered with the TO clause.

WITH GRANT OPTION
This clause allows users with the authorization IDs named in the prior clause to grant the same privileges to others.

- **Usage**: Interactive and application programs.

- **Example**
  The following example grants the BIND privilege to users OAKS and THOMASLO on application plan BIND01.

```
GRANT BIND
   ON BIND01
   TO OAKS, THOMASLO;
```

◘ GRANT—Grant system privileges

- **General format**
```
GRANT system-privilege,...
   TO <PUBLIC or auth-id,...>
   [WITH GRANT OPTION]
```

- **Description**
  This GRANT statement gives one or more users privileges to use a resource at the system level of DB2. With this statement you can specify one or more privileges.

  system-privilege is one of the following keywords:

Keyword	Privilege
SYSADM	Perform system administration
SYSOPR	Perform system operation
BINDADD	Create application plans

BSDS	Issue the -RECOVER BSDB command
CREATEDBA	Create databases and have DBADM privileges
CREATEDBC	Create storage groups
DISPLAY	Issue the -DISPLAY THREAD and -DISPLAY DATABASE commands.
RECOVER	Issue the -RECOVER INDOUBT command
STOPALL	Issue the -STOP DB2 command
STOSPACE	Use the STOSPACE utility
TRACE	Issue the -START TRACE and -STOP TRACE commands

TO <PUBLIC or *auth-id,...*>
This specifies who gets the privilege: individual users or all users.

PUBLIC means all users.

auth-id is an authorization ID. One or more IDs can be entered with the TO clause.

WITH GRANT OPTION
This clause allows users with the authorization IDs named in the prior clause to grant the same privileges to others.

- **Usage**: Interactive and application programs.

- **Example**
The following example grants the DISPLAY privilege to users Z1335MG and Z0880MG.

```
GRANT DISPLAY
   TO Z1335MG, Z0880MG;
```

◘ GRANT—Grant table privileges

- **General format**
```
GRANT < ALL or
      ALL PRIVILEGES or
      table-privilege,...>
   ON [TABLE] <table-name,... or view-name,... >
   TO <PUBLIC or auth-id,...>
   [WITH GRANT OPTION]
```

• **Description**

This GRANT statement gives one or more users privileges to use a resource at the table level of DB2. With this statement you can specify one or more privileges and tables or views.

ALL or ALL PRIVILEGES means to grant all privileges on tables or views mentioned with the ON clause.

table-privilege is one of the following keywords:

Keyword	Privilege
ALTER	Issue the ALTER statement
DELETE	Issue the DELETE statement
INDEX	Issue the INDEX statement
INSERT	Issue the INSERT statement
SELECT	Issue the SELECT statement
UPDATE	Issue the UPDATE statement

ON TABLE <*table-name,...* or *view-name,...* >
This specifies one or more tables or one or more views.

table-name is the name of a table.

view-name is the name of a view.

TO <PUBLIC or *auth-id,...*>
This specifies who gets the privilege: individual users or all users.

PUBLIC means all users.

auth-id is an authorization ID. One or more IDs can be entered with the TO clause.

WITH GRANT OPTION
This clause allows users with the authorization IDs named in the prior clause to grant the same privileges to others.

• **Usage**: Interactive and application programs.

● **Example**

The following example grants all table privileges to users Z1335MG and Z0880MG.

```
GRANT ALL PRIVILGES
   ON TABLE RBA.CLIENTS
   TO Z1335MG, Z0880MG;
```

■ **GRANT—Grant USE privileges**

● **General format**

```
GRANT USE OF < BUFFERPOOL <buffer-pool,... > or
          STOGROUP  <storage-group-name,...>  or
            TABLESPACE[database-name.]tablespace,...>
    TO <PUBLIC or auth-id,...>
    [WITH GRANT OPTION]
```

● **Description**

This GRANT statement gives one or more users privileges to use resources such as buffer pools, storage groups, or table spaces.

BUFFERPOOL *buffer-pool,...*
This specifies one or more buffer pools.

buffer-pool is one of the four buffer pools: BP0, BP1, BP2, and BP32K.

STOGROUP *storage-group-name,...*
This specifies one or more storage groups.

storage-group-name is the name of the storage group for which USE privileges are granted.

TABLESPACE *database-name.tablespace,...*
This specifies one or more table spaces for which USE privileges are granted.

database-name is the name of the database where the table space is defined. The default is DSNDB04.

tablespace-name is the name of the table space for which USE privileges are granted.

TO <PUBLIC or *auth-id,...*>
This specifies who gets the privilege: individual users or all users.

PUBLIC means all users.

auth-id is an authorization ID. One or more IDs can be entered with the TO clause.

WITH GRANT OPTION
This clause allows users with the authorization IDs named in the prior clause to grant the same privileges to others.

- **Usage**: Interactive and application programs.

- **Example**
The following example grants all USE privileges to users Z1335MG and Z0880MG.

```
GRANT USE OF BUFFERPOOL BP1,BP2
   TO Z1335MG, Z0880MG;
```

■ **INCLUDE—Insert code or declarations into a source program**

- **General format**
```
INCLUDE < SQLCA or
          SQLDA or
          member-name>
```

- **Description**
The INCLUDE statement causes the precompiler to get a named member and merge it into a source program during the precompile time.

SQLCA
This is required to access DB2 from a program. It a set of fields that DB2 updates after each SQL statement is executed. For example, in COBOL the INCLUDE SQLCA statement specifies:

```
01  SQLCA.
    05 SQLCAID         PIC X(8).
    05 SQLCABC         PIC S9(9) COMP-4.
    05 SQLCODE         PIC S9(9) COMP-4.
    05 SQLERRM.
```

```
     49 SQLERRML            PIC S9(4) COMP-4.
     49 SQLERRMC            PIC X(70).
  05 SQLERRP                PIC X(8).
  05 SQLERRD     OCCURS 6 TIMES PIC S9(9) COMP-4.
  05 SQLWARN.
     10 SQLWARN0            PIC X(1).
     10 SQLWARN1            PIC X(1).
     10 SQLWARN2            PIC X(1).
     10 SQLWARN3            PIC X(1).
     10 SQLWARN4            PIC X(1).
     10 SQLWARN5            PIC X(1).
     10 SQLWARN6            PIC X(1).
     10 SQLWARN7            PIC X(1).
  05 SQLEXT                 PIC X(8).
```

SQLDA
This specifies a data declaration to be included. It must not be specified in a FORTRAN or COBOL program.

member-name is the name of a PDS member whose content is to be included where the INCLUDE statement is found.

- **Usage**: Application programs.

- **Example**
The following example makes the precompiler fetch data declaration SQLCA and insert it in your program.

```
EXEC SQL
   INCLUDE SQLCA
END-EXEC
```

▣ INSERT—Insert a row into a table or view

- **General format**
```
INSERT INTO <table-name or view-name>
   [column-name,...]
   VALUES (constant          or
           host-variable  or
        NULL            or
           USER,...)
   subselect statement
```

- **Description**
The INSERT statement inserts a row into a view or table. If the row is inserted into a view, then it is also added to the table which is the basis for the view.

table-name is the name of a table already described in the DB2 catalog.

view-name is the name of a view already described in the DB2 catalog.

column-name is the name of a row of a table or view. You can have one or more columns, in any order. The column list is optional; if it is omitted, the columns defined in the named view or table are used.

VALUES (*constant*   or
　　　host-variable   or
　　　NULL   or
　　　USER,...)
This specifies the values for the row you are inserting. Each value must correspond with the column name. The values can be keywords, constants, variables, NULL, or USER.

constant is a specific value; it can be one of the following: integer, floating point, decimal, character string, and graphic string.

host-variable is the name of a structure or variable that follows the rules of the host program.

NULL is a keyword that represents a null value.

USER is a keyword that specifies the authorization ID to DB2.

subselect statement
This is a SELECT statement, and the result of this statement is an insert to the table or view.

● **Usage**: Interactive and application programs.

● **Example**
The following example inserts a row into a table RBA.CLIENTS. The columns are NAME, CITY, POSTAL_C, and PROV, and the values are RBC, NEWMARKET, L3X1F0, and ONTARIO.

```
INSERT INTO RBA.CLIENTS
  (NAME, CITY, POSTAL_C, PROV)
  VALUES ('RBC','NEWMARKET','L3X1F0','ONTARIO');
```

◘ **LABEL—Add or replace labels for tables, views, and columns**

● **General format**
```
LABEL ON
   <TABLE <table-name or view-name> IS string    or
      COLUMN <table-name.column-name> IS string    or
      COLUMN <view-name.column-name>  IS string
   <table-name or view-name> (column-name IS string,...)
```

● **Description**
The LABEL ON statement changes or adds labels for individual tables, views, and columns or sets of columns.

TABLE *table-name* or *view-name*
This specifies the table or view for which the label is to be changed or added. The label column of the SYSIBM.SYSTABLES catalog is affected by this clause.

table-name is the name of a table already defined in the DB2 catalog.

view-name is the name of a view already defined in the DB2 catalog.

COLUMN *table-name.column-name* or
      view-name.column-name
This specifies an individual column of a table or view.

column-name is the name of the named table or view.

IS *string*
This gives the label.

string is any SQL character string less than 30 characters in length.

● **Usage**: Interactive and application programs.

● **Example**
The following example enters a label on the NAME column of table RBA.CLIENTS.

```
LABEL ON COLUMN  RBA.CLIENTS.NAME IS 'Client name';
```

◘ LOCK TABLE—Lock a table space

● General format
```
LOCK TABLE table-name
   IN <SHARE MODE or EXCLUSIVE MODE>
```

● Description
The LOCK TABLE command locks the table space, either in shared mode or in exclusive mode. The lock can be released with a BIND command and an SQL RELEASE statement.

table-name is the name of the table for which the table space is locked.

IN <SHARE MODE or EXCLUSIVE MODE>
This specifies the type of locking.

SHARE MODE means to acquire a lock on the table for the unit of work (program) where this statement is executed that will allow other programs to access the table in read-only mode.

EXCLUSIVE MODE means to acquire a lock on the table for the unit of work (program) where this statement is executed that will not allow any other program to access the table at all.

● Usage: Interactive and application programs.

● Example
The following example acquires an exclusive lock on the table RBA.CLIENTS.

```
LOCK TABLE  RBA.CLIENTS IN EXCLUSIVE MODE;
```

◘ OPEN—Open a cursor

● General format
```
OPEN cursor-name
   [USING host-variable,...]
```

● Description
The OPEN statement is used after a cursor has been declared. This statement executes the SELECT statement associated with the

DECLARE CURSOR statement; it creates the result table to which the cursor points. Subsequent to the OPEN statement, the cursor is initialized to point to a row with a FETCH statement.

cursor-name is the name of a cursor already DECLAREd.

USING *host-variable,...*
This specifies user-defined variables.

host-variable is the name of a structure or variable that follows the rules of the host program.

- **Usage**: Application programs.

- **Example**
The following example opens a cursor called CLIENTS_C.

```
EXEC SQL
   OPEN CLIENTS_C
END-EXEC
```

◻ REVOKE—Revoke database privileges

- **General format**
```
REVOKE database-privilege,...
   ON DATABASE database-name,...
   FROM <PUBLIC or auth-id,...>
   [BY <ALL or auth-id,...>]
```

- **Description**
This REVOKE statement removes from one or more users privileges to use a resource at the database level of DB2. With this statement you can specify one or more privileges or databases.

database-privilege is one of the following keywords:

Keyword	Privilege
DBADM	Administer a database
DBCTRL	Control a database
DBMAINT	Maintain a database
CREATETAB	Create a table
CREATETS	Create a table space

DISPLAYDB	Issue the -DISPLAY DATABASE command
DROP	Drop a database
IMAGCOPY	Run the COPY and MERGECOPY utilities
LOAD	Run the LOAD utility
RECOVERDB	Run the RECOVER utility
REORG	Run the REORG utility
REPAIR	Run the REPAIR utility
STARTDB	Issue the -START DATABASE command
STATS	Run the RUNSTART and CHECK utilities
STOPDB	Issue the -STOP DATABASE command

ON DATABASE *database-name,...*
This specifies one or more databases for which privileges are to be revoked.

database-name is the name of a database already described in the DB2 catalog.

FROM <PUBLIC or *auth-id,...*>
This specifies from whom the privileges are revoked; individual users or all users.

PUBLIC means all users.

auth-id is an authorization ID. One or more IDs can be entered with the TO clause.

BY <ALL or *auth-id,...*>
This specifies grantors who explicitly grant privileges to others.

ALL means to revoke the privileges of all users who were explicitly granted privileges.

auth-id is the authorization ID of a grantor.

• **Usage**: Interactive and application programs.

• **Example**
The following example revokes the REPAIR privilege of users LAILA and SANJIV on database RBA001.

REVOKE REPAIR

```
ON DATABASE RBA001
FROM LAILA, SANJIV;
```

◘ REVOKE—Revoke plan privileges

● General format
```
REVOKE plan-privilege,...
   ON PLAN plan-name,...
   FROM <PUBLIC or auth-id,...>
   [BY <ALL or auth-id,...>]
```

● Description
This REVOKE statement revokes from one or more users privileges to use resource at the application plan level of DB2. With this statement you can specify one or more privileges or plans.

plan-privilege is one of the following keywords:

Keyword	Privilege
BIND	Issue the BIND, REBIND, and FREE commands against the plans named in this statement
EXECUTE	Run programs belonging to the plan named in this statement

ON PLAN *plan-name,...*
This specifies one or more application plans for which privileges are revoked.

plan-name is the name of an application plan.

FROM <PUBLIC or *auth-id,...*>
This specifies from whom the privileges are revoked; individual users or all users.

PUBLIC means all users.

auth-id is an authorization ID. One or more IDs can be entered with the TO clause.

BY <ALL or *auth-id,...*>
This specifies the grantors who explicitly granted privileges to others.

ALL means to revoke the privileges of all users who were explicitly granted privileges.

auth-id is the authorization ID of a grantor.

- **Usage**: Interactive and application programs.

- **Example**
The following example revokes the BIND privilege of users OAKS and THOMASLO on application plan BIND01.

```
REVOKE BIND
    ON BIND01
    FROM OAKS, THOMASLO;
```

◻ REVOKE—Revoke system privileges

- **General format**
```
REVOKE system-privilege,...
   FROM <PUBLIC or auth-id,...>
   [BY <ALL or auth-id,...>]
```

- **Description**
This REVOKE statement revokes from one or more users privileges to use a resource at the system level of DB2. With this statement you can specify one or more privileges.

system-privilege is one of the following keywords:

Keyword	Privilege
SYSADM	Perform system administration
SYSOPR	Perform system operation
BINDADD	Create application plans
BSDS	Issue the -RECOVER BSDB command
CREATEDBA	Create databases and have DBADM privileges
CREATEDBC	Create storage groups
DISPLAY	Issue the -DISPLAY THREAD and -DISPLAY DATABASE commands

RECOVER	Issue the -RECOVER INDOUBT command
STOPALL	Issue the -STOP DB2 command
STOSPACE	Use the STOSPACE utility
TRACE	Issue the -START TRACE and -STOP TRACE commands

FROM <PUBLIC or *auth-id,...*>
This specifies from whom the privileges are revoked; individual users or all users.

PUBLIC means all users.

auth-id is an authorization ID. One or more IDs can be entered with the TO clause.

BY <ALL or *auth-id,...*>
This specifies grantors who explicitly granted privileges to others.

ALL means to revoke the privileges of all users who were explicitly granted privileges.

auth-id is the authorization ID of a grantor.

- **Usage**: Interactive and application programs.

- **Example**
The following example revokes the DISPLAY privilege of users Z1335MG, Z0880MG, and CTB11905.

```
REVOKE DISPLAY
   FROM Z1335MG, Z0880MG, CTB11905;
```

◻ REVOKE—Revoke table privileges

- **General format**
```
REVOKE < ALL or  ALL PRIVILEGES or
      table-privilege,...>
   ON [TABLE] <table-name,... or
                     view-name,... >
   FROM <PUBLIC or auth-id,...>
   [BY <ALL or auth-id,...>]
```

● **Description**
This REVOKE statement revokes from one or more users privileges to use a resource at the table level of DB2. With this statement you can specify one or more privileges and tables or views.

ALL or ALL PRIVILEGES means grant all privileges on tables or views mentioned with the ON clause.

table-privilege is one of the following keywords:

Keyword	Privilege
ALTER	Issue the ALTER statement
DELETE	Issue the DELETE statement
INDEX	Issue the INDEX statement
INSERT	Issue the INSERT statement
SELECT	Issue the SELECT statement
UPDATE	Issue the UPDATE statement

ON TABLE *<table-name,... or*
              view-name,... >
This specifies one or more tables or one or more views.

table-name is the name of a table.

view-name is the name of a view.

FROM <PUBLIC or *auth-id,...*>
This specifies from whom the privileges are revoked; individual users or all users.

PUBLIC means all users.

auth-id is an authorization ID. One or more IDs can be entered with the TO clause.

BY <ALL or *auth-id,...*>
This specifies grantors who explicitly granted privileges to others.

ALL means to revoke the privileges of all users who were explicitly granted privileges.

auth-id is the authorization ID of a grantor.

- **Usage:** Interactive and application programs.

- **Example**
  The following example revokes all table privileges from users
  Z1335MG and Z0880MG.

  ```
  REVOKE ALL PRIVILEGES
     ON TABLE RBA.CLIENTS
     FROM Z1335MG, Z0880MG;
  ```

◘ REVOKE—Revoke user privileges

- **General format**
  ```
  REVOKE USE OF <BUFFERPOOL buffer-pool,...  or
       STOGROUP storage-group-name,...   or
           TABLESPACE [database-name.]tablespace,...>
     FROM <PUBLIC or auth-id,...>
     [BY <ALL or auth-id,...>]
  ```

- **Description**
  This REVOKE statement revokes from one or more users
  privileges to use resources such as buffer pools, storage groups, or
  table spaces.

  BUFFERPOOL *buffer-pool,...*
  This specifies one or more buffer pools.

  buffer-pool is one of the four buffer pools: BP0, BP1, BP2, and
  BP32K.

  STOGROUP *storage-group-name,...*
  This specifies one or more storage groups.

  storage-group-name is the name of the storage group for which
  USE privileges are revoked.

  TABLESPACE *database-name.tablespace,...*
  This specifies one or more table spaces for which USE privileges
  are revoked.

  database-name is the name of the the database where the table space is defined. The default is DSNDB04.

tablespace-name is the name of the table space for which USE privileges are revoked.

FROM <PUBLIC or *auth-id,...*>
This specifies from whom the privileges are revoked: individual users or all users.

PUBLIC means all users.
auth-id is an authorization ID. One or more IDs can be entered with the TO clause.

BY <ALL or *auth-id,...*>
This specifies grantors who explicitly granted privileges to others.

ALL means to revoke the privileges of all users who were explicitly granted privilege.

auth-id is the authorization ID of a grantor.

- **Usage**: Interactive and application programs.

- **Example**
The following example revokes all USE privileges of users Z1335MG and Z0880MG.

```
REVOKE USE OF BUFFERPOOL BP1,BP2
   FROM Z1335MG, Z0880MG;
```

◘ ROLLBACK—Back out database changes

- **General format**
```
ROLLBACK
```

- **Description**
The ROLLBACK statement backs out all changes to the database up to the point of last execution of a COMMIT statement. If the COMMIT statement was not issued in a program and ROLLBACK is executed, then all changes will be backed out. DB2 issues a ROLLBACK if a program abends or if a timeout or lock occurs.

- **Usage**: Interactive and application programs.

- **Example**

The following is an example of how to issue the ROLLBACK statement.

```
EXEC SQL
   ROLLBACK
END-EXEC.
```

◘ SELECT—Retrieve data

- **General format**

```
subselect [ORDER BY
          <column-name or integer> <ASC or DESC>,...
                       [FOR FETCH ONLY]      or
              FOR UPDATE OF column-name,... or
          FOR FETCH ONLY]

     or

fullselect [ORDER BY
          <column-name or integer>  <ASC or DESC>,...
                       [FOR FETCH ONLY]   or
              FOR UPDATE OF column-name,... or
          FOR FETCH ONLY]
```

subselect is

```
SELECT [ALL or DISTINCT] <* or column-name,...>
   FROM <table-name or view-name,...>
   [WHERE <search-condition> ]
   [GROUP BY column-name,...]
   [HAVING <search-condition> ]
```

fullselect is

```
<subselect or fullselect> <UNION or UNION ALL>
```

Embedded SELECT is

```
SELECT [ALL or DISTINCT]<* or column-name,...>
   INTO host-variable,...
   FROM <table-name or view-name,...>
   [WHERE search-condition]
```

- **Description**

The SELECT statement is used to retrieve rows of data from a database. There are two types of SELECT statement; they are interactive and embedded, and both are complete statements.

fullselect is part of an interactive SELECT statement or a DECLARE CURSOR statement.

subselect is part of *fullselect*, a CREATE VIEW statement, or an INSERT statement.

ORDER BY <*column-name* or *integer*>
      <ASC or DESC>,...
This clause specifies the sequence in which the rows are presented. If this clause is not used, the rows are returned in the order in which they are stored physically. With this clause you can specify a column name or column number and the order of presentation. This specification can be repeated many times.

column-name is the name of the column according to which the result table is ordered.

integer is the number which identifies the position of a column. This number should be greater than zero and not greater than the number of columns in the result table.

ASC is the keyword for ordering the column in an ascending sequence. ASC is the default.

DESC is the keyword for ordering the column in a descending sequence.

FOR UPDATE OF
This clause is effective only in application programs. and used with the DECLARE CURSOR statement.

ALL
This keyword is used in the SELECT clause to return all rows, including duplicate ones.

DISTINCT
This keyword is used in the SELECT clause to return only unique rows and discard any duplicate ones.

FROM <*table-name* or *view-name,...*>
This clause specifies one or more tables or views from which the data are extracted. In processing a SELECT statement, a result table is created, although the actual data are stored in the objects called tables. This result table exists temporarily and is only a conceptual file. It contains all the possible rows.

table-name is the name of a table already defined in the catalog.

view-name is the name of a view already defined in the catalog.

WHERE *search-condition*
This clause determines the number of rows the result table will have.

search-condition is made up of columns, operators, and constants, composed in a logical manner. Each row that satisfies the search condition is found in the result table. The following operators, conditions, and keywords may be used as part of the search condition.

Type	Operator	Meaning
Comparison	=	Equal
	¬ = or < >	Not equal
	>	Greater than
	¬ > or < =	Not greater than
	¬ < or > =	Not less than
Arithmetic	+	Addition
	-	Subtraction
	*	Multiplication
	/	Division
Boolean	AND	Logical AND
	OR	Logical OR
Keyword	BETWEEN	A value is equal to or between two other values
	IN	Combine one or more OR operators

NOT or ⌐	Negative search condition
LIKE	Compare similar values

GROUP BY *column-name,...*
This clause causes the rows in the intermediate result set to be grouped according to the values of one or more columns named in the GROUP BY clause. It is commonly used when there are one or more column functions in the SELECT clause.

column-name is the name of a column of the table or view.

HAVING *search-condition*
This specifies a search condition which each group of rows must satisfy in order to be passed to the column function.

search-condition is made up of columns, operators, and constants, composed in a logical manner. Each row that satisfies the search condition is found in the result table. The operators AND, OR, BETWEEN, IN, and LIKE may be used as part of the search condition.

UNION
This clause merges two results of two or more SELECT statements into one result table. With this clause, each SELECT statement is processed individually; they are then combined into one result table. All duplicate rows are discarded except when UNION ALL is used.

INTO *host-variable,...*
This clause specifies one or more host variables into which DB2 is to place the data retrieved by an embedded SELECT statement. SELECT...INTO works only if no rows or one row is retrieved. If SELECT...INTO results in more than one row, it will fail with a negative code (-811), and it will retrieve no data.

host-variable is the name of a structure or variable declared in your program. The variable is referenced by DB2 when SQL statements are executed. It is a good programming practice to provide variables that are compatible in data type and scale with the columns they receive. The following is a list of DB2 data types that correspond to COBOL data types.

DB2   COBOL

```
FIELD_A   CHAR(n)        01 FIELD-A  PIC X(n)
FIELD_A   VARCHAR(n)     01 FIELD-A
                            10 FIELD-A-LEN PIC S9(4) COMP
                            10 FIELD-A-TEXT  PIC X(n)
FIELD_A   SMALLINT       01 FIELD-A  PIC S9(4) COMP
FIELD_A   INTEGER        01 FIELD-A  PIC S9(9) COMP
FIELD_A   DECIMAL(p,q)   01 FIELD-A PIC S9(a)V9(q) COMP-3
FIELD_A   DATE           01 FIELD-A  PIC X(10)
FIELD_A   TIME           01 FIELD-A  PIC X(8)
FIELD_A   TIMESTAMP        01 FIELD-A  PIC X(26)
```

Column functions

The following is a list of built-in column functions supplied by SQL. They operate on the entire column to produce one value in the result table.

Function	Description	Restrictions
SUM	Sum of values in column	Numeric data only
AVG	Average of values in column	Numeric data only
MIN	Minimum value within column	
COUNT	Count of the number of rows	

Scalar functions

The following is a list of built-in scalar functions supplied by SQL.

Function	Description
SUBSTR	Extract a subset of a string of characters
LENGTH	Find the length of a value of any data type
DECIMAL	Convert any number to a decimal representation
INTEGER	Convert any number to an integer
DIGITS	Convert numeric values to characters
HEX	Return result in hexadecimal format
FLOAT	
VARGRAPHIC	

Concatenation

The concatenation operator (| |) combines character values into one string.

● **Usage**: Interactive and application programs.

● **Example**
The following example returns all unique rows with values for the CL_NAME and CL_LANG columns.

```
SELECT DISTINCT CL_NAME, CL_LANG
   FROM RBA.CLIENTS
```

The following example returns rows with values for the CL_NAME and CL_LANG columns according to a search condition. The condition is that the value of the CL_CITY column is 'TORONTO' and the first character of the CL_LANG column is 'E'.

```
SELECT CL_NAME, CL_LANG
   FROM RBA.CLIENTS
   WHERE CL_CITY='TORONTO' AND SUBSTR(CL_LANG,1,1)='E';
```

In the following example, two SELECT statements are executed using the UNION clause.

```
SELECT CL_NAME, 'CLIENT NAME'
   FROM RBA.CLIENTS
   WHERE CL_CITY='TORONTO' AND SUBSTR(CL_LANG,1,1)='E'
UNION
SELECT CL_NAME, 'CLIENT LANGUAGE'
   FROM RBA.CLIENTS
   WHERE CL_CITY='TORONTO' AND SUBSTR(CL_LANG,1,1)='E';
```

In the following example, all the rows of the CLIENTS table are first grouped together according to the values in CL_BRANCH. Then the highest CL_RATING of each group is found.

```
SELECT MAX(CL_RATING)
   FROM RBA.CLIENTS
   GROUP BY CL_BRANCH;
```

◻ UPDATE—Update columns of a table or view

● General format

```
Not using cursor:

  UPDATE  <table-name or view-name> [correlation-name]
    SET column-name = <expression or NULL,...>
    WHERE search-condition

Using cursor:

  UPDATE <table-name or view-name>
    SET column-name = <expression or NULL,...>
    WHERE CURRENT OF cursor-name
```

● Description

The UPDATE statement updates the values of one or more columns of a table or view. The update can be done in two ways: using a search condition or using the cursor.

table-name is the name of a table already defined in the DB2 catalog.

view-name is the name of a view already defined in the DB2 catalog.

SET *column-name* = <*expression* or NULL,...>
This specifies a list of columns and values.

column-name is the name of a column already defined in the table or view.

expression is any valid SQL expression.

NULL means a null value.

WHERE *search-condition*
This clause determines how many rows will be updated.

search-condition is the same as the search condition used in the WHERE clause of the SELECT statement. Depending on the condition, no rows or many rows may be updated.

WHERE CURRENT OF *cursor-name*
This clause determines how many rows will be updated using a cursor.

cursor-name is the name of a cursor, defined previous to using it in the UPDATE statement. The DECLARE CURSOR statement defines the cursor. When this statement is executed, it updates the row where the cursor is positioned. After the update, the cursor points to before the next row.

- **Usage**: Interactive and application programs.

- **Example**
  The following example updates columns of the table RBA.CLIENTS. The columns are NAME, CITY, POSTAL_C, and PROV, and the values are RBC, NEWMARKET, and L3X1F0.

  For all the rows that have column ADDRESS equals to '330 MAIN ST', the update will take place.

```
UPDATE INTO RBA.CLIENTS
  SET  NAME='RBC', CITY='NEWMARKET', POSTAL_C='L3X1F0'
    WHERE ADDRESS='330 MAIN ST';
```

◻ WHENEVER—Conditional processing

- **General format**
```
WHENEVER <NOT FOUND              or
          SQLERROR               or
        SQLWARNING>
        <CONTINUE                or
            GO TO host-label     or
        GOTO host-label>
```

- **Description**
  The WHENEVER statement causes the DB2 translator to generate the code needed to check SQLCODE and/or SQLWARN0 after each SQL statement is executed. If a certain condition is met, a specific action is taken. The condition may be an error, an exception, or a warning that exists in SQLCA. The following describes the conditions triggered after a statement is executed and the actions that can be taken.

NOT FOUND is a condition where SQLCODE is +100.

SQLERROR is a condition where SQLCODE is negative.

SQLWARNING is a condition where SQLCODE is greater than zero but not equal to 100 or where SQLWARN0 is 'W'.

CONTINUE means to ignore the exception and continue processing.

GO TO *host-label*
This means to branch to the paragraph or section named and begin processing the statements found there.

host-label is a paragraph or section.

- **Usage**: Application programs.

- **Example**
  The following example cuases control to branch to paragraph PARA-WARNING if the condition SQLWARNING occurs after any SQL statement is executed.

```
EXEC SQL
    WHENEVER SQLWARNING GO TO PARA-WARNING
END-EXEC.
```

VSAM AND IDCAMS

This chapter is a reference for programmers using VSAM and IDCAMS. IDCAMS is a utility program for managing VSAM and non-VSAM files. IDCAMS provides many access method services; some of them are:

- Create a VSAM dataset.
- Create a VSAM alternate index.
- Create a generation data group (GDG).
- List catalog information for a dataset.
- Print the content of a dataset in hex or character form.
- Do backups of VSAM and non-VSAM datasets.
- Change the attributes of a catalog or dataset.
- Delete a catalog or an entry in a catalog.
- Delete a VSAM or non-VSAM dataset.

This chapter also discusses, with practical examples, how to use some of the services of IDCAMS using JCL. It gives step-by-step procedures for estimating space for VSAM datasets.

Notational Conventions: In the general format of the IDCAMS control statements used in this chapter, there are a few symbols that are not part of the syntax, therefore they must not be included when you code your program. These symbols and their meanings are:

Symbol	Meaning
[]	The option enclosed by the brackets ([]) is not required but can be included.
<>	Only one of the alternatives enclosed by the angle brackets (<>) must be chosen.
or	The alternatives enclosed by the angle brackets (<>) are separated by "or."
____	The underlined word is the default value.
...	The vertical or horizontal ellipsis means that the preceding can be coded more than once.
Uppercase characters	All keywords of the command are written in uppercase characters; they must be coded as shown.
Lowercase characters	All strings in lowercase characters and italic are variables that can be changed to any other strings to suit your programming style. In your code they represent values that you supply to commands.

11.1 IDCAMS CONTROL STATEMENTS

This section contains the syntax of all the IDCAMS control statements.

■ **ALTER—Change attributes of datasets and catalogs**

● **General format**
```
ALTER entryname[/password]
    [ADDVOLUMES(vol1,vol2,...)]
    [ATTEMPTS(n)]
    [AUTHORIZATION(entrypoint [string])]
    [BUFFERSPACE(size)]
    [BUFND(n)]
    [BUFNI(n)]
    [CODE(code)]
    [CONTROLPW(password)]
    [DESTAGEWAIT or NODESTAGEWAIT]
    [EMPTY or NOEMPTY]
    [ERASE or NOERASE]
    [EXCEPTIONEXIT(entrypoint)]
    [FILE(ddname)]
    [FREESPACE(ci% ca%)]
    [INHIBIT or UNINHIBIT]
    [KEYS(length offset)]
    [LIMIT(limit)]
    [LOCK or NOLOCK]
    [MASTERPW(password)]
```

```
[NEWNAME(newname)]
[NULLIFY(info...)]
[OWNER[ownerid)]
[READPW(password)]
[RECORDSIZE(avg max)]
[REMOVEVOLUMES(voll,...)]
[ROLLIN]
[SCRATCH or NOSCRATCH]
[SHAREOPTIONS(region [system])]
[STAGE or BIND or CYLINDERFAULT]
[STRNO(n)]
[TO(date) or FOR(days)]
[TYPE(LINEAR)]
[UNIQUEKEY or NONUNIQUEKEY]
[UPDATE or NOUPDATE]
[UPDATEPW(password)]
[UPGRADE or NOUPGRADE]
[WRITECHECK or NOWRITECHECK]

[CATALOG(catalogname[/password])]
```

◘ BLDINDEX—Build alternate indexes for existing datasets

• General format
```
BLDINDEX <INFILE(ddname[/password]) or
          INDATASET(entryname[/password])>
        <OUTFILE(ddname[/password]) or
          [OUTDATASET(entryname[/password])]>
        [EXTERNALSORT or INTERNALSORT]

        [CATALOG(catalogname[/password])]
```

◘ CHKLIST—List tape datasets opened during a checkpoint

• General format
```
CHKLIST INFILE(ddname)
        [CHECKID(checkid...)]
        [OUTFILE(ddname)]
```

◘ CNVTCAT—Convert a catalog

• General format
```
CNVTCAT <INFILE(ddname[/password]) or
         INDATASET(entryname[/password])>
        <OUTFILE(ddname[/password]) or
         OUTDATASET(entryname[/password]) or
         CATALOG(catalogname[/password])>
        [CVOLEQUATES (catalogname1 (voll vol2 ...))
               (catalogname2 (voll vol2 ...))]
        [FILE(ddname)]
        [LIST or NOLIST]
        [MASTERCATALOG(catalogname[/password])]
```

◘ DEFINE ALIAS—Define an alternate name for a non-VSAM dataset or catalog

- **General format**

```
DEFINE ALIAS (
    NAME(aliasname) RELATE(entryname))

    [CATALOG(catalogname[/password])]
```

◘ DEFINE ALTERNATEINDEX—Define an alternate index

- **General format**

```
DEFINE ALTERNATEINDEX (
    NAME(aliasname) RELATE(entryname)
    [CYLINDERS(primary [secondary])  or
        RECORDS(primary [secondary]) or
        TRACKS(primary [secondary])]
    VOLUMES(vol1 [vol2 vol3...])
    [ATTEMPS(n or 2)]
    [AUTHORIZATION(entrypoint string)]
    [BUFFERSPACE(size)]
    [CODE(code)]
    [CONTROLINTERVALSIZE(size)]
    [CONTROLPW(password)]
    [DESTAGEWAIT or NODESTAGEWAIT]
    [ERASE or NOERASE]
    [EXCEPTIONEXIT(entrypoint)]
    [FILE(ddname)]
    [FREESPACE(ci% ca%)]
    [IMBED or NOIMBED]
    [KEYRANGES((lowkey highkey) (lowkey highkey) ...)]
    [KEYS(length offset)]
    [MASTERPW(password)]
    [MODEL(entryname[/password]catalogname[/password])]
    [ORDERED or UNORDERED]
    [OWNER(ownerid)]
    [READPW(password)]
    [RECATALOG or NORECATALOG]
    [RECORDSIZE(avg max)]
    [REPLICATE or NOREPLICATE]
    [REUSE or NOREUSE]
    [SHAREOPTIONS(region system)]
    [SPEED or RECOVERY]
    [STAGE or BIND or CYLINDERFAULT]
    [TO(date) or FOR(days)]
    [UNIQUEKEY or NONUNIQUEKEY]
    [UPDATE or NOUPDATE]
    [UPDATEPW(password)]
    [UPGRADE or NOUPGRADE]
    [WRITECHECK or NOWRITECHECK] )
```

```
[ DATA (
[ATTEMPTS(n)]
[AUTHORIZATION(entrypoint string)]
[BUFFERSPACE(size)]
[CODE(code)]
[CONTROLINTERVALSIZE(size)]
[CONTROLPW(password)]
[CYLINDERS(primary [secondary]) or
   RECORDS(primary [secondary]) or
   TRACKS(primary [secondary])]
[DESTAGEWAIT or NODESTAGEWAIT]
[ERASE or NOERASE]
[EXCEPTIONEXIT(entrypoint)]
[FILE(ddname)]
[FREESPACE(ci% ca%)]
[KEYRANGES((lowkey highkey) (lowkey highkey) ...)]
[KEYS(length offset)]
[MASTERPW(password)]
[MODEL(entryname[/password]catalogname[/password])]
[NAME(entryname)]
[ORDERED or UNORDERED]
[OWNER(ownerid)]
[READPW(password)]
[RECORDSIZE(avg max)]
[REUSE or NOREUSE]
[SHAREOPTIONS(region system)]
[SPEED or RECOVERY]
[STAGE or BIND or CYLINDERFAULT]
[UNIQUEKEY or NONUNIQUEKEY]
[UPDATEPW(password)]
[VOLUMES(vol1 [vol2 ...])]
[WRITECHECK or NOWRITECHECK]
) ]

[ INDEX (
[ATTEMPTS(n)]
[AUTHORIZATION(entrypoint string)]
[CODE(code)]
[CONTROLINTERVALSIZE(size)]
[CONTROLPW(password)]
[CYLINDERS(primary [secondary]) or
   RECORDS(primary [secondary]) or
   TRACKS(primary [secondary])]
[DESTAGEWAIT or NODESTAGEWAIT]
[EXCEPTIONEXIT(entrypoint)]
[FILE(ddname)]
[IMBED or NOIMBED]
[MASTERPW(password)]
[MODEL(entryname[/password]catalogname[/password])]
[NAME(entryname)]
[ORDERED or UNORDERED]
[OWNER(ownerid)]
[READPW(password)]
[REPLICATE or NOREPLICATE]
[REUSE or NOREUSE]
[SHAREOPTIONS(region system)]
```

```
    [STAGE or BIND or CYLINDERFAULT]

    [UPDATEPW(password)]
    [VOLUMES(vol1 [vol2...])]
    [WRITECHECK or NOWRITECHECK ]
    ) ]

  [CATALOG(catalogname[/password])]
```

◘ DEFINE CLUSTER—Define a cluster for KSDS, ESDS, or RRDS

● General format
```
DEFINE CLUSTER (
    NAME (aliasname)
    [CYLINDERS(primary [secondary]) or
        RECORDS(primary [secondary]) or
        TRACKS(primary [secondary])]
    VOLUMES(vol1 [vol2 vol3])
    [ATTEMPTS(n or 2)]
    [AUTHORIZATION(entrypoint string)]
    [BUFFERSPACE(size)]
    [CODE(code)]
    [CONTROLINTERVALSIZE(size)]
    [CONTROLPW(password)]
    [DESTAGEWAIT or NODESTAGEWAIT]
    [ERASE or NOERASE]
    [EXCEPTIONEXIT(entrypoint)]
    [FILE(ddname)]
    [FREESPACE(ci% ca%)]
    [IMBED or NOIMBED]
    [INDEXED or LINEAR or NONINDEXED or NUMBERED]
    [KEYRANGES((lowkey highkey) (lowkey highkey)...)]
    [KEYS(length offset)]
    [MASTERPW(password)]
    [MODEL(entryname[/password]catalogname[/password])]
    [ORDERED or UNORDERED]
    [OWNER(ownerid)]
    [READPW(password)]
    [RECATALOG or NORECATALOG]
    [RECORDSIZE(avg max)]
    [REPLICATE or NOREPLICATE]
    [REUSE or NOREUSE]
    [SHAREOPTIONS(region system)]
    [SPANNED or NONSPANNED]
    [SPEED or RECOVERY]
    [STAGE or BIND or CYLINDERFAULT]
    [TO(date) or FOR(days)]
    [UPDATE or NOUPDATE]
    [UPDATEPW(password)]
    [WRITECHECK or NOWRITECHECK] )

    [ DATA (
    [ATTEMPTS(n)]
    [AUTHORIZATION(entrypoint string)]
```

```
                        [BUFFERSPACE(size)]
                        [CODE(code)]
                        [CONTROLINTERVALSIZE(size)]
                        [CONTROLPW(password)]
                        [CYLINDERS(primary [secondary]) or
                           RECORDS(primary [secondary]) or
                           TRACKS(primary [secondary])]
                        [DESTAGEWAIT or NODESTAGEWAIT]
                        [ERASE or NOERASE]
                        [EXCEPTIONEXIT(entrypoint)]
                        [FILE(ddname)]
                        [FREESPACE(ci% ca%)]
                        [KEYRANGES((lowkey highkey) (lowkey highkey) ...)]
                        [KEYS(length offset)]
                        [MASTERPW(password)]
                        [MODEL(entryname[/password]catalogname[/password])]
                        [NAME(entryname)]
                        [ORDERED or UNORDERED]
                        [OWNER(ownerid)]
                        [READPW(password)]
                        [RECORDSIZE(avg max)]
                        [REUSE or NOREUSE]
                        [SHAREOPTIONS(region system)]
                        [SPEED or RECOVERY]
                        [STAGE or BIND or CYLINDERFAULT]
                        [UNIQUEKEY or NONUNIQUEKEY]
                        [UPDATE or NOUPDATE]
                        [UPDATEPW(password)]
                        [VOLUMES(vol1 [vol2 ...])]
                        [WRITECHECK or NOWRITECHECK]
                        ) ]

                         [ INDEX (
                        [ATTEMPTS(n)]
                        [AUTHORIZATION(entrypoint string)]
                        [CODE(code)]
                        [CONTROLINTERVALSIZE(size)]
                        [CONTROLPW(password)]
                        [CYLINDERS(primary [secondary]) or
                           RECORDS(primary [secondary]) or
                           TRACKS(primary [secondary])]
                        [DESTAGEWAIT or NODESTAGEWAIT]
                        [EXCEPTIONEXIT(entrypoint)]
                        [FILE(ddname)]
                        [IMBED or NOIMBED]
                        [MASTERPW(password)]
                        [MODEL(entryname[/password]catalogname[/password])]
                        [NAME(entryname)]
                        [ORDERED or UNORDERED]
                        [OWNER(ownerid)]
                        [READPW(password)]
                        [REPLICATE or NOREPLICATE]
                        [REUSE or NOREUSE]
                        [SHAREOPTIONS(region system)]
                        [STAGE or BIND or CYLINDERFAULT]
                        [UPDATEPW(password)]
                        [VOLUMES(vol1 [vol2...])]
                        [WRITECHECK or NOWRITECHECK ]
                        ) ]
```

```
[CATALOG(catalogname[/password])]
```

◘ DEFINE GENERATIONDATAGROUP—Create a catalog entry for a generation data group

● General format
```
DEFINE GENERATIONDATAGROUP(
   NAME(entryname)
   LIMIT(n)
   [EMPTY or NOEMPTY]
   [OWNER(ownerid)]
   [SCRATCH or NOSCRATCH]
   [TO(date) or FOR(days)] )

   [CATALOG(catalogname[/password])]
```

◘ DEFINE NONVSAM—Define a catalog entry for a non-VSAM dataset

● General format
```
DEFINE NONVSAM(
   NAME(entryname)
   DEVICETYPES(devtype [devtype...])
   VOLUMES(vol1 [vol2...])
   [FILESEQUENCENUMBERS(n1 [n2...])]
   [OWNER(ownerid)]
   [RECATALOG or NORECATALOG]
   [TO(data) or FOR(days)] )

   [CATALOG(catalogname[/password])]
```

◘ DEFINE PAGESPACE—Define an entry for a page space dataset

● General format
```
DEFINE PAGESPACE (
   NAME(entryname)
   [CYLINDERS(primary) or
     RECORDS(primary) or
     TRACKS(primary)]
   VOLUME(volser)
   [ATTEMPTS(n or 2)]
   [AUTHORIZATION(entrypoint string)]
   [CODE(code)]
   [CONTROLPW(password)]
   [FILE(ddname)]
   [MASTERPW(password)]
   [MODEL(entryname[/password]catalogname[/password])]
   [OWNER(ownerid)]
   [READPW(password)]
```

```
[RECATALOG or NORECATALOG]
[SWAP or NOSWAP]
[TO(date) or FOR(days)]
[UPDATEPW(password)] )

[CATALOG(catalogname[/password])]
```

◼ DEFINE PATH—Define a path directly to a base cluster or an alternate index and its related base cluster

● General format
```
DEFINE PATH (
  NAME(entryname)
  PATHENTRY(entryname[/password])
  [ATTEMPTS(n or 2)]
  [AUTHORIZATION(entrypoint string)]
  [CODE(code)]
  [CONTROLPW(password)]
  [MASTERPW(password)]
  [MODEL(entryname[/password]catalogname[/password])]
  [OWNER(ownerid)]
  [READPW(password)]
  [RECATALOG or NORECATALOG]
  [TO(date) or FOR(days)]
  [UPDATE or NOUPDATE]
  [UPDATEPW(password)] )

  [CATALOG(catalogname[/password])]
```

◼ DEFINE USERCATALOG or MASTERCATALOG—Define a user catalog

● General format
```
DEFINE USERCATALOG or MASTERCATALOG (
    NAME(entryname)
    [CYLINDERS(primary [secondary]) or
       RECORDS(primary [secondary]) or
       TRACKS(primary [secondary])]
    VOLUME(volser)
    [ATTEMPTS(n or 2)]
    [AUTHORIZATION(entrypoint string)]
    [BUFFERSPACE(size or 3072)]
    [BUFND(n)]
    [BUFNI(n)]
    [CODE(code)]
    [CONTROLINTERVALSIZE(size)]
    [CONTROLPW(password)]
    [DESTAGEWAIT or NODESTAGEWAIT]
    [FILE(ddname)]
    [FREESPACE(ci% ca%)]
    [IMBED or NOIMBED]
    [LOCK or UNLOCK]
```

```
[MASTERPW(password)]
[MODEL(entryname[/password]catalogname[/password])]
[OWNER(ownerid)]
[READPW(password)]
[RECORDSIZE(avg max)]
[REPLICATE or NOREPLICATE]
[SHAREOPTIONS(region system)]
[STRNO(n or 2)]
[TO(date) or FOR(days)]
[UPDATEPW(password)]
[VSAMCATALOG or ICFCATALOG]
[WRITECHECK or NOWRITECHECK] )

[ DATA (
[BUFFERSPACE(size)]
[CYLINDERS(primary [secondary]) or
   RECORDS(primary [secondary]) or
   TRACKS(primary [secondary])]
[BUFND(n)]
[CONTROLINTERVALSIZE(size)]
[DESTAGEWAIT or NODESTAGEWAIT]
[FREESPACE(ci% ca%)]
[RECORDSIZE(avg max)]
[WRITECHECK or NOWRITECHECK]
) ]

[ INDEX (
[CYLINDERS(primary) or
   RECORDS(primary) or
   TRACKS(primary)]
[BUFNI(n)]
[CONTROLINTERVALSIZE(size)]
[DESTAGEWAIT or NODESTAGEWAIT]
[IMBED or NOIMBED]
[REPLICATE or NOREPLICATE]
[WRITECHECK or NOWRITECHECK]
) ]

[CATALOG(mastercatalogname[/password])]
```

◘ DELETE—Delete catalogs, VSAM datasets, and non-VSAM datasets

● General format
```
DELETE (entryname[/password] entryname[/password]...)
   [ALIAS or ALTERNATEINDEX or CLUSTER or
    GENERATIONDATAGROUP or NONVSAM or NVR or PAGESPACE
    or PATH or TRUENAME or USERCATALOG or VVR]
   [ERASE or NOERASE]
   [FILE(ddname)]
   [FORCE or NOFORCE]
   [PURGE or NOPURGE]
   [RECOVERY or NORECOVERY]
   [SCRATCH or NOSCRATCH]

[CATALOG(catalogname[/password])]
```

◘ **DIAGNOSE—Scan a basic catalog structure or a VSAM volume dataset**

● **General format**
```
DIAGNOSE [ICFCATALOG or VVDS]
  [INFILE(ddname) or INDATASET(datasetname)]
  [COMPAREDD ddname [ddname] ...) or
      COMPAREDS dsname [dsname] ...) ]
  [DUMP or NODUMP]
  [ERRORLIMIT(value)]
  [EXCLUDE (
   ENTRIES(entryname [entryname] ..) or
   CATALOG(catalogname (catalogname) ...) or
   LEVEL(levelname) ) or
   INCLUDE (
   ENTRIES(entryname [entryname] ..) or
   CATALOG(catalogname (catalogname) ...) or
   LEVEL(levelname) )]
  [LIST or NOLIST]
  [OUTFILE(ddname)]
```

◘ **EXAMINE—Analyse and report on the structural consistency of index and data of KSDS**

● **General format**
```
EXAMINE NAME(clustername[/password])
    [INDEXTEST or NOINDEXTEST]
    [DATATEST or NODATATEST]
    [ERRORLIMIT(value)]
```

◘ **EXPORT DISCONNECT—Disconnect a user catalog**

● **General format**
```
EXPORT usercatalogname[/password]
```

◘ **EXPORT—Copy data from a cluster or index.**

● **General format**
```
EXPORT entryname[/password]
    [OUTFILE(ddname) or [OUTDATASET(entryname)]
    [CIMODE or RECORDMODE]
    [ERASE or NOERASE]
    [INFILE(ddname)]
    [INHIBITSOURCE or NOINHIBITSOURCE]
    [INHIBITTARGET or NOINHIBITTARGET]
    [PURGE or NOPURGE]
    [TEMPORARY or PERMANENT]
```

```
[TEMPORARY or PERMANENT]
[INFILE(ddname[/password]) or
       INDATASET(entryname[/password])]
[OUTFILE(ddname) or [OUTDATASET(entryname)]
[ERASE or NOERASE]
[INTOEMPTY]
[OBJECTS
   entryname
   [FILE(ddname)]
   [KEYRANGES((lowkey highkey)
              (lowkey highkey) ...)]
   [NEWNAME(newname)]
   [ORDERED or UNORDERED]
   [VOLUMES(vol1 [voln] ...)] )
   (entryname ...) ]
[PURGE or NOPURGE]
[SAVRAC or NOSAVRAC]

[CATALOG(catalogname[/password])]
```

◘ LISTCAT—List catalog entries

● General format
```
LISTCAT [ENTRIES(entryname[/password]
        entryname[/password] ...) or
        LEVEL(levelname)]
  [ALIAS]
  [ALTERNATEINDEX]
  [CLUSTER]
  [DATA]
  [GENERATIONDATAGROUP]
  [INDEX]
  [NONVSAM]
  [PAGESPACE]
  [PATH]
  [USERCATALOG]
  [CREATION(days)]
  [EXPIRATION(days)]
  [FILE(ddname)]
  [NAME or HISTORY or VOLUME or ALLOCATION or ALL]
  [OUTFILE(ddname)]

  [CATALOG(catalogname[/password])]
```

◘ PRINT—Print contents of VSAM datasets, non-VSAM datasets, and catalogs

● General format
```
PRINT <INFILE(ddname[/password]) or
       INDATASET(entryname[/password])]
  [CHARACTER or DUMP or HEX]
  [FROMKEY(key) or
   FROMADDRESS(address) or
   FROMNUMBER(number)    or
```

```
      SKIP(number)]
   [OUTFILE(ddname)]
   [TOKEY(key)   or
     TOADDRESS(address) or
     TONUMBER(number)    or
     SKIP(number) ]
```

◘ REPRO—Copy VSAM and non-VSAM datasets

● General format

```
REPRO <INFILE(ddname[/password] [ENVIRONMENT(DUMMY)] or
   INDATASET(entryname/[password][ENVIRONMENT(DUMMY)]>

   <OUTFILE(ddname[/password]) or
     OUTDATASET(entryname[/password])>

   [ENTRIES(entryname[/password]entryname[/password]...)
     or LEVEL(levelname)]
   [FILE(ddname)]
   [FROMKEY(key)      or      FROMADDRESS(address)      or
     FROMNUMBER(number) or SKIP(number)]
   [MERGECAT or NOMERGECAT]
   [REPLACE or NOREPLACE]
   [REUSE or NOREUSE]
   [TOKEY(key) or TOADDRESS(address) or
     TONUMBER(number) or SKIP(number)]

   /* The following keywords are used in an installation
   where cryptographic is supported. */

   [ENCIPHER (
        <EXTERNALKEYNAME(keyname) or
         INTERNALKEYNAME(keyname) or
         PRIVATEKEY>
     [CIPHERUNIT(number or 1)]
     [DATAKEYFILE(ddname) or DATAKEYVALUE(value)]
     [SHIPKEYNAME(keyname [keyname])]
     [STOREDATAKEY or NOSTOREDATAKEY]
     [STOREKEYNAME(keyname)]
     [USERDATA(value)]    )]

   [DECIPHER (
     <DATAKEYFILE(ddname) or
      DATAKEYVALUE(value) or SYSTEMKEY>
     [SYSTEMDATAKEY(value)]
     [SYSTEMKEYNAME(keyname)]   )]
```

◘ VERIFY—Verify a cluster or alternate index

● General format

```
VERIFY [FILE(ddname[/password])   or
   DATASET(entryname[/password])   ]
```

◘ IF—Conditional execution of commands

● General format

```
IF   [LASTCC or MAXCC] operator number

     THEN [command] or [DO command-list END]

[ELSE [command]     or [DO command-list END] ]

where (1)     operators are =, EQ, |=, NE, >, GT, <,
              LT,>=, GE, <=,  or LE.

      (2)     values for LASTCC and MAXCC are set by
              IDCAMS to 0, 4, 8, 12, or 16.
```

◘ SET—Set value of condition code

● General format

```
SET [LASTCC or MAXCC] = number

PARM [TEST (
              [TRACE]
              [AREAS(areaid [areaid]...)]
              [FULL(dumpid [number1 [number2]])]
              [OFF]    )]

     [GRAPHICS(CHAIN(chain) or TABLE(mname))]
     [MARGINS(leftbound rightbound)]
```

11.2 USING IDCAMS WITH JCL

The following is a general form for a JCL to execute the IDCAMS program. Following it is the explanation of the JOB, EXEC, and DD statements.

```
//jobname    JOB (acct),'IDCAMS',MSGCLASS=C,NOTIFY=tsoid
//stepname   EXEC PGM=IDCAMS,REGION=1024K,PARM=parameters
//STEPCAT    DD DSN=dataset-name,DISP=SHR
//anyname    DD DSN=dataset-name
//SYSPRINT   DD SYSOUT=*
//SYSIN      DD *
  control statements
/*
```

JOB   Initiates the batch job.

EXEC	Specifies execution of the program IDCAMS.
STEPCAT DD	Is an optional DD statement that specifies the user catalog to access during execution of IDCAMS.
anyname DD	Specifies a DD statement which is referenced in the FILE control statement and used in one of many IDCAMS functions, such as REPRO, DEFINE, or PRINT.
SYSPRINT DD	Specifies a message output dataset. It can be a system output device, tape, or disk.
SYSIN DD	Is used to pass the control statements to IDCAMS.

11.3 SAMPLE IDCAMS JCL

The following job step called STEP01 executes IDCAMS to create a VSAM KSDS. The dataset has the following characteristics:

- The cluster name is PROD.VSAM.CUST.
- Free space allocated is 10% for *ci* and *ca*.
- Key size is 10 bytes.
- Variable record size is from 100 to 150 bytes.
- Sharing option is 2.
- It is stored in volume CEL121.
- All keys are unique.
- Data name is PROD.VSAM.CUST.DATA.
- Primary space is 10 cylinders, and secondary space is 2 cylinders.
- Index name is PROD.VSAM.CUST.INDEX.
- Space for index is 1 cylinder.

```
//STEP01    EXEC PGM=IDCAMS
//SYSPRINT  DD SYSOUT=*
//SYSIN     DD *
DEFINE CLUSTER( NAME(PROD.VSAM.CUST ) -
            FREESPACE(10 10) -
     KEYS(10 0)   -
     RECORDSIZE(100 150) -
```

```
      SHR(2)
      VOL(CEL121) -
      UNIQUE)
   DATA( NAME(PROD.VSAM.CUST.DATA) -
      CYLINDER(15 2)) -
   INDEX(NAME(PROD.VSAM.CUST.INDEX) -
      CYLINDER(1))
/*
```

In the following example, the non-VSAM dataset TEMP.CUST.FILE is uncataloged but not deleted.

```
//STEP01    EXEC PGM=IDCAMS
//SYSPRINT  DD SYSOUT=*
//SYSIN     DD *
 DELETE -
      TEMP.CUST.FILE -
      NOSCRATCH
/*
```

In the next job step, IDCAMS is used to copy a portion of a VSAM KSDS PROD.VSAM.CUST to a sequential dataset TEMP.CUST.FILE. All the records with keys in the range BBBB0000 through GGGG0000 are copied to the output file.

```
//STEP01    EXEC PGM=IDCAMS
//SYSPRINT  DD SYSOUT=*
//TESTFIL   DD DSN=TEMP.CUST.FILE,DISP=SHR
//SYSIN     DD *
 REPRO -
  INDATASET(PROD.VSAM.CUST) -
     OUTFILE(TESTFIL) -
  FROMKEY(BBBB0000) -
  TOKEY(GGGG0000) -
/*
```

In the next example, IDCAMS is used to print 200 records from VSAM KSDS PROD.VSAM.CUST and sequential dataset TEMP.CUST.FILE.

```
//STEP01    EXEC PGM=IDCAMS
//SYSPRINT  DD SYSOUT=*
//SYSIN     DD *
 PRINT -
  INDATASET(PROD.VSAM.CUST) -
  COUNT(200) -
  DUMP
 PRINT-
  INDATASET(TEMP.CUST.FILE,DISP) -
  COUNT(200) -
  DUMP
/*
```

In the next example, IDCAMS is used to create three GDG bases.

```
//JS001     EXEC PGM=IDCAMS
//SYSPRINT DD  SYSOUT=*
//SYSIN    DD  *
 DEF GDG (NAME(CNCLP.PS00.TSA0.CWSO) LIMIT(7) SCRATCH)
 DEF GDG (NAME(CNCLP.SAA.REPORT.CSC1) LIMIT(7) SCRATCH)
 DEF GDG (NAME(CNCLP.SAA.REPORT.CSC2) LIMIT(7) SCRATCH)
```

11.4 SPACE ESTIMATION FOR VSAM DATASETS

11.4.1 Estimation for a KSDS

There are five steps in calculating the space required for a VSAM KSDS for both fixed-length and variable-length records. In each case a formula is supplied along with a explanation of the variables.

11.4.1.1 Estimating Space for Fixed-Length Records

◼ **Step 1: Calculate the number of records per CI.**

● **Formula:**

$$\text{Records per CI} = \frac{\text{DCISZ}-10}{\text{RECSZ}} \times \frac{100-\text{CIPERCENT}}{100}$$

DCISZ is the data component CI size.

RECSZ is the data record size.

CIPERCENT is the CI percent value of FREESPACE.

● **Example**
Let's say the data CI is 4096 bytes, the record size is 200 bytes, and the free space is coded as FREESPACE(30,40). The number of records that a single CI can hold is

$$\text{Records per CI} = \frac{4096-10}{200} \times \frac{100-30}{100}$$

$$= 14.301 \text{ or } 14 \text{ records}$$

CI Size	Index option	3330	3350	3380	3370*	9332*	9335*
			CIs per Cylinder for Different Devices				
512	IMBED	360	783	644	682	222	355
	NOIMBED	380	810	690	744	296	426
1,024	IMBED	198	435	434	341	111	177
	NOIMBED	209	450	465	372	148	213
2,048	IMBED	108	232	252	170	55	88
	NOIMBED	114	240	270	186	74	106
4,096	IMBED	54	116	140	85	27	44
	NOIMBED	57	120	150	93	37	53
6,144	IMBED	36	77	84	56	18	29
	NOIMBED	38	80	90	62	24	35
8,192	IMBED	27	58	70	42	13	22
	NOIMBED	28	60	75	46	18	26
12,288	IMBED	18	38	46	28	9	14
	NOIMBED	19	40	50	31	12	17
16,384	IMBED	13	29	35	21	6	11
	NOIMBED	14	30	37	23	9	13
32,768	IMBED	6	14	17	10	3	5
	NOIMBED	7	15	18	11	4	6

*IBM 3370 is an FBA device used with DOS/VSE.
IBM 9332 and IBM 9335 are FBA devices used with the 9370 series of computers and the DOS/VSE system.

Fig. 11.1 Table giving relationship among different CI sizes, types of DASD, and CIs per cylinder.

◼ Step 2: Calculate the number of CIs per CA.

The number of CIs that a CA can hold depends upon the following two factors: the type of DASD and the number of tracks per CA. The tabulation in Fig. 11.1 shows the relationship among the type of DASD, CI size, and number of CIs that can be contained in a cylinder with or without use of IMBED. Use this table when allocation space is specified in cylinders, thereby making a data CA one cylinder in size.

If the CA size is less than a cylinder, use the information in Figure 11.2 to determine the number of tracks per cylinder, and calculate the number of CIs per track to determine the number of CIs per CA.

IBM Device   Tracks per Cylinder

3380	19
3350	30
3375	12
3380	15
3370*	12
9332*	4
9335*	6

---

*FBA device.

Fig. 11.2   Track capacities of some IBM DASDs.

◻ **Step 3: Calculate the number of effective CIs per CA.**

● **Formula:**

$$\text{Effective CIs per CA} = \text{TOTCI} \times \frac{100 - \text{CAPERCENT}}{100}$$

TOTCI is the total number of CIs per CA, determined in step 2.

CAPERCENT is the second value (CA%) of the FREESPACE parameter.

● **Example**
In our example, the FREESPACE parameter was coded as FREESPACE(30,40); therefore CAPERCENT is 40. From Fig. 11.1, we determine that there are 140 CIs per CA. The effective number of CIs per CA is calculated as follows:

$$\text{Effective CIs per CA} = 140 \times \frac{100 - 40}{100}$$

$$= 84$$

▣ Step 4: Calculate the number of records per CA:

● Formula:

```
Records per CA = records per CI × Effective CIs per CA
```

where records per CI was calculated in step 1 and effective CIs per CA was caculated in step 3.

● Example
In our example there are 14 records per CI and 84 effective CIs per CA. Therefore,

```
Records per CA = 14 x 84 = 1176
```

▣ Step 5: Calculate the primary and secondary space requirements:

● Formula:

$$\text{Primary space value} = \frac{\text{EXPRECS}}{\text{RECSCA}} \times \frac{100 + \text{GRFACT}}{100}$$

EXPRECS is the expected number of records at the time of initial load.

RECSCA is the number of records per CA calculated in step 4.

GRFACT is the growth factor, given as a percentage of CAs to accommodate CA splits before getting a secondary allocation.

● Example
In this example, during the initial load there will be 200,000 records. The growth factor is 5%.

$$\text{Primary space value} = \frac{200,000}{1176} \times \frac{100 + 5}{100}$$

$$= 178.5 \text{ cylinders}$$

This calculated value is rounded to 180. The secondary space allocation can be 10% of 180 cylinders, which is 18 cylinders. The space parameter for this example will be coded as

```
CYLINDER(180,18)
```

11.4.1.2 Estimating Space for Variable-Length Records

To calculate the space requirements for a variable-length record for a VSAM KSDS, first find the average record length based on your judgment. Then use the five steps oulined for fixed-length records.

11.4.2 Estimation for an Alternate Index

An alternate index can be considered a KSDS. Therefore the space requirements for an alternate index can be calculated the same way as for a of KSDS. The unique key of the alternate index can be compared to a fixed-length record and the nonunique key to a variable-length record.

The alternate index record size can be calculated with the following formula:

Alternate index record size = 5 + AKL + (N x PRTLEN)

where AKL is the length of the alternate key.

N is the average number of occurrences of the pointer or primary key. For a unique key alternate index, the value of N is always 1. For a nonunique key alternate index, N is the average number of occurrences of a base cluster pointer for each alternate key value.

PRTLEN is the length of the primary key.

After calculating the alternate index record size, use the five steps described for KSDS to estimate the primary and secondary space requirements for the alternate index.

11.4.3 Estimation for an ESDS

The space requirements for an ESDS are the same as those for a KSDS. Therefore, use the five steps described for KSDS to estimate the primary and secondary space requirements for an ESDS.

11.4.4 Estimation for an RRDS

To calculate the space requirement for an RRDS, the following will be required:

- Type of DASD
- CI size
- CA size
- Record size
- Highest RRN supported

Then use the following three steps to calculate the space requirement.

◻ **Step 1: Calculate the number of records per CI.**

- **Formula:**

$$RECSPERCI = \frac{CISZ - 4}{RECLEN + 3}$$

RECSPERCI is the number of records per CI.

CISZ is the control interval size.

RECLEN is the record length.

◘ **Step 2: Calculate the number of records per CA.**

● **Formula:**

```
RECSPERCYL  =  CISPERCYL x RECSPERCI
```

RECSPERCYL is the number of records per cylinder.

CISPERCYL is the number of CIs per cylinder.

RECSPERCI is the number of records per CI calculated in step 1.

◘ **Step 3: Calculate space requirements**

● **Formula:**

$$\text{Space requirement (cylinders)} = \frac{\text{HRRN}}{\text{RECSPERCYL}}$$

HRRN is the highest RRN supported.

RECSPERCYL is the number of records per cylinder calculated in step 2.

XEDIT is an editor running under CMS (Conversational Monitor System). This chapter is a reference for users of XEDIT. It contains the general format and description of the command, subcommands, and macros. There is only one XEDIT command; it is used to invoke the editor from CMS. While in an editing session, there are many subcommands and macros that you can issue, and both follow the same syntax rules and conventions.

General Format: The general format starts with a subcommand name or macro name, followed by one or more operands. The format is

```
<subcommand-name or macro-name> operand...
```

The *subcommand-name* or *macro-name* is a symbolic name that represents a function that you want XEDIT to perform. *operand* can be a keyword and/or a positional operand.

Notational Convention: In the general format of the XEDIT command, subcommands, or macros used in this chapter, there are a few symbols that are not part of the syntax; therefore they must not be included when you code your program. These symbols and their meanings are:

Symbol	Meaning
[]	The option enclosed by the brackets ([]) is not required but can be included.
<>	Only one of the alternatives enclosed by the angle brackets (<>) must be chosen.
or	The alternatives enclosed by the angle brackets (<>) are separated by "or."
____	The underlined word is the default value.
...	The vertical or horizontal ellipsis means that the preceding can be coded more than once.
Uppercase characters	All keywords of the command are written in uppercase characters; they must be coded as shown.
Lowercase characters	All strings in lowercase characters and italic are variables that can be changed to any other strings to suit your programming style. In your code they represent values that you supply to commands.
fn	Filename.
ft	Filetype.
fm	Filemode.

Abbreviation: In many cases an abbreviated form of the subcommand or operand is permitted. The acceptable part is in uppercase characters. For example, the subcommand Down has a short form D; however, DO, DOW, and DOWN are also valid specifications.

12.1 XEDIT—INVOKE THE EDITOR FROM CMS

The XEDIT command invokes the editor from CMS. This editor can be used to create or change a CMS file. The editor also has many subcommands, prefix subcommands, and built-in macro that can be issued to manipulate a file. The rest of the chapter describes the subcommands and macros.

The general format is

```
Xedit [fn] [ft] [fm] [(options...[)]]
```

where *options* are   [Width   *nn*]   [NOSCreen] [PROFile
                         macroname]   [NOPROFil]   [NOCLear]
                         [NOMsg] [MEMber *membername*] [WINdow
                         wname] [<u>LOCK</u> or NOLOCK]

fn is the name of the file to be edited.

ft is the type of the file to be edited.

fm is the file mode of the file to be edited, which specifies where the file is to be found. If it is omitted, XEDIT assumes the file to be on minidisk A1.

WIDTH specifies the record length of the file to be edited. if *nn*, the line width, is too small, it is possible some lines may be trucated. If this parameter is omitted, XEDIT will either use the logical record length (LRECL) of the file or the default logical record length, which ever is larger.

NOSCREEN means that a 3270 display terminal is used in a typewriter mode.

PROFILE specifies the profile macro to be executed first by XEDIT.

NOPROFIL tells XEDIT not to execute the default PROFILE macro.

NOCLEAR tells XEDIT not to clear the screen when it is executed, rather it should place the screen in the waiting status (MORE..).

NOMSG means that XEDIT go into editing mode after setting MSGMODE OFF.

MEMBER specifies the name of member in the nacro library. This member is specified in *fn ft fm*.

WINDOW specifies the name of the virtual screen and window that XEDIT must use.

LOCK tells XEDIT to prevent other users to change the file you are currently working with.

UNLOCK allows a file that you are using to be changed by other users.

12.2 XEDIT SUBCOMMANDS

This section contains all the XEDIT subcommands. For each subcommand, it gives the syntax, followed by an explanation of the subcommand.

◘ ADD—Add lines

- **General format**

  ADD [n or 1]

- **Description**

  The ADD subcommand is used to insert one or more blank lines. The lines are added right after the current line. If the number of blank lines to be added is omitted, the default value is 1.

◘ BACKWARD—Scroll backward

- **General format**

  BAckward [n or * or 1]

- **Description**

  The BACKWARD subcommand is used to scroll one or many screens of display towards the top of the file. If the number of screens is omitted, then 1 screen of display is scrolled backward. If an asterisk (*) is specified, then the display starts from the beginning of the file.

◘ BOTTOM—Bottom of the file

- **General format**

  Bottom

- **Description**

  The BOTTOM subcommand is used to make the last line of the file the current line.

◘ CDELETE—Delete character

- **General format**
  CDelete [*column-target* or 1]

- **Description**
  The CDELETE subcommand is used to delete one or more characters of the current line. The deletion starts with the column at the column pointer and *column-target* specifies the number of characters to be deleted.

◘ CFIRST—Move column pointer to the beginning

- **General format**
  CFirst

- **Description**
  The CFIRST subcommand is used to change the column pointer to point to the beginning of the zone.

◘ CHANGE—Change characters

- **General format**
  Change /*string-1*/*string-2*/ [*target* or * or 1]
        [*p* or * or 1] [*g* or 1]

- **Description**
  The CHANGE subcommand is used to substitute nothing or a group of characters in a file for one or more characters. You can also specify the number of lines in which the change is to take place, which can vary from one to all lines.

  / is a delimiter.

  string-1 is the string to be changed.

  string-2 replaces *string-1*.

  target is the number of lines to be changes.

  p is the number of occcurrences of *string-1* in every line.

* means all occurrences.

q is the relative number of the first instance of *string-1* in every line.

◘ CINSERT—Insert a string

• **General format**
```
Cinsert string
```

• **Description**
The CINSERT subcommand is used to insert a string. The insertion starts at the column pointer of the current line.

◘ CLAST—Move column pointer to the end

• **General format**
```
CLast
```

• **Description**
The CLAST subcommand is used to change the column pointer to point to the end of the zone.

◘ CLOCATE—Search for column target

• **General format**
```
CLocate column-target
```

• **Description**
The CLOCATE subcommand is used to search a file to find a specified column target. If it is found, then the column pointer is copied to the target. The column target can be one of the following: an absolute column number, a relative column number, a string expression, or a complex string expression.

◘ CMS—Execute CMS a command

• **General format**
```
CMS [command]
```

- **Description**

  The CMS subcommand is used to execute a CMS command. If the command is not specified, then the editor enters into a CMS subset mode.

◘ **CMSG—Command-line message**

- **General format**

  CMSG [text]

- **Description**

  The CMSG subcommand is used to show a message in the command line of a terminal.

  text is the message to be displayed; if it is omitted, a blank line is shown.

◘ **COMMAND—Execute XEDIT subcommand**

- **General format**

  COMMAND [XEDIT-command]

- **Description**

  The COMMAND subcommand is used to execute an XEDIT subcommand even if SET SYNONYM ON or SET MACRO ON is in effect. In other words, no checking of synonyns and macros is done.

  XEDIT-command is the name of any XEDIT command, except ? and &.

◘ **COMPRESS—Reposition data**

- **General format**

  COMPress [target or * or 1]

- **Description**

  The COMPRESS subcommand is used to reposition data after a new tab setting. The repositioning starts from the current line, and the number of lines affected depends on the *target* parameter.

* means the rest of the file is to be compressed.

◘ COPY—Copy lines

- **General format**
COpy *from-target* *to-target*

- **Description**
The COPY subcommand is used to copy one or more lines from the current line to a specified target line.

◘ COUNT—Count occurrences of a string

- **General format**
COUnt /*string*[/*target* or * or 1]

- **Description**
The COUNT subcommand is used to count the number of occurrences of a string. The scanning starts from the current line and is done for the specified number of lines. After the specified string is located, the number of occurrences is displayed.

string is the string to be counted.

target is the number of lines to be searched.

* means to search to the end of the file.

◘ COVERLAY—Overlay a character string

- **General format**
COVerlay *string*

- **Description**
The COVERLAY subcommand is used to replace characters in the current line with a specified character string. The overlay starts at the column position.

string contains characters to be overlayed; if it contains a blank character, it does not replace corresponding character in the current line.

◘ CP—Issue CP a command

- **General format**
  ```
  CP [cp-command]
  ```

- **Description**
  The CP subcommand is used to issue CP commands while using XEDIT.

◘ CREPLACE—Replace a character string

- **General format**
  ```
  CReplace string
  ```

- **Description**
  The CREPLACE subcommand is used to overwrite characters in the current line with a specified character string. The replacement starts at the column position.

◘ CURSOR—Move the cursor

- **General format**
  ```
  CURsor CMdline  [colno or 1] [Priority n]
       Column  [Priority n]
       File    lineno [colno] [Priority n]
       Home    [Priority n]
       Screen  lineno [colno] [Priority n]
  ```

- **Description**
  The CURSOR subcommand is used to move the cursor to a specified position. The positioning of the cursor occurs only after any prending prefix subcommand is processed, any pending macro is executed and the screen is refreshed.

  CMDLINE positions the cursor under the command line.

  COLUMN positions the cursor under the current line.

  FILE positions the cursor from the top of the file.

HOME positions the cursor from the command line to the screen, or from the screen to the command line.

SCREEN positions the cursor relative to the beginning of the screen.

PRIORITY specifies the priority to be assigned to the specific position.

lineno is either the file line or the screen line.

colno is the column number where the cursor is moved to.

◘ DELETE—Delete line

● General format
```
DELete [num-line or * or 1]
```

● Description
The DELETE subcommand is used to delete one or more lines from a file. It deletes the specified number of lines starting with the current line. If an asterisk (*) is specified, then all the lines from the current line to the end of the file are removed from the file.

◘ DOWN—Move the line pointer down

● General format
```
Down [n or * or 1]
```

● Description
The DOWN subcommand is used to move the line pointer a specified number of lines towards the end of the file.

◘ DUPLICAT—Duplicate lines

● General format
```
DUPlicat [n or 1 [target or 1]]
```

● **Description**
The DUPLICAT subcommand is used to duplicate lines starting
from the current line. It duplicates the specified number of lines
the specified number of times.

◘ **EMSG—Display a message and sound an alarm**

● **General format**
EMSG [*message*]

or

EMSG [*mmmnnn*[*n*]*s*]

● **Description**
The EMSG subcommand is used to display a specified message
and sound the alarm at the terminal.

message is the text to be shown; if none is specified, a blank line
is displayed.

mmm is the name of a macro or module that produced the
message.

nnn[n] is the message number.

s specifies the severity and is one of the following:

R	Response
I	Information
W	Warning
E	Error
S	Sever error
T	Terminal error

◘ **EXPAND—Reposition data**

● **General format**
EXPand [*target* or * or 1]

● **Description**

The EXPAND subcommand is used to reposition data after a new tab setting. The repositioning happens wherever there is a tab character starting from the current line; the number of lines affected depends on the *target* parameter.

◼ **EXTRACT—Get information about XEDIT variables and file data**

● **General format**

```
EXTract /operand [/operand...]

operand is one of the following:
```

ACTion	ALT	APL	ARBchar	AUtosave	BASEft
BRKkey	CASE	CMDline	COLOR<* or *field*>		COLPtr
COLumn	CTLchar [*char*]		CURLine	CURSor	DISPlay
EDIRName	EFMode		EFName	EFType	ENTer
EOF	EOL		ESCape	ETARBCH	ETMODE
FILler	FMode		FName	FType	
FULLread	HEX		IMage	IMPcmscp	
LASTlorc	LASTmsg		LENgth	LIBName	LIBType
Line	LINENd		LRecl	LSscreen	MACRO
MASK	MEMber		MSGLine	MSGMode	NBFile

```
NONDisp   NULls    NUMber    PA [n or *]
PACK      PENDing [BLOCK] [OLDNAME] <name or *>
PF [n or *]          Point [*]
PREfix [Synonym * or name]
```

RANge	RECFm		REMOte	RESERved	RING
SCALE	SCOPE		SCReen	SELect	Seq8
SERial	SHADow		SIDcode	SIZe	SPAN
SPILL	STAY		STReam		
SYNonym [* or *name*]					
TABLine	TABS		TARGet	TERMinal	TEXT
TOF	TOFEOF		TOL	TRANSLat	TRunc
UNIQueld	UNTil		UPDate	VARblank	Verify
VERShift	Width		WRap	Zone	=

```
PENDing [BLOCK][OLDNAME <name or *>
                        [target-1 [target-2]]
PREfix [Synonym name or Synonym *]
```

● **Description**

The EXTRACT subcommand is used to retrieve information about internal XEDIT variables or file data. The information is placed in one or more variables. This command is used within a macro. The forward slash (/) is a delimiter.

◘ FILE—Write to file

● **General format**
FILE [*fn* or =] [*ft* or =] [*fm* or =]

● **Description**
The FILE subcommand is used to write data from an XEDIT session to a file in minidisk.

◘ FIND—Find a character string in a file

● **General format**
Find *string*

● **Description**
The FIND subcommand is used to search a file for a specified character string. The search starts from the current line.

◘ FINDUP—Find a character string in a file backward

● **General format**
<FINDUp or FUp> *string*

● **Description**
The FINDUP subcommand is used to search a file backward for a specified character string. The search starts from the current line.

◘ FORWARD—Scroll forward

● **General format**
FOrward [*n* or * or 1]

● **Description**
The FORWARD subcommand is used to scroll one or many screens of display towards the bottom of the file. If the number of screens is omitted, then 1 screen of display is scrolled forward. If an asterisk (*) is specified, then the last screen of the file is displayed.

◙ GET—Retrieve file

- **General format**
```
GET [fn or =] [ft or =] [fm or =]
     [firstrec or 1] [numrec or *]
```

- **Description**

The GET subcommand is used to retrieve a specified CMS file and insert it after the current line. If no operand is listed, then GET retrieves the lines saved by a previous PUT or PUTD subcommand.

firstrec is the record number which is first record that is inserted.

numrec is the number of records to be inserted.

◙ INPUT— Input data

- **General format**
```
Input [line]
```

- **Description**

The INPUT subcommand is used to input a line of data to a file.

◙ LEFT—Move text to left

- **General format**
```
LEft [n or 1]
```

- **Description**

The LEFT subcommand is used to move data so that columns to the left are visible.

◙ LOAD—Load a file into virtual storage

- **General format**
```
LOAD [fn] [ft] [fm] [(options...[)]]
```

where *options* are   [Width nn] [NOSCreen] [PROFile
                           macroname] [NOPROFIL] [NOCLear]
                           [NOMsg]   [MEMber   membername]
                           [WINdow wname] [LOCK or NOLOCK]

Note: In update mode, the following are valid options:

[Update or NOUpdate] [Seq8 or NOSeq8]
[Ctl *fn* 1 or NOCtl] [Merge] [UNtll *filetype*]
[Incr *nn*] [SIDcode *string*]

● **Description**
The LOAD subcommand is used to read a copy of the file being edited in XEDIT into virtual storage.

fn is the name of the file to be edited.

ft is the type of the file to be edited.

fm is the file mode of the file to be edited, which specifies where the file is to be found. If it is omitted, XEDIT assumes the file to be on minidisk A1.

WIDTH specifies the record length of the file to be edited. if *nn*, the line width, is too small, it is possible some lines may be trucated. If this parameter is omitted, XEDIT will either use the logical record length (LRECL) of the file or the default logical record length, which ever is larger.

NOSCREEN means that a 3270 display terminal is used in a typewriter mode.

PROFILE specifies the profile macro to be executed first by XEDIT.

NOPROFIL tells XEDIT not to execute the default PROFILE macro.

NOCLEAR tells XEDIT not to clear the screen when it is executed, rather it should place the screen in the waiting status (MORE..).

NOMSG means that XEDIT go into editing mode after setting MSGMODE OFF.

MEMBER specifies the name of member in the nacro library. This member is specified in *fn ft fm*.

WINDOW specifies the name of the virtual screen and window that XEDIT must use.

LOCK tells XEDIT to prevent other users to change the file you are currently working with.

UNLOCK allows a file that you are using to be changed by other users.

◘ LOCATE—Locate and change the current line

- **General format**
  Locate *target* [*subcommand*]

- **Description**
  The LOCATE subcommand is used to search the file for a specified target; if it is found, the line becomes the current line. The scanning of the file starts with the line after the current line.

◘ LOWERCAS—Convert to lowercase

- **General format**
  LOWercas [*target* or * or 1]

- **Description**
  The LOWERCAS subcommand is used to convert uppercase characters to lowercase. The conversion starts from the current line. If asterisk (*) is specified, the rest of the file is converted.

◘ LPREFIX—Write in prefix area

- **General format**
  LPrefix [*text*]

- **Description**
  The LPREFIX subcommand is used to write a five-character string into the prefix area of the current line.

◘ MACRO—Execute a macro

● General format
MACRO [*macro-name*]

● Description
The MACRO subcommand is used to execute a specified XEDIT macro. All the XEDIT macros are discussed later in this chapter.

◘ MERGE—Merge lines

● General format
MErge *target1 target2* [*col*]

● Description
The MERGE subcommand is used to combine one group of lines with another group. The first group, specified as *target1*, is deleted and replaced by the second group, specified as *target2*. The first group starts with the current line.

◘ MOVE—Move lines

● General format
MOve *target1 target2*

● Description
The MOVE subcommand is used to move one or more lines from the current line to a specified destination line.

◘ MSG—Display a message

● General format
MSG [*text*]

● Description
The MSG subcommand is used to display a specified text in the message area of a screen.

◘ NEXT—Move the line pointer forward

● General format
NEXT [n or * or 1]

● Description
The NEXT subcommand is used to move the line pointer a specified number of lines towards the bottom of the file.

◘ NFIND—Search forward for a line not starting with a string

● General format
NFIND string

● Description
The NFIND subcommand is used to scan the file forward for the first line that does not start with the specified *string*. The search is done from one line after the current line.

◘ NFINDUP—Search backward for a line not starting with a string

● General format
<NFINDUp or NFUp> string

● Description
The NFINDUP subcommand is used to scan the file backward for the first line that does not start with the specified *string*. The search is done from one line before the current line.

◘ OVERLAY—Replace characters

● General format
Overlay string

● Description
The OVERLAY subcommand is used to replace one or more characters in the current line with a specified character string.

◘ POWERINP—Enter input line

● **General format**
POWerinp

● **Description**
The POWERINP subcommand is used to start the input mode. In this mode you type the input data as a long line and the editor justifies it into lines appropriately.

◘ PRESERVE—Save values of XEDIT variables

● **General format**
PREServe

● **Description**
The PRESERVE subcommand is used to save the values of most of the XEDIT variables until a RESTORE subcommand is executed.

◘ PURGE—Remove a macro from storage

● **General format**
PURge *macroname*

● **Description**
The PURGE subcommand is used to delete a copy of a macro that has been loaded into virtual storage.

◘ PUT—Write lines to file

● **General format**
PUT [*target* or * or 1] [*fn* or =] [*ft* or =] [*fm* or =]

● **Description**
The PUT subcommand is used to write one or more lines starting with the current line to one of the following:

● The end of an existing file
● A new permanent file

- A temporary file

The original lines are not deleted.

◘ PUTD—Write lines to file and delete

- **General format**
  PUTD [*target* or * or 1] [*fn* or =] [*ft* or =] [*fm* or =]

- **Description**
  The PUTD subcommand is used to write one or more lines starting with the current line to one of the following:

  - The end of an existing file
  - A new permanent file
  - A temporary file

  The original lines are deleted.

◘ QUERY—Query editing options

- **General format**
  Query *option*

  where *option* is one of the following:

ACTion	ALT	APL	ARBchar	AUtosave	BASEft
BRKkey	CASE	CMDline	COLOR<* or *field*>		COLPtr
COLumn	CTLchar [*char*]		CURLine	CURSor	DISPlay
EDIRName	EFMode		EFName	EFType	ENTer
EOF	EOL		ESCape	ETARBCH	ETMODE
FILler	FMode		FName	FType	
FULLread	HEX		IMage	IMPcmscp	
LASTlorc	LASTmsg		LENgth	LIBName	LIBType
Line	LINENd		LRecl	LSscreen	MACRO
MASK	MEMber		MSGLine	MSGMode	NBFile
NONDisp	NULls		NUMber	PA [*n* or *]	
PACK	PENDing[BLOCK][OLDNAME]<*name* or *>				
PF [*n* or *]			Point [*]		
PREfix [Synonym * or *name*]			RANge	RECFm	REMOte
RESERved	RING		SCALE	SCOPE	SCReen
SELect	Seq8		SERial	SHADow	SIDcode
SIZe	SPAN		SPILL	STAY	STReam
SYNonym [* or *name*]			TABLine	TABS	TARGet
TERMinal	TEXT		TOF	TOFEOF	TOL
TRANSLat	TRunc		UNIQueId		UNTil
UPDate	VARblank		Verify	VERShift	Width
WRap	Zone		=		

- **Description**

  The QUERY subcommand is used to retrieve the current setting of a specified XEDIT setting and display it in the message area.

◘ QUIT—End an editing session

- **General format**

  QUIT [n]

- **Description**

  The QUIT subcommand is used to end the current editing session without saving the data to the file. If the file has been changed, then XEDIT will prompt with a warning and request for a confirmation.

◘ READ—Read data from the terminal

- **General format**

  READ [_cmdline_ or ALL [Number] or Nochange [number]]
       [Tag or Notag]

- **Description**

  The READ subcommand is used to read data from the terminal and place them in the terminal stack. The stack data can be retrieved by a REXX PULL instruction.

  CMDLINE means to move data from the command input area to the stack.

  ALL means to move all lines changed on the screen to the stack.

  NOCHANGE means that all lines changed on the screen to the stack; this changes are not made to the file being edited.

  NUMBER means that the lines that are changed must have their line numbers in the prefix area.

  TAG means to add a tag at the beginning of each line written to the stack. The tag identifies the origin of the line.

NOTAG means not to insert a tag at the beginning of each line written to the stack.

◘ RECOVER—Recover data

● **General format**
```
RECover [n or * or 1]
```

● **Description**
The RECOVER subcommand is used to restore a specified number of lines that were previously deleted with one of the following subcommands: MERGE, DELETE, or PUTD.

◘ REFRESH—Redisplay data on the screen

● **General format**
```
REFRESH
```

● **Description**
The REFRESH subcommand is used to redisplay data on the screen. The data shown are those that are available at the moment REFRESH is issued.

◘ RENUM—Renumber lines

● **General format**
```
RENum [start-num or 10 [increment]]
```

● **Description**
The RENUM subcommand is used to renumber the lines of a VSBASIC or FREEPORT file.

◘ REPEAT—Execute the last subcommand again

● **General format**
```
REPEat [target or * or 1]
```

● **Description**

The REPEAT subcommand is used to accomplish the following two tasks: advance the line pointer by one and reexecute the previous subcommand entered.

◘ **REPLACE—Replace the current line**

● **General format**
```
Replace [text]
```

● **Description**

The REPLACE subcommand is used to replace the current line. If input text is specified, then the current line is automatically replaced. Otherwise, XEDIT replaces the current line with data received in input mode.

◘ **RESET—Remove all prefix subcommands or macros**

● **General format**
```
RESet
```

● **Description**

The RESET subcommand is used to remove all prefix subcommands or macros. This happens only when the screen status is "pending."

◘ **RESTORE—Recover XEDIT variable values**

● **General format**
```
RESTore
```

● **Description**

The RESTORE subcommand is used to reset the values of XEDIT variables to their settings when the last PRESERVE subcommand was issued.

◘ RIGHT—Move text to right

● **General format**
RIght [n or 1]

● **Description**

The RIght subcommand is used to move data so that columns to the right are visible.

◘ SAVE—Write an edited file to disk

● **General format**
SAVE [fn or =] [ft or =] [fm or =]

● **Description**

The SAVE subcommand is used to write a file that is being currently edited to disk.

◘ SET—Set editing options

● **General format**
SET option

where option is one of the following:

ALT	APL	ARBchar	AUtosave	BRKkey
CASE	CMDline	COLOR	COLPtr	CTLchar
CURLine	DISPlay	ENTer	ESCape	ETARBCH
ETMODE	FILler	FMode	FName	FType
FULLread	HEX	IMage	IMPcmscp	LASTLorc
LINENd	LRecl	MACRO	MASK	MSGLine
MSGMode	NONDisp	NULls	NUMber	PAn
PACK	PENDing	PFn	Point	PREfix
RANge	RECFm	REMOte	RESERved	SCALe
SCOPE	SCReen	SELect	SERial	SHADow
SIDcode	SPAN	SPILL	STAY	STReam
SYNonym	TABLine	TABS	TERMinal	TEXT
TOFEOF	TRANSLat	TRunc	VARblank	Verify
WRap	Zone	=		

● **Description**

The SET subcommand is used to initialize a value for a specified XEDIT option while editing is in progress. The next part of this section provides more information on each option of the SET subcommand.

◘ SET ALT—Change the alteration count

● General format
SET [ALT] *n* [*p*]

● Description
The SET ALT subcommand is used to reset the number of alterations made to a file. The parameters *n* and *p* are the counts since the last AUTOSAVE or SAVE command, repectively, was issued.

◘ SET [APL]—Set APL character option

● General format
SET APL <ON or OFF>

● Description
The SET APL subcommand is used to set an ON or OFF value to indicate to CMS or XEDIT whether or not to use APL characters.

◘ SET ARBCHAR—Set an arbitary character

● General format
[SET] ARBchar <ON or OFF> [*char*]

● Description
The SET ARBCHAR subcommand is used to set an ON or OFF value to indicate whether or not to use an arbitary character in a target definition.

◘ SET AUTOSAVE—Set the autosave option

● General format
[SET] AUtosave <*n* or OFF> [mode or A]

● Description
The SET AUTOSAVE subcommand is used to set or reset the automatic save option of XEDIT. If the option is set, XEDIT saves the file being edited to disk after *n* alterations.

◘ SET BRKKEY—Set the break key option

- **General format**

```
[SET] BRKkey <ON or OFF> key
```

- **Description**

The SET BRKKEY subcommand is used to set an ON or OFF value to indicate whether or not CP should break when the BRKKEY is pressed.

◘ SET CASE—Set the case option

- **General format**

```
[SET] CASE <Uppercase or Mixed> [Respect or Ignore]
```

- **Description**

The SET CASE subcommand is used to indicate whether a file should contain uppercase only, or both uppercase and lowercase characters. If the uppercase option is chosen, then lowercase input characters are translated to uppercase characters.

RESPECT means not to treat lowercase and uppercase characters as the same when executing a search subcommand.

IGNORE means to treat lowercase and uppercase characters as the same when executing a search subcommand.

◘ SET CMDLINE—Position the command line

- **General format**

```
[SET] CMDline <ON or OFf or Top or Bottom>
```

- **Description**

The SET CMDLINE subcommand is used to set the position of the command line on the screen.

◘ SET COLOR—Specify a color for certain screen areas

- **General format**

```
[SET] COLOR <field or *> [color][exthi]
            [High or Nohigh] [PSs]
```

● **Description**

The SET COLOR subcommand is used to set the color and intensity of certain areas of the screen.

* means all of the fields on the screen, listed below.

field is one of the areas on the screen as follows:

ARROW is arrow at the command line.

CMDLINE is the area where a command is entered.

CURLINE is the current line.

FILEAREA is data area of a file, excluding TOF, EOF, and current line.

IDLINE is the first line on the screen where the file name is found.

MSGLINE is the line where a message is shown.

PENDING is the prefix area where pending macro and subcommands are shown.

PREFIX is prefix area, either on the left of right side of line of a file. The side is determined by SET PREFIX subcommand.

SCALE is the scale line.

SHADOW refers to shadow line(s).

STATAREA is the status area.

TABLINE is the line that shows a T in every tab column.

TOFEOF are the lines that show "TOP OF FILE" and "END OF FILE" messages.

color is one of the following:

Blue	Turquoise
Red	Yellow
Pink	White
Green	Default

exthi specifies highlighting and is one of the following:

BLInk
REVvideo
Underline
NONe

High means to highlight the field.

Nohigh means not to highlight the field.

PS*s* specifies the programmed symbol and is on of the following:

PS0	PSD
PSA	PSE
PSB	PSF
PSC	

◘ **SET COLPTR—Set the column pointer option**

● **General format**
```
[SET] COLPtr <ON or OFF>
```

● **Description**
The SET COLPTR subcommand is used to set an ON or OFF value to indicate whether or not to display the column pointer.

◘ **SET CTLCHAR—Define control characters**

● **General format**
```
[SET] CTLchar
       <char
           [[OFF or Escape or Protect or Noprotect]
           [color exthi [High or Nohigh or Invisible]]
           PS s]
       or
       OFF>
```

● **Description**

The SET CTLCHAR subcommand is used to define a control character. This character is used with the following features:

● Color
● Ordinary and extended highlighting
● Protection
● Visibility
● Programmed symbol set

char is uppercase or lowercase control character.

OFF means to reset all control characters or a specific character if used with *char*.

Escape specifies a character as a the control character name; if this character appears in text, the following character is interpreted as a control character.

Protect means that the string following *char* is to be shown in a protected mode.

Noprotect means that the string following char is to be shown in an unprotected mode.

color is one of the following:

Blue	Turquoise
Red	Yellow
Pink	White
Green	Default

exthi specified highlighting and is one of the following:

BLInk
REVvideo
Underline
NONe

High means to highlight the field.

Nohigh means not to highlight the field.

Invisible means the characters belonging to this field are not to be shown, for example, a password.

PS*s* specifies the programmed symbol and is one of the following:

PS0	PSD
PSA	PSE
PSB	PSF
PSC	

◘ SET CURLINE—Define the position of the current line

● General format
```
[SET] CURLine ON M [+n or -n]
```

● Description
The SET CURLINE subcommand is used to define the position of the current line and display the line on the screen.

◘ SET DISPLAY—Define the selection level

● General format
```
[SET] DISPlay n1 [n2 or *]
```

● Description
The SET DISPLAY subcommand is used to choose the selection level of lines to be displayed. The selection level is defined with the SET SELECT subcommand.

◘ SET ENTER—Define a meaning for ENTER key

● General format
```
[SET] ENTer [BEFORE or AFTER or ONLY or IGNORE]
   [string or NULLKEY or COPYKEY or TABKEY]
```

- **Description**

  The SET ENTER subcommand is used to associate a meaning with the ENTER key or remove the previous association.

  BEFORE means to process the key definition before executing the command entered at the command line.

  AFTER means to process the key definition after executing the command entered at the command line.

  ONLY means to only process the key definition and not execute the command entered at the command line.

  IGNORE means not to process the key definition and only execute the command entered at the command line.

  string is an XEDIT subcommand or macro that is executed when ENTER is pressed.

  NULLKEY means that blank characters found at the cursor are translated to nulls.

  COPYKEY means to copy the content of the virtual screen to the printer spool when ENTER is pressed.

  TABKEY means to move the cursor to the next tab when ENTER is pressed.

◻ SET ESCAPE—Turn the ESCAPE character on or off

- **General format**
  ```
  [SET] ESCape <ON or OFF> [char]
  ```

- **Description**

  The SET ESCAPE subcommand is used to turn on or off the use of the ESCAPE character.

◘ SET ETARBCH—Turn the use of DBCS on or off

● General format
```
[SET] ETARBCH  <ON or OFF> [char]
```

● Description
The SET ETARBCH subcommand is used to turn on or off the use of the double-byte character set (DBCS).

◘ SET ETMODE—Set extended mode

● General format
```
[SET] ETMODE <ON or OFF>
```

● Description
The SET ETMODE subcommand is used to enable XEDIT to display and manipulate DBCS strings or to disable it.

◘ SET FILLER—Define a filler character

● General format
```
[SET] FILler  [char]
```

● Description
The SET FILLER subcommand is used to specify to the editor a character to be used as a filler when tabs are removed from a file.

◘ SET FMODE—Change the filemode of a file

● General format
```
[SET] FMode fm
```

● Description
The SET FMODE subcommand is used to change the filemode of a file that is currently being edited.

◘ SET FNAME—Change the filename of a file

- **General format**
  [SET] FName *fn*

- **Description**
  The SET FNAME subcommand is used to change the filename of a file that is currently being edited.

◘ SET FTYPE—Change the filetype of a file

- **General format**
  [SET] FType *ft*

- **Description**
  The SET FTYPE subcommand is used to change the filetype of a file that is currently being edited.

◘ SET FULLREAD—Accept null characters

- **General format**
  [SET] FULLread <ON or OFF>

- **Description**
  The SET FULLREAD subcommand is used to set the option so that XEDIT will accept or reject null characters in the middle of a line.

◘ SET HEX—Set hexadecimal mode

- **General format**
  [SET] HEX <ON or OFF>

- **Description**
  The SET HEX subcommand is used to turn on or off the option to specify operands or targets in a hexadecimal string.

◘ SET IMAGE—Set type-like mode

● General format
```
[SET] IMage <ON or OFF or Cannon>
```

● Description
The SET IMAGE subcommand is used to turn on or off the type-like mode. If it is turned on, when a line is entered, tab characters are expanded with filler characters. Otherwise tab and backspace characters are left as they are entered.

Cannon means to leave tabs as they are found in the text—in other words, do not expand tabs to blanks or filler characters.

◘ SET IMPCMSCP— Execute an unrecognized subcommand

● General format
```
[SET] IMPcmscp <ON or OFF>
```

● Description
The SET IMPCMSCP turns on or off the option of sending a subcommand to CMS or CP for execution. If the option is turned on, XEDIT sends the subcommands that it cannot recognize. If the option is turned off, such subcommands are not sent to CMS or CP.

◘ SET LASTLORC—Initialize the buffer

● General format
```
[SET] LASTLorc line
```

● Description
The SET LASTLORC subcommand is used to initialize the value for the last locate or change (LASTLORC) buffer.

◘ SET LINEND—Initialize the line-end character

● General format
```
[SET] LINENd <ON or OFF> [char]
```

- **Description**

  The SET LINEND subcommand is used to initialiaze a specified character as the line-end character. If a character is not specified, then the pound sign (#) is the default value.

◘ SET LRECL—Initialize the logical record length

- **General format**
  ```
  [SET] LRecl <n or *>
  ```

- **Description**

  The SET LRECL subcommand is used to define a new logical record length for a file to be written to disk.

◘ SET MACRO—Set the search order for macros

- **General format**
  ```
  [SET] MACRO <ON or OFF>
  ```

- **Description**

  The SET MACRO subcommand is used to define the order in which macros and subcommands are executed. If the option is ON, then macros are searched for and executed before subcommands. Otherwise, XEDIT executes subcommands before macros.

◘ SET MASK—Initialize a mask

- **General format**
  ```
  [SET] MASK <Define or Immed [text] or Modify>
  ```

- **Description**

  The SET MASK subcommand is used to change the content of the mask. This mask is initially blanks and is used when inserting a new line.

  Define means to define a new mask.

  Immed replaces the current maks with a new mask.

  text is the new mask that replaces the current one.

Modify displays the current masks and lets you type over it.

◘ SET MSGLINE—Define the location of the message line

● General format
```
[SET] MSGLine <ON or OFF> [M [+n or -n]] [p or 1]
[Overlay]
```

● Description
The SET MSGLINE subcommand is used to define the position and size of the message line on the screen.

◘ SET MSGMODE—Control the message display

● General format
```
[SET] MSGMode <ON or OFF> [Short or Long]
```

● Description
The SET MSGMODE subcommand is used to control the message display. It is used to display short or long messages on the screen or not to display any data.

◘ SET NONDISP—Define a character to replace a nondisplayable character

● General format
```
[SET] NONDisp [char]
```

● Description
The SET NONDISP subcommand is used to define a character to replace a character that cannot be displayed. If no character is specified, then blank is used as the default value.

◘ SET NULLS—Define trailing blanks

● General format
```
[SET] NULls <ON or OFF>
```

- **Description**

  The SET NULL subcommand is used to define whether or not to replace trailing blanks with nulls.

☐ SET NUMBER—Display line numbers

- **General format**

  ```
  [SET] NUMber <ON or OFF>
  ```

- **Description**

  The SET NUMBER subcommand is used to indicate whether or not to display line numbers in the prefix area.

☐ SET PAn—Associate a meaning with an attention key

- **General format**

  ```
  [SET] PA n [BEFORE or AFTER or ONLY or IGNORE]
       [string or NULLKEY or COPYKEY or TABKEY]
  ```

- **Description**

  The SET PAn subcommand is used to associate a meaning with a specified attention key. It can also be used to remove a previously associated meaning.

  BEFORE means to process the key definition before executing the command entered at the command line.

  AFTER means to process the key definition after executing the command entered at the command line.

  ONLY means to only process the key definition and not execute the command entered at the command line.

  IGNORE means not to process the key definition and only execute the command entered at the command line.

  string is an XEDIT subcommand or macro that is executed when a PA key is entered.

  NULLKEY means that blank characters found at the cursor are translated to nulls.

COPYKEY means to copy the content of the virtual screen to the printer spool when a PA key is entered.

TABKEY means to move the cursor to the next tab when a PA key is pressed.

◘ SET PACK—Set the pack option

● **General format**
[SET] PACK <ON or OFF>

● **Description**
The SET PACK subcommand is used to indicate whether or not to pack a file before it is written to disk.

◘ SET PENDING—Control the execution of a macro

● **General format**
[SET] PENDing <ON or BLOCK or ERROR or OFF> *string*

● **Description**
The SET PENDING subcommand is used to control the execution of a prefix macro. It also displays the status of the macro being executed.

ON shows *string* in the prefix area of the current line and a pending message in the status area.

BLOCK shows *string* in prefix area of blocked lined abd a pending message in the status area.

ERROR displays question mark (?) followed by *string*.

OFF removes all pending subcommands or macros from the prefix area.

string is either a prefix subcommand or macro or a block form of a prefix subcommand or macro.

◘ SET PFn—Associate a meaning with a function key

● General format
```
[SET] PFn [BEFORE or AFTER or ONLY or IGNORE]
     [string or NULLKEY or COPYKEY or TABKEY]
```

● Description
The SET PF*n* subcommand is used to associate a meaning with a specified function key. It can also be used to remove a previously associated meaning.

BEFORE means to process the key definition before executing the command entered at the command line.

AFTER means to process the key definition after executing the command entered at the command line.

ONLY means to only process the key definition and not execute the command entered at the command line.

IGNORE means not to process the key definition and only execute the command entered at the command line.

string is an XEDIT subcommand or macro that is executed when a PF key is entered.

NULLKEY means that blank characters found at the cursor are translated to nulls.

COPYKEY means to copy the content of the virtual screen to the printer spool when a PF key is entered.

TABKEY means to move the cursor to the next tab when a PF key is pressed.

◘ SET POINT—Define a name for the current line

● General format
```
[SET] Point .symbol [OFF]
```

● Description
The SET POINT subcommand defines a name for the current line.

More than one name can be defined for a line by executing the SET POINT subcommand several times.

◘ SET PREFIX—Control and define the prefix area

● **General format**
```
[SET]   PREfix <ON Nulls or OFF> [Left or Right]
    or
[SET]   PREfix Synonym newname oldname
```

● **Description**
The SET PREFIX subcommand is used for the following two reasons:

- To control the display of the prefix area
- To define the synonym for a prefix

ON is used to display a prefix area either on the left or right side of a line on the screen. Where the prefix is displayed depends on the LEFT or RIGHT operand you choose. The prefix area is five-characters long (=====).

Nulls shows nulls in the prefix area. This operand also enables the insert key.

OFF removes the prefix area from the screen.

Synonym defines a synonym for a prefix subcommand or macro.

newname is the new name to be associated with a prefix subcommand or macro.

oldname is an old name of a prefix subcommand or macro to be replaced.

◘ SET RANGE—Define the range for the line pointer

● **General format**
```
[SET] RANge target1 target2
```

● **Description**

The SET RANGE subcommand defines the range for the line pointer movement. By specifying a new top or bottom of the file, the RANGE subcommand sets new limits.

◘ SET RECFM—Define a record format

• General format
    [SET] RECFm <F or V or FP or VP>

• Description
The SET RECFM subcommand is used to define a new record format for a file. The formats are fixed, variable, fixed packed, and variable packed.

◘ SET REMOTE—Control the display for data transmission

• General format
    [SET] REMOte <ON or OFF>

• Description
The SET REMOTE subcommand is used to control the transmission of data. If it is ON, it specifies that XEDIT should compress display data, thus minimizing the amount of data transmission and enhancing speed. Otherwise, data are not compressed.

◘ SET RESERVED—Reserve a line

• General format
    [SET] RESERved <M [+n or -N] [color] [exthi or NONE]
    [PS s] [High or Nohigh] [text]>
       or
    OFF

• Description
The SET RESERVED subcommand is used to reserve lines on the screen, thus not allowing XEDIT to use them.

M indicates the line to be reserved.

color is one of the following:

Blue	Turquoise
Red	Yellow
Pink	White
Green	Default

exthi specified highlighting and is one of the following:

BLInk
REVvideo
Underline
NONe

High means to highlight the field.

Nohigh means not to highlight the field.

PS*s* specifies the programmed symbol and is on of the following:

PS0	PSD
PSA	PSE
PSB	PSF
PSC	

text is the string to be shown in the reserved line.

OFF means to cancel a reserved line and giving back to XEDIT.

■ **SET SCALE—Display a scale**

● **General format**
```
[SET] SCALe <ON or OFF> [M [+n or -n]]
```

● **Description**
The SET SCALE subcommand is used to display a scale under the current line.

□ SET SCOPE—Define the scope of operations

- **General format**
  ```
  [SET] SCOPE <Display or All>
  ```

- **Description**

  The SET SCOPE subcommand is used to define a set of lines upon which the editor should operate. The choice is either all the lines in the file or only the lines displayed.

□ SET SCREEN—Split the screen

- **General format**
  ```
  [SET] SCReen n [Horizontal or Vertical]
        Size s1...
        Width w1...
        Define [sl1 sw1 sh1 sv1]...
  ```

- **Description**

  The SET SCREEN subcommand is used to split the screen into two or more portions. Each can be used to edit a file.

  n is the number of portions a virtual screen is split into.

  Horizontal specifies to split the screen horizontally—one on top of other.

  Vertical specifies to split the screen vertically—one next to the other from left to right.

  Size specifies the size of the screen to be created horizontally.

  Width specifies the size of the screen to be created vertically.

  Define specifies a layout, such as number of lines, number of columns, row position of the upper-left corner, and column position of the upper-left corner.

◘ SET SELECT—Designate a selection level

● **General format**

```
[SET] SELect [+ or -] n [target or * or 1]
```

● **Description**

The SET SELECT subcommand is used to designate a selection level for specified lines.

◘ SET SERIAL—Control serial numbers

● **General format**

```
[SET] SERial    <ON [incrno or 10] [startno or 10]> or
         <ALL [incrno or 1000] [startno or 1000]> or
         <string [incrno or 10] [startno or 10]> or
         <OFF>
```

● **Description**

The SET SERIAL subcommand is used to turn on or off serialization of files. If it is turned on, an incremental value and starting number are specified, and these form part of the file name.

◘ SET SHADOW—Show a shadow line

● **General format**

```
[SET] SHADow <ON or OFF>
```

● **Description**

The SET SHADOW subcommand is used to turn on or off a shadow line. A shadow line is only an indication of how many lines are not displayed. Its effect depends on the previous setting of the DISPLAY subcommand.

◘ SET SIDCODE—Insert code in lines

● **General format**

```
[SET] SIDcode [string]
```

● **Description**

The SET SIDCODE subcommand is used to instruct the editor to insert a specified string in every line of a file being updated. The string is placed in the first eight positions of the last 17 columns of each line.

◘ SET SPAN—Search one or a number of lines

- **General format**
  ```
  [SET] SPAN <ON or OFF> [Blank or Noblank] [n or *]
  ```

- **Description**
  The SET SPAN subcommand specifies that, during a search for a string, the search should span either one line or many lines of a file. If the value ON is specified, then several lines are concatenated for searching. Otherwise, a string is searched for within a line.

  Blank adds one blank character between consecutive lines of the file during concatenation and search.

  Noblank means consecutive lines are concatenated without blanks.

◘ SET SPILL—Spill data to a new line

- **General format**
  ```
  [SET] SPILL <ON or OFF or WORD>
  ```

- **Description**
  The SET SPILL subcommand is used to instruct the editor to either truncate data or spill them into a new line when executing the following subcommands: CHANGE, CINSERT, COVERLAY, CREPLACE, EXPAND, GET, INPUT, MERGE, OVERLAY, REPLACE, and SHIFT.

  WORD means not to split a word if a line is spilled into a new line.

◘ SET STAY—Do not move the line pointer

- **General format**
  ```
  [SET] STAY <ON or OFF>
  ```

● **Description**

The SET STAY subcommand is used to instruct the editor whether to move the line pointer or to stay when executing the following subcommands: CHANGE, COUNT, COMPRESS, EXPAND, LOWERCASE, SELECT, SHIFT and UPPERCAS. If the operand is ON, the pointer is not moved; otherwise it is moved.

■ **SET STREAM—Search the file or the current line**

● **General format**

```
[SET] STRream <ON or OFF>
```

● **Description**

The SET STREAM subcommand is used to instruct the editor to search either the entire file or the current line when executing the following subcommands: CLOCATE and CDELETE. If the operand is ON the, editor searches the whole file starting with the column pointer; otherwise it searches the current line.

■ **SET SYNONYM—Maintain synonyms**

● **General format**

```
[SET] SYNonym <ON or OFF>
            or
[SET] SYNonym [LINEND char] newname [n] oldname
            or
[SET] SYNonym [LINEND char] newname [n] [format...]
                  oldname[&1...]
```

● **Description**

The SET SYNONYM subcommand does the following:

● Instructs the editor to search or not to search for synonyms.
● Assigns synonyms to subcommands or existing macros.
● Rearranges operands as expected by XEDIT.

ON means to look for synonyms.

OFF means not to look for synonyms.

LINEND spcifies a character to be interpreted as a line-end character.

char is a line-end character.

newname is the name of a synonym to be given to a subcommand or macro.

n is the minimum length of a synonym.

oldname is the name of a subcommand or macro for which a synonym is created.

format specifies the format of the new operands.

◧ SET TABLINE—Indicate tabs

● **General format**
```
[SET] TABLine <ON or OFF> [M [+n or -n]]
```

● **Description**
The SET TABLINE subcommand is used to instruct the editor whether or not to place the character T in every column indicating the current tab setting. If the operand is ON, the editor displays the tab line; otherwise it does not.

◧ SET TABS—Define tabs

● **General format**
```
[SET] TABS n1...n28
```

● **Description**
The SET TABS subcommand is used to define tab stops for a file.

◧ SET TERMINAL—Select line or screen mode

● **General format**
```
[SET] TERMinal <Typewriter or Display>
```

● **Description**
The SET TERMINAL subcommand is used to specify whether a terminal is to be used in line mode or full-screen mode.

◘ SET TEXT—Select text mode

- **General format**
  ```
  [SET] TEXT <ON or OFF>
  ```

- **Description**
  The SET TEXT subcommand is used to instruct CMS and XEDIT to use data as text. If the operand is ON, the editor does conversion; otherwise no conversion takes place.

◘ SET TOFEOF—Show notices

- **General format**
  ```
  [SET] TOFEOF <ON or OFF>
  ```

- **Description**
  The SET TOFEOF subcommand is used to instruct XEDIT to show or not show the following messages:

  Top of File
  End of File
  Top of Range
  End of Range

◘ SET TRANSLAT—Translate characters

- **General format**
  ```
  [SET] TRANSLat <char1 char2>... or OFF
  ```

- **Description**
  The SET TRANSLAT subcommand is used to instruct XEDIT to translate one or more specified pairs of characters. If the operand is ON, the editor translates the characters to uppercase; otherwise no translation takes place.

◘ SET TRUNC—Define the truncation column

- **General format**
  ```
  [SET] TRunc <n or *>
  ```

- **Description**

  The SET TRUNC subcommand defines the truncation column. It is the last column in which data are either modified or entered.

◻ **SET VARBLANK—Define blanks in between words**

- **General format**

  [SET] VARblank <ON or OFF>

- **Description**

  The SET VARBLANK subcommand is used to specify that blanks in between words are or are not significant when searching for a target. If the operand is ON, the editor does not consider the number of blanks between words; otherwise blanks are significant.

◻ **SET VERIFY—Show changed lines**

- **General format**

  [SET] Verify <ON or OFF> [[Hex] *startcol endcol*]...

- **Description**

  The SET VERIFY subcommand is used to instruct XEDIT to show lines that are changed by a subcommand. Optionally, you can also specify a pair of column numbers as an area to be displayed, and call for hexadecimal notation.

◻ **SET WRAP—Turn wrap-around on or off**

- **General format**

  [SET] WRap <ON or OFF>

- **Description**

  The SET WRAP subcommand is used to instruct XEDIT to, or not to, wrap around or not a file when the end of file is reached while executing the following subcommands: LOCATE, CLOCATE, FIND, FINDUP, NFIND, and NFINDUP.

◘ SET ZONE—Define the search zone

● General format
```
[SET] Zone zone1 [zone2 or *]
```

● Description
The SET ZONE subcommand is used to define the search zone. The search zone is the starting and ending columns of each record.

◘ SET =—Initialize the equal buffer

● General format
```
[SET] = <subcommand or macro>
```

● Description
The SET = subcommand is used to initialize the equal (=) buffer with the name of an XEDIT subcommand or macro.

◘ SHIFT—Move data

● General format
```
SHift <Left or Right> [cols or 1] [target or * or 1]
```

● Description
The SHIFT subcommand is used to move data either to the left or to the right. It defines the number of columns and lines to be shifted.

◘ SOS—Screen operation simulation

● General format
```
SOS option
```

```
    where option is one of the following:

    Alarm        NUlls OFF          TABCmd            CLEAR
    PFn          TABCMDB[n or 1]    LINEAdd           POP
    LINEDel      PUsh               TABCMDF[n or 1]
    NUlls        TABB[n or 1]       NUlls ON
    TABF[n or 1]
```

- **Description**
  The SOS subcommand is used to provide screen functions that can be used within XEDIT macros or associated with PF keys.

◻ **STACK—Copy lines to the stack**

- **General format**
  STAck [*target* or * or 1] [*startcol* or 1] [*length* or *]

- **Description**
  The STACK subcommand is used to copy a specified number of lines to the terminal stack.

◻ **TOP—Move to the top of file**

- **General format**
  TOP

- **Description**
  The TOP subcommand is used to move the line pointer to the beginning of a file.

◻ **TRANSFER—Access XEDIT variables**

- **General format**
  TRAnsfre *option*

  where *option* is one of the following:

```
APL        ARBchar      AUtosave     BRKkey
CASE       CMDline      COLPtr       COLumn
CTLchar[char]           CURLine      CURSor
EOF        ESCape       FILler       FMode
FName      FType        HEX          IMage
IMPcmscp   LASTmsg      LENgth       Line
LINENd     LRecl        LScreen      MACRO
MASK       MSGMode      NBFile       NONDisp
NULls      NUMber       PACK         PFn
Point      PREfix       RANge        RECFm
RESERved   SCALe        Seq8         SERial
SIDcode    SIZe         SPAN         STAY
STReam     SYNonym[name]             TABLine
TABS       TARGET       TERMinal     TEXT
TOF        TOFEOF       TRunc        UPDate
VARblank   Verify       VERShift     WRap
Zone       =
```

- **Description**
The TRANSFER subcommand is used to get values of XEDIT variables from macros.

◻ **TYPE—Display lines**

- **General format**
Type [*target* or * or 1]

- **Description**
The TYPE subcommand is used to display lines starting from the current line.

◻ **UP—Move line the pointer up**

- **General format**
Up [*n* or * or 1]

- **Description**
The UP subcommand is used to move the line pointer a specified number of lines towards the beginning of the file.

◻ **UPPERCAS—Convert to uppercase**

- **General format**
UPPercas <*target* or * or 1>

- **Description**
The UPPERCAS subcommand is used to convert all lowercase characters to uppercase characters. The conversion starts from the current line, and the number of lines affected depends on the operand, which specifies the number of lines.

◻ **XEDIT—Edit multiple files**

- **General format**
Xedit [*fn*] [*ft*] [*fm*] [(*options*...[)]]

where *options* are	[Width *nn*] [NOSCreen]
	[PROFile *macroname*]
	[NOPROFil] [NOCLear]
	[NOMsg] [MEMber *membername*]
	[WINdow *wname*]

- **Description**

  The XEDIT subcommand is used to edit multiple files. Note that the options are the same as those used when invoking XEDIT from CMS.

  fn is the name of the file to be edited.

  ft is the type of the file to be edited.

  fm is the file mode of the file to be edited, which specifies where the file is to be found. If it is omitted, XEDIT assumes the file to be on minidisk A1.

  WIDTH specifies the record length of the file to be edited. if *nn*, the line width, is too small, it is possible some lines may be trucated. If this parameter is omitted, XEDIT will either use the logical record length (LRECL) of the file or the default logical record length, which ever is larger.

  NOSCREEN means that a 3270 display terminal is used in a typewriter mode.

  PROFILE specifies the profile macro to be executed first by XEDIT.

  NOPROFIL tells XEDIT not to execute the default PROFILE macro.

  NOCLEAR tells XEDIT not to clear the screen when it is executed, rather it should place the screen in the waiting status (MORE..).

  NOMSG means that XEDIT go into editing mode after setting MSGMODE OFF.

  MEMBER specifies the name of member in the macro library. This member is specified in *fn ft fm*.

WINDOW specifies the name of the virtual screen and window that XEDIT must use.

LOCK tells XEDIT to prevent other users to change the file you are currently working with.

UNLOCK allows a file that you are using to be changed by other users.

■ & (ampersand)—Redisplay subcommand

● General format
& [subcommand]

● Description
The & (ampersand) subcommand is used to retrieve a subcommand. The retrieved subcommand can be reexecuted as is, or after any modification by pressing the ENTER key.

■ = (equal sign)—Reexecute the last subcommand

● General format
= [subcommand]

● Description
The = (equal sign) subcommand is used for the following reasons:

- To reexecute the previous subcommand or macro
- To reexecute the previous CP or CMS command
- To execute a subcommand and then reexecute the previous subcommand

■ ? (question mark)—Display the last subcommand, macro, or command

● General format
?

- **Description**

  The ? (question mark) subcommand is used to display the previous XEDIT subcommand, macro, CP command, or CMS command that was executed from the command line. The subcommand or command is displayed in the command area and can be reexecuted by pressing the ENTER key.

12.3 XEDIT MACROS

This section contains all the XEDIT macros. For each macro, it gives the syntax, followed by an explanation of the function.

▣ ALL—Edit specific lines

- **General format**

  ALL [rtarget]

- **Description**

  The ALL macro displays lines specified by a target; those are the only ones that are possible to edit. The display starts from the top of the file and is repeated until the bottom is reached.

▣ ALTER—Change a character

- **General format**

  ALter char1 char2   [target or * or 1]
                         [n or * or 1]
                         [p or 1]

- **Description**

  The ALTER macro is used to change one character to another. It allows hexadecimal notation and is intended for characters not found on a terminal keyboard.

  char1 is the character to be changed to *char2*.

  target specifies the number of lines to be searched for *char1*.

  n is the number of occurrences of *char1* changed in each line.

p is the relative number of the first occurrences of char1 to be changed.

◘ CANCEL—Terminate editing

- **General format**
  CANCEL

- **Description**
  The CANCEL macro is used to end editing of all files. This macro is equivalent to issuing the QUIT subcommand for each file.

◘ CAPPEND—Add text

- **General format**
  CAppend [*text*]

- **Description**
  The CAppend macro adds a specified text after the current line.

◘ HELP—Get online information

- **General format**
  Help [MENU or HELP or TASK or *name*]

- **Description**
  The HELP macro is used to retrieve online information about XEDIT subcommands. Depending on the operand, one of the following is displayed:

  - A list of all XEDIT subcommands
  - Information about how to use the HELP macro
  - A list of task-oriented HELP lines
  - Information about a specific subcommand or macro

◘ HEXTYPE—Display in HEX and EBCDIC

- **General format**
  HEXType [*target* or * or 1]

- **Description**
The HEXTYPE macro is used to display a specified number of lines in hexadecimal notation and EBCDIC.

◻ **JOIN—Join lines and replace**

- **General format**
```
Join [Aligned] <Column or CURSOR> or
          <colno or /string/>
```

- **Description**
The JOIN macro is used to join one or more lines into one replacement line. There are two ways of specifying the join. One is at the column pointer or at the cursor, and the other is by specific column numbers or specific character strings.

◻ **MODIFY—Display a subcommand**

- **General format**
```
MODify  keyword
```

where *keyword* is one of the following:

ALT	APL	ARBchar	AUtosave
BRKkey	CASE	CMDline	COLOR *field*
COLPtr	CTLchar[*char*]		CURLine
DISPlay	ENTer	ESCape	ETARBCH
ETMODE	FILler	FMode	FName
FType	FULLread	HEX	IMage
IMPcmscp	LASTlorc	LINENd	LRecl
MACRO	MASK	MSGLine	MSGMode
NULls	NUMber	PAn	PACK
PFn	PREfix	Synonym[*name*]	
RANge	RECFm	REMOte	SCALE
SCOPE	SCReen	SELect	SERial
SHADow	SIDcode	SPAN	SPILL
STAY	STReam	SYNonym	TABLine
TABS	TERMinal	TEXT	TOFEOF
TRunc	VARblank	Verify	WRap
Zone			

- **Description**
The MODIFY macro is used to first display a subcommand and its operands, then reenter the subcommand after new operands are typed.

◘ PARSE—Check an operand in the console stack

● **General format**
```
PARSE startcol <Alphaword or Number or String or
               Dblstring or Target or Word or Line>
```

● **Description**

The PARSE macro is used to parse a line already in the console stack. It verifies the format of an operand.

◘ RGLEFT—Move text to left

● **General format**
```
RGLEFT n
```

● **Description**

The RGLEFT subcommand moves data so that columns to the left are visible.

◘ SCHANGE—Selective change

● **General format**
```
SCHANGE [keynumber]
```

● **Description**

The SCHANGE macro is used to selectively find all the occurrences of a specified string and change them.

◘ SI—Structured input

● **General format**
```
SI
```

● **Description**

The SI macro is used to enter data in continuous mode. A new line is added when ENTER is pressed.

◘ SORT—Sort a file

• General format
```
SORT <target or *> [A or D] col1 col2 [col1 col2] ...
```

• Description
The SORT macro is used to rearrange a file according to sort fields in an ascending or descending order. The order depends on EBCDIC.

◘ SPLIT—Split two or more lines

• General format
```
SPlit [Aligned] <Column or CURSOR>
                or
        <colno or [Before or After] /string/>
```

• Description
The SPLIT macro is used to split two or more lines. There are two ways of specifying the split. One is at the column pointer or at the cursor, and the other is through specific column numbers or specific character strings.

◘ SPLTJOIN—Split or join

• General format
```
SPLTJOIN
```

• Description
The SPLTJOIN macro is used to split or join lines. The operation depends on the position of the cursor. The split operation is done when the cursor is positioned before or at the last nonblank character. The join operation takes place when the cursor is positioned after the end of data of a line. The split or join takes place at the cursor position.

◘ STATUS—Display options and settings

• General format
```
STATus [filename]
```

● **Description**

The STATUS macro displays the options set by the SET subcommand and the values of each option. The subcommands for which settings are displayed are

ALT	APL	ARBchar	AUtosave
BRKkey	CASE	CMDline	COLOR
COLPtr	CTLchar	CURLine	DISPlay
ENTer	ESCape	ETARBCH	ETMODE
FILler	FMode	FName	FType
FULLread	HEX	IMage	IMPcmscp
LASTlorc	LINENd	LRecl	MACRO
MASK	MSGLine	MSGMode	NULls
NUMber	PAn	PACK	PENDing
PFn	Point	PREfix	RANge
RECFm	REMOte	RESERved	SCALE
SCOPE	SCReen	SELect	SERial
SHADow	SIDcode	SPAN	SPILL
STAY	STReam	SYNonym	TABLine
TABS	TERMinal	TEXT	TOFEOF
TRANSLat	TRunc	VARblank	Verify
WRap	Zone		

12.4 PREFIX SUBCOMMANDS AND MACROS

This section contains all the XEDIT line subcommands and macros. They are entered in the prefix area to perform various editing functions. For each subcommand or macro, the section gives the syntax, followed by an explanation of the function.

◻ **A—Add one or more line**

● **General format**

```
A      One line
nA     n lines
An     n lines
```

● **Description**

The A prefix subcommand adds one or many lines anywhere in the file. The addition occurs immediately following the line where the subcommand is entered. The A prefix subcommand is the same as the I prefix subcommand.

☐ C—Copy lines

● General format
```
C       One liney
Cn      n lines
nC      n lines
CC      A block of lines
C*      Lines to the end of the file
```

● Description
The C prefix subcommand is used to copy one line, a number of lines, or a block of lines. With the C prefix subcommand, a destination prefix subcommand, either   F (following) or P (preceding) must be entered. For block copy, CC should appear in the prefix area of the first and last lines to be copied.

☐ D —Delete lines

● General format
```
D       One line
Dn      n lines
nD      n lines
DD      A block of lines
D*      Lines to the end of the file
```

● Description
The D prefix subcommand is used to remove one line, a number of lines, or a block of lines. When a block is deleted, DD should appear in the prefix area of the first and last lines to be removed.

☐ E—Extend a logical line

● General format
```
E
```

● Description
The E prefix subcommand is used to extend a line by one more screen lines. The maximum length of the visible screen is defined by the SET VERIFY and SET SCREEN subcommands.

◘ F—Following a line

● General format
```
F
```

● Description
The F prefix subcommand is always used with C or M prefix subcommands. It specifies the line after which a move or copy operation should take place.

◘ I—Insert one or more lines

● General format
```
I       One line
nI      n lines
In      n lines
```

● Description
The I prefix subcommand is used to insert one or many lines anywhere in the file. The addition occurs immediately following the line where the subcommand is entered. The I prefix subcommand is the same as the A prefix subcommand.

◘ M—Move lines

● General format
```
M       One line
Mn      n lines
nM      n lines
MM      A block of lines
M*      Lines to the end of the file
```

● Description
The M prefix subcommand is used to move one line, a number of lines, or a block of lines. With the M prefix subcommand, a destination prefix subcommand, either F (following) or P (preceding) must be entered. For block copy, MM should appear in the prefix area of the first and last lines to be copied.

◘ P—Preceding line

● **General format**
P

● **Description**
The P prefix subcommand is always used with C or M prefix
subcommands. It specifies the line before which a move or copy
operation should take place.

◘ S Macro—Redisplay one or more lines

● **General format**
```
S       All lines
S*      All lines
Sn      The first n lines
S+n     The first n lines
nS      The first n lines
S-n     The last n lines
```

● **Description**
The S prefix macro is used to redisplay either all or a selected
number of lines.

◘ SCALE—Display a scale

● **General format**
SCALE

● **Description**
The SCALE prefix subcommand displays a scale under a
corresponding line.

◘ SI—Structured input

● **General format**
SI

● **Description**
The SI macro is used to enter data in continuous mode. A new
line is added when ENTER is pressed.

◻ TABL—Display tab line

● General format
TABL

● Description
The TABL prefix subcommand shows the character T in every tab column for the corresponding line.

◻ X macro—Exclude one or more lines

● General format
```
X        All lines
Xn       n lines
nX       n lines
XX       A block of lines
X*       The rest of the file
```

● Description
The X prefix macro is used to exclude from the display either all or a selected number of lines.

◻ < macro—Shift left

● General format
```
<        One line one column
<n       One line n columns
n<       One line n columns
<<       A block of lines one column
<<n      A block of lines n columns
n<<      A block of lines n columns
```

● Description
The < prefix macro is used to shift data to the left in the following ways: one line one column, one line many columns, a block of lines one column, and a block of lines many columns.

◻ /—Set the current line

● General format
/[n] or [n]/

- **Description**

The / (diagonal) prefix subcommand is used to set the current line.

■ > **Macro—Shift right**

- **General format**

```
>        One line one column
>n       One line n columns
n>       One line n columns
>>       A block of lines one column
>>n      A block of lines n columns
n>>      A block of lines n columns
```

- **Description**

The > prefix macro is used to shift data to the right in the following ways: one line one column, one line many columns, a block of lines one column and a block of lines many columns.

■ " **—Duplicate**

- **General format**

```
  "        Duplicate one line
 "n        Duplicate one line n times
 n"        Duplicate one line n times
 " "n      Duplicate a block n times
 n" "      Duplicate a block n times
```

- **Description**

The " (double quote) prefix subcommand is used to duplicate lines in the following ways: one line once, one line many times, a block of lines once, and a block of lines many times.

Index

ABOUT THE AUTHOR

V. Mitra Gopaul has more than 20 years' experience in such mainframe disciplines as CICS, IMS, MVS, and VM, and is a leading consultant at IBM, Merrill Lynch, Royal Bank of Canada, and several other large corporations. He has played a major role in the development, programming, and maintenance of numerous on-line and batch systems while serving as a consultant, project leader, and programmer analyst. A specialist in C language programming and MVS application software development, Gopaul is the author of *Personal Computers and the Baha'i Community*, *C Programming in the MVS Environment*, and the forthcoming *C/C++ Programming in the OS/2 Environment* and *OS/2 Programmer's Desk Reference*. He holds a bachelor's degree in computer science from York University, Canada.